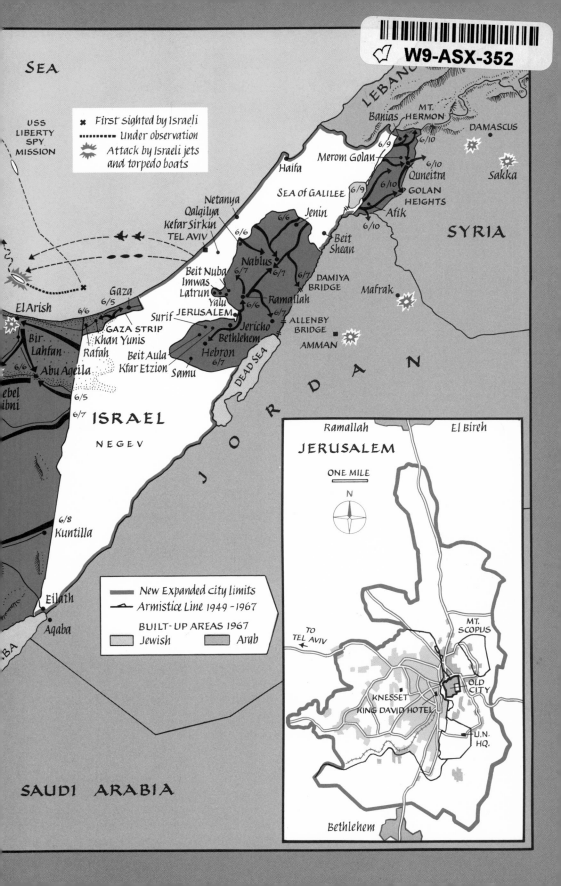

SEA

USS
LIBERTY
SPY
MISSION

Legend:
- ✕ First sighted by Israeli
- ····· Under observation
- ☀ Attack by Israeli jets and torpedo boats

LEBANON

MT.
HERMON

Banias   6/10

DAMASCUS

Merom Golan   6/9

Haifa

Netanya
Qalqilya
kefar Sirkin
TEL AVIV

SEA OF GALILEE

Jenin   6/6

6/9

6/10   Quneitra

6/10   GOLAN
HEIGHTS

Sakka

Afik   6/10

SYRIA

Beit
Shean

Nablus   6/7   6/7   6/7

DAMIYA
BRIDGE

Mafrak

Beit Nuba   6/7
Imwas
Latrun   Yalu
Surif   JERUSALEM   6/6   Ramallah
Gaza   6/5   Jericho   ALLENBY
BRIDGE

Gaza   6/6
El Arish

Bethlehem

AMMAN

GAZA STRIP
Khan Yunis
Rafah
Bir
Lahfan
Abu Ageila   6/6
6/5

Beit Aula
Kfar Etzion   Samu

Hebron   6/7

DEAD SEA

J O R D A N

ebel
ibni

6/5

6/7   **ISRAEL**

N E G E V

6/8
Kuntilla

Eilath

Aqaba

BA

SAUDI ARABIA

Inset map:

Ramallah   El Bireh

JERUSALEM

ONE MILE

N

TO
TEL AVIV

MT.
SCOPUS

KNESSET
KING DAVID HOTEL

OLD
CITY

U.N.
HQ.

Bethlehem

Legend (inset):
- ━━ New Expanded city limits
- ▴▴▴ Armistice Line 1949-1967
- BUILT-UP AREAS 1967
  - ☐ Jewish   ☐ Arab

Also by Donald Neff

WARRIORS AT SUEZ

WARRIORS FOR JERUSALEM

The Six Days That Changed the Middle East

DONALD NEFF

LINDEN PRESS/SIMON & SCHUSTER
New York 1984

Published by Linden Press / Simon & Schuster
A Division of Simon & Schuster, Inc.
Simon & Schuster Building
Rockefeller Center
1230 Avenue of the Americas
New York, New York 10020
LINDEN PRESS / SIMON & SCHUSTER and colophon are trademarks of Simon
& Schuster, Inc.
Designed by Karolina Harris
Manufactured in the United States of America

1 3 5 7 9 10 8 6 4 2

Library of Congress Cataloging in Publication Data

Neff, Donald, date.
Warriors for Jerusalem.

Bibliography: p.
Includes index.
1. Israel-Arab War, 1967—Diplomatic history.
I. Title.
DS127.2.N43   1984   956'.046   83-26746

ISBN 0-671-45485-4

FOR

ABIGAIL TRAFFORD

AND

THE COMING GENERATION:

ABBIE, GREG, TRISH AND TORIA

A Note to the Reader

Much of the new material for this book comes from documents released under the Freedom of Information Act. Although the bureaucracy in recent years has been making increasing inroads into the act's liberal provisions for declassifying government documents, the act remains viable as of late 1983. A number of significant documents concerning the 1967 war have been released in the past three years, and they form the basis for portions of this book.

I am grateful to David C. Humphrey, archivist at the Lyndon Baines Johnson Library in Austin, Texas, for his generous and uncomplaining assistance. As in my work with the Eisenhower Library on an earlier book, the Johnson Library proved to be the single most helpful institution. These presidential libraries remain the best-organized and most convenient gathering places of a wealth of diverse research material that would be unavailable otherwise. As such they perform a valuable function for the American democracy.

The other major source of new information came from interviews with officials of the period. In those cases where the sources refused to be publicly identified with a viewpoint or event but where I had confirmed their version and felt it insightful or critical to the understanding of events, I have clearly signaled the circumstances for anonymity. On the whole, however, I have refrained from using nonattributable information, no matter how tempting it was to do so.

CONTENTS

PART ONE: COUNTDOWN
January 1, 1965, to June 4, 1967

PART TWO: WAR
June 5 to June 10, 1967

PART THREE: AFTERMATH
June 11 to November 22, 1967

CAST OF
___ CHARACTERS ___

AMERICA

Walworth Barbour, ambassador to Israel
Lucius D. Battle, assistant secretary of state
McGeorge Bundy, special assistant to the President
Abraham Feinberg, Democratic Party fund raiser
Abraham Fortas, associate justice of the Supreme Court
Arthur J. Goldberg, ambassador to the United Nations
Richard Helms, director, Central Intelligence
Lyndon B. Johnson, President
Arthur B. Krim, finance chairman, Democratic National Committee
Mathilde Krim, wife of Arthur Krim
Robert S. McNamara, secretary of defense
Richard H. Nolte, ambassador-designate to Egypt
Eugene V. Rostow, under secretary of state
Walt W. Rostow, national security adviser
Dean Rusk, secretary of state
Harold H. Saunders, Mideast expert, National Security Council

BRITAIN

Lord Caradon, ambassador to the United Nations
Harold Wilson, prime minister

EGYPT

Abdel Hakim Amer, commander in chief
Mohamed Heikal, journalist
Mohamed A. Kony, ambassador to the United Nations
Gamal Abdel Nasser, president
Mahmoud Riad, foreign minister
Anwar Sadat, legislator

FRANCE

Charles de Gaulle, president
Maurice Couve de Murville, foreign minister

ISRAEL

Menachem Begin, opposition leader
David Ben Gurion, former prime minister
Moshe Dayan, defense minister
Abba Eban, foreign minister
Levi Eshkol, prime minister
Ephraim Evron, minister to the United States
Yitzhak Rabin, chief of staff
Ezer Weizman, chief of operations

JORDAN

Mohammad H. Farra, ambassador to the United Nations
Hussein ibn Talal, king

PALESTINE

Yasser Arafat, leader of Fatah
Anwar Khatib, governor of Jordanian Jerusalem
Ahmed Shukairy, chairman, Palestine Liberation Organization
Raymonda Tawil, writer

SOVIET UNION

Nikolai Fedorenko, ambassador to the United Nations
Aleksei N. Kosygin, premier
Vasily V. Kuznetsov, first deputy foreign minister

SYRIA

Hafez Assad, defense minister
Nureddin Attassi, president
Yousef Zayyen, prime minister

UNITED NATIONS

Odd Bull, chief of staff, Truce Supervision Organization
Indar Jit Rikhye, commander, Emergency Force
U Thant, secretary-general

Hear my prayer, O Lord, and let
my cry come unto thee.
                    —Psalm 102:1

Lord, accept my prayer.
                    —The Koran 14:40

Beware lest stern heaven hate
    you
enough to hear your prayers!
                    —Anatole France

___PROLOGUE___

T hey began arriving in Palestine in the early 1880s, refugees from the pogroms of tsarist Russia seeking safety and a new life. What these early Jewish immigrants found was not encouraging. Palestine was still a neglected backwater of the Turkish Ottoman Empire. The first rough road between the major port at Jaffa to the storied city of Jerusalem had been cut only in 1869, the same year the far more glamorous Suez Canal was opened in Egypt. Jerusalem itself was a small and dusty village of fewer than twenty thousand persons, nearly equally split between Arabs and Jews.

There had always remained some Jews in the ancient land, but they were few and mainly "Arabized," Sephardic Jews speaking Arabic, living in poverty and suspicious of their European counterparts. Their total number in Palestine in the middle of the nineteenth century was not much more than twenty-five thousand, about 6 percent of the Arab population. Within ten years of the start of the wave of new immigrants, as many Jews arrived as had been living there in the past quarter century.

The sudden influx of Jews caused immediate apprehension. Turkish authorities, fearful of conflict between the inhabitants and the newcomers, outlawed all Jewish immigration in May 1882, just as the new immigrants began arriving in numbers. Yet so desperate was their plight that by stealth and by bribery the homeless Jews continued to arrive. The concern of native Palestinians grew so great that before the end of the century some Arabs were already calling for the halt of all land sales to Jews.

Many of the early immigrants did not remain long. Unaccustomed to farming and disillusioned by Palestine's poverty and backwardness, most of them moved on in their search for a home and a livelihood. But their trek had not been without significance. It marked the beginning of a relentless struggle between Arab and Jew to create their own nation in Palestine, a struggle that was to bring suffering and bloodshed to an ancient land that already had more than its share of human tragedy.

To most Jews of the 1800s, as well as to many other peoples, the promised land was not Palestine but the United States. Before the founding of the republic there were barely 2,500 Jews in America. That began to change after 1815 when the conservative reaction in Europe to the French Revolution began to set in. Napoleon Bonaparte's invasion army had brought legal equality for Jews at the point of the sword throughout much of Southern and Eastern Europe. Now, with his final downfall, the pendulum swung the other way. German Jews began emigrating to America in large numbers in the first half of the nineteenth century, reaching a peak after the European revolutions of 1848. By the time the mass emigration of Russian Jews started in 1881, there were about 250,000 Jews in the United States, most of them of German and Austrian descent. They had settled throughout the United States, quickly establishing themselves, particularly in retail businesses, and blending with other immigrants into the American landscape.

By World War I, Jews in America numbered more than two million, the vast majority of them recent arrivals from Eastern Europe. Unlike the earlier tradesmen immigrants from Germany who came as individuals or in families, the new immigrants arrived in America by groups, sometimes by whole villages, and established instant ghettos in the metropolises along the eastern seaboard. Though many of them soon assimilated the mores of the American melting pot, large groups remained in the ghettos, heightening the awareness of their ethnic uniqueness and producing communities, like other ethnic groups before and after, that became voting blocs sensitive to issues affecting their lives.

Jewish immigrants were only one group of a massive movement of immigration into America at the turn of the century, and Congress, sensing among other things the potential change in voting patterns, reacted by trying to limit the number of the newcomers. In 1897, it passed a measure to restrict immigration, but President Grover Cleveland vetoed it. Other attempts followed with regularity and also met the same fate under Presidents William H. Taft and Woodrow Wilson. National policy remained that there should be unlimited immigration except for "Orientals, paupers, imbeciles, and prostitutes."

Unrestricted by law, Jews and others continued to move to the United States, flooding parts of the country with cheap labor, strange customs and, in the minds of some "Hundred Percenter" Americans, questionable associations. The East Europeans, emerging from the region where the new ideology of Communism had conquered tsarist Russia, were suspected of being Communists, and the South Europeans from Sicily and Italy of importing organized crime in the form of a shadowy organization called the Mafia.

In 1921, Congress finally got its way. It passed the first of a series of new immigration laws setting quotas on the number and nationalities of persons allowed in the country. The Johnson Act, passed May 19 and signed by President Warren G. Harding, limited aliens admitted to the United States to 3 percent of each nationality already in the country according to the 1910 census. Total immigration was restricted to 358,000 annually, with 200,000 admissions allotted to Northern Europe and 155,000 to Southern and Eastern Europe. Three years later, the law was toughened by the 1924 Johnson Act, which reduced the quota to 2 percent of those nationalities in the country in 1890, which was before the great migrations from Southern and Eastern Europe. Then in 1929, a third, even harsher, act established 152,000 as the number of new aliens to be admitted annually, with 132,000 allotted to Northern Europe and only 20,000 to Southern and Eastern Europe as well as Asia. Africa had no quotas at all.

Suddenly, Jews found that entry to the promised land of America was essentially closed.

In the decades that followed, many Jews turned to another promised land. It was a land that had a potent and unique meaning for them—Palestine. The first Jewish state had existed in Judea and Samaria in Palestine, then called Canaan, nearly three thousand years earlier, founded by King Saul around 1025 B.C., enlarged to its greatest extent by King David between 1004 and 965 B.C., and brought to its apogee of riches and grandeur by King Solomon between 965 and 928 B.C. It was King David who captured Jerusalem and made it the religious and political center of Jewish national life, and it was in Jerusalem that the Jews first established their Temple to worship Yahweh.

Over the centuries the Jews came under the sway of one powerful empire after another—Egyptian, Assyrian, Babylonian—until, in 586 B.C., Emperor Nebuchadnezzar of Babylonia avenged a Jewish rebellion by destroying Jerusalem and its Temple and ordering all Jews slain or deported to Babylon. Thus ended, seemingly forever, Jewish life in Palestine, an event known in Jewish history as the end of the First Temple.

It was this early diaspora that created the longing echoes in the haunting lyrics of Psalm 137:

> How shall we sing the Lord's song
> in a strange land?
> If I forget thee, O Jerusalem, let my
> right hand forget her cunning.
> If I do not remember thee, let my tongue
> cleave to the roof of my mouth;
> if I prefer not Jerusalem above my chief joy.

The Jews did not forget Jerusalem. Fifty years after their exile, the great Persian Emperor Cyrus captured Babylon and gave the Jews their choice to remain or to return to Palestine. Many returned, and they soon had rebuilt their Temple in Jerusalem under Persian rule, completing it in 516 B.C., thus inaugurating what became known as the epoch of the Second Temple.

Over the following centuries more invaders, the Greeks under Alexander the Great, the Ptolemies of Egypt, the Seleucids of Syria, came and went in what became known as Palestine, a name meaning the land of the sea people, the Palestinians; the name "Palestine" was already in common usage by Herodotus by the fifth century B.C. It was only in 164 B.C. that the Jews became strong enough to recapture Jerusalem as their own. By 142 B.C. they proclaimed the establishment of a new Jewish nation ruled by priest-kings under the Hasmonean family and free of their Syrian Seleucid masters. The Jewish nation fell to Rome in 63 B.C. In 70 A.D. a rebellion was brutally suppressed by the Roman Legion; many thousands of Jews were slain, thousands of others were sold into slavery, and the Temple in Jerusalem was destroyed.

Yet the Jews did not give up. By 132 A.D., the survivors again rose up against Rome. This time the Jews were totally eradicated from Palestine. Thousands were killed in the revolt that ended three years later. So many were sold off into slavery that their value declined to the price of a horse's ration. Emperor Hadrian ordered the rebuilt Temple destroyed totally, changed Jerusalem's name to Aelia Capitolina and Judea's to Syria-Palestina, and scattered nearly all of the surviving Jews into the great Diaspora, to wander the world for the next two thousand years.

Jewish nationalism—Zionism—grew in the nineteenth century as a response to anti-Semitism. The pogrom of 1881 in Russia gave urgency to the idea that "there is something unnatural about a people without a territory, just as there is about a man without a shadow," as one of Zionism's pioneer writers, Leo Pinsker, a Russian physician, wrote in his 1882 seminal work, *Auto-Emancipation.* The movement was at first focused mainly on gaining territory for a Jewish homeland regardless of the location. Such diverse regions as Argentina, Asiatic Turkey, North America and Uganda were at one time or another mentioned as a suitable site for the new Jewish nation.

By the time the Zionist Organization was officially founded on August 29, 1897, in Basle, Switzerland, Palestine with its historic associations for Jews was the generally accepted choice for the Jewish homeland. The aim of Zionism, the founders declared, was the establishment of a "Jewish homeland openly recognized, legally secured." The leading figure of the movement was Theodor Herzl, a native of Budapest who became a Vienna journalist and wrote Zionism's most important book, *Der Judenstaat (The Jewish State).* It had been published the year before the founding of the Zionist Organization and had galvanized European Jews with its clarion message: "We shall at last live as free men on our own soil and die peacefully in our own homeland."

As attention focused on Palestine, a powerful Zionist slogan soon became popular: "A people without a land for a land without a people."

But there was a problem. Palestine already had a people: Arabs.

Britain claimed Palestine from Turkey as part of its booty from World War I. When it officially established its mandate under the League of Nations and conducted the first formal census in 1922, it was determined there were 83,790 Jews in the region living among 598,177 Moslems and 71,464 Christians, mainly Palestinians but some Westerners as well.

Organized Zionist immigration, openly dedicated to establishing a Jewish homeland, had begun eight years after the founding of the Zionist Organization. The first of the new immigrants, members of the second *aliyah* (literally "ascent" in Hebrew), as it became known in the Jewish community, had added thirty thousand more Jews to Palestine between 1905 and 1914. There followed the third and fourth *aliyahs,* the former bringing thirty-seven thousand newcomers between 1919 and 1924 and the latter seventy thousand between 1924 and 1928.

Palestinians, both Moslems and Christians, viewed the immigration of Jews with alarm. By a historic coincidence, a wave of nationalism was sweeping the Arab world, sharpening the Arabs' sensitivities to the threat posed by Zionism. The first anti-Jewish riots came in 1920, and they were to continue sporadically throughout the quarter century of the British Mandate. The British repeatedly established royal commissions to study the cause of the Palestinians' violence, and repeatedly the commissions came to the same conclusion: The Palestinians feared the Jews were trying to take their land and deny them the opportunity to establish their own state.

The rise of Adolf Hitler in 1933 brought the fifth and greatest prewar *aliyah* to Palestine. With persecution rising in Germany and entry to America restricted, large numbers of German Jews for the first time emigrated to Palestine. Though East Europeans continued to dominate the immigration rolls in most years, the proportion of Germans among the immigrants of the 1930s rose from an average of 2.5 percent to a high of 71 percent. Total immigration leaped from 9,553 in 1932 to 30,327 the next year and a high of 61,854 in 1935. Yet the surge in immigrants still left the Jewish community in Palestine a minority, 320,358 against 826,457 Moslems and 103,371 Christians in 1935. Nevertheless, the *Yishuv,* the Jewish community, was finally a viable group, capable of defending itself and cohesive enough to more than dream that one day soon a Jewish nation might arise in Palestine.

Britain, like Turkey before it, increasingly found itself the target of hatred by both sides in Palestine. It was caught between the aspirations of the Jews and the resentment of the Palestinians, both of whom believed they had a commitment from London supporting their claims to form a nation. A series of armed revolts by Palestinians in the late 1930s finally convinced London that it must take bold actions to try to reconcile the two sides.

In a far-ranging White Paper issued in 1939, Britain declared flatly that the United Kingdom's policy had never supported the creation of either an Arab state or a Jewish state in Palestine. Instead, the White Paper announced, Britain would set up one independent Palestinian state in ten years "in which Arabs and Jews share in government in such a way as to ensure that the essential interests of each community are safeguarded." In order to preserve the current proportion of Jews to Arabs, which would be reflected in each community's representation in the government, Britain declared that it would limit Jewish immigration to a total of seventy-five thousand over the next five years. After that, "no further Jewish immigration will be permitted unless the Arabs of Palestine are prepared to acquiesce in it."

The White Paper was a devastating blow to Zionists. First the United States had all but slammed its door on Jews. Now they were being denied entry into the region they considered at least partly theirs by history and pioneering effort.

Britain's plan was swept aside by the horrors of the Holocaust of World

War II. Revelations of the death camps transformed the issue of a home for the Jews into one of the most pressing questions of the postwar period. The incredible stories of crematoria and the pitiful flood of Jewish refugees elicited an enormous outpouring of sympathy for the persecuted Jews. But Britain, torn by its promises to Arabs to control Jewish immigration and its hope to create one state in Palestine, continued to enforce its quotas on the number of Jewish newcomers. The saga of tens of thousands of homeless Jews desperately trying to reach the shores of Palestine in the face of British opposition evoked still more empathy for Jews in the Western world.

Britain, shattered by Arab resentment, international condemnation, growing terrorist attacks from Jewish extremists, and the cost of maintaining a 100,000-man peace-keeping army in Palestine, finally threw up its hands. In desperation, London turned the thorny Palestine issue over to the United Nations at the beginning of 1947.

The world body's solution to the Palestine conundrum was to create two nations, one Arab, one Jewish. On November 29, 1947, the United Nations voted to partition Palestine, awarding the Jewish state 56.47 percent of the land and the rest to the Palestinians. Jerusalem was to be an international city, controlled by neither Jews nor Moslems, in which there would be free access for worship in Christian, Islamic and Jewish shrines and holy places.

The Jews accepted partition but the Arabs refused. They bitterly noted that while the Jews owned only 5.67 percent of the land and made up less than a third of the population (608,000 Jews to 1,327,000 Arabs), the partition plan gave the *Yishuv* more than 50 percent of Palestine. The Palestinians would not accept partition, and they were strongly backed by the Arab nations.

The next year, on May 14, 1948, the Jews declared the establishment of the state of Israel. Fighting between Arabs and Jews had been sputtering for months; now full-scale war broke out between the new Jewish state and its Arab neighbors. The fighting ended in 1949 with armistice agreements concluded between Israel and Egypt, Jordan, Lebanon and Syria.*

The old Palestinian fear that had first manifested itself in riots twenty-nine years earlier had come true. As a result of the war, Israel now controlled half of Jerusalem, though not the revered Old City, and a total of 77.4 percent of the land. Nearly 60 percent of the Palestinians—725,000 men, women and children—had been uprooted from their homes. While Jews, many of them recently arrived from Europe, moved into the houses

* Iraq also fought against Israel, but it had no frontiers with the young country and found it unnecessary to sign an armistice.

that Palestinians had lived in for generations, and in some cases for centuries, the displaced Palestinians huddled in crude refugee camps, homeless, landless and filled with hatred. Another group of Palestinians, about 160,000, remained on their land within Israel's frontiers, now second-class citizens within a Jewish state.

The remaining Palestinians lived within the 22.6 percent of the territory that the Israelis had failed to capture. The cease-fire lines separating Palestinians from Israelis were a Mad Hatter's pattern. They curved irregularly around the heart of the West Bank of the River Jordan, over desert and wadis and the rocky hills of Judea and Samaria, slicing through the center of Jerusalem itself, curling like a half-inflated balloon inside the body of Palestine, which was now largely the land of Israel.

This West Bank bulge at some points stretched to within less than twenty miles of the Mediterranean, narrowing Israel's territory to a thin and vulnerable waist. Artillery located on the West Bank had in its range nearly every major Israeli city except the port town of Haifa in the northwest, a source of constant worry to Israelis.

The United States immediately exhibited its friendly feelings toward Israel by becoming the first to recognize the new country diplomatically. It looked on Israel as a fellow democracy amid the Moslem nations of the Middle East, an image Israel encouraged, and many people around the world rejoiced that at last the Jews had their own promised land.

The establishment of Israel and the crushing defeat it inflicted on its Moslem neighbors set off a series of reverberations throughout the Arab world. Arabs viewed Israel with bitterness, the cause of their humiliation and cultural disgrace. The Jewish state was widely perceived in the Arab capitals of the Middle East as a Western enclave in the Islamic heartland and a direct threat to Moslem regimes. Repeatedly, the Arab nations threatened to wrest the land back for the Palestinians, but as the years passed, the boasts proved to be empty, and the Palestinian refugees were left bitter and landless.

Israel's birth sparked a decade of dramatic change in the Middle East. Arab countries, emerging into postcolonial freedom and swept by discontent, suffered convulsions as the disaffected populaces sought effective governments to eradicate the humiliation of their defeat by Israel. The first leader to fall to this wave of discontent was Egypt's corrupt King Farouk, who was deposed in 1952 in a nationalist coup engineered by Colonel Gamal Abdel Nasser. Within three years, Nasser, suspicious of the West's support of Israel, began strengthening Egypt's ties with the Soviet Union, up to that time a minor player in the Middle East, but one which had long nurtured ambitions to gain influence in the region. Syria and Iraq also soon slipped from the West's exclusive grip as their regimes fell to local nationalists.

This period also saw the momentous dissolution of the old European empires. Libya, once an Italian colony, gained its independence in 1951. British troops were finally removed from Egypt in 1956, ending an unwelcome stay of seventy-four years. Morocco, Sudan and Tunisia all received independence from their British and French colonial masters that year. Britain's suzerainty in Jordan came to an end in the same year when young King Hussein unceremoniously deported Sir John Bagot Glubb, the legendary Glubb Pasha of the Arab Legion. Cyprus was in open rebellion against British rule, and Algeria was already two years into a bloody civil war that would take hundreds of thousands of lives, nearly destroy France, and provide a model and an inspiration for Arab revolutionaries throughout the Middle East.

Amidst this historic upheaval, Britain and France colluded with Israel to try to topple Gamal Abdel Nasser. The resulting Suez war in the fall of 1956, the second Arab-Israeli conflict, ruined the reputations (and displayed the weakness) of Britain and France, accelerated the dismemberment of the European colonial empires, and elevated Nasser as the symbol of Arab aspirations. It also brought about the entry of the United States into the Middle East.

Britain and France, which at the end of World War I had controlled nearly all of the Arab nations, were swept aside. Almost by default, the United States and the Soviet Union found themselves the new superpower arbiters in the Middle East at the end of the brief Suez war.

Eisenhower established a neutral posture for the United States by refusing to countenance Israel's conquest by force of the Sinai Peninsula during the war. Under his intense pressure Israel was made to return the Sinai to Egypt, earning America, briefly, the reputation of being a fair and evenhanded broker in Arab capitals.

This rapidly changed as first John F. Kennedy and then Lyndon B. Johnson took a more openly pro-Israel position. It was Kennedy who first breached Washington's long-standing policy of refusing to sell major weapons systems to Israel. In 1962, he took the precedent-breaking action of providing the tiny state with Hawk antiaircraft missiles, a purely defensive weapon but an action nonetheless notable because it set the pattern for future sales.

Johnson went further. He opened the doors of America's non-nuclear armory to Israel. As he became more bogged down in Vietnam and desperately needed domestic political support, Johnson, the consummate politician, became increasingly attentive toward Israel and its numerous American supporters, especially the influential Jewish American community. The community represented a potent bloc of voters, a fact not lost on Johnson when he became the first American President openly to sell major offensive weapons systems to Israel. In 1965 he agreed to provide Israel with battle tanks; a year later he took the unprecedented step of selling sophisticated A-4 Skyhawk combat jets to Israel.

Inevitably, some of the newly emerging Arab nations reacted by embracing the Soviet Union even more closely as their protector and provider. Moscow was more than happy to respond to the opportunities presented by Washington's increasing tilt toward Israel. The result was that as the 1967 war approached, Russia was firmly entrenched in the Middle East as the powerful backer of such socialist Arab countries as Egypt and Syria.

By then, Lyndon Johnson was a weak and confused President, totally mired in Vietnam, beset at home by antiwar and race riots and increasingly distrusted abroad. He was desperate to garner all the support he could. It was in these circumstances that Johnson threw all of America's mighty support behind Israel. He was in a way merely reflecting the overwhelming popularity of Israel at the time in the United States. But in the long run, as leader of the strongest democracy, the man responsible for the nation's guidance as well as the mentor of its friends, especially its weakest ones, he made a tragic mistake. For it was the war of six days, as brief as it was, that brought about the impasse in the Middle East that persists today and the problems that are likely to plague the world in the years ahead.

And it was the Johnson Administration's conduct during the war that marked the beginning of an intimate and symbiotic relationship between the United States and Israel that ultimately harmed the national interests of both.

In Israel, the uncritical and unprecedented financial, diplomatic and moral support of the United States soon encouraged the most recalcitrant and militant elements of the Jewish nation. With the proof of continuing American support showing that their hard line was both effective and tolerated, these militant leaders—so unrepresentative of the humanism of Israel's founding fathers—came to govern the state of Israel.

As for the United States, its blind support of such reckless leaders left the country with little influence among the Arab states, and tarnished its reputation as a champion of human rights in many lands. Because of the events of 1967, America today is more deeply involved than ever in the Middle East, and the region itself is more torn by factional, religious and superpower rivalries than at any time in its modern history.

Three times in less than thirty years—during the 1956, 1967 and 1973 wars—the United States and the Soviet Union have found themselves, despite their best efforts, drawn into direct confrontation in the Middle East. Today they are dangerously poised opposite each other, with Soviet advisers and missiles in Syria and U.S. Marines in Lebanon and major elements of the U.S. Navy offshore. It is a parlous and extremely volatile mixture, one that makes all the more urgent the necessity to understand how the United States and the region arrived at the current hazardous position.

PART ONE
COUNTDOWN

January 1, 1965, to June 4, 1967

I
FATAH LIGHTS THE FUSE

The Sinai Peninsula sits like a keystone supporting the continents of Africa and Asia, separating the Mediterranean Sea and the Indian Ocean, Europe and Asia, the symbolic middle between the West and East and the natural land bridge between Cairo and Jerusalem. It is an arid, barren land of sandy wastes and stark granite mountains, of furnace heat and feverish mirages. Although its landscape is so poor and forbidding that it has always been largely uninhabited, this sere and harsh peninsula is uniquely rich in history.

It was in the Sinai that Jews expelled from Egypt millennia ago wandered aimlessly and where Moses was said to have received the Ten Commandments. It was across the Sinai that Alexander the Great marched to capture Egypt in 332 B.C., a feat repeated in 641 A.D. by an Arab army that brought Islam to the Middle East and half of the Mediterranean world. It was across the Sinai that Napoleon Bonaparte led French troops in 1799 to bring back into Palestine the first major invasion of Christian forces since the Crusades.

It was also in this trackless desert that Egyptian troops unexpectedly began to mass in the spring of 1967. Their presence there evoked a powerful and historic reaction from Israel.

Shortly after 7 A.M. Monday, June 5, 1967, radar screens of several nations began picking up the blips of airplanes taking off from Israeli airfields and heading out over the Mediterranean, off the north coast of the Sinai Peninsula. The planes flew in flights of four and in complete radio silence. Soviet and American warships patrolling the eastern Mediterranean were capable of tracking the Israeli aircraft as flight after flight formed up in the cloudless azure skies. So too were sixteen Egyptian radar stations in the Sinai as well as other stations in Jordan and in Cyprus, where Britain maintained sophisticated installations.

But the Israeli planes were visible for only a brief instant. When the Mirage, Mystère, Ouragans, Fouga Magisters and Vatour craft reached the blue waters of the Mediterranean they dived low, disappearing from the radar screens as they skillfully skimmed the waves at altitudes as low as thirty feet.

All this was familiar to the radar operators. For the past two years the Israeli Air Force had been practicing massed early-morning flights westward over the Mediterranean at altitudes so low as to be undetectable by radar. But this time there was a dramatic difference. When they reappeared on radar screens the Israeli planes were over Egypt and in attack formation.

The third Arab-Israeli war in nineteen years was about to begin.

It had been a decade since war had raged between Arabs and Israelis. The Suez war of 1956 had brought minor benefits to Israel but no major territorial changes. The same tortuous, happenstance lines that had existed since the armistice agreements of 1949 remained, a nightmare for both Arab and Israeli security forces and for the anxious citizens who lived on both sides of them.

Although the armistice lines remained the same, a far-reaching change of a different kind had occurred since the second Arab-Israeli war: The embittered Palestinian refugees had at last managed to begin forming an effective resistance organization.

The 725,000 Palestinians left homeless by the creation of Israel in 1948 now numbered about 1.3 million refugees still living in the hovels of refugee camps, 430,000 of them on the West Bank alone.* They were a constant source of trouble for the Arab nations as well as for Israel.

Time and time again Palestinian causes were lost and forgotten in the larger disputes between the competing Arab governments and their jealous leaders. The Palestine Liberation Organization was a good example. The groundwork for its creation had been laid at the first Arab summit meeting in January 1964 as a means to give the Palestinians an organization of their own; it officially came into being in September that year. But, in fact, it was under the control of Egypt, and President Gamal Abdel Nasser kept its ac-

---

* In addition to the West Bank refugees, 300,000 others were on Jordan's East Bank, 300,000 in the Gaza Strip, 160,000 in Lebanon and 136,000 in Syria.

tivities tightly reined in and directed away from guerrilla actions against Israel. More than any other Arab leader, Nasser had reason to respect Israel's power, which he had painfully experienced in 1956. He was cautious to the point of being accused of cowardice in avoiding any actions that might bring about war with the Jewish state. His caution was well founded. A secret study commissioned during the 1964 Arab summit revealed that it would take the Arabs at least until 1969 to reach a level of military strength equal to Israel's.

After listening for nearly twenty years to the vapid boastings of the Arab countries, the Palestinians had not gotten one inch of their land back. They had grown disillusioned and impatient. Out of this mass of restless and angry people emerged a small group who decided they could no longer wait for help from the Arab nations. They had been encouraged by the examples of the final success, in 1962, of the Algerian rebellion against France and by the Viet Cong's tactics against the United States in Southeast Asia, and they finally resolved to carry the fight themselves. As one of their early statements declared: The battle "must be today, not tomorrow."

The name of the new organization was Fatah, a double acronym from Harakat Tahrir Falestini, Movement for the National Liberation of Palestine. The initials HTF mean death in Arabic; when reversed they mean victory, which in turn is the title of the forty-eighth Sura of the Koran, which extols the capture of the holy city of Mecca in 630 A.D. by Mohammed. The Fatah Palestinians had as their ultimate goal the capture of another holy city as the capital of a Palestinian nation—Jerusalem.

Fatah's leader was known by a nom de guerre, Abu Ammar, actually Yasser Arafat, a round-faced, soft-voiced Palestinian refugee from Jerusalem in his mid-thirties who was by profession an engineer and by passion and dedication a totally devoted fighter against Israel. Since the late 1950s, he and a small group of other Palestinian refugees had been conspiring in various Arab nations to form an effective guerrilla campaign against Israel.

By 1964, despairing of ever having the fractious Arab governments unify enough to carry the war against Israel, Arafat and his colleagues evolved an ingenious strategy. Fatah would eschew all intra-Arab disputes and allegiances and devote itself solely to one aim: attacks on Israel. The theory was simple. Arafat and his cohorts believed that from these attacks would emerge Arab unity and from Arab unity would come the strength to defeat the Jewish state.

It was this theory that separated Fatah from all earlier guerrilla organizations and from Nasser and his many followers in the Arab world. Nasser believed that unity had to be achieved first, then recovery of Palestinian land. Arafat believed that Nasser was wrong. Unity would come only with the battle, not before it.

Thus Fatah's goal was clear: provoke war between Israel and its Arab neighbors.

The first public notice of the new terror organization came on New Year's Day 1965 when leaflets were distributed to the offices of newspapers in Beirut announcing "Military Communiqué No. 1 of the General Command of the Asifah [Storm] Forces." Asifah was the name that Fatah had given to its strike forces. The leaflet declared: "On the night of Friday 31 December—1 January 1965, detachments of our strike forces went into action, performing all the tasks assigned to them in the occupied territories and returning safely to their bases."

Actually, the announcement was premature. Lebanese security forces had arrested the Fatah raiders as they tried to cross into Israel from Lebanon. It appeared that Fatah, like other groups of Palestinian would-be fighters over the years, was just another band of posturing braggarts. But then on February 28 a small band of Fatah guerrillas finally did penetrate into the central sector of Israel from Jordan and placed explosives at a grain silo at Kfar Hess, a village about three miles from the Jordanian frontier. A hole was blown in the silo and one of the village's houses was also partly demolished.

The damage was minor and no injuries were caused, but that mattered less than one outstanding fact: Fatah had scored its first successful attack against Israel.

Other attacks soon followed. Materially, they were pinpricks; psychologically, they were deeply disturbing and highly provocative to the anxious Israeli population.

As early as March 16, it was clear that Israel was faced with a new, more extensive and worrisome threat than it had ever experienced from the Palestinians. A U.N. observer reported on that date that "it appears that these acts were planned and executed by a group, and were not the spontaneous acts of a single individual. It appears also from the evidence that the perpetrators of these acts escaped to the armistice demarcation line with the intention of crossing into Jordan."

Communiqués by Fatah, like Communiqué No. 1, frequently embroidered the extent of damage inflicted by the guerrilla raids and struck heroic poses about the valor of Fatah fighters. But still, as Israel's ambassador to the United Nations, Michael Comay, later noted before the Security Council, they usually had some basis in reality. "Although boastful and exaggerated, these communiqués are reasonably accurate about times and places. . . . The raids follow fairly standard procedures. They are usually carried out by a squad of three armed men who have crossed the border under cover of darkness and have returned before dawn. Demolition charges of a uniform type, with time fuses, are attached to village dwelling houses, water installations and other civilian targets, or different roadways are mined in the same fashion. The techniques and equipment used make clear that these men have been specially trained for such exploits, and operate under special direction."

Although Fatah was puny in numbers (later estimated at fewer than two hundred in 1965–66) and weak, its emergence carried grave implications for Israel. It meant that for the first time since the brief period before the 1956 Suez war Israel was being confronted by trained and organized guerrilla units. *Fedayeen* (self-sacrificers) trained by Egyptian forces had operated briefly against Israel in 1955–56, but they were eliminated by the Suez war. Otherwise, the numerous incursions and acts of sabotage inflicted on Israel since its existence had been mainly the work of untrained individuals and unorganized small bands seeking revenge and the recovery of their confiscated property. They had been desperate acts of insignificant efficacy.

Now, with Fatah, Israel was faced with a far more formidable enemy, and Israel's leaders knew better than anyone the problem posed by the serpentine frontiers. The long and winding armistice lines stretched for a distance of 590 miles around Israel and were nearly impossible to guard against a trained and determined foe. Even though the damage that Fatah could inflict remained comparatively minor and its threat as a military force was nonexistent, Fatah was a menacing challenge to Israel as a symbol of Palestinian and Arab resistance. Each new exploit won attention in the news media, spreading the name of Fatah, earning it increasing respect and support among restive Palestinians, and even spawning other fledgling guerrilla organizations.

Nothing could so demoralize the Israeli populace and discourage potential immigrants as repeated and unrestrained attacks on its civilian population. Nor could anything be more threatening to the achievement of the Zionist goal of making Israel into a beacon and a safe haven for the Jews of the world.

As the months passed and Fatah's exploits grew bolder, Israel's leaders came to an inescapable conclusion: Fatah had to be eliminated. The question was, how?

Israel at first employed its old tactic of nighttime retaliatory raids, initially developed in the early 1950s, sending military commandos against suspected guerrilla camps in Jordan and Lebanon. But Fatah proved as persistent as it was elusive. Its raids continued into 1966, and by April the pace of the hit-and-run sabotage operations was picking up.

Israel responded by calling an emergency meeting of the Israel-Jordan Mixed Armistice Commission, an arbitration panel made up of Israelis, Jordanians and U.N. observers that was established by the 1949 armistice to determine responsibility for armistice-line violations. At the meeting on April 20, Israel's representative warned: "I want to stress that my authorities are gravely concerned by this new outbreak of sabotage perpetrated by persons coming from Jordan. . . . We urgently request the Jordan authorities to take immediate measures to have this kind of activity stopped in good time."

But that, as Israeli authorities knew, was nearly impossible. Jordan's armistice line with Israel was the longest, stretching 392 miles. Jordan tried to police the frontier but was no more able to stop the guerrillas from crossing its long frontier than Israel was to keep them out. As Israeli Ambassador Comay later told the Security Council: "A glance at the map will show that Israel is long and narrow in shape, with nearly . . . [600] miles of open border, much of it winding through hills and desert. These borders are incapable of being sealed up physically."

That point was proved again on April 25 when three Israeli dwellings were blown up near the Jordan River at Beit Yosef in the Beit Shean area in northeast Israel. Three days later an army truck was damaged by a mine near the tourist attraction of Masada on the Dead Sea. Two buses, one of them filled with children, were directly behind the truck. Although they escaped damage, the possibility that one of them might have hit the mine caused a spasm of anger among the Israeli public.

On the night of April 29–30, Israel took its revenge by sending commandos to attack two Jordanian villages, killing eleven civilians and causing considerable damage. The Mixed Armistice Commission condemned Israel for the attack at Tel Arabain and said of the other at Rafat that the commission "calls upon the Israel authorities in the strongest terms to desist from their aggressions against Jordan which constitute a threat to peace and security."

But Israel's troubles with Fatah were not confined to the Jordanian frontier. Neighboring Syria, with a population of nearly six million, actively supported the guerrilla group. The radical regime in Damascus believed along with Arafat that the only way to achieve Arab unity was to provoke a war with Israel.

Up until 1966 Damascus had severely limited attacks from its territory in fear of Israeli retaliation. But on February 23 of that year, the thirteenth coup d'état in seventeen years brought to power an extreme pro-Palestinian government dedicated to Israel's destruction. Ironically, one of the factors that had weakened the administration of Amin Hafez and eased the way for the coup makers was the revelation the previous year that an Israeli spy had deeply penetrated his government. The spy, Eliahu Cohen, an Egyptian Jew who had emigrated to Israel in the 1950s, had been arrested in Damascus at the beginning of 1965 and subjected to public trial between February 28 and March 19. Carefully selected portions of the testimony were televised to limit damage to the Hafez regime, but nonetheless the revelations from the trial were explosive.

The fact that an Israeli agent could operate so successfully inside Syria gave the regime's enemies strength and other Arab nations an opportunity to heap scorn on the unpopular Hafez. Egypt, always ready to criticize its competing brother nation, accused Hafez of corruption and inefficiency. Other Arab states followed Egypt's lead. Iraq, Jordan, Kuwait, Lebanon and Saudi Arabia described Cohen as the "wizard spy" and the "master Zionist agent," and questioned Syria's capacity to contribute to Arab security.

Indeed, Cohen's accomplishments had been phenomenal. He had provided the spymasters in Tel Aviv with top political and military intelligence from the very core of the Hafez government, including detailed descriptions and photographs of Syria's heavily fortified positions along the Golan Heights overlooking Israel. It was information of immense value to Israel, and would be used with stunning effect in the 1967 war.

Cohen was publicly hanged in Martyrs Square on May 19, 1965, and his body, draped in a white sheet with a poster carrying his death sentence, was left to hang for six hours. Heavy radio and television coverage was given to the proceedings, which inflamed passions in Israel and elicited demands for revenge—demands that would reverberate until they were drowned out by the sounds of war.

In the meantime, the change of government in Syria in 1966 brought about a dramatic change of Syrian policy toward the Palestinian guerrillas. Syria's new leaders allowed Fatah to operate from their territory, an open provocation to Israel. On April 18 and May 16, mining incidents originating in Syria took the lives of two Israeli farmers and wounded a third. Tensions rapidly increased and Israel warned Syria that "this state of affairs cannot continue."

But it did. Within one twenty-four-hour period in July, Israel charged, four acts of sabotage and minelaying occurred from Syrian territory, taking the lives of two more Israelis and wounding two others. Israel retaliated on July 14 by sending airplanes eight miles inside Syria to attack earth-moving equipment being used to divert waters of the Baniyas River. Damascus complained to the U.N. Security Council about the attack but, much to Syria's disappointment, most members felt that any condemnatory resolution should be balanced by condemnation of the activities of Fatah as well.

On August 15, another clash occurred between Israel and Syria and quickly escalated into a battle involving planes, artillery and patrol boats in the Sea of Galilee. Israel announced it had shot down two Syrian MiGs; Syria said it had damaged ten gunboats and their base. Both sides accused the other of starting the fighting.

Afterward, Syria, still angered by the Security Council's failure to condemn Israel the previous month, vowed that henceforth it would ignore the United Nations and adopt a "new strategy" against Israel. No longer, announced Damascus, would Syria confine itself to defensive action but would "attack defined targets and bases of aggression within" Israel. Syrian Prime Minister Yousef Zayyen declared that Syria could not be expected to guard Israel against attacks from Fatah guerrillas.

The threats brought stern counterwarnings from Israel. Prime Minister Levi Eshkol, one of Israel's legendary founding fathers, was under increasing public pressure to combat the Fatah raids, and now he was moved to caution Syria that aggression would be met with "effective countermeasures." Major General Yitzhak Rabin, the military chief of staff, declared on September 11 in an interview with the Israeli Army's official organ, *Bamahane:* "The Syrians are the spiritual fathers of the Fatah group. . . . The military engagements which Israel has to conduct in Syria in reprisal for sabotage raids she suffers are therefore directed against the Syrian regime. . . . Our aim is to make the Syrian government change its mind, and to eliminate the cause of the raids."

Despite the warnings, Fatah raids originating in Syria continued. On October 7, four Israeli policemen were killed and two others wounded by a land mine in the Upper Galilee near the Syrian border. To Israeli complaints about Syria's failure to control the Fatah guerrillas, Prime Minister Zayyen repeated at a press conference in Damascus on October 10 that

Syria had no intention of curbing Fatah. "We are not sentinels over Israel's security and are not the leash that restrains the revolution of the displaced and persecuted Arab Palestinian people."

Tensions between Israel and Syria grew so great that the Soviet Union publicly came to Syria's support by verbally attacking Israel. It declared on October 12 that it had received information that Israel was concentrating troops along the Syrian frontier, and indicated that Moscow would support Syria. The next day *Pravda* printed an inflammatory version of Rabin's *Bamahane* interview, saying he had hinted that Israel planned to overthrow Zayyen's new Syrian government. Privately, the Soviets urged Syria and Egypt to draw closer together in defense against Israel.

By now the atmosphere was so charged by the raids, the diplomatic activity, the public taunts and posturings, that a major attack by Israel on Syria seemed an imminent likelihood. On November 4, Syria and Egypt reacted by taking a momentous action. They concluded a mutual-defense treaty.

Nasser, always skittish about provoking Israel, may have been motivated more by concern to gain some restraining influence over the reckless Syrian government than by an interest in forging the unified Arab front the Soviets desired. But whatever the case, one thing seemed clear: Fatah's strategy was working. Syria, the region's most radical and anti-Israel regime, was now formally linked with Egypt, the largest and most powerful Arab nation, with a population of thirty-one million.

The pact was highly disturbing to Israel, where it appeared the Soviet ambition to forge unity among the Arabs was succeeding.

On the same day that the Syrian-Egyptian pact was concluded Israel suffered another setback. The U.N. Security Council failed to act on its complaint about the October 7 mining incident that had taken the lives of four policemen. Ten members approved a draft resolution to "deplore" the incident, call on Syria to prevent Fatah raids, and to urge both Israel and Syria to desist from provocative acts. But the Soviet Union, seeking to show its friendship to the Arabs, vetoed the resolution on the grounds that it was not balanced since it did not condemn Israeli aggressiveness. It was the first Soviet veto in two years.

Just as Syria had been disappointed with the Council's failure to support its case in July, Israel was greatly perturbed by the Soviet veto. Emotions were by now feverish in Israel. In addition to the newfound unity between Syria and Egypt, there had in the meantime been new Fatah raids. These, combined with Syrian and Soviet threats and the Council's failure to chastise Syria, fueled Israelis' sense of indignation and isolation. It also gave new ammunition to Israeli hardliners, particularly in the intelligence community and the Army, who hotly argued that Israel could not depend on outside help and that Eshkol had to act more firmly.

Public anger had been especially aroused by the dynamiting of two homes in the Romema quarter of Jerusalem on October 8 in which four civilians were wounded. The sabotaged houses were only a mile from Prime Minister Eshkol's residence. Then on October 27 a freight train had been derailed, injuring one Israeli. Finally, on November 12 a land mine exploded under a military vehicle in the southern Hebron hills, killing three Israeli soldiers and wounding six. All three operations had originated in Jordan.

Under pressure from hardliners, Eshkol decided to hit back hard.

———————

At dawn on November 13, a large force of Israeli tanks and armored personnel cars accompanied by air cover sped across the border in the Hebron area into Jordan's West Bank, about thirty miles southwest of Jerusalem, smashed a police post and descended on the village of Samu. Firing their rifles and using loudspeakers, they routed the population of five thousand from their homes and then calmly spent the next four hours planting charges and blowing up 125 homes, the village clinic, a school and a workshop. Damaged were twenty-eight other houses and the village mosque.

A force of twenty trucks filled with Jordanian troops rushed to the village but ran into an Israeli ambush. None of the trucks got through. Four Jordanian Hunter Hawk airplanes also rose to the battle. One was shot down by Israeli planes.

When U.N. observers arrived at the site later that day, they found a scene of desolation. Fifteen soldiers and three Jordanian civilians had been killed and fifty-four persons wounded, including seventeen civilians. The body of one woman was still lying in a pool of blood in front of a home. The house next to it had been hit by twenty bullets. The observers reported they counted twenty domestic animals that had been killed "either by explosions or by small arms fire." They also observed in the area "one Bedouin dwelling tent and three Jordanian army tents completely destroyed."

In the nearby village of Khirbet Jinba, they found fifteen stone houses destroyed, seven damaged and one water well blown up. The police post at Rujm Madfaa was completely destroyed.

Israeli losses were one killed and ten wounded.

———————

The Samu attack, Israel's first boldly undertaken in daylight and conducted by an overwhelming force of regular army units, was Israel's answer to the question of how to combat Fatah. It represented a portentous decision by Israel and it meant the triumph of a new breed of Israelis. They were for the most part the native-born sabras and self-confident younger generation of military leaders. Instead of depending on the world powers, hat in hand, seeking approval and support, these Israelis stood tall and disdained the caution of their immigrant founding fathers. Illustrative of this audacious and proud son of the Israeli nation was Ezer Weizman, dashing air force hero and the number two leader of the Israel Defense Forces, who had largely influenced the decision to abandon stealthy night raids and conduct the daylight assault on Samu. His reasoning was typical of the boldness of the new breed.

"When a sovereign state decides to strike at its foes, it ought to act differently than night [raids]," Weizman wrote in his memoirs. "We have armor, and we have an air force. Let's go in by day, operating openly and in force."

His advice reflected Israel's might and brought an easy victory that boosted the morale of the public and Israel's military forces.

But in terms of achieving the goal of eliminating Fatah, it failed. Fatah continued to grow in strength and popularity among the restless Palestinian masses. And, without anyone yet recognizing it, the incident at Samu had given the region another push toward the war that Fatah and Syria desired and some hardliners like Weizman in Israel welcomed.

II
MOSCOW SEARCHES FOR ARAB UNITY

The boldness and destructiveness of the Israeli raid on Samu outraged the Arab world and nearly brought about the fall of the monarchy in Jordan. Riots swept the nation. There were loud protests that the government had failed to provide security for the villagers and had refused to arm them to protect themselves.

Particularly distraught were the defenseless Palestinians who had been the direct victims. Correspondent Joe Alex Morris, Jr., of the Los Angeles *Times,* visited the devastated village the day after the raid and found the villagers angry and bitter. Their passions were directed not only at Israel but at the king of Jordan and at the United States, on which they blamed their plight because of America's support for Israel.

"If America did not support the Jews, you would see what we would do," one embittered villager told Morris. Others complained about their defenselessness, which they blamed on the king. "What do they expect us to fight with—with women? With children? Or with stones?"

Not only was the ease with which the Israeli force had brought off the raid humiliating, but it had come the day before the state visit of President Mohammad Ayub Khan of Pakistan. Samu and other towns throughout Jordan had been festooned with the flags of Jordan and Pakistan in celebration of the visit. Khan's visit coincided with the celebration of the thirty-first birthday of King Hussein ibn Talal ibn Abdullah ibn Hussein Al Hashimi.*

* The name denotes the king's genealogy: son (ibn) of King Talal, the grandson of King Abdullah, the great-grandson of Hussein, Sharif of Mecca and keeper of the holy places, from the clan of Hashimi, indicating descent from the Prophet Mohammed.

Short, muscular, ruggedly handsome and personally courageous, an alumnus of Harrow and Sandhurst, Hussein was a moderate toward Israel and a friend of the West. But by no means was he a sycophant, although for years he had accepted secret CIA funds.* When he thought his cause was just, as he was later to view Arab retaliation for Israeli attacks, he did not hesitate to part company with his American sponsors.

Over the years, Hussein had survived countless assassination attempts, the displeasure of Britain when he ousted Glubb Pasha in 1956, and incendiary verbal attacks by Egypt and Syria. He usually carried a pistol for his own protection. Except for Nasser, he had ruled longer (since August 12, 1952) than any other living leader in the Middle East. He flew his own plane, drove fast cars and liked the company of beautiful women. But in diplomacy he was as cautious as a high-wire walker.

His circumspection was well founded. At fifteen years of age, he had been at his grandfather Abdullah's side at the Al Aqsa Mosque in Jerusalem for Friday prayers when the aged monarch was shot and killed on July 20, 1951, by a disgruntled Palestinian. One of the assassin's bullets hit a medal on Hussein's chest but caused him no serious injury.

Abdullah, a moderate in his attitude toward Israel, had been disliked by many Palestinians. As the first ruler of Transjordan, which Britain created in 1921, he had since then steadily strengthened his small realm. He took advantage of Israel's failure to capture a large portion of the West Bank in 1948–49 by formally annexing it, including east Jerusalem and all of the Old City, in April 1950. He gave his new Palestinian subjects Jordanian passports and changed the country's name to the Hashemite Kingdom of Jordan. The annexation was recognized by only two nations, Britain and Pakistan, and was resented by many Palestinians. They felt Abdullah's Arab Legion had let them down in the war and that he now was capitalizing on their misery by expanding his kingdom by taking their land.

Annexation of the West Bank gave Jordan a large Palestinian population. Originally populated mainly by Bedouins fiercely loyal to the Hashemites, Jordan had been flooded by a half million refugees as a result of the 1948–49

---

* Hussein received the money from 1957 to 1977, when it was stopped after the Washington *Post*'s Bob Woodward learned of the arrangement and broke the story on February 18, 1977. It was never established exactly how much the king received in this arrangement, but estimates ranged up to a total of $15 million. His supporters said the money was used to finance his security services; his detractors said it was to support his royal life-style. Whatever the case, such arrangements by the CIA were not uncommon—although by no means routine—and usually were used to buttress a friendly head of state who might have had difficulty receiving open aid because of congressional opposition.

war. By the mid-1960s, they made up as much as half of Jordan's population of two million. This large group, already disaffected and dispossessed, was especially unhappy with Hussein because of his inability to protect Palestinians from Israel's heavy raids.

Ever since Fatah's operations had begun, Israel's retaliatory attacks had been primarily against West Bank Palestinian villages suspected of harboring guerrillas. The attacks stoked Palestinian resentment of Hussein for not stopping the Israelis and for failing to provide adequate protection for the West Bankers. Still, Hussein's rule had seemed secure as late as May 1966 when a visiting journalist wrote about Jordan's "remarkable spell of political tranquility. The benefits can be seen in the tourist boom, the well-stocked shops, the high rate of building and the newly planted fields and orchards."

After Samu, all this changed. The Palestinians' lingering resentment erupted in massive antigovernment riots that continued throughout November and had to be put down forcefully. One of the worst days of rioting was November 24, when ten thousand Palestinians, mainly refugees, surged through the streets of Hebron, near Samu, demanding weapons to fight Israel. They burned cars, including the local governor's, and scuffled with police and Jordanian troops for seven hours before they were finally dispersed. Three rioters were wounded during the confrontation and many were arrested. Similar demonstrations occurred that day in other major Palestinian cities. Curfews were widely imposed.

Jerusalem had been quiet, but the next day, Friday the twenty-fifth, the day of worship for Moslems, all mosques held prayers for the "martyrs of Samu." Afterward, huge riots erupted near the Damascus Gate in the Old City. Hussein's pictures were torn down, rocks were thrown, and antigovernment slogans were shouted, "Down with monarchy!" "Give us arms!" Jordanian police and soldiers fired into the crowds, killing three persons and wounding many. The riots spread outside the Old City when the demonstrators carried over their heads to the office of Anwar Khatib, governor of Jordanian Jerusalem, the body of one of the victims. Police waded into the crowd with clubs flailing and eventually were able to quell the demonstration and turn the body over to the victim's family. But Palestinian passions remained high.

On the same day as the Jerusalem riot, the U.N. Security Council passed Resolution 228 censuring Israel "for this large-scale military action in violation of the United Nations Charter and of the General Armistice Agreement between Israel and Jordan." The vote was 14 to 0, with New Zealand abstaining. The United States supported the censure, declaring that America "respects the sovereignty and territorial integrity of all countries in the Middle East." It was a phrase that was to be much heard in the developing crisis.

After the November 25 vote, the ambassadors of Israel and Jordan engaged in an illuminating dialogue that succinctly summed up the Israelis' and the Arabs' opposing views of their conflict in the Middle East.

Ambassador Michael Comay, deploring the resolution, presented Israel's case. He charged that the "fundamental cause of Arab-Israeli tension . . . lies in Arab belligerence and military threat to Israel." Second, he added, "In the last two years these Arab policies have spawned a pattern of organized terrorist and sabotage raids from the territory of neighboring states into the territory of Israel, resulting in death, destruction and insecurity within our borders." The duty of Israel's government, he pointed out, was to provide security for its citizens. "We are open to the consideration of any effective means of ensuring this result," he told the Council. "What we cannot accept is that our neighbors should deem that they have a right to kill us and violate our territory with impunity."

Comay deplored the fact that none of Israel's complaints against the Arabs were ever adopted by the Council and expressed his belief that the resolution would fail to help solve the region's problems. "These problems cannot be solved so long as the people of Israel are not permitted to live peaceful and secure lives within their own borders and so long as the international community does not insist on neighboring states conducting themselves towards Israel in accordance with Charter principles, armistice commitments and the concept of peaceful coexistence."

Jordan's Ambassador Mohammad H. Farra directly disputed the Israeli version of the fundamental causes of the Middle East conflict. "The causes behind the tension . . . are, first, the forcible occupation of an area belonging to its inhabitants, to its rightful people, by foreigners coming from outside," Farra said. "The second cause is the refusal of the occupiers to permit repatriation of refugees. . . . If one wishes to look deeper, one will find that the real causes are the ideology and the acts, deeds and behavior based on that destructive thinking—the thinking of Zionism calling for more immigration, more expansion, more expelling of Arabs, acquiring more of their lands."

Farra expressed gratitude for the passage of the censuring resolution, but he complained that it was merely a warning and had not been tough enough. "We do not see the need for any more warnings," he said, referring to the five previous times Israel had been censured, condemned or found by the

Council to be acting inconsistently with the terms of the U.N. Charter.*
"We feel that, with this background of condemnation and repeated defiance, sanctions should have been invoked immediately."

Passage of the resolution brought outrage in Israel, where resentment still lingered over the Soviet Union's veto of Israel's complaint against Syria earlier that month. Prime Minister Levi Eshkol called the Security Council's action a "one-sided decision" and asserted that it was "the duty and right of an attacked state to defend itself." Eshkol's remarks were made at the regular Sunday Cabinet meeting on November 27, 1966, and, in an unusual departure from practice, broadcast over national radio.

"Our experience teaches us that self-defense is imperative for our survival," Eshkol declared. He added that Israel had not been created "in order that it should be left defenseless against sabotage and murder."

Eshkol's remarks were meant to mollify his frustrated countrymen, who were shocked by worldwide criticism of the Samu raid without similar criticism being directed at the terror raids. The criticism was also mixed with some provocative sneers that Israel had struck against defenseless Jordan instead of the real villain, Syria, because Israelis were afraid of the Syrians. It was a taunt that Israel's activist military men were unlikely to appreciate.

Israelis were especially frustrated because they feared that world criticism and the censure resolution would encourage more terrorist attacks. That fear was quickly realized. Only a day after the Council vote, and a day before Eshkol's remarks, an Israeli was wounded near the Jordanian frontier by a burst of automatic weapons fire. It was the first terrorist attack since the Samu raid. For Israelis, especially the hardliners in intelligence and the Army, the message was clear. Guerrillas could attack them without condemnation from the world community, but Israel could retaliate only at the risk of international criticism.

From this time on, the voices of activists like Major General Weizman, who advocated strong retaliatory raids, grew louder and increasingly more respected in political councils at the expense of Prime Minister Levi Eshkol.

Weizman was the flamboyant nephew of Chaim Weizmann (Ezer dropped the extra *n*), the first president of Israel. Born in 1924 in Tel Aviv, handsome, charming, and charismatic, Weizman was a brilliant Royal Air Force–trained pilot, a daredevil from the age of the flowing silk scarf and

* The other times: May 18, 1951, SC Resolution 93; November 24, 1953, #101; March 29, 1955, #106; January 19, 1956, #111; and April 9, 1962, #171.

clipped British accent. Considered by some military men to be Israel's greatest general, he was at this time the chief of operations of the Israel Defense Forces and one of Israel's most vocal nationalists.

It was not fashionable in the 1960s for Israelis to talk about claims to Arab lands in Judea and Samaria, the biblical names of the West Bank, but Weizman, like the other outspoken nationalist of the time, opposition leader Menachim Begin,* was unabashedly open about his desire to capture those areas. His outspokenness made him less than popular with the leading Labor Party politicians. As he later wrote: "To them I was a wild man, with horrifying opinions: a senior commander who claimed that we have the right to Hebron and Nablus and all of Jerusalem, and that we must endeavor to implement that right by force of arms, if there is no other alternative; a character who could influence young people with his claim that Zionist rights cannot be divided between Beersheva and Hebron, but between hypocrisy and honesty and who said that anyone who claimed we had the right to Beersheva [inside Israel] but not to Hebron [on the West Bank] was sinning against Zionism, against the state and against his own conscience.

"They viewed me as a 'national desperado' who preached that the best pilot in the world isn't just a man who knows how to squeeze the right button and send off his missile at the right moment, but must believe in the justice of his deeds in defense of the rights of the Jewish people to the land of Israel."

To a large measure, it was Weizman and other young, usually native-born, Israelis like him in senior military and intelligence positions who formed the chorus of activists demanding tougher and more direct confrontation with the Arabs. They believed, along with Begin and his philosophy of Revisionist Zionism, that *Eretz Yisrael*, the ancient land of Israel, which to them meant not only the West Bank of Palestine but the East Bank too, belonged to the Jews by birth and biblical prophecy. Like Begin's mentor, the late Vladimir Jabotinsky, a Ukrainian journalist from Odessa who had espoused a militant, mystical Zionism that was abhorrent to most of Israel's founding fathers, they believed there could be no accommodation with the Arabs.

Weizman and the other activists, small in number but powerful and vocal, wanted all the land. And of all the land, they especially wanted all of Jeru-

---

* When Begin became prime minister in 1977, he appointed Weizman as his defense minister. But Weizman over the years had become less hawkish. His only son, Shaul, had been seriously wounded in 1970, and Weizman, after playing a significant role in achieving the peace treaty with Egypt in 1978, finally resigned his post in 1980 because of disillusionment with the inflexible policies of Begin.

salem, including the Old City, the ancient, golden symbol of the original Jewish nation.

It was against these emotions so unabashedly proclaimed by believers in *Eretz Yisrael* like Weizman and Begin that Levi Eshkol, Abba Eban and the traditional leaders of the old ruling Labor Party, the repository of the humanistic ideals of the original pioneers and founders of Israel, now had to compete.

Theirs was a competition nearly as old as Zionism itself. It was a profound struggle over the very nature of the Zionist state, voiced in terms of contending viewpoints and attitudes toward the Arabs and about the legitimate goals of Israel's destiny. At its heart was the old argument between the early humanism of the founding fathers and the militant mysticism of Jabotinsky and Begin, who had waged some of the bloodiest terrorism against Arabs and the British in the 1940s before the establishment of Israel.

Prime Minister Eshkol was a hesitant, cautious, kindly and moderate leader. Now seventy-one years of age, squat, unpretentious and a lover of Yiddish jokes, Eshkol had been prime minister since succeeding in 1963 the grand Old Man of Israel, David Ben Gurion. Like Ben Gurion, he was one of the pioneer immigrants of the second *aliyah,* that legendary group of turn-of-the-century settlers who had done so much to establish the Jewish state and who had ruled Israel since its founding. Born Levi Shkolnik in the village of Oratovo in the Ukraine on October 25, 1895, he emigrated to Palestine in 1914, where he took the nearest Hebrew equivalent of his name, Eshkol, which literally meant "a bunch." In Palestine, Eshkol worked on a kibbutz, helped found in 1921 the Histadrut, the General Federation of Labor, and spent the rest of his career with the Jewish Agency and as an official of the socialist Mapai Party. Ben Gurion appointed him minister of finance in 1952, a powerful post he held until becoming prime minister.

Eshkol was an excellent finance minister, a superb organizer and a shrewd politician. His deceptive lack of charisma, his frequent indecisiveness and his halting, wooden speaking style hid his talents as a moderate and thoughtful leader. He spoke six languages, Hebrew, Yiddish, English, French, German and Russian, had a knowledge of Latin, and was an indefatigable worker. He became the first Israeli prime minister to visit the United States officially when President Johnson received him at the White House in 1964. He loved good food, good company, an occasional cognac and, though seemingly few of his colleagues knew it, power.

In the eyes of the young native-born Israelis, impatient for rule themselves and intolerant of the old immigrants' Diasporic ways, Eshkol was increasingly coming to symbolize what they considered tired and old-fashioned leadership. To them, Eshkol was too hesitant, too homey and remindful of the obsequiousness of the Diaspora Jew, too tolerant of their Arab enemies. They criticized him harshly for his indecisiveness, and repeated with glee a current joke about him. The joke asked how Eshkol responded when he was questioned whether he wanted coffee or tea. After hesitating, he answered: half and half.

Eshkol's tragedy was that he had come to power too late, too old. Israel had changed. It was no longer a small settlement of Diaspora Jews fleeing persecution and depending on outside powers for their security. It was now a power in its own right in the Middle East, a sovereign nation of dedicated, ambitious, native-born sons anxious to make names for themselves and sure of their ability to defend themselves and take what they considered theirs.

Eshkol had disturbed many of these Israeli activists in February 1966 when he appointed the moderate Abba Eban, Israel's longtime ambassador in the United States, as his foreign minister. Eban, like Eshkol, sought accommodation, not confrontation, with Israel's Arab neighbors. As late as May 31, less than six months before the Samu raid and in the midst of mounting Fatah raids, Eshkol and Eban had been actively searching for a peaceful solution to the Arab-Israeli conflict.

Their efforts were appreciated in Washington, as were the difficulties they faced from the militants. A National Security Council memorandum that spring observed: "Since Eban took over, he has set up his own task force to study the whole Arab-Israeli problem. Eshkol is fully aboard. They are looking for ways to break down the 'fortress Israel' idea and to build bridges to the Arabs. A lot of good ideas are forming."

But, the memorandum noted, the Eban-Eshkol effort was not without political risk. "The steps Eban's people are considering—greater contact between Arabs and Israelis—lay them open to the charge of letting down Israel's defenses."

Now, with the Samu raid and the Security Council censure, these conciliatory efforts began to atrophy as Israel's hardliners grew in power and Israel's policy moved toward a new aggressiveness.

King Hussein immediately detected the change, and openly worried whether the new policy was aimed at gaining more land for Israel. President Lyndon B. Johnson tried to quiet these fears in a letter to the king shortly after the Samu raid.

"... Ambassador [Findley] Burns has informed me of Your Majesty's concern that Israel's policies have changed and that Israel now intends to occupy territory on the West Bank of the Jordan River," Johnson wrote on November 23. "While I can understand the reason for this concern, we have good reason to believe it highly unlikely that the events you fear will in fact occur. In this connection my government's opposition to the use of force to alter armistice lines or borders in the Near East has been made unmistakably clear to all parties concerned. The strong private representations we have made in Israel as well as our forthright public statements make clear that should Israel adopt the policies you fear it would have the gravest consequences. There is no doubt in my mind that our position is fully understood and appreciated by the Israelis."

These soothing words from the superpower were welcomed by Hussein, as was the Security Council censure of Israel. But even if they reassured him about the perceived threat from Israel, they did nothing to redress his grievances—or to protect him from his many other enemies in the region. These included such socialist Arab states as Egypt and Syria, with their support by the Soviet Union, and the Palestinian nationalist groups like Fatah and the Palestine Liberation Organization.

Egypt, as the leader of the socialist Arab states, had long been at odds with the conservative, pro-Western monarchies of Jordan and Saudi Arabia, which were supported by the United States. Over the years Cairo and Amman had heaped a colorful catalogue of epithets on each other's leader, Hussein being called, among other things, the "harlot of Amman" and the "CIA dwarf," while President Nasser was labeled the "arch-villain, the sinister plotter, the man who ... had betrayed the cause of the Palestinian people." After the Samu raid, Cairo broadcasts accused Hussein of weakness and failure to protect his citizens. The king's radio lashed back by taunting Cairo for failure to come to Jordan's aid and for hiding behind the lines of UNEF, the United Nations Emergency Force, which since the 1956 Suez war had patrolled the Egyptian-Israeli frontier. It was a painful charge for Nasser; the stationing of these several thousand troops in the Sinai had been one of the few gains Israel scored in the war.

No less bitter were Hussein's relations with his northern neighbor, Syria. The new Syrian regime left little doubt that it also believed the battle against Israel could begin only after Hussein was replaced by a ruler more aggressive in his attitude toward Israel.

Fatah and the Palestine Liberation Organization also sought Hussein's overthrow. As Palestinian organizations, both groups had to operate among the hundreds of thousands of refugees in Jordan, yet Hussein severely limited their activities.

The PLO took its case to the public and poisoned the atmosphere with provocative statements calling for Hussein's overthrow. The PLO leader, Ahmed Shukairy, a windy, white-haired Palestinian attorney who was totally subservient to Egypt's Gamal Abdel Nasser, referred to Hussein as the "tyrant of Amman" and branded him a traitor to the Palestinian cause. Shukairy was publicly advised by Cairo's semiofficial newspaper *Al Gomhuria* that "the Palestine Liberation Organization has no alternative but to enter a battle to the finish with the Jordanian ruler."

PLO agitators were behind many of the riots following the Samu raid, and Hussein struck back on November 26 by closing the PLO's office in Jerusalem and arresting hundreds of PLO members. "In this country there will be one army with one loyalty," Hussein insisted.

That was certainly his desire, but in the turbulent climate created by the Fatah attacks and the Samu raid neither he nor anyone else could be certain where the volatile emotions of the refugees would carry their allegiance.

As Hussein's unhappy relations with his Arab neighbors demonstrated, unity was the Arab nations' elusive will-o'-the-wisp. Much rhetoric was devoted to it, but only once had a formal union actually been attempted. That had occurred in the late 1950s when Baathists came to power in Syria. The Baathists were socialists who believed in secular nationalism tinged by a mystical belief in the "Arab nation," by which was meant the unity of all the Arab nations much as it existed during the splendor of Mohammed's Arab Empire more than a thousand years earlier. But unity could never come without the cooperation of the largest and most influential Arab nation, Egypt. The Baathists began to woo Gamal Abdel Nasser, then at the height of his popularity as a result of the Suez war, urging him to form a united nation incorporating Egypt and Syria. Despite many misgivings on Nasser's part, not the least of them his reluctance to get involved in Syria's internecine politics and complex religious and tribal rivalries, the emotional appeal of Arab unity swept all before it. Nasser finally gave in to Syrian blandishments and popular demand and formed the United Arab Republic with Syria on February 1, 1958.

His hesitations were soon justified. After a rocky and unhappy union of three and a half years, the Syrians, brawling among themselves and angry at being treated like an insignificant northern province of Egypt, proclaimed their secession from the United Arab Republic on September 28, 1961.

Egypt officially retained the name United Arab Republic, but ever since, relations between the two countries had been strained. Syria under the Baathists became increasingly strident in its opposition to Israel and openly impatient with Nasser's cautious attitude. The attacks piqued Nasser, who of course realized that the combined might of the Arabs did not match Israel's. At a session of the Palestinians' representatives, called the Palestine National Conference, convened in May 1965 in Cairo, he angrily lashed back at a Syrian complaint about Egypt's timidity in "hiding" behind the lines of UNEF. "They say, 'Drive out UNEF.' Suppose that we do, is it not essential that we have a plan? If Israeli aggression takes place against Syria, shall I attack Israel? Then Israel is the one which determines the battle for me. It hits a tractor or two to force me to move. Is this a wise way? We have to determine the battle."

His wise counsel held the day. But then the Syrian government fell in a military coup and was replaced by the fire-breathing leftist Baathist regime of President Attassi and Prime Minister Zayyen in February 1966. The new government was hailed almost immediately by Moscow. On March 6, *Pravda* gave a hint of the Soviet Union's ambitions when, noted an observer, it "made special mention of the Syrian leadership's foreign policy objectives, notably the achievement of an alliance of all progressive Arab elements, including especially the UAR. . . ."

By April 18, Prime Minister Zayyen was in Moscow for a series of high-level meetings that resulted in Russia pledging around $120 million for construction of a Euphrates River dam and other aid. The final communiqué, issued April 25, said the two countries "confirmed their solidarity with Palestinian Arabs . . . their determined support for the Arab people in Aden . . . and the Arab Yemeni people."

Without apparently realizing the elusiveness and difficulty of achieving Arab unity, the Soviets now embarked on a major campaign to bring the socialist Arab nations together under the tutelage of Moscow. From the strategic perspective of the Soviet Union, the Syrian coup had been a windfall. It had, the Soviets believed, suddenly created the opportunity for Moscow to achieve the long-cherished goal of bringing into Russia's zone of influence the strategic Persian Gulf with its rich oil resources and an opening to the Indian Ocean.

Indeed, everywhere Moscow looked in the Middle East that winter of 1966, opportunity seemed to be beckoning. Foremost was the vacuum left by the inactivity of the United States because of its total involvement in Vietnam. The war was consuming the attentions of Washington to the exclusion of all other foreign issues. The United States could not afford another war, and while the Soviet Union was not seeking one, the situation was an invitation to Soviet adventurism.

The Middle East was ripe for political exploitation. The new Syrian government of President Nureddin Attassi openly sought alliance with the Soviet Union and, to prove its leftist credentials, appointed a Communist to the Cabinet, the first Communist ever to serve in such a high post in any Arab country. The Syrians also professed a strong desire for unity among the Arab socialist countries, by which were meant, foremost, Egypt, Iraq and Yemen. Such a coalition, supported and guided by the Soviet Union, would be a formidable bloc of friendly nations in the center of the Arab heartland.

Beyond that, the southwest section of the barren Arabian Peninsula seemed ready for plucking by Moscow. Civil wars raged in both Yemen and the British Crown Colony of Aden at the southern tip of the peninsula bounded by the Red Sea and the Persian Gulf. Egypt was deeply involved in both wars.

The capping opportunity for Moscow was Britain's Labour government's announcement on February 22, the day before the Syrian coup, that in 1968 it would withdraw its troops from Aden, where it had ruled since 1839. This would leave a vacuum that Moscow apparently believed it could fill.

From this time on, Russia made a concerted effort to secure unity among the socialist Arab states with the aim of influencing them and extending its own influence into the Arabian Peninsula.

Israeli intelligence immediately sensed the increased activity of Moscow in the region and quickly perceived what the Russians were out to accomplish. It was an alarming and frightening prospect for the beleaguered country. For if Moscow was successful, Israel's hostile Arab neighbors would be strengthened by unity and the Soviet Union would become a power in the region. This would be at the expense of U.S. influence, which Israel depended on for its ultimate security.

The fears of the Israeli intelligence community were communicated in the strategic estimates routinely shared with the Central Intelligence Agency. From now until the war, the Israeli estimates expressed "intense and growing alarm," in the words of James Critchfield, who throughout the 1960s was chief of the CIA's Middle East division within the Deputy Directorate for Plans, better known as the clandestine services.

"The Israelis were very worried," Richard Helms, director of Central Intelligence, said later. "In a sense, they shared Moscow's appreciation of the situation. But what the Soviets saw as an opportunity, the Israelis regarded as a threat. They could see the Soviets sitting in southwest Arabia, blocking the Red Sea and denying them access to the Indian Ocean and at the same time their Arab enemies unifying against them with Soviet support. They were getting scared in the early part of 1966 and they got increasingly so as the months passed. There was a note of rising anxiety in their estimates."

Israel's apprehensions—particularly rife in the Army and the intelligence community—and Russia's ambitions were to play an important role in explaining Israeli actions over the following months leading to war.

Support of the Palestinians became a major policy of the new Syrian regime. President Attassi publicly declared within three weeks of coming to power that the "liberation of Palestine" was the central goal of his revolutionary government, a goal that could be achieved only with Arab unity. "We believe that postponement of the liberation battle will increase the enemy's chances of survival," he declared at a Baathist Party congress on that day, echoing Fatah's position. "Through its call for the liberation war, the revolution believes that the chances of unity will increase. Unity will be forged in the flames of the liberation war, which will be a decisive factor in providing the psychological, political and military atmosphere."

Two months later, on May 23, he told army units stationed on the southwestern frontier with Israel: "We want a full-scale, popular war of liberation ... We want a policy of scorched earth, and it is only through this policy that we can hope to build a new life for the Arab masses."

Syria's zealous rhetoric against Israel was fueled in part by a sense of injustice. For almost two decades, Israelis and Syrians had been dueling over ownership of a demilitarized zone between their two countries. It was made up of three sectors comprising only 66.5 square kilometers around the Sea of Galilee in the northeast part of Israel, but it caused more trouble over the years than any other issue between Israel and Syria. The zone had been created out of Arab and Israeli farmland at the end of the 1948–49 war to keep Israeli and Syrian troops apart. The armistice between the two countries called for continued farming of the zone by Arabs and Jews, each cultivating their land under the supervision of the chairman of the U.N. Syrian-Israeli Mixed Armistice Commission, which was headed by a U.N. officer and had representatives from both Israel and Syria.

Suddenly, in March 1951, Israel declared that the part of the zone lying within the former international boundary of Palestine, now under Israeli control, belonged solely to Israel. Athough Arab farmers had been cultivating the land for centuries, the Israelis demonstrated their resolve later that year by forcefully evicting the two thousand Syrian inhabitants of three villages, Baggara, Ghanname and Khouri Farm, lying within the zone. The villages were destroyed and the villagers were not allowed to return until the U.N. Security Council ordered Israel to let them back. Only about 350 returned, but not for long. During the Suez war they were again pushed out by

Israel into Syria proper, where they remained, their lands being tilled from that time on by Israelis.

In order to prevent Israeli cultivation of the Arab land in the zone, Syria began to shell Israeli tractors from the Golan Heights, a towering plateau overlooking the northern Jordan Valley and the Sea of Galilee. The Israelis responded by putting amored plate on their tractors, arming their farmers and countering Syrian artillery fire with artillery salvos of their own. In their turn, the Syrians dug deep fortifications and converted the Heights into a mini Maginot Line that eventually consisted of a half million mines, two-level underground operations bases, and miles of trenches and communications tunnels.

Over the years, the exchanges of fire between Israel and Syria in the Golan Heights area were a constant source of friction between the two countries. They soon were to lead to a battle even more incendiary than the Samu raid.

A fire fight between Israel and Syria at the Golan Heights erupted on the first day of 1967, opening another round of battles and guerrilla raids. Although casualties were minor, the skirmishes kept tensions high. Both sides complained to the Security Council about violations of the armistice agreement, but the Council confined its action to calling on Israel and Syria to talk over their troubles. Then on January 14, a Fatah mine exploded at a soccer field at Dishon near the Syrian frontier and took the life of one Israeli youth and wounded two others.

Israelis were outraged and demands for firm retaliation increased. Israel's hardliners upped their pressure on Eshkol. Walworth Barbour, the U.S. ambassador in Israel, cabled Washington: "Eshkol is reported to have expressed himself . . . as at a loss as to what course he should take. . . . My feeling is that Eshkol really finds himself in a serious dilemma and would appreciate as much hand-holding as is possible in a position where he is trying to find a peaceful way out in face of considerable pressures for direct action."

Israel launched a diplomatic campaign to warn Syria that there was a "legitimate limit even to self-restraint." It also agreed to attend for the first time since February 16, 1960, a meeting of the Syrian-Israeli Mixed Armistice Commission. But after three contentious sessions, beginning on January 25, in which Israel insisted on talking only about cultivation within the demilitarized zone and Syria spent its time demanding that Israel remove its forces from the zone, the talks broke off without achieving anything except more rancor.

Israel's sense of being besieged was increased on January 23 when a new guerrilla group, identifying itself as Heroes of the Repatriation and suspected of being associated with the PLO, openly boasted of dynamiting an ammunition dump near Jerusalem.

The tense atmosphere was kept charged by inflammatory threats from both sides. By February 4, correspondent Alfred Friendly was reporting to the Washington *Post* from Jerusalem that "the Israeli government is energetically advertising its intent to give Syria a bloody nose by strong military action. . . . Government officials talk freely . . . of what the action will be. They speak of an armed thrust in relatively large force. . . . It would be begun by a heavy air attack on the Syrian gun positions that command [the Golan Heights]."

Syria's President Attassi was no less provocative. He repeated his statement that Syria would not limit guerrilla actions and, on February 22, he publicly declared that "it is the duty of all of us now to move from defensive positions to offensive positions and enter the battle to liberate the usurped land. . . . Everyone must face the test and enter the battle to the end."

Unwillingly, but inevitably, King Hussein was being dragged ever deeper into the boiling controversy. Members of the Arab League, the official organization of Arab states, were calling on him to allow troops volunteered by Iraq and Saudi Arabia to be stationed in Jordan to defend Palestinians against Israeli raids. When Hussein refused, prudently suspecting they might be used against him rather than Israel, Nasser taunted the king by calling him a puppet of the United States. Hussein responded by withdrawing his ambassador from Cairo on February 22. He also stepped up his charges that Nasser was hiding behind UNEF's skirts. Hussein's prime minister, Wasfi Tell, now went so far as to charge that Nasser had colluded in 1956 with Israel and Dag Hammerskjold, at the time secretary-general of the United Nations, to abandon its "role in the struggle for Palestine." The proof of this conspiracy, claimed Tell, was the continued presence of UNEF troops on Egyptian territory at the Egyptian-Israeli frontier.

The repeated airing of these charges encouraged some Egyptian officials to propose that Nasser expel UNEF, but this he refused to do. He well recognized that such an act could lead to war. But just as the mounting tensions were goading Israeli activists to advocate tougher measures, so too were Egyptian military men becoming outspoken in urging war.

Nasser, like Hussein and like Eshkol, was beginning to feel the pressure of attacks from all sides. He was being taunted not only by "rightist" Jordan but by "leftist" Syria, which openly wanted him to act more boldly against Israel and work harder for Arab unity. But still the cautious Egyptian leader refused to be goaded into taking action against Israel. Of all the Arab states, his had the most to lose by provoking Israel and the least to gain. His army was vulnerable to Israel's air force, he sought no land from Israel, and he had comparably few Palestinians living in Egypt and exerting political pressure on him.

Nasser answered his critics in a newspaper interview on March 26 by asserting that victory over Israel could only come with Arab unity. "Israel can be attacked only from the territory of Jordan and Syria," he declared. "But conditions in Jordan and Syria have to be in order so that we in Egypt can be sure we will not be stabbed in the back. . . ."

Nasser's position became even more tenuous on April 7, when the largest battle since the Samu raid erupted. Syrian gunners fired from their Golan Heights positions on an Israeli tractor farming in the demilitarized zone. Artillery fire was exchanged and the fight quickly escalated. Israel sent airplanes against the Syrian gun positions and several Syrian villages. The Syrians responded by sending up MiG jets, and an all-out dogfight ensued. Before it was over, Israel downed six of the MiGs and forced others back into Syria, chasing them all the way to Damascus.

The Arab world was outraged at the sight of Israeli planes flying over Syria's capital, and Nasser was strongly criticized for tolerating Israel's aggressiveness. Jordan was unmerciful in its jeers. *Al Quds,* a Palestinian daily located in Jerusalem, unkindly asked: "What has Cairo done in face of this flagrant air aggression on Damascus?" Many Arabs were asking the same thing. After all, Egypt was committed to come to Syria's defense under its mutual-defense treaty signed the previous November.

Nasser took to the radio to defend himself. "King Hussein was very angry, and he and his mother were weeping because the [mutual-defense] agreement had not been implemented," Nasser said sarcastically. Then he explained: "Fighter planes have a limited range. Our fighter planes cannot reach the Syrian border."

The criticism was taking its toll. Nasser was increasingly being forced on the defensive to justify his continued acceptance of UNEF troops and his inaction against Israel, relentlessly being pushed closer to Syria to demonstrate his loyalty to Arab unity and the Palestinian cause.

From Syria's perspective, the battle had been welcome. Information Minister Mahmoud Zubi declared the next day that the battle would be "followed by more severe battles until Palestine is liberated and the Zionist

57

presence ended." President Attassi boasted on April 17 that the fight had been "very useful to us."

What he meant by that was illustrated on the same day he made his remarks. Egypt's prime minister arrived in Damascus that day, the highest official to visit since the 1961 rupture between the two countries. He was there for talks on mutual defense. Five days later a communiqué was released saying the two sides had agreed "to carry out joint plans under the joint defense agreement between them." It added that they were in agreement in considering the "battle for the liberation of Palestine" as the main cause around which the Arab masses should rally.

The goals sought by the Soviet Union and Fatah seemed on their way to consummation. Syria and Egypt were drawing closer together. With proper skill, Moscow might soon be in a position to wield increased influence through this strengthened alliance of its two main clients in the Middle East. Similarly, the Arab states and Israel were now acting so belligerently toward each other that the war Fatah sought was nearing reality.

By now, the hardliners in Israel had grown more vocal, and the increasing accord between Egypt and Syria only gave more credence to their views. Observers in the U.S. intelligence community and the U.N.'s General Odd Bull, chief of U.N. forces in the Middle East, believed they were itching for a war.

"I don't think Eshkol wanted a war," Bull said later. "But it was quite clear the military establishment, including the intelligence services, badly wanted a showdown with the Arabs."

Even Moshe Dayan, Israel's hero of the Sinai war, thought that the military's aggressiveness during this period was provocative.

"Are you people out of your minds?" Dayan demanded of Ezer Weizman as Israel's retaliatory raids became more fierce. "You're leading the country to war!"

Then came two more guerrilla incidents on May 5 and May 8 which took no lives but renewed Israeli anger. Tensions were now so high that on May 11 U Thant, the secretary-general of the United Nations, personally condemned the latest raids as "very deplorable."

Israeli officials responded to the raids by issuing bellicose statements that strongly indicated they had plans to overthrow the government in Syria. On May 12, United Press International reported from Jerusalem that "a high Israeli source said today Israel would take limited military action designed to topple the Damascus army regime if Syrian terrorists continue sabotage raids inside Israel." The next day, *The New York Times* reported on its front page that Israeli leaders had "decided that the use of force against Syria may be the only way to curtail increasing terrorism.... The comments being heard in recent weeks in Tel Aviv, and especially since last weekend, are stronger than those usually heard in responsible quarters."

That same day Prime Minister Eshkol attacked Syria on Israeli radio, charging that Israel "may have to teach Syria a sharper lesson than that of 7 April." He added that "it is quite clear to the Israeli government that the focal point of the terrorists is in Syria, but [we] have laid down the principle that we shall choose the time, the place and the means to counter the aggressor."

Syria was concerned enough about the threats that it drew the Security Council's attention to them on May 15. In a letter, Damascus charged that "the kind of language used, the insistence on accusing Syria again and again of incidents for which she is not responsible, the pretexts created in order to justify further aggression, all point to one conclusion supported by recent lessons of history: that another 1956 Suez is in the making."

Behind the threats and complaints by both sides were more worrisome reports. Both Syria and the Soviet Union informed Egyptian officials that Israel was concentrating troops on the Syrian frontier. Nasser tended to dismiss the Syrian reports, but he took seriously the Russian claims, particularly one that had been delivered personally by Premier Aleksei N. Kosygin to National Assembly Speaker Anwar Sadat on April 29 in Moscow, where Sadat was on a visit. The Soviets informed Sadat that they had evidence Israel had massed two brigades on the Syrian border and planned to attack in mid-May.

Israel denied the charge and invited the Soviet ambassador to Tel Aviv, Dmitri Chuvakhin, to inspect the frontier area himself on May 12. He declined. U Thant ordered U.N. observers to look into the widely circulating report, but, he reported to the Security Council on May 14, they found no evidence of an Israeli buildup.

If the Soviet report was false, it may not have been entirely a deliberate falsehood. As the National Security Council's Middle East expert, Harold H. Saunders, wrote in a memorandum, "... an Israeli attack seemed imminent whenever one of these Fatah attacks spilled Israeli blood. In this sense, the Soviet advice to the Syrians that the Israelis were planning an attack was not far off, although they seem to have exaggerated the magnitude. The Israelis probably were planning an attack—but not an invasion."

Whatever Israeli intentions were, the Soviet reports and other rumors neatly fit in with Russia's strategy. They increased Nasser's apprehensions and made him more conscious of the need to honor his mutual-defense pact with Syria.

The fall of the Syrian government would be a calamity, a "blow against the front of progressive Arab states," as one Communist commentator put it. Even setting aside Moscow's strategic goals, the destruction of Soviet-made jets by Israel in April had been a public embarrassment, and another heavy blow against its client would be more humiliating. If Moscow could get Nasser to show his support for Syria, then Israel might be deterred from further attacks.

Throughout April and early May the Soviets repeatedly urged unity among their two allies and encouraged Egypt to help Syria. Unity was one of the subjects discussed even earlier by Soviet Foreign Minister Andrei A. Gromyko during a week-long visit to Cairo just prior to the April 7 air battle. The Egyptians had been pressing for a high-level Russian visit and Gromyko finally arrived on March 29 for talks with Nasser. Details of the discussions remained unusually secret, and even journalist Mohamed Heikal, a friend of Nasser's and one of the best-informed men in Egypt, reported merely that Gromyko assured the Egyptians that Moscow was not coordinating its Middle East policy with Washington. The only leak about the substance of the talks was one in Yanyug, the Yugoslav news agency, which reported that the two men discussed the problems of UNEF.

In fact, the CIA had learned that Gromyko had expressed bitterness at the slowness Nasser was showing in achieving the Arab unity the Soviets sought. The problem with Gromyko's line was that the Soviets were badly overestimating their own ability and that of the Arab leaders to bring about the unity of the socialist states. Instead of unity, they were contributing to the region's rush to war. But in May 1967 they did not know that yet. When they discovered their error, it was too late.

III
EGYPT MOVES
INTO THE SINAI

Israel's nineteenth Independence Day parade was held in Jerusalem on May 15, a gesture to symbolize the nation's claim to the ancient city as its capital. The parade was a modest display with no artillery or heavy armor so as not to breach the 1949 armistice agreement with Jordan, which strictly limited the weapons allowed in Jerusalem, or inflame more the already hot atmosphere.

Prime Minister Levi Eshkol's caution had infuriated his many critics, who said that the parade was so modest that they scornfully called it "Eshkol's mini-parade." Former Prime Minister David Ben Gurion deliberately boycotted the celebration as a demonstration of his disgust. He thought Eshkol was far too timid and had urged that the full array of Israel's might be shown off. But Eshkol refused.

Eshkol was satisfied that the small demonstration was sufficient to maintain Israel's claim to Jerusalem. It was a claim that no major nation accepted and which most actively rejected. The U.S. ambassador and nearly every other envoy assigned to Israel had refused to attend the parade to avoid giving even tacit acceptance of the claim.

For the world community, Tel Aviv was Israel's legitimate capital and that is where nearly every nation located its embassy and insisted on conducting official business. Jerusalem was considered no one's capital, a *corpus separatum,* as the 1947 U.N. Partition Plan decreed and as the United Nations General Assembly had reiterated on December 9, 1949, a city to be administered as an international municipality for the protection of the holy places sacred to three great religions.

But the Israelis' emotional commitment to Jerusalem was larger than resolutions, greater than the United Nations.

For Israelis, Jerusalem, more than any other city or symbol, was the embodiment of the Jewish nation. It had been the Jews' first capital three millennia earlier, and the failure to capture the Old City during the 1948 war had been one of the great disappointments of the war for Israelis. No people had ever been so attached to one city for so long. When Jews prayed, they prayed toward Jerusalem and when they uttered their ritual felicitations they promised: "Next year in Jerusalem."

The Old City contained the Western Wall (the Wailing Wall) of the Second Temple built nearly two thousand years earlier, the wall of Herodian blocks where Jews prayed and felt at one with their tragic past. But, since 1948, Jews had been prevented from visiting their holiest of shrines. Jordan refused to honor its armistice agreement and all Jews, whether Israeli or not, were denied permission to pray at the venerated shrine.

Yet the Western Wall was only yards from Israeli territory, the Temple Mount clearly visible from Jewish Jerusalem, a beckoning and irksome scene to the religious who longed to pray there. If the opportunity ever presented itself, there could be little doubt that the wellspring of Israeli longing would demand the capture of all of Jerusalem.

A vivid example of Israelis' desire for Jerusalem had been demonstrated on January 23, 1950, when the Israeli parliament had defiantly declared that Jerusalem would "always" be Israel's capital. Despite vigorous protests from the United States and other nations, government offices soon thereafter began moving to Jerusalem from Tel Aviv.

Since then Israel had persisted in treating Jerusalem as its capital, although the reality was that at most it was only half a capital. The armistice line dividing Jerusalem for all nineteen years of Israel's existence remained an ugly no-man's slash of barbed wire, walls, minefields and sniper positions. The line cut the city's population into hostile Arab and Jewish sectors, both claiming it their own, both worshiping in holy places that made the ancient city of golden rock sacred to them. The crenellated walls of the western edge of the Old City, the site of the most venerated shrines for Jews and Moslems as well as Christians, defined the two uneasy sectors. To the east, including all of the Old City, lay Arab Jerusalem of 70,000 Christians and Moslems. To the west was Jewish Jerusalem, a new city of 200,000 Jews built over the past century.

On May 15, 1967, it was in Jewish Jerusalem, against a background of mounting tension, that Israel was celebrating the miracle of its existence. Only the day before, Israel had learned that Egyptian troops had been put on alert and had begun reinforcing units in the Sinai. It was a worrisome but by no means dire development—yet. Israeli officials were carefully monitoring the troop movements, but in the meantime the parade went on. Colored lights formed canopies over the gay streets and at the Municipal Stadium flags fluttered and a band oompahed as infantry and light armored units paraded before a cheering, happy crowd.

On the reviewing stand were the nation's leaders, Prime Minister Levi Eshkol and the members of the Cabinet. Next to Eshkol was the young chief of staff, Major General Yitzhak Rabin, proudly saluting a fleet of jeeps flying service banners as they passed the grandstand. At that moment, as the parade was drawing to a close, Eshkol leaned over to Rabin and whispered in his ear. As soon as the parade was over, he murmured, they must hold an emergency meeting.

Eshkol had just learned that the Egyptian Army was now moving in full force into the Sinai Peninsula along Israel's western frontier. The movement into the Sinai was suddenly taking place in impressive proportions and with unusual openness, artillery-towing trucks filled with combat-equipped soldiers rolling through Cairo's streets in broad daylight. The column ostentatiously passed through the embassy section of Cairo, hopelessly snarling traffic but also announcing its presence to foreign governments. One of the embassies the column passed was that of the United States. Foreign correspondents placed the size of the unit at a full army division.

At the end of the parade, Eshkol and Rabin passed up a special Independence Day reception being hosted by the mayor of Jerusalem and went directly to the prime minister's home. They were joined there by Foreign Minister Abba Eban. After reviewing the situation, the three men decided the Egyptian action deserved continued attention but still was not alarming. They speculated that the Egyptians were probably just putting on a demonstration of their own in response to Israel's parade.

In addition, once before, in January 1960, Egyptian President Gamal Abdel Nasser had massed his troops along the frontier with Israel to help Syria. Israel responded by massing its troops, and forces of the United Nations Emergency Force stationed in the Sinai were reduced to looking on helplessly. Until the end of the crisis two months later in March, the two armies had glared and feinted at each other, but withheld their fire. Nasser finally withdrew his forces and was wildly and exaggeratedly acclaimed throughout the Arab world for standing up to Israel's army and deterring an attack on Syria. It was an easy victory that cost him no serious casualties and won him much praise.

Although the Israeli leaders were not yet unduly concerned, they nonetheless ordered some regular army armored units to reinforce the Sinai front. They also drafted a message to make sure that Egypt understood that Israel was responding to Egypt's buildup and not massing troops on its own initiative.

"Israel wants to make it clear to the Government of Egypt that it has no aggressive intentions whatsoever against any Arab state at all."

Eshkol then went back to his Independence Day activities. He presented awards at the annual Bible Quiz contest and later was the guest of honor at a party for servicemen. In Israel, life continued in its normal routine.

Eshkol, Eban and Rabin met again that night to reassess the situation. They remained convinced that Nasser was putting on a show. But, as in the afternoon, they sent more regular army units south in order to keep pace with the Egyptian buildup.

The United Nations' senior military man in the Middle East was not unduly concerned about the large movement of Egyptian troops either. At his Gaza headquarters, Major General Indar Jit Rikhye was feeling confident that war was a long way away. As commander of the United Nations Emergency Force, he had 3,378 international troops stationed between Israel and Egypt on the 164-mile frontier, which had remained quiescent since their arrival nearly eleven years earlier.

Rikhye, an Indian career officer and an old Middle East hand, was used to periodic posturing in the region. The movement of Egyptian forces appeared to be more of the same empty bluffing.

"We in UNEF were . . . accustomed to all this," Rikhye later wrote. "It was the season for an exchange of verbal threats, demonstrations, parades across the border and high tension."

The atmosphere was tranquil enough the next day, May 16, that General Rikhye was more concerned about playing a round of golf than the outbreak of war. As he prepared to go out, he was stopped by a telephone call. It was from the Egyptian liaison officer attached to the U.N. force at Gaza headquarters and his voice was urgent. The Supreme Command of the United Arab Republic (Egypt) had an important message for the general, he said. A special courier was being dispatched from Cairo, and Rikhye was requested to await his arrival in Gaza.

"Never before had any communications taken the form of a special courier," Rikhye observed in his memoirs. "I decided against playing golf, and settled down in my study to wait."

It was not until shortly before 10 P.M. that the courier finally arrived and

Rikhye was summoned to the Office of the U.A.R. Liaison Staff in downtown Gaza. There he was greeted perfunctorily by Brigadier General Eiz Din Mokhtar, who without any small talk handed him a message from General Mahmoud Fawzi, chief of staff of the Egyptian Army. Rikhye's amazement grew as he read it.

COMMANDER UNEF (GAZA)

To your information, I gave my instructions to all U.A.R. forces to be ready for action against Israel the moment it might carry out any aggressive action against any Arab country. Due to these instructions our troops are already concentrated in Sinai on our eastern border. For the sake of complete security of all U.N. troops . . . I request that you issue your orders to withdraw all these troops immediately. . . .

Rikhye realized immediately that compliance would mean the end of the United Nations Emergency Force and with that, he thought to himself, "war would be inevitable."

In the heavy silence, General Mokhtar said: "I would like to have your reply, General. I have to communicate it immediately to General Fawzi."

Rikhye, in a near state of shock, stalled. "I wanted to say, 'Do you know what you are doing, do you know that this will lead to war, a war that is bound to have grave consequences not only for you, but for the people of this area?' " Instead, he said: "I have noted the contents of General Fawzi's letter to me. I will immediately report to the secretary-general [of the United Nations] for instructions."

General Mokhtar was insistent. He demanded that UNEF troops begin withdrawing that night.

"Our Supreme Command anticipates that when Israel learns of our request to you they will react immediately," he said.

Rikhye was still trying to gather his thoughts and, in order to gain more time, he reread the astonishing message. Finally he informed Mokhtar that he could not take such a momentous decision on his own. He repeated that it would have to be made in New York by the secretary-general.

During the confrontation, Rikhye's old friend Brigadier General Ibrahim Sharkawy, head of the Egyptian liaison office in Gaza, had sat silent. Now as Rikhye rose to rush back to his headquarters, Sharkawy insisted that Arab custom be observed and the three men share coffee. Rikhye, despite his impatience to cable his urgent news to New York, felt he could not ignore etiquette. Thus the three generals sat in a small Gaza office and sipped thick Turkish coffee while Rikhye's dramatic news went unreported.

Rikhye did not get back to his headquarters until around midnight. He immediately dispatched a high-priority cable to the secretary-general, then called an emergency meeting of his senior staff. It was about 3 A.M. before the U.N. commander finally fell into bed to get the rest he knew he would need in the approaching crisis.

The startling Egyptian request for UNEF's withdrawal started a chain reaction that swept reason before it and led to a devastating conclusion that was unwanted by its author, President Gamal Abdel Nasser. Although only forty-nine, the Egyptian leader was the elder statesman of the Arab world, a master at maneuvering between the superpowers and intriguing in the Byzantine hothouse of Arab politics. During his fifteen-year rule of Egypt, he had freed his country of British colonial troops for the first time since 1882, had defied the combined might of Britain, France and Israel in the 1956 Suez war, and now was a respected and founding member of the Third World's nonaligned movement.

It now seemed to most observers that he had in mind something similar to his ploy of 1960, when he had moved troops into the Sinai in aid of Syria. What almost no one knew that May 16, however, was that Nasser had embarked on a far more adventurous course than in 1960.

The man responsible for deciding how to handle Nasser's explosive demand was U Thant, a gentle, hesitant fifty-eight-year-old former schoolteacher from Burma who had been the United Nation's secretary-general since 1961. His supporters admired his honesty and humility; his detractors accused him of being too timid. U Thant's immediate reaction that May 16 was much the same as Rikhye's: stall. He received Rikhye's cable in the early evening (because of the six-hour time difference between Gaza and New York) and responded instantly with orders to do nothing. He added: "Be firm in maintaining UNEF position while being as understanding and as diplomatic as possible in your relations with local United Arab Republic officials."

Then U Thant called in Egypt's ambassador to the United Nations, Mohamed A. Kony, and gave him a lecture on elementary U.N. protocol: A request for withdrawal of UNEF must come from the government of Egypt directly to the secretary-general. Such a momentous action could not be dealt with at a lower level.

In effect, U Thant, by demanding a request directly from the government, was giving Egypt a chance to reconsider its rash demand and gaining time for diplomacy to work. At this time, the United Nations was still a major force in world diplomacy and the secretary-general spoke with authority.

Until receiving Rikhye's cable, U Thant's main concern, like most of the world's outside of the Middle East, had been directed toward a wholly different part of the globe—America's war in Vietnam. Although he was acutely aware that his effectiveness as the first non-European secretary-general depended on treading a precarious course between the Soviet Union and the United States, he increasingly found himself unable to contain his distress at the mounting level of violence in Vietnam. As an Asian and a Buddhist, sensitive to Third World suspicions and fears, U Thant considered the Vietnam war the most dangerous conflict of the time. The war occupied his gloomiest thoughts and brought forth his harshest criticism against the United States.

Just five days before Nasser's demand, U Thant had publicly warned that America's escalating war in Vietnam was leading to a disaster of global proportions. "We are witnessing today the initial phase of World War III," he told a meeting of U.N. news correspondents on May 11 in New York City. "If the present trend continues, I am afraid direct confrontation, first of all between Washington and Peking, is inevitable."

His concern did not seem exaggerated at the time. U.S. policy in the spring of 1967 had become uncompromising and bellicose, and increasingly violent and destructive in Vietnam. In the same week that U Thant spoke, China, which was still not recognized diplomatically by the United States, issued a threat through the news media that it would intervene in the war if American troops invaded North Vietnam. This conjured up the bloody specter of a repeat of the Sino-American battles in Korea less than two decades earlier. U Thant had even graver fears. He warned that if China intervened, then the Soviet Union, despite its antithetical relations with China at the time, might feel it necessary to invoke its mutual-defense pact with Peking. That would mean that behind the threat of Chinese hordes stood the lethal reality of the Soviet Union's large arsenal of nuclear-equipped intercontinental ballistic missiles.

The sense of superpower crisis, of looming tragedy, was intense that spring. The world seemed unstably poised at a precipice. Any new crisis could tip it into the chasm.

Israel's initial sanguinity at Egypt's sending massive reinforcements into the Sinai was already turning to active concern by May 16, even before it learned of Nasser's decision to remove the UNEF troops. By that afternoon, the Egyptian buildup in the Sinai had become impressive. About thirty thousand troops and two hundred tanks had already been added to the thirty thousand to thirty-five thousand troops permanently stationed on Egyptian territory in the peninsula and reinforcements continued pouring in. Although Eshkol informed the Cabinet in an afternoon meeting that the Egyptian deployment remained defensive, he and Rabin that evening decided to take their mobilization one step further. They ordered the activation of a reserve, as opposed to regular army, regiment of armor and some units of reserve artillery.

When Israel learned the next day of Egypt's demand for the withdrawal of UNEF and of the continued movement of Egyptian troops into the Sinai, the situation began to appear even more serious. A series of emergency meetings was again held throughout the day by members of the Cabinet and parliament. Israeli apprehensions increased when the head of military intelligence, Major General Aharon Yariv, a highly regarded career officer, reported to army headquarters, apparently mistakenly, that the Egyptian troops were equipped with poison gas.

"At that time we were unprepared for chemical warfare, and our anxiety deepened," recalled Chief of Staff Yitzhak Rabin. It deepened even more when Yariv and his colleagues in military intelligence concluded that if U.N. troops were actually withdrawn, Israel should interpret that as a "clear indication of Egypt's aggressive intentions."

That May 17 night, Israel called up more reserve units and sent them to the southern front to face Egypt's gathering forces.

Even before U Thant had received an answer to his demand for a formal request for UNEF's withdrawal, the Egyptians acted, wasting little time in moving in on U.N. positions in the Sinai. On Wednesday, May 17, Egyptian soldiers took up stations at the El Sabha and El Amr U.N. posts along a demilitarized zone in the center of the frontier. Egyptian, Israeli and UNEF troops now faced one another in an atmosphere so volatile that violence could erupt with the slightest provocation.

Rikhye notified U Thant of the growing confrontation and in return received instructions "to do what you reasonably can to maintain the position of UNEF and to avoid having the Force or elements of it humiliated, without, however, going so far as to risk an armed clash." Rikhye was reminded that UNEF was stationed on Egyptian territory and could remain there only with the consent of Cairo.

Meanwhile, the secretary-general was informally canvassing the countries contributing troops to UNEF and other U.N. members about their opinions on the crisis. He found them badly divided. Of the seven nations representing UNEF, India, Pakistan and Yugoslavia maintained that if Egypt asked the troops to leave, then they had no choice but to do so, since they were on sovereign Egyptian territory. The four other members, Brazil, Canada, Denmark and Norway, all opposed withdrawal. A similar division existed among members of the Security Council. The Soviet Union favored withdrawal, and Britain and the United States opposed it.

With such sharp division, U Thant was left in lonely isolation to await Cairo's reply.

By the next morning, May 18, U Thant was informed that Egyptian Foreign Minister Mahmoud Riad had called to his office in Cairo the ambassadors of the UNEF countries and declared that they must withdraw their troops forthwith. They, of course, like General Rikhye, were not authorized to undertake such an action.

———

That morning Rikhye flew in a slow Caribou transport plane to inspect the security of UNEF positions along the frontier between Egypt and Israel in the Sinai. The plane was clearly marked as the U.N.'s, and stayed within Egyptian territory. Suddenly, as it lumbered over the desert sands, it was confronted by Israeli planes. Two French-built Mystères flew dangerously close passes, then fired a warning burst of machine-gun bullets in an effort to direct it to Israel and make it land.

Rikhye's plane escaped only by resorting to "daredevil tactics by sand dune hopping, sharp turns, steep climbs with the engines sputtering and revving their guts out, sudden low dives and skimming over the cactus in the sand in order to avoid a situation which might lead to the crash of our aircraft and brought about by the pushing, shoving and jostling of the high-speed Israeli jet fighters," Rikhye wrote in his memoirs. He ordered the plane to land immediately at Gaza and lodged a forceful protest with Israel.

Though visibility had been "perfect," according to Rikhye, and his plane had been flying more than a kilometer inside Egyptian territory, Israeli authorities claimed their aircraft had intercepted him because his plane was twenty kilometers inside Israel. Rikhye was outraged by the charge and he brought the matter to the attention of Chief of Staff Rabin, who soon apologized but gave no explanation for the Israeli action.

Rikhye let the incident drop, but he concluded that Israel "had something to conceal and felt that aircraft even though flying well inside U.A.R.-controlled territory could perhaps pick it up in their innocent passage." His suspicions were correct. On the previous day Israel had secretly infiltrated a reconnaissance battalion into Egyptian territory to scout out the intentions of the gathering Egyptian Army. By now, much of the world was also wondering what those intentions were.

Foreign Minister Abba Eban sought passionately to convince U Thant not to allow UNEF to be withdrawn. He argued through his U.N. ambassador that the matter must first be taken up by the General Assembly. He also insisted that withdrawal was contrary to Israel's understanding when it agreed to pull its troops out of the Sinai in 1957. For U Thant, however, there was a major problem with Eban's position. It was that the original UNEF plan had envisioned locating the peace-keeping troops on both sides of the frontier. But this Israel had firmly opposed because of its deep suspicions about the objectivity of the international organization, which it considered prejudiced against the Jewish state. As a result, Israel had never allowed U.N. forces, either observers or peace-keepers, to be stationed on its territory.

In an effort to keep UNEF in the region, U Thant now called to his office on May 18 Israeli Ambassador Gideon Rafael, who had replaced Michael Comay at the beginning of the month. He asked Rafael whether Israel would accept the UNEF force on its side of the frontier. Rafael replied that his country would find such a situation "entirely unacceptable."

Repeated requests over the next several days by Britain, Canada and the United States for Israeli acceptance of UNEF were similarly rebuffed.

Thus one more option was denied U Thant. He was increasingly finding his choices narrowed, the pressure to find a solution, a saving gesture, becoming urgent.

Shortly after U Thant's disappointing meeting with Gideon Rafael, Egyptian Ambassador Kony arrived at the secretary-general's office at noon, bringing the tensely awaited response from Cairo. It was ominous. Foreign Minister Riad informed the secretary-general that Egypt "has decided to terminate the presence of the United Nations Emergency Force from the territory of the United Arab Republic and Gaza Strip. Therefore, I request that the necessary steps be taken for the withdrawal of the Force as soon as possible."

Kony took the occasion to impress on U Thant "the strong feeling of resentment" building up in Cairo. He pointed out that UNEF was in the Sinai at Egypt's invitation. Now, he charged, there was an apparent effort to turn it into an "occupation force" of Egypt's own territory.

With his sensitivities to Third World suspicions and acutely aware of the clouded legal justification of UNEF's presence in Egypt but not Israel, this was a charge that greatly worried U Thant. The effectiveness of the United Nations would be severely impaired if it ever became suspected that it was willing to trample on the sovereign rights of one of its weak members.

Desperately seeking some way out of the impasse, U Thant asked Kony to check Riad's reaction to the idea of U Thant's making a personal visit to Cairo to speak directly with Nasser. Apparently finding U Thant's attention flattering, Riad a short time later informed him through Kony that such a visit would be welcome "as soon as possible."

With that note of encouragement, U Thant held a meeting of the UNEF Advisory Committee that afternoon. However, the seven members were still sharply split over what course he should take and the meeting ended inconclusively. With no firm alternative available, U Thant sadly decided that he had no choice but to comply with Egypt's demand.

At 7 P.M. that Thursday, he sent a cable to Cairo advising that UNEF would be withdrawn. Unmentioned but implicit in his action was the fact that the withdrawal of so many troops could not be accomplished before U Thant's trip to Cairo. Thus his tactic gave him one last chance to reverse Nasser's decision.

To his Cairo cable, U Thant added a cautionary warning: "Irrespective of the reasons for the action you have taken, in all frankness, may I advise you that I have serious misgivings about it for . . . I believe that this Force has been an important factor in maintaining relative quiet in the area of its deployment during the past ten years and that its withdrawal may have grave implications for peace."

However, Egypt was not acting as though it wanted peace. That same day Cairo Radio's Voice of the Arabs program broadcast one of its inflammatory commentaries, which were to become more extreme and more frequent as the crisis deepened. "The Zionist barrack in Palestine is about to collapse and be destroyed," said Cairo Radio. "Every one of the hundred million Arabs has been living for the past nineteen years on one hope—to live to see the day Israel is liquidated. . . . There is no life, no peace nor hope for the gangs of Zionism to remain in the occupied land."

Despite such provocations, Abba Eban assured the United States that Israel's hawks were still being held in check. U.S. Ambassador to Israel Walworth Barbour saw the foreign minister on May 18 and cabled Washington that "... we could be assured Israeli Government does not rpt not intend any military action and that GOI [Government of Israel] fully in control its military. As he put it, there no rpt no 'automatic switches open.' "

True, the switches may not yet have been open, but the pressures from the military were exerting increasing influence on Eshkol to act firmly.

The next day U Thant warned the Security Council of the perils ahead. "I do not want to cause alarm," he said, "but it is difficult for me not to warn the Council that, as I see it, the position in the Middle East is more disturbing ... indeed more menacing than at any time since the fall of 1956."

Though many of the Council members were critical of U Thant's course, none of them stepped forward to propose a viable alternative. UNEF would be withdrawn—unless U Thant could persuade Nasser to change his mind.

Shortly before dusk in the Middle East that May 19, General Rikhye drove to the United Nations' observation post at King's Gate on the Gaza–Tel Aviv road. A small guard of honor was awaiting him as he delivered his somber message. "In accordance with instructions I have received from the Secretary-General of the United Nations, you will withdraw your guards and observation posts at 5 o'clock."

At the stroke of 5 P.M., the guard of honor presented arms, the pipe band played a salute, and a young Swedish soldier lowered the blue-and-white U.N. flag. Colonel Stig Lindskog, commander of the Swedish unit assigned to the post, presented the flag as a souvenir to Rikhye, who accepted it with a heavy heart. Rikhye walked the short distance to the armistice demarcation line and informed the Israeli liaison officer to report to Israeli military headquarters that the withdrawal of UNEF had begun.

A platoon of the Palestine Liberation Army, the military arm of the PLO attached to the Egyptian Army, had watched the ceremony with relish. The PLA soldiers now saluted Rikhye before taking over the UNEF post, the first regular Palestinian military unit to take up positions directly confronting Israel in the Sinai since the Palestinians' expulsion in 1948. They were ecstatic.

"The young Palestinian officer in command was grinning from ear to ear on assuming the responsibility for the security of the Gaza Strip from us,"

Rikhye noted later. "I saluted back, thinking to myself, 'It's all yours now.' I suddenly felt very sorry for him."

That same May 19 evening Israel took the portentous step of ordering an immediate large-scale mobilization of reserves. Egyptian troops in the Sinai were now estimated at forty thousand soldiers and five hundred tanks. Chief of Staff Rabin advised all Israeli commanding officers "to make clear to their men that we were heading for war."

IV
THE PRESSURES ON JOHNSON BEGIN

T he reaction in Washington to the sudden crisis in the Middle East was at first low-keyed. Secret messages were sent to Egypt and Syria urging restraint, and a personal letter was dispatched to Israel on May 17 over the signature of President Lyndon B. Johnson.

Aware of Israel's strength and its prickly impatience in the face of Arab threats, the President cautioned Prime Minister Levi Eshkol: "I would like to emphasize in the strongest terms the need to avoid any action on your side which would add further to the violence and tension in your area. I urge the closest consultation between you and your principal friends. I am sure that you will understand that I cannot accept any responsibilities on behalf of the United States for situations which arise as the result of actions on which we are not consulted."

Neither Johnson nor his top officials appeared unduly concerned at this stage, although they were aware of the reasons behind Nasser's action and its potential gravity, as a memorandum to Johnson demonstrated.

The UAR's brinksmanship stems from two causes [the National Security Council memorandum written May 17 observed]. (1) The Syrians are feeding Cairo erroneous reports of Israeli mobilizations to strike Syria. Regrettably, some pretty militant public threats from Israel by Eshkol and others have lent credibility to the Syrian reports. (2) Nasser probably feels his prestige would suffer irreparably if he failed a third time to come to the aid of an Arab nation attacked by Israel. Moderates like Hussein have raked him over the coals for not coming to Jordan's aid in November or to Syria's when Israel shot down 6 of its MiG's last month.

The President's Daily Diary for the day on which he received this memorandum and wrote Eshkol shows that he kept a dental appointment in the morning, met for political discussions with the Democratic Senate leadership in the White House and later with officers of the American Bar Association, then chatted with an aide about the Model Cities Program, and discussed politics and patronage with Senator William Spong of Virginia. At an hour-long meeting of the Cabinet at noon, the agenda was dominated by the war raging in Vietnam. There apparently was no discussion of the Middle East.

It was understandable that Vietnam dominated the Cabinet meeting. The war by now had become the consuming obsession of Lyndon Johnson to the point of threatening to destroy the visionary programs of his Great Society and indeed his presidency as well. A natural political conniver and congressional manipulator, Johnson was a man of social vision but international myopia. When it came to foreign affairs, he was an American innocent abroad, as he was proving in Vietnam—and was about to demonstrate in the Middle East.

As the fifty-eight-year-old President desperately pursued military victory in the Asian war, he was losing the support of his countrymen. There already were 440,000 American soldiers in South Vietnam, and now commanding General William C. Westmoreland was reported to have urged on May 2 that 160,000 reinforcements be sent "as soon as possible."

His request stunned the country. Week after dismal week the American public had been reassured of victories and progress in the war. Yet each week brought higher casualties and another escalation in the violence. The American air war against North Vietnam had burgeoned to an unprecedented level. Hanoi and Haiphong were under daily aerial attack. The Soviet Union had provided North Vietnam with one of the densest antiaircraft missile systems in the world, and by May 6 U.S. losses over the north had reached an astonishing 553 planes since the air campaign began February 7, 1965. In the south, troop casualties were running in the hundreds weekly as America unleashed practically everything in its lethal arsenal short of nuclear weapons. Forests were being defoliated, villages wiped out and the countryside ruined all in the name of a victory that grew more elusive each year.

The amount of firepower employed by U.S. forces defied comprehension. America's mightiest bombers, the eight-engine B-52s, had been converted from their nuclear duties to drop hundreds of thousands of bombs on Vietnam, turning the lush countryside into a moonscape. Swimming-pool-size craters were gouged in the earth by 15,000-pound monster bombs, so destructive that they could wipe out the center of a city. In one brief operation alone, Masher/White Wing, fighter-bombers flew 1,126 sorties and they and B-52s unloaded 1.5 million pounds of bombs and 292,000 pounds of napalm. The operation was supported by artillery and naval guns which added to the devastation by firing an unreported number of additional shells. Masher/White Wing was only one of scores of similar operations launched by the Johnson Administration.

The war seemed to have turned reason upside down and reality into a nightmare, as typified by the memorable comment of an unidentified army major after the devastation of a village in Vietnam's Delta region. "We had to destroy it to save it," he said amid the rubble to visiting reporters. The comment received front-page attention across the country and seemed to many Americans to encapsulate the madness of the war.

Such massive destruction was sickening many Americans. Civil rights leader Martin Luther King and others that spring announced formation of an antiwar group called Negotiation Now and launched a nationwide peace drive scheduled to last throughout the summer. King declared that the war was "abominable and unjust," and many Americans agreed. At least 100,000 volunteered to help organize the summer protests.

There was abundant other evidence of the nation's disillusionment with Johnson's Vietnam war that spring as the crisis developed in the Middle East. Trustees of the University of Pennsylvania on May 6 had terminated all research contracts with the Army and the Air Force. The week before, a thousand Protestant, Catholic and Jewish seminarians had sent Defense Secretary Robert S. McNamara a petition urging more lenient treatment of conscientious objectors to the war. On May 10, an antiwar teach-in was conducted simultaneously at more than eighty universities across the country with such participants as Harvard economist John Kenneth Galbraith and historian Henry Steele Commager. The next day, the same day as U Thant's speech warning of World War III, 321 faculty members of Columbia University sent a letter to Congress and President Johnson demanding that they "extricate the nation from a detestable war."

Expressing both his frustration and his determination, and perhaps also his disingenuousness, Johnson had vowed on April 26 that he was ready to negotiate a settlement on Vietnam but "I just can't negotiate with myself. . . . Maybe someday, somehow, sometime, somewhere, someone will want to sit at a table and talk instead of fight, reason instead of murder, and when they do, I will be the first to come to that table, wherever it is." It was standard political rhetoric for Johnson, and it was unpersuasive to his critics. His countrymen were acutely aware that as the President spoke his military commanders were waging a campaign of escalating violence in Vietnam that showed no sign of either victory or abatement.

Yet there was one thing that spring for which Lyndon Johnson could count himself fortunate: During all of his presidency he had never been faced with a serious crisis in the volatile Middle East. And now of all times, with the Vietnam war absorbing his obsessive attention and the country feverish in its dissent, a Middle East war was the last thing he needed.

In the Middle East, both sides were moving closer to war.

Israel, parallel with the partial mobilization of its armed forces, had begun conducting an intensive diplomatic campaign to assure that if war erupted Israel would not be blamed. On May 18, Foreign Minister Abba Eban drafted a letter for Eshkol to send as his reply to Johnson's letter of the previous day. In it, Eshkol sought assurances of America's commitment to Israel's security and requested the President to inform the Soviet Union of the U.S. position.

But Johnson could not give Eshkol a security pledge in the form he wanted, since, in fact, there was no defense treaty between Israel and the United States, nor was there any formal written guarantee specifically of Israel's security. This was emphasized a day after the receipt of Eshkol's cable when the President's national security adviser, Walt Whitman Rostow, sent Johnson a memorandum entitled *The US Commitments to Israel.*

"Our main formal public commitment to Israel," Rostow wrote, underlining "formal public commitment," had been expressed by President John F. Kennedy during a press conference on May 8, 1963, when he said: "We support the security of both Israel and her neighbors."

The most recent expressions of the commitment, Rostow added, had been made by President Johnson. On June 3, 1964, at the end of Eshkol's visit to Washington, Johnson had said in a joint communiqué: "[Johnson] reiterated to Prime Minister Eshkol U.S. support for the territorial integrity and political independence of all countries in the Near East and emphasized the firm opposition of the U.S. to aggression and the use of force or the threat of force against any country." Finally, on August 2, 1966, Johnson during a toast to the visiting president of Israel, Zalman Shazar, had repeated Kennedy's 1963 statement.

That was the total of U.S. pledges. They were, on their face, as applicable to the Arab nations as they were to Israel. But that was not how most Americans interpreted them. For those Americans, the U.S. commitment was solely to Israel, a country that by 1967 had become so popular in the United States that it was only half laughingly referred to as the fifty-first state. And why not? Israel was almost universally perceived in America as a fellow democracy sharing common ideals, a beleaguered and courageous outpost of the West in the midst of inhospitable infidels, a nation of hard-working and God-fearing pioneers who defied not only Arabs but the mighty British Empire. The images evoked by the novel *Exodus,* of bedraggled and longing wretches trying to reach the sanctuary of the shores of Palestine against forceful British opposition, had been kept fresh by a thousand reminders of Israelis' suffering and achievements, not the least of which was the movie version of *Exodus,* starring Paul Newman, which shaped for many years Americans' idea of Israel and its people.

So strong was the pro-Israel mood of the country that from now on Johnson and the American public acted as though there were a formal U.S. guarantee of Israel's security, but not of the Arab states'.

In addition to the security commitment, Eshkol apparently also sought more in his letter, as indicated by a memorandum from Harold Saunders, the National Security Council's Middle East expert, written on the same day as Rostow's memorandum.

"The President may be so deeply involved in working out the final answer on the Israeli aid package that you may *not* want to send up the attached," wrote Saunders.

The contents of "the attached" remain classified, as does any information on the aid package. But according to items later sent, the aid probably consisted of at least the gas masks Israel feared it needed, ammunition and other military material.

Whatever the aid consisted of, Israel could count on generous treatment from the Johnson Administration. No Administration up to that time had been as generous in financial support and the transfer of advanced military weapons to Israel as Johnson's.

This was no surprise since Lyndon Johnson had been a consistent supporter of Israel throughout his career. As majority leader of the Senate in 1956, he had fought vigorously against President Dwight D. Eisenhower's effort to make Israel return the Sinai Peninsula to Egypt at the end of the Suez war. Over the years he repeatedly supported Israel in public and in the Senate.

As a result of his pro-Israel stance, Johnson profited by receiving powerful support from the well-organized and vocal Jewish community in the United

States. By 1967, when Johnson was still planning to run for re-election, there were 5.5 million Jews in the country, the largest Jewish community in the world, and they had acquired a level of success and education far beyond the average American's. Jews in white-collar jobs were three times the national average and anti-Semitism was so scarce that the *American Jewish Year Book* of 1965 did not include it as a subject in its major articles for the first time in its more than sixty-year history. For U.S. Jews America had turned out to be a true promised land.

Such assimilation had from the beginning created a strain between the Jewish American community and Israel. Few Jewish Americans emigrated to the new country, and some even ignored it. Up until World War II and the revelations of the horrors of the Holocaust, substantial numbers actively opposed the concept of Zionism. Only 187 emigrated to Israel in 1956, 271 the next year and 378 the following year. It was not until 1964 that for the first time more than a thousand Jewish Americans made *aliyah* in one year. This comparative lack of support by the largest Jewish community was deeply resented in Israel, where it was seen as a loss of "Jewishness" and a lack of faith in Zionism and the ideals of the Zionist pioneers. Israelis responded by proselytizing among Jewish Americans, warning of future holocausts and urging them to join the great experiment in creating a modern Jewish state.

The Jewish American community reacted over the years not by moving to Israel in large numbers but by awarding it unprecedented financial and political support.

With their prosperity, their dedication to education and sense of community, Jewish Americans by the mid-1960s had become more assertive in the country's political processes. Many of them enthusiastically threw themselves into all aspects of the political system, often becoming the leaders in liberal causes from civil rights to labor reform and important contributors or editors in the whole spectrum of publishing. Some of their voices were particularly powerful in the news media, where Jewish Americans were among the best reporters, editors and writers on the largest newspapers, newsmagazines and television shows. They were tireless in working for political parties, mainly the Democrats, and they frequently were the intellectual activists who helped define the issues of campaigns.

Substantial contributions by wealthy Jewish Americans became a significant factor in the hopes of any presidential contender. Similarly, because Jews by the mid-1960s were concentrated in large numbers in only a few cities, their votes could carry a disproportionate influence in races that were close. Thus concentrations of Jews in six cities—New York, Los Angeles,

Philadelphia, Chicago, Boston and Newark—gave them the political power to help swing those states which in turn had 169 of the 270 electoral votes necessary to elect a President.

The Jewish vote had played a significant role in the election of Kennedy, especially in helping him carry the important states of Illinois and New York. When Kennedy informally met Prime Minister David Ben Gurion in 1961, he told him: "I know I was elected by the votes of American Jews and I would like to do something for the Jewish people." He did in 1962 by becoming the first President to break with traditional U.S. arms control in the Middle East when he gave Israel its first major American weapons system, Hawk antiaircraft missiles.

After Kennedy's assassination, Lyndon Johnson told an Israeli diplomat: "You have lost a very great friend, but you have found a better one." Commented Jewish lobbyist Isaiah L. Kenan in his memoirs: "I would say that everything he did as President supported that statement."

As the Vietnam war heated up and Johnson's popularity cooled, the Jewish American–Israel connection became increasingly important to him. Administration officials spent considerable amounts of time trying to enlist Jewish American support for the war—which many Jews violently opposed—by extending support to Israel. The effort had two aims. One was to receive the backing of the Jewish American community and, by extension, the support or at least the understanding of the liberal community, where Jews exerted a major influence. The other was to secure Israel's support for the war in international forums where the United States was becoming increasingly isolated from the world community.

The ways in which the Administration strove to achieve these twin goals was illustrated by a memorandum written in the spring of 1966 by Walt Rostow for the President, informing Johnson that "I have been canvassing new things we might do in Israel." Already in the pipeline, he observed, was the historic announcement of the sale of A-4 warplanes, an event that "will probably stand out as the major US-Israeli event of 1966, though we will not want to crow about it because we do not want to invite any more Arab reaction than is inevitable."

Implicit in Rostow's memorandum was the extremely close relationship that had grown between Israel and the United States and that by 1966 manifested itself at every level of government and cultural relations. Thus he was able to advise the President that if he wanted to send a message of friendship to Israel he could do it through Chief Justice Earl Warren, who was about to visit Israel with his wife for the opening of the Kennedy Forest. The Truman Peace Center in Israel was also about to be inaugurated, an event to which former President Truman had been invited. Rostow suggested that the occasion could be used to "endow a professorship or set of fellowships, perhaps in the name of a non-controversial Israeli figure like Martin Buber." Rostow also reminded Johnson that he had agreed to meet in the White House with Israeli President Zalman Shazar while Shazar was in the country on a private visit.

Though the list of friendly gestures to Israel was already impressive, Rostow proposed that more could be done during the summer of 1966, an off-year election period in which the Administration was determined to retain the support of Jewish Americans. "We might finance several prestigious chairs at US universities for leading Israeli scholars on a rotational basis. . . . Establish a scientific or medical institute in Israel to concentrate on training public health careerists. . . . Stimulate a partnership between US medical school and the Hebrew University-Hadassah Hospital medical school. . . . Fund research at an Israeli hospital in disease control. . . . Help Hadassah Hospital more. . . . Allow Israel to bid on AID [Agency for International Development] contracts for purchase of potash."

Rostow concluded by writing: "My question at this stage is whether you judge the things on my illustrative list as useful. If so, I will get the departments down to work on details." He left two tick-off spaces for Johnson to indicate his preference: "This is the right approach" and "See me." The President put a check mark behind the "right approach."

Another study, written in the winter of 1966–67 by an unidentified author, was prepared for the President under the title of "1968—American Jews and Israel." It was a preliminary draft of a study of how the Administration could best capitalize on the Jewish vote in the 1968 presidential elections, in which Johnson expected former Vice President Richard M. Nixon to be his Republican challenger.

In assaying attitudes of Jewish Americans toward Israel, the study noted that "they were among the first to espouse the idea of the re-establishment of a Jewish state in Israel. From the days of Justice Brandeis and Justice Frankfurter to the days of Justice Goldberg and Justice Fortas, American Jewish leaders have deliberately identified themselves with this effort. Since the establishment of Israel in 1948, Jewish leaders have constantly sought to promote the economic and social consolidation of the state and its physical security."

The voting pattern of Jewish Americans, the study observed, had in recent decades favored Democrats. Jews supported Harry S. Truman "partly because they believed that Truman was more likely than Dewey to support an independent state of Israel. They preferred Stevenson to Eisenhower." John

F. Kennedy had initial problems with Jewish voters, the study noted, but "he took active steps to deal with them. In 1960 he spoke before a Zionist convention and made clear that his support for Israel was unequivocal. He met regularly with important groups of representative Jewish leaders throughout the United States. . . . He took these steps even though he could rely upon the fact that to most Jewish voters Nixon was generally unacceptable partly for what he was and partly because he was identified with what most Jewish voters regarded as the Eisenhower-Dulles double-standard policy against Israel during the Suez crisis."

The study pointed out that Nixon, after his defeat in 1960, had made an effort to increase his support in the Jewish community. He visited Israel in 1966 and was planning another visit. "In 1968 we are likely to see the Republican candidate portrayed not only as a progressive but as deeply concerned with Israel and its problems. In 1968, therefore, the Democratic candidate must not simply rely upon the record but make clear, by action, that he truly understands—and will seek to deal with—the deep-seated historic Jewish concerns."

The study spent fourteen single-spaced typewritten pages detailing those concerns, including everything from Israel's desire for more military and economic aid to support for encouraging Jewish emigration from the Soviet Union and the possibility of establishing an American university in Israel. "The establishment in Israel of an American University would constitute a new and important symbolic American presence," said the study.

In addition to supporting implicitly most of Israel's positions, the study recommended that the Democrats could further enhance their standing among Jewish Americans if more Jews were regularly invited to the White House for meals and ceremonies. It also suggested that high officials of the Administration visit Israel, mentioning the Vice President and the secretary of state as two likely candidates for this function. It added that it "would be very useful" if the President invited Israel's prime minister for "a day or two at Blair House, with conversations covering the more important problem areas." It further recommended that the President appear "before a Jewish forum, using the occasion to define his views of the proper relations between Israel and the United States, and setting forth actions taken and practical proposals for future action."

Although the President did not follow all of this advice, the mere existence of the study was indicative of how sensitive his aides were to the importance of the Jewish vote and its intimate connection with the security and prosperity of Israel.

Indeed, the aides were simply reflecting the sensitivity exhibited by the

President himself. This was demonstrated just before the elections of 1966 in a memorandum from the NSC's Hal Saunders to Walt Rostow. "This is the last chance to do something for Israel . . . before elections. Do you want to give the President a crack at it?" Attached was a prepared statement announcing a $6 million Export-Import Bank loan to Israel to help medium-sized manufacturers. The loan was part of an effort to win Jewish American voters in a campaign whose "principle is to space out our pro-Israel gestures between now and November," as Walt Rostow put it in a memorandum.

The President authorized the loan and ordered that a cable be sent to Abraham Feinberg advising him of the action "if he's over there." "Over there" meant Israel, where Feinberg had extremely close ties. Feinberg was one of the most powerful Jewish American leaders in the country, president of the American Bank & Trust Company of New York and the first major Jewish fund raiser for national politics. He gained influence in the Democratic Party in 1948 when he solicited substantial funds for the seemingly hopeless 1948 election campaign of Harry S. Truman. According to Stephen D. Isaacs' study entitled *Jews and American Politics,* "Feinberg's activities started a process of systematic fund raising for politics that has made Jews the most conspicuous fund raisers and contributors to the Democratic Party."

Feinberg was influential not only in national Democratic politics but in Israel also. He funded the School for Advance Studies at Israel's Weizmann Institute, and at various times he owned the Coca-Cola franchise in Israel as well as being a part owner of the Jerusalem Hilton Hotel. (When his bank fell into trouble and two of its officers were convicted of misappropriation of funds, an Israeli firm, Bank Leumi Company, in a generous act of reverse foreign aid, purchased American Bank & Trust Company.)

Just before the election, Johnson approved another $6 million loan, this one to finance an Israeli power plant at Haifa. To assure that he milked the maximum political profit from Israel's supporters, he then used it as the basis to write a letter to Feinberg, reminding him how generous to Israel the Administration had been. His "Dear Abe" letter on November 3, 1966, promised additional assistance for Israel and included an attachment reviewing U.S. aid to Israel over the previous three years. "The depth and breadth of these programs are impressive," Johnson wrote. "So is the fact that our total aid to Israel last year was higher than in any previous single year because of significant military credits."

Indeed, Johnson was not exaggerating in calling the list of U.S. aid impressive. The list reported that economic aid to Israel in the first three years of Johnson's presidency totaled $134 million, a record to that time. This did not include military aid, much of which was secret but substantial. In addition to direct aid to Israel, the study pointed out, the United States also supported Israel's security by giving "full financial support ($87.3 million since 1949 and $25.3 million FY 1967) for the elaborate U.N. peace-keeping machinery on Israel's borders and has helped support over a million Arab refugees at a cost of some $71 million 1964–1966 (over $387 million since 1948)."

Far more significant than economic support was the Johnson Administration's unprecedented transfer of arms to Israel. It became the first to ignore a long-standing policy against selling offensive weapons in the Middle East when in 1965 it agreed to transfer to Israel 210 M-48 battle tanks at a cost of $34 million. Then in 1966 it took a fateful step in escalating the Middle East arms race. It sold forty-eight A-4 Skyhawk attack aircraft for $72.1 million, the first combat planes sold by the United States to Israel. Up to this time American direct weapons sales to Israel had been severely limited and mainly of defensive items.

Instead of sending the letter enumerating all these concessions directly to Feinberg, Johnson handed it to his close friend Arthur B. Krim and asked him to telephone the banker and read it to him. Krim, a frequent guest of the President's, was another powerful Jewish American fund raiser, a New York attorney, president of a profitable Hollywood studio, United Artists Corporation, and chairman of the Democratic National Party Finance Committee. He, like Feinberg, was an ardent supporter of Israel.

In the tradition of American politics, both men and the many other supporters of Israel surrounding the President used their influence in behalf of the Jewish state as the crisis in the Middle East developed. This is, of course, a time-honored practice, the essence of a living democracy. But in this case, as the crisis developed, the President found himself deep in political debt to a pressure group that felt strongly about a foreign-policy issue in which the U.S. was nominally neutral. Such influence and partisanship tended to blind the President, along with a great many other Americans, to the claims of the Arabs, which the country was also pledged to protect.

To be sure, all Presidents accrue political debts—to labor unions, to corporations, to ethnic groups, to various lobbies—but seldom, if ever, has one group exerted such sustained and direct influence on a sitting President as Israel's supporters did on Johnson. The crisis was to prove beyond any doubt that the power, the influence and the direct involvement of Israel in U.S. politics are unique.

But it was not all a one-way street. While he was being lobbied to aid Israel, Lyndon Johnson was trying to use Israel's supporters to win backing for his Vietnam policy. Vice President Hubert H. Humphrey, also a staunch friend of Israel throughout his career, involved himself in the effort, but somehow he seemed unable to get the issues straight. He had been told, apparently by supporters of Israel, that South Vietnam could gain some popularity in the Jewish American community if it would extend diplomatic recognition to Israel. The Jewish state needed all the international support it could receive, and a formal endorsement by even South Vietnam seemed desirable.

To this end, on March 15, 1966, Humphrey wrote to Secretary of State Dean Rusk: "Because of the disaffection on the Viet Namese issue in the American Jewish community, it might be well for us to encourage the government of South Viet Nam to promptly recognize Israel and go through whatever formalities are necessary to let the whole world know that the exchange of diplomats has taken place—also that other developments of mutual benefit are underway. I am sure this would have a salutary effect in the United States. . . . I have mentioned this to the President and he suggested that I get in touch with you at once."

Rusk tried to explain to the Vice President in a March 31 reply that it was Israel that showed no desire for relations with South Vietnam rather than the other way around. ". . . all information available to the Department indicates that it is Israel, not Viet Nam, which is delaying a diplomatic exchange between the two countries," Rusk wrote. "Israel's reluctance apparently stems from the opposition of Israeli left-wing coalition parties to any Israeli involvement in Viet Nam."

Despite Rusk's letter, Humphrey continued to push the idea in the same mistaken belief that it was Vietnam that did not want relations. On May 1 he wrote to the NSC's Walt Rostow: "I have good reason to believe that a number of Jewish intellectuals here in the United States and other Jewish leaders are very unhappy over the manner in which South Viet Nam has treated Israeli overtures for better relationships."

The White House now did its own study of the affair and came up with the same conclusion as the State Department. ". . . There is a rather tortuous history to the problem which, on balance, reveals that the Israeli [sic] are the ones dragging their feet," said the May 2 report entitled *Israeli-Vietnamese Relations*. "About two months ago there was reason to believe that our overtures to the Israeli to enter relations with the GVN [Government of Viet Nam] might be successful. The Viet Namese and Israeli representatives in Bangkok had held exploratory talks on diplomatic recognition, and the

GVN was fully in favor. Then the local Jewish Telegraphic Agency correspondent filed a story to the Israeli press alleging that the GVN was antiSemitic. . . . The fat was in the fire and left-wing opposition in Tel Aviv prevailed on Foreign Minister Eban not to press recognition before the Knesset [parliament]. We made repeated overtures since to Prime Minister Eshkol and Eban, but with no success."

That same day the State Department asked the National Security Council for permission "to cite the President's disappointment over Israel's failure to make any gesture toward Viet Nam. This sharp reaction is in keeping with the pressure we have applied."

All this effort failed to move the Israeli government to extend diplomatic recognition to the unsavory South Vietnamese regime during Johnson's presidency.* But the U.S. pressure no doubt contributed to Israel's generally supportive stance toward America at the United Nations and elsewhere throughout the war. It was support, however modest, that the beleaguered Administration badly needed in the increasingly hostile international community and at home, and now, at the beginning of the 1967 crisis in the Middle East, Washington once again showed its appreciation.

The secret aid package Israel sought on May 18 had been quickly worked out by President Johnson and it obviously was generous. A note six days later from National Security Adviser Walt Rostow informed the President that Israeli Embassy Minister Ephraim Evron, who was extremely close to Johnson, had called to say "he deeply appreciates—as does his government—the final form of the Israeli aid package."

Johnson took one other action at this time to gird the government for the developing crisis. He sent a letter May 19 to Soviet Premier Aleksei Kosygin, as requested by Eshkol, spelling out America's commitment to Israel's security and suggesting a "joint initiative of the two powers to prevent the dispute between Israel and the U.A.R. and Syria from drifting into war."

The withdrawal of UNEF focused Israel's attention on a tantalizing question: What would Nasser do next? The logic of the accelerating momentum pointed to a dire answer. He would occupy Sharm el Sheikh at the tip of the Sinai Peninsula and blockade the Straits of Tiran. The straits led from the Red Sea to the Gulf of Aqaba and Israel's port city of Elath, the

---

* It was not until December 21, 1972, that Israel finally announced it would exchange ambassadors with South Vietnam.

Jewish state's only direct maritime access to the markets of East Africa and Asia. The opening of the waterway to Israeli flagships had been the one major reward Israel had earned for its collusion in the 1956 attack on Egypt. Partly in return for evacuating the Sinai Peninsula, Israel had received a written guarantee from the United States that it considered the straits an international waterway and was ready to help secure "free and innocent" passage for all countries' shipping through them.

Egypt had acquiesced to the stationing of UNEF at Sharm el Sheikh and had not attempted to interfere with Israeli ships using the straits since 1956, but the situation remained as sensitive for Egyptians as did the presence of UNEF along the Egyptian-Israeli frontier. The straits were bound on one side by Saudi Arabia and on the other by Egypt and lay within the three-mile limit of Egypt's territorial waters. Cairo asserted that even without the technical state of war that had existed between Egypt and Israel since 1948 it had a legal right to deny usage of the straits to Israel or any other nation because the waterway was within Egyptian sovereign territory.

The question had never been adjudicated by the International Court of Justice or in any other world forum and it remained an open issue between those who considered it an international waterway and those who believed the straits were Egyptian territorial waters. The opening of the narrow straits as a result of the 1956 Suez war rankled in the Arab world as yet another Israeli victory over the Arabs, another humiliation of Egypt and Nasser.

Israeli officials considered continued access to the straits vital, though more as a symbol of Israeli determination than as an immediate economic asset, except for the importation of Iranian oil, which came through Elath at considerable savings. No Israeli flagship had used the straits in nearly two years. On the other hand, a widely held tenet in Israel maintained that once the country surrendered what it considered to be one of its rights, "It was only a question of time before it would be faced with fresh demands and renewed pressure . . . the beginning of the end, the slow strangulation of the Jewish state," as historian Walter Laqueur succinctly expressed it.

Thus, Israel now turned its attention to letting it be widely known that closure of the straits would be considered an act of aggression and cause for war. Foreign Minister Abba Eban asserted that imposition of a blockade would "take us to a point of no return." As he noted: "Troop movements, after all, could be ordered and later dispersed without loss of face or implication of retreat. But if a blockade was imposed, its cancellation was inconceivable except under pressure or threat of physical force."

As part of Israel's diplomatic campaign, Prime Minister Levi Eshkol sent a message on May 19 to France's President Charles de Gaulle, an old friend of Israel's. He assured de Gaulle that he could count on Israel not to initiate hostilities "until or unless [Egyptian forces] close the Straits of Tiran to free navigation by Israel." In separate messages to the leading maritime powers, Eshkol warned: "Israel would stop short of nothing to cancel the blockade. It is essential that President Nasser should not have any illusions."

By now illusions were rampant in the excited Arab world. The publicity, the world attention, the apparent success of Nasser in forestalling an Israeli attack on Syria all contributed to a euphoric atmosphere. Even such traditional enemies of the socialist states as the Kingdom of Saudi Arabia were joining the Syrian-Egyptian axis. The Saudis announced they were ready to support the struggle on grounds of "our religion, Arabism, and brotherly bonds." On May 20, the Syrian defense minister, General Hafez Assad, said, ". . . it is necessary to adopt at least the minimum measures required to deal a disciplinary blow to Israel, which should restore its senses and bring it to its knees, humiliated and terrified to live in an atmosphere of awe and fear which will prevent it from contemplating another aggression."

On May 21, Egypt announced total mobilization of its reserves. Nasser also said he had accepted an offer by Iraq to send units of its armed forces to assist in the struggle.

Illusions were so rife in Egypt that the top pop singer, Um Kalthoum, already had a hit with a song that had these lyrics:

> We are going back by force of arms.
> We are going back like morning
>   after the dark night.
> Army of Arabism, may God be with you.
> O, how great, splendid and brave you are.
> The tragedy of Palestine pushes you
>   toward the borders.
> All are with you in the flaming battle.

Nasser, by now "carried away by his own impetuosity," in the words of Anwar Sadat, called a meeting of his top officials and candidly said: "Now with our concentrations in Sinai, the chances of war are fifty-fifty. But if we close the Straits war will be a one-hundred-percent certainty." Turning to Minister of War Abdel Hakim Amer, Nasser asked: "Are the armed forces ready, Abdel Hakim?"

"On my head be it, Boss!" replied Amer blithely. "Everything's in tiptop shape."

U Thant, desperate to head off the coming tragedy, boarded a plane the evening of May 22 to fly to Cairo. It was his only hope to dissuade Nasser from taking the fateful step of blockading the Straits of Tiran. While he was in the air Nasser took the momentous decision.

"Under no circumstances will we allow the Israeli flag to pass through the Aqaba Gulf," he announced. "This water is ours."

V
ISRAEL AGREES TO WAIT

Chief of Staff Rabin, already dead tired and tense from the mounting crisis, was the first Israeli leader to receive word of Nasser's closing of the straits. The message came in a telephone call to his Tel Aviv home at 3:45 A.M. He immediately rushed to general headquarters in Tel Aviv and met with his headquarters staff. Then he alerted his southern commanders and ordered them to refrain from any threatening military moves. It was 4:30 o'clock before he finished these basic tasks and telephoned Prime Minister Eshkol at his Jerusalem home.

Next to get the word was Foreign Minister Abba Eban, who was awakened a few minutes after 5 A.M. in his Jerusalem home as the first shafts of dawn's light shone through his bedroom window. After hearing the message, delivered in a dry, emotionless voice by an Israel Defense Forces headquarters officer, the anxious thought passed through Eban's mind that "nothing in our life or history would ever be the same."

Eban immediately called his senior aides to his house and together they listened to a recording of the closure statement. Nasser had delivered it in a speech the previous night at the Advanced Air Headquarters at the Bir Gafgafa air base in the Sinai, but Cairo Radio had not broadcast the talk until after midnight. In the early-morning light, Eban and his aides now heard the fateful words for the first time.

"We are now face-to-face with Israel. In recent days Israel has been making threats of aggression and it has been boasting. On 12 May a very impertinent statement was made. Anyone reading this statement must believe that these people are so boastful and deceitful that one simply cannot remain silent. . . . On 13 May we received accurate information that Israel was concentrating on the Syrian border huge armed forces. . . . The decision made by Israel at this time was to carry out an aggression against Syria as of 17 May. On 14 May we . . . contacted our Syrian brothers. . . . We told them that we have decided that if Syria was attacked, Egypt would enter the battle from the first minute. . . . Our forces are now in Sinai, and we are in a state of complete mobilization in Gaza and Sinai."

Nasser told the cadets that "there is talk of peace now. What is peace? . . . Does peace mean that we should ignore the rights of the Palestinian people because of lapse of time? Does peace mean that we should concede our rights because of the lapse of time? . . . The peace talk is heard only when Israel is in danger. But when Arab rights and the rights of the Palestinian people are lost, no one speaks about peace, rights, or anything."

Then he delivered a reckless taunt. "The armed forces yesterday occupied Sharm el Sheikh. What is the meaning? . . . It is an affirmation of our rights and our sovereignty over the Aqaba Gulf. The Jews threaten war. We tell them you are welcome, we are ready for war."

Even the moderate Eban, reflecting the heightened sense of crisis gripping Israel, concluded extravagantly that Nasser's words presented Israel with a drastic choice: "slow strangulation or rapid, solitary death." Others, especially the impatient senior military and intelligence officers, experienced the same overwrought emotion.

Eshkol, after meeting with his own staff in his home, called a meeting of the Ministerial Committee on Defense for 9 A.M. in Tel Aviv. But first he drove to The Pit, the underground headquarters for the IDF, the Israel Defense Forces, in Tel Aviv where he met with General Rabin and his staff. The generals were in a fighting mood. They were also confident of victory.

In the eleven years since the Suez war, the IDF had been immeasurably strengthened by sophisticated weapons from France, West Germany and the United States. The members of the Israel Defense Forces were highly motivated, enormously competent professional soldiers, sure of their mission and unencumbered by doubts.

The civilian-fighter of previous wars had been largely replaced by the young career soldier who was introverted and had an "icy matter-of-factness," in Israeli reporter Amos Elon's words. This new Israeli was more impressed with fighters like Meir Har-Zion than with the farmers of the fading kibbutzim. Har-Zion, a professional paratrooper of the 1950s, "began to personify an Israeli version of the Indian Fighters in the American Wild West," observed Elon. "Laconically killing Arab soldiers, peasants, and townspeople in a kind of fury without hatred, he remained cold-blooded and thoroughly efficient, simply doing a job and doing it well, twice or three times a week for months . . ." It was Har-Zion who became "a sort of culture hero, the living symbol of a 'new,' cold-blooded, fighting Jew with an armor-plated conscience," wrote Elon. General Ariel Sharon, who fought by Har-Zion's side many times in violent retaliatory raids against Arab villages, called Har-Zion "the fighting symbol not only of the paratroopers, but of the entire Israel Defense Forces."

The generals meeting with Eshkol in The Pit were confident of the fighting talents of these new professionals as well as the effectiveness of the rigorous training they had undergone. One of the contingency plans they had repeatedly practiced had been maneuvers aimed at chasing Egypt out of the Sinai.

Eshkol informed Rabin's staff that President Johnson had already requested in a letter, received only that morning, but written the day before, that Israel not fire the first shot. But, as Rabin later wrote, "As far as we were concerned, Nasser had already fired off much more than a first shot. . . ."

Indeed, the other generals wanted to go to war immediately. Major General Ezer Weizman, as the nation's number two general, urged Eshkol to approve instant air attacks against Egypt.

And Aharon Yariv, the brilliant chief of military intelligence, soberly declared: "The post-Sinai Campaign period has come to an end. It's no longer just a matter of freedom of navigation. If Israel takes no action in response to the blockade of the straits, she will lose her credibility and the IDF its deterrent capacity. The Arab states will interpret Israel's weakness as an excellent opportunity to threaten her security and her very existence."

Eshkol demurred. "There may be no further point in waiting," he told the impatient generals. "But first we must send a message to the President of the United States, honoring his request to consult before taking critical steps."

Rabin, more cautious than his aides, agreed with Eshkol. "If we ignored [Johnson] and war broke out, we would find ourselves alone in the international arena," he said. "And without the United States to keep Soviet involvement in check, Israel would be in a tough predicament."

At about 9:30 A.M., the meeting of the Ministerial Committee on Defense finally got under way with all eighteen sober-faced ministers in attendance. They soon were joined by such opposition figures as Moshe Dayan and Shimon Peres of David Ben Gurion's splinter Rafi faction and Menachem Begin of the extremist Gahal Party, all brought in because of the gravity of the situation. Eban, like others, arrived at the meeting with darkling thoughts of ancient disasters that the Jews had suffered: ". . . our minds revolved around the question of survival; so it must have been in ancient days, with Babylon or Assyria at the gates."

Despite their deepened concern, the actual military situation had not changed significantly. Rabin informed the ministers that the Egyptian Army remained in a defensive posture and the crack 4th Egyptian Armored Division still had not crossed into the Sinai. Nor, he added, had there been any threatening moves on the Jordanian or Syrian fronts. According to Eban's memoirs, Rabin reported that the most outward threat was "the ecstatic mood sweeping over the Arab world. Masses of people, long elated by dreams of vengeance, were now screaming for Israel's blood."

In summing up, Rabin did not urge the immediate launching of war, but nonetheless he did point out that the sooner Israel attacked the easier it would be to win. This was a widely shared view, especially by the generals, and it gave a special urgency to the deliberations.

Adding to the crisis was a consideration totally divorced from Egypt—Israel's foundering economy. The routine annual growth by 10 percent of the Gross National Product and total employment that Israel had enjoyed since 1949 had suddenly halted. In the past year the GNP had plummeted to barely 1 percent growth and unemployment, always a sensitive issue in a nation trying to attract immigrants, had shot up to a dangerous 10.3 percent. Riots had broken out on March 14 during a protest march by two thousand unemployed workers in Tel Aviv and seven policemen and four rioters were injured. Worse, since it struck at the very core of the Jewish state, immigration had sunk from sixty-five thousand in 1964 to twenty-three thousand in 1965 and to a mere twelve thousand in 1966. Added to that was the distressing fact that an estimated ten thousand Israelis in 1966 had pulled up stakes and sought a new life elsewhere. The mood in the country was so depressed that a popular black-humor joke had it that there was a sign at the international airport reading: "Will the last to leave kindly turn out the light."

In addition to these domestic political and economic problems, there was another imperative pressing for urgency. The nation's standing army stood at only around 50,000 regular soldiers; to get to full strength it had to mobilize all of the 200,000 reservists. This meant pulling more civilians away from their jobs and disrupting the economy even further, putting it under a nearly unsuperable strain.

Like the majority of generals, some of the officials at the ministerial meeting favored going to war immediately; others were less certain of Israel's strength. As the meeting dragged on through the morning, it appeared that the hawks might prevail. U.S. Ambassador Walworth Barbour, who had been assigned to the country since 1961 and had excellent sources among the Israeli Establishment, grew increasingly concerned that Israel was about to launch a war. From his Tel Aviv embassy, he telephoned in Washington Eugene V. Rostow, the State Department's under secretary for political affairs, the department's number three position, and said in an emotional voice: "I don't think I can hold this much longer without a new idea."

Rostow managed to get off a flash cable to Barbour within half an hour. He asked Barbour to urge the Israelis to delay any action for forty-eight hours, saying the time was necessary to give the United States a chance to pursue various schemes for opening the straits, including the use of an international naval force.

The urgent formal request put the ministers in an awkward position. With Israel's need of U.S. support, they could hardly ignore a direct request by Washington for a two-day delay. As Eban warned them, "We should be careful not to make the mistake of 1956 again. . . . At that time Eisenhower protested strongly that America had not been kept informed of our intentions." He added that it was imperative "to secure a warmer American understanding. Otherwise . . . we could well win a war and lose the victory."

Moshe Dayan, the one-eyed hero of the Suez war, reflected the impatience of many of the participants at the meeting. "If the United States has asked for forty-eight hours, we can give it to them. But I mean forty-eight, not forty-nine. . . . After that delay we ought to go to war with Egypt and fight a battle that will destroy hundreds of tanks and planes."

Eban's advice carried the day. Despite misgivings, the ministers agreed to put off a decision about whether to go to war. Instead, they decided to seek international support in the capitals of the West. But the committee formally expressed its determined mood by passing unanimously a policy statement:

1. The blockade is an act of aggression against Israel.
2. Any decision on action is postponed for 48 hours, during which time the Foreign Minister will explore the position of the United States.
3. The Prime Minister and Foreign Minister are empowered to decide, should they see fit, on a journey by the Foreign Minister to Washington to meet President Johnson.

When they learned that morning of the closure, the Israeli public reacted with alarm and determination. Housewives, who had displayed restraint up until then, stormed the grocery stores that May 23, stocking up on canned goods, flour, oil and sugar in preparation for a long war. Thousands of Israelis paid up their taxes and others donated cash and jewelry to the Defense Ministry to provide extra funds to purchase weapons. Neighborhood groups formed on their own to build bomb shelters, dig trenches and volunteer for essential services.

The nation's mobilization was by now far advanced and the newspapers were filled with columns of canceled meetings and postponed weddings "because of the situation." Old men and women now drove the public buses since the young drivers had been called up. Thousands of Israeli mothers baked cakes and tarts and sent them off to the Negev so their fighters would have something fresh to eat besides canned combat rations. Civilians appeared in the outposts handing out cigarettes, soft drinks and magazines.

Israelis were digging in, getting ready for war.

That May 23 afternoon, Levi Eshkol went before the parliament and unintentionally provided the hawks with more ammunition. "I demand that the great powers respect without delay the right of free passage to our southern port, a legal right for all states without exception."

It was not the tone or the message that Israelis girding for war wanted to hear. As Israeli historian Michael Bar-Zohar observed: "[Eshkol's remark] characterized the essential differences between the generation of leaders who had come to Israel from foreign lands—those of the Diaspora—and the generation that had been born and raised in the land. During the Diaspora it had been customary for Jews to seek aid and protection from persons in high office. To the young Israelis, however, it had been clear from the beginning ... that Arabs and Israelis would confront each other alone. No one was going to pull Israel's chestnuts out of the fire. Only Israel, relying on its own strength, could do that."

Reflecting the urgency felt by the government, Eban boarded a chartered El Al Boeing 707 at 3:30 o'clock on the morning of May 24, sleepless since the disturbing phone call he had received at 5 A.M. the previous day. He was off on a war-or-peace tour that would take him to Paris, London and, most importantly, Washington.

VI
NASSER'S GRUDGE
AGAINST WASHINGTON

Like Abba Eban, U Thant also was traveling to find a solution to the crisis. He landed aboard a Pan American commercial flight at Cairo International Airport on May 23 with the knowledge that the action he had come to prevent had already been taken. To his chagrin, he had learned of the straits' closure during a stopover in Paris.

U Thant found Cairenes in a festive mood because of Nasser's dramatic gesture, and they lustily cheered and waved at the secretary-general and his U.N. colleagues during the drive to the Nile Hilton Hotel. The Egyptians felt that the last of the lingering scars of the 1956 Suez crisis had finally been eradicated by the withdrawal of U.N. forces from the Sinai and the reoccupation of Sharm el Sheikh by Egyptian troops. Egypt for the first time since November 1956 was again free of all foreign forces and its people were in a happy, celebratory mood.

U Thant met for most of the evening with his U.N. staff to discuss the new development and then, exhausted, he went to bed to rest up for his meeting with Nasser the next day.

On the same day as U Thant's arrival, a letter for Nasser arrived from President Johnson. The letter had been written the day before Nasser had closed the straits. But even if it had reached him earlier it was unlikely to have deterred the Egyptian leader. Relations were badly strained between the two men, as Johnson's letter openly acknowledged.

"Various of our common friends, including Ambassador [Lucius D.] Battle, have told me of your concern that the United States may have indicated our unfriendliness toward the UAR," said the second paragraph of the letter. "This, I would wish you to know directly, is far from the truth."

But, from Nasser's perspective, it was the truth. The U.S. Congress and the American people had shown little understanding and no support for Egypt over the years. The Executive branch, particularly the professionals in the National Security Council and in the State Department were more aware of Egyptian needs. But they were repeatedly hampered by congressional opposition and they eventually lapsed into acquiescence.

The letter gave Nasser no hope that this attitude of indifference would change. While it said the "transcendent objective" was "the avoidance of hostilities," the letter then implicitly questioned Egypt's rights and intentions by warning it not to launch an attack: "The great conflicts of our time are not going to be solved by the illegal crossing of frontiers with arms and men—neither in Asia, the Middle East, Africa, or Latin America. But that kind of action has already led to war in Asia, and it threatens the peace elsewhere.

"Whatever differences there may be in the outlook and interests of your country and mine, we do share an interest in the independence and progress of the UAR and the peace of the Middle East. I address you at this critical moment in the hope that you share that assessment. . . ."

Johnson offered to help mediate the crisis by sending Vice President Humphrey to see Nasser and other Arab leaders in the Middle East and Eshkol in Israel. It was an idea whose time never came, because it, like the letter itself, was overtaken by the rush of events.

While Nasser was correct to sense no intimacy, and even some enmity, in his relations with the Johnson Administration, he was wrong in ascribing it solely to the President. Johnson had gone through the motion of fostering better relations over the years by such efforts as writing a series of personal letters to the Egyptian leader about the two countries' broad aims in the Middle East and by warmly entertaining Nasser's daughter, Mona, and her new husband, Lieutenant Ashraf Marawan, at the White House on September 12, 1966. At that time, Johnson with typical Texan effusiveness said to the newly married woman: "You are a bride . . . I have a daughter who is also a bride . . . therefore I am like your father . . . come to the ranch . . . tell your father I want to be his friend."

But Nasser, a private and somewhat prudish family man, was more confused than swayed by such behavior. He was unhappily aware of the imbalance shown by Johnson in his different attitudes to Israel and to Egypt. "He felt that Johnson was giving him nice words but that American deeds were completely different from those nice words," observed his biographer and confidant, journalist Mohamed Heikal.

Beyond that, Nasser had an instinctive dislike of Lyndon Johnson, though the two were never to meet. Nasser thought of him as gross, a petty politician who was ignorant about foreign affairs and irretrievably committed to Israel's cause.

The popularity and respect that the United States had enjoyed in Egypt at the end of the 1956 Suez crisis because of its intercession on the side of Cairo against London, Paris and Tel Aviv had long since evaporated. Partly this was an inevitable result of superpower rivalry in the Middle East. From the time of its first significant entry into the region with a massive sale of arms to Egypt in 1955, the Soviet Union had been extending its influence at the expense of Western interests, and was now actively involved in efforts to strengthen its position in Egypt and Syria.

In addition to the natural tensions flowing from Egypt's friendship with Russia, events around the globe tended to pit Egypt and the United States on opposite sides of most issues. Foremost among these festering problems was Egypt's intervention with as many as seventy thousand troops in the civil war in Yemen. The war had erupted on September 27, 1962, when a group of army officers staged a coup d'état against the royal family of Imam Saif Badr. The Saudi and Jordanian royal families immediately backed the deposed Imam and Nasser threw his support to the rebels; predictably the United States lined up behind the royalists and the Soviet Union behind Nasser and the rebels. It was an enervating and costly war that was to drag on until 1970 and be a constant irritant between Cairo and Washington.

The American press roundly damned Nasser for his intervention and readily accepted royalist charges that his army was using poison gas although United Nations observers on the scene could not verify such reports.

Nasser's image was further tarnished in the United States in 1964 when Washington mounted a large rescue operation of white civilians in the war-torn Congo and in reaction black African students in Cairo showed their outrage by burning down the U.S. Information Service Library on November 26, Thanksgiving Day. Then, three weeks later, on December 19, an airplane belonging to a personal friend of President Johnson's, Texas oilman John W. Mecom, was shot down by Egyptian MiGs and its two-man crew was killed when it flew through Egyptian airspace.

Though the public impression was that the plane had been downed by trigger-happy Egyptians, it turned out that through a mix-up the plane had failed to seek permission to fly over Egyptian territory. In addition, it was the same type of lumbering boxcar aircraft used by Israel to gather intelligence along the Egyptian frontier. When the Mecom craft penetrated Egyptian airspace it was shot down in the apparent belief that it was conducting an Israeli spy mission, yet all this was unknown at the time and passions in America were stirred by the event.

The destruction of the plane and the burning of the library were disruptive enough in the best of times, but relations between Cairo and Washington suffered from an even more corrosive and long-term problem—Egypt's constant and desperate need for U.S. wheat. Egypt depended on American wheat to supply nearly half of its grain requirements, a reality that had become a humiliation for Nasser and a subject of resentment for Congress. Nasser, ever sensitive about Egypt's endemic poverty, bridled at his dependency; Congress, overwhelmingly supportive of Israel, felt Nasser was biting the hand that fed him by not making peace with the Jewish state. It was a situation certain to create ill will, and it did.

During this uneasy period in mid-December 1964, Egypt was anxiously trying to clear up several technical details of a new wheat deal with Washington. Ambassador Luke Battle, a tall, genial Georgian who enjoyed working with Egyptians, knew it was a doomed proposition in the current heated climate. He forcefully let Egyptian officials know his views and also vented his anger over the plane and library incidents.

Battle's plain words got back to Nasser in a highly exaggerated form on December 23. The Egyptian leader was traveling to Port Said that day to give a speech, accompanied by Prime Minister Ali Sabry, Moscow's strongest advocate in the Egyptian government. Sabry missed no chance to undermine the United States' position in Egypt and he now gave such an inflammatory version of Battle's comments that Nasser's blood was boiling by the time they arrived at Port Said. When he finally stood up to speak, Nasser, who was a stirring extemporaneous speaker, let his venom flow.

"The American ambassador says that our behavior is not acceptable," he shouted. "Well, let us tell them that those who do not accept our behavior can go and drink . . ." Here he shouted to the audience: "From where?" and the mass responded: "From the sea!" Nasser continued: "And if the Mediterranean is not enough to slake their thirst, they can carry on with the Red Sea.

"What I want to say to President Johnson is that I am not prepared to sell Egyptian independence for thirty million pounds or forty million pounds or fifty million pounds.... We are not going to accept gangsterism by cowboys."

A Central Intelligence Agency assessment of the speech noted that it was "Nasser's bitterest attack on the U.S. since 1956. Some of its extravagances suggest that he had thrown away his text and was speaking extemporaneously.... In any case, the speech reflects both Nasser's recognition of Egypt's economic problems and his determination nonetheless to back 'national liberation' movements at whatever cost."

Another reason for the speech's extravagances not mentioned by the CIA report was that Nasser was trying to strengthen his relations with the Soviet Union. It had been only the previous October 15 that Nikita S. Khrushchev had been deposed and replaced by Leonid I. Brezhnev as secretary-general of the party and Aleksei N. Kosygin as prime minister. Khrushchev's fall had been a heavy blow to the Egyptians, who looked on him as a friend and protector, the man who had threatened the West at the time of the Suez war, who had given them the Aswan High Dam, and who had provided Egypt with arms and vast amounts of aid.

The natural anxieties of having to deal with a new leadership of unknown attitude toward Egypt were heightened by rumors that it was Khrushchev's Middle East policies that helped bring about his removal from office. Unconfirmed reports had it that resentment in the Kremlin centered on complaints about Khrushchev's generosity to Egypt. He was reportedly accused of extending far too much aid to Egypt, at the expense of East European Communist countries, and of failing to get in return better treatment of Communist parties in the region. Indeed, one of the conditions Nasser had imposed in creating the U.A.R. with Syria had been the outlawing of all political parties, including the Communist Party. The party fared no better inside Egypt itself. It was kept weak and was eventually abolished. In Iraq, it was outlawed.

In the Port Said audience listening to Nasser's speech that December 23 was Soviet Deputy Prime Minister Alexander Shelepin, sent to discuss the new leadership's relations with Egypt. His presence may have encouraged Nasser's venom to flow a bit freer to demonstrate to the new Soviet leaders that the United States could not kick him around.

There were yet other strains in U.S.-Egyptian relations. Nasser strongly opposed America's war in Vietnam and also Britain's failure to depose the white regime of Ian Smith in Rhodesia. The Egyptian leader repeatedly spoke out on these issues and condemned both countries. He became so suspicious of Britain that he joined with black African countries and broke relations with London on December 15, 1965, over the Rhodesian issue. He also had a further, lacerating quarrel with Britain over Aden—still, at this point, a Crown Colony.

As if all this were not enough to strain to the limit his dealings with the United States and its friends, Nasser also broke off relations in 1965 with West Germany when that country finally decided to extend diplomatic recognition of Israel.

The move had been long in coming. At least as early as 1958, Israel had established secret ties with the Federal Republic of Germany, much as it had with France, for the supply of weapons. These included vast stores of sophisticated arms and ammunition, eventually including U.S.-built battle tanks that were sold by Germany with secret permission from the Johnson Administration. By 1960 Nasser had suspected what the West Germans were up to, but he kept his peace because he had a German connection of his own—he was employing German scientists to build missiles for Egypt. Like Israeli leaders, Nasser was wary about depending totally on outside support for weaponry. Thus he had decided to make an effort to build up a local armaments industry based on the technological expertise of German scientists, who since World War II had been fair game for all countries who could afford them.

Nasser wanted a short-range ground-to-ground missile much like one Israel was developing. About one hundred German scientists and technicians were put to work secretly at a factory code named 333 and located near Heliopolis. Israel was the first to test-fire its missile, the Shavit 2, which it launched with great fanfare on July 6, 1961, claiming it was a meteorological research tool. The next year, on July 21, Egypt launched four missiles, two Al Kahirs and two Al Zafirs. Nasser recklessly boasted that the missiles had a range (from 175 to 350 miles) that could take them to any target "south of Beirut." The reaction in Israel was instantaneous. Soon highly exaggerated stories were appearing in the world press claiming that Egypt's German scientists were producing not only rockets but atomic bombs, death rays, chemical-warfare microbes and other amazing devices that would soon render Israel helpless.

The Israeli secret service, the Mossad (Central Institute for Intelligence and Special Missions), planted many of these stories and, judging by the ferocity of the terror campaign it soon unleashed, it may even have begun to believe some of its own exaggerated claims. Starting September 11, 1962, with the abduction of a German purchasing agent of rocket parts in Munich, Dr. Heinz Krug (his body has never been found), Mossad waged a violent campaign called Operation Damocles against the German scientists. Threatening letters were sent to the scientists and even some letters that contained bombs. One of the letter bombs addressed to the manager of Factory 333 exploded and badly injured the man's secretary, Hannelore Wende, on November 27. The next day another bomb sent to the factory exploded and killed five persons. Other bombs were discovered and defused. The terror continued until March 2, 1963, when an Israeli, Joseph Ben-Gal, and an Austrian colleague were arrested in Basle, Switzerland, for threatening Heidi Goerke, the daughter of Professor Paul Goerke, who was the leading scientist at Factory 333.

Though German scientists remained in Egypt, the terror had its intended effect in dampening their enthusiasm for working in Nasser's employ. Years later it was generally agreed that Mossad and Israel's supporters worldwide had vastly exaggerated the danger posed by the Egyptian missiles. The CIA had assessed the missiles as primitive, ineffective and a waste of resources, a judgment that one of Israel's chief arms buyers, Shimon Peres, who later was defense minister, eventually confirmed. "I confess that the American estimates proved closer to reality than our own."

Nonetheless, the affair had important ramifications. The continued presence in Egypt of a handful of German electronics specialists was cited as late as 1965 as an excuse for the United States to ignore Nasser and increase its arms shipments to Israel, even though the Jewish state had hundreds of Western scientists routinely visiting there on fellowships and contributing significantly to its sophisticated defense effort and its advanced nuclear program. The brouhaha also greatly embarrassed the West German government and undoubtedly contributed to that country's decision to prove to the world that its anti-Semitism of World War II no longer existed by officially recognizing Israel on May 12, 1965. The move infuriated Nasser and he (and most other Arab countries) broke relations with West Germany the next day.

By the time of his confrontation with West Germany, Nasser was already so abhorred in the U.S. Congress that Secretary of State Dean Rusk was referring to "two years of congressional criticism of [Egypt]." The month before Nasser's break with Bonn, McGeorge Bundy, Walt Rostow's predecessor as head of NSC, received a staff note lamenting the "spate of anti-Nasser amendments being offered in Congress. No less than EIGHT are being offered. . . . Mac, believe me when I stress the real depth of my conviction that we've got to have some room to maneuver with Nasser if we're going to avert a major crisis in the Middle East. I may not know my Congress but I do know my Arabs."*

Still the floor of Congress in the mid-'60s rang with anti-Nasser histrionics. Typical was a statement on June 29, 1965, by Donald Rumsfeld, congressman from Illinois, who said: "Nasser has not proved reliable in the past and cannot be counted upon today to promote peace and amity among nations." The next day Congressman William F. Ryan of New York declared: "Let us recognize once and for all that Nasser aims only to dominate the Middle East and that his goals have nothing in common with America's." So it went through the summer, a campaign of vilification spurred both by Nasser's own open criticism of the United States and by Israel's effective propaganda aimed at keeping his relations with America in a constant state of animosity.

Nor was anti-Nasser, anti-Arab sentiment confined to the halls of Congress. Parts of the bureaucracy seemed infested with it too, as illustrated by a stinging cable from Ambassador Battle complaining about a Central Intelligence Agency analysis of a Nasser speech. "CIA piece is shot full of distortions," Battle wrote, and then went on to cite an impressive list of distortions. He concluded with an impatient lecture:

"I am aware that US-UAR relations are generally a controversial subject in Washington and have been for some time. At same time, many important US interests involved in that relationship and it essential that decision makers have full and unvarnished facts. US-UAR relations are neither football games nor western movies with 'bad guys chasing good guys.' "

Even a visit to the White House by Anwar Sadat did nothing to assuage the widespread distaste for Nasser and his country. Sadat, as speaker of the National Assembly, had planned to visit the United States in the summer of 1965 but had to cancel the trip. When he finally decided to make it the following winter, the State Department and the NSC strongly urged the President to see him.

"Dean Rusk again recommends that you see Anwar Sadat," wrote Robert Komer of the National Security Council staff in a memo on January 21 to the President. "Sadat ain't Nasser, but he's the highest ranking Egyptian ever to visit officially. . . . We'd suggest . . . a straight 10-minute protocol appointment. The Egyptians constantly are received in Moscow, so it makes sense to let them see that the door is open here too. There wouldn't be much local reaction, but Israel's new Foreign Minister Eban will be here in early

---

* Although unsigned, the memo's tone and style indicate strongly that it was written by Robert Komer, known as "Blowtorch Bob" because of his uninhibited style. Komer was the NSC's Middle East expert preceding Hal Saunders.

February if you want a balancing act. In fact, I'd advise giving Eban 10 minutes in any case, though he's not here officially."

Johnson agreed, but as usual with the star-crossed relations between the two countries, a minor storm erupted the day before Sadat's appointment. Nasser had made a speech and the newspapers were playing it as being a direct attack on the United States. In a memorandum to the President sent on the morning of Sadat's February 23 visit, Komer warned Johnson that "the NYT [*New York Times*] account is grossly inflated, in the opinion of the experts." He recommended the President reassure Sadat of America's desire to have friendly relations, observe that he was impressed with self-help measures being taken in Egypt and caution that both sides must be more conscious of the other's public relations problems. Komer added:

"We are surprised at Nasser's fears that Israel is going nuclear. We don't think so, though we are watching closely too as we oppose nuclear proliferation anywhere."

In fact, as the Central Intelligence Agency later determined, Israel was far along in its nuclear development by this time. Once again Nasser's suspicions were correct. He had tried to head off Israel's nuclear drive by offering to sign an inspection agreement with the International Atomic Energy Agency if Israel would also sign. But this Israel refused to do, thereby heightening Nasser's suspicions.

Finally, Komer advised Johnson to urge Sadat to confine his remarks to the media after their meeting to a simple statement that the talks were friendly. "We don't want him popping off in the West Lobby," cautioned Komer.

As was his habit with foreign leaders, Johnson was friendly and outgoing with Sadat. He talked with him in the Oval Office, pointing out a number of autographed photographs of world leaders on the wall and remarking: "Now look, I have a space here waiting for a picture of President Nasser. Why doesn't he send me one? Why do we make enemies of each other? We should be friends."

Sadat then delivered his message. It was a poignant and revealing one. "President Nasser has asked me to tell you that we want one thing. It's not that we want wheat or that we want aid. What we want . . . is understanding. We don't want anything more than understanding. I have no other message."

Johnson replied by saying that what was needed in the relationship was less public feuding. "Why does President Nasser stand up and openly attack me and the policy of the United States?" he asked.

He received his answer some days later after Sadat reported the meeting to Nasser. The Egyptian leader called in Ambassador Battle and asked him to explain to Johnson that quiet diplomacy was not in Egypt's interests. "You have got money and atom bombs, riches and power without limit. These are your means," Nasser said. "What have I got? The main weapon of the Revolution is its masses, the conviction of the masses and the mobilization of those masses. . . . Quiet diplomacy would not suit us because I would be cut off from the support of my masses."

Not even Johnson's friendly request for a photograph of Nasser helped improve relations. When the Egyptian ambassador to Washington asked for one, Nasser refused on the grounds that Johnson was trying to confuse him with what one Egyptian characterized as "nice words which had no bearing on his policies." Several weeks later the Egyptian ambassador made a special trip to Cairo to carry a personal message from Johnson. When it was delivered to Nasser it turned out to be a photograph of Johnson on which the President had written: "I hope to convince you that one day we can be friends."

Much to the detriment of the Egyptian people and the delight of Nasser's enemies, he never did.

———————

In the beginning of 1966 a series of coincidental events plunged U.S.-Egyptian relations even deeper into animosity and mutual suspicions. On February 23 the army coup brought to power in Syria the extreme neo-Baathist government that was openly determined to challenge Israel. The next day the radical president of Ghana, Kwame Nkrumah, a colleague of Nasser's in the nonaligned movement, was overthrown in what was perceived as a pro-Western military coup while he was on a visit to Communist China. During the same period, it was becoming obvious that President Sukarno of Indonesia, another leader of the nonaligned world, was slowly being isolated from power by Indonesia's military leaders. Hundreds of thousands of Communists were being indiscriminately slain throughout the country. Though Nasser despised the philandering Sukarno because he had tried to convince the Egyptian Foreign Ministry to provide a woman for his bed during a 1960 visit, the Egyptian leader nonetheless saw the Indonesian's eclipse as part of a larger pattern of a renewed campaign by Western nations to impose their will on the Third World nations of Africa, Asia and the Middle East.

On the global scoreboard, then, Cairo and Washington looked at the early part of 1966 as one victory for the Arabs and the Socialist Camp (Syria) and two victories for the West (Ghana and Indonesia). Although that was not a bad batting average for either side, it worried Nasser and did not please the hawks in Congress. When it came to Egypt, they were beyond pacification.

Over the next year leading up to the Straits of Tiran crisis, relations became increasingly cooler and Nasser's suspicions that the United States had adopted a new, unfriendly policy grew into conviction. American agreement to sell weapons to Egypt's royalist Arab enemies, Jordan and Saudi Arabia, and to his powerful neighbor, Israel, had all added to Nasser's disillusionment. An invitation to Dean Rusk to visit Cairo went ignored and attempts by the U.S. Embassy in Cairo to have some high official visit to show the flag failed.

Then in 1967 two more events outside of Egypt contributed to the American-Egyptian strain. A colonels' coup d'état on April 21 overthrew Greece's leftist regime and inaugurated a long period of repression under military rule. Nasser believed the coup was part of a U.S. plan to isolate him and build up rightist governments throughout the Middle East, not an improbable surmise. Only a short time earlier he had been informed by his ambassador in Brussels, Amin Shaker, that the United States had decided it could no longer work with Egypt. Shaker, quoting Belgian Foreign Minister Paul Henri Spaak as his source, said an American official had told a secret meeting of NATO representatives that Nasser's repeated attacks on U.S. policy and his close cooperation with the Soviet Union had made it impossible for Washington to deal with him. U.S. policy in the Middle East, Shaker reported, would now be based on the pro-Western governments of Iran, Israel and Turkey.

In the context of this alarming report, Nasser now saw the coup in Greece as part of a larger U.S. design. Greece would become a rear base for Turkey while Israel, which was dramatically stepping up its attacks on Syria (it had shot down the six Syrian jets only two weeks earlier), would cause a coup in Damascus and bring about Washington's long-sought goal of turning Syria into a pro-Western nation. This would neutralize the most aggressive of Israel's neighbors and give the United States a string of allies stretching across the northeastern tier of the Mediterranean, a goal the West had been trying to achieve since the days of the ill-starred Baghdad Pact alliance that Britain had formed in the mid-1950s.

In Nasser's eyes, the next step in this ambitious concept would be his overthrow so Egypt could be added to the chain of pro-Western nations along the rim of the Mediterranean. It was not a thought likely to give him any comfort or add to his small fund of pro-American feelings.

Then yet another strain was put on U.S-Egyptian relations five days after the Greek coup. A mob stormed the U.S. Consulate and the offices of the

Agency for International Development in Taiz in Yemen and uncovered a large number of secret documents, which were made available to Egyptian intelligence. Yemen charged the AID mission was a CIA cover and that its compound had been used to fire two bazooka shells at an ammunition dump in an attempt "to completely destroy the city." The truth was that British commandos had staged a covert raid to deter attacks into Aden, but presumably in the eyes of the revolutionary government there was little difference between blaming London or Washington. The Yemen revolutionary government arrested four Americans, threatening to execute them, and immediately ended the U.S. AID program. Washington retaliated by withdrawing all 160 Americans stationed in Yemen and refusing to allow Yemen's ambassador and his embassy counselor to leave Washington. Behind this incident was seen Nasser's hand, since the revolutionary government was his client, another reason for Washington to bear no love for him.

It was during this same mid-decade period when aid was being denied Egypt, when the country was being attacked almost daily in Congress and the news media, that the Johnson Administration was opening America's armory to Israel. Nasser could not help feeling he was being slighted and belittled by Washington. As he watched this ripening relationship between the American superpower and the tiny Jewish state become broader and deeper, his apprehensions and resentment mounted. But Washington showed little concern about the Egyptian leader's frustrations.

Then in March 1967, the State Department promoted Luke Battle, who had been ambassador to Egypt since 1964, back to Washington to become assistant secretary of state for Near Eastern and South Asian affairs. Battle, good-natured and tough-minded, liked Nasser personally, as did most Americans who dealt with him. The two men were about the same age, both big and easy-going, and Battle felt a special sadness during his last meeting, on March 4, with Nasser before returning to Washington. Despite the warmth between the two men, the forces keeping their two nations apart were too great for them to bridge. Each in his way had tried but they were caught in what Battle called a Greek tragedy. American support for Israel was so overwhelming that it blinded the President and Congress to Egypt. Yet Nasser's resentment of congressional opposition, his unquenchable suspicions of the West and his need for Soviet aid all tended to justify congressional opposition. It was a destructive rondo that the best of will seemed incapable of halting.

In their long, final meeting, Battle asked Nasser if he foresaw war erupting with Israel. The Egyptian leader said that if war came it would be at his timing and his choosing. But he did not want war now. He had nearly seventy thousand troops in Yemen and he was not strong enough to take on Israel.

The next day Battle wrote his last cable to Washington from Cairo. He noted that Egypt was on a "disaster course" because of its expensive involvement in Yemen, its tattered economy and its loss of American wheat. Battle predicted that Nasser would do one of three things soon to reverse this deteriorating trend: 1) intensify the Yemeni war, 2) start an adventure against neighboring Libya, or 3) "least likely," heat up the Arab-Israeli conflict. He added that Nasser did not want war but he needed to win back political prestige.

The man selected to replace Battle was Richard H. Nolte, a choice deeply resented among State Department professionals and especially by the current deputy chief of mission in Cairo, David G. Nes, an outspoken career officer. The forty-six-year-old Nolte had a brilliant academic background, had lived and studied in the Middle East for many years, spoke Arabic, and was the executive director of the Institute of Current World Affairs in New York and a close personal friend of the State Department's number two man, Under Secretary Nicholas DeB. Katzenbach. But foreign service officers were appalled because he had no previous diplomatic experience. Nes openly called him an "amateur" and a poor choice to represent the United States in the Arab world's most important country. Despite the grumbling, Dean Rusk and the President seemed barely concerned about Nolte's assignment. Rusk, consumed like the President with Vietnam, met with Nolte for only fifteen minutes before he departed for Cairo. That was more than the President did. He never met with Nolte privately.

To Nasser, Nolte's selection was one more example, if he needed any more at this point, of how little Washington cared for him or valued his country's friendship. Yet some influence in Cairo would have helped as the crisis of 1967 unfolded. As Nes later noted, when Nasser made his decision to blockade the straits he "might have thought twice if relations with the United States had been better and he had had hope he could profit from American friendship."

Indeed, when Nasser read Johnson's letter on May 23, he turned to Foreign Minister Riad and said: "I gravely doubt the sincerity of Johnson. For a man who has always sided with Israel it is inconceivable that, all of a sudden, he would become evenhanded."

Nasser did not know how right he was going to be proved.

VII
RABIN HAS A BREAKDOWN

Nasser had no trouble getting Washington's attention after closing the Straits of Tiran. Announcement of the closure sent the Johnson Administration into a flurry of activity. It was immediately obvious that the President, who up to this point had kept a discreet silence, would now have to speak out on the crisis to enunciate the nation's position and to try to divert the rush to war. Because of the seven-hour time difference between Cairo and Washington, it was still the evening of May 22 in Washington when word of the blockade was received. The lights burned late that night at the White House and the State Department as the Administration reacted to the latest jolt from the Middle East.

One of the first actions taken was to order the Sixth Fleet with its aircraft carriers U.S.S. *America* and U.S.S. *Saratoga* to sail toward the eastern Mediterranean. Next, the State Department quickly worked up a draft of Johnson's proposed statement for the next day and then a special White House aide was brought in to put it into presidential rhetoric. He was John P. Roche, a history professor known as Johnson's intellectual-in-residence and an avid supporter of Israel. He was appalled by the noncommittal State Department draft and immediately set to work rewriting it.

Roche labored on a new draft until around 3 A.M. and then sent it off to the President with a note: "Studied ambiguity is an art form much loved by statesmen, but I have tried to eliminate as much of the conditional-subjective tense as is possible short of issuing an ultimatum. It is still a bit mushy for my taste, but I confess I look on the Israelis as Texans and Nasser as Santa Ana."

The dawn of May 23 found the Jewish American community in full outcry demanding that the President openly declare America's support of Israel. A special edge of anxiety went with the demands because it was known that Johnson was going to make a statement that night but its contents remained secret.

"Jewish pressure groups in this country were lined up all the way from Washington to California," Roche later stated, "and Johnson engaged in one of his malicious little games. The various Jewish groups would call him, and what he did was he'd fish out the State Department draft and read it to them and say, 'Well, how do you feel about that? . . .' So boom! The phones are ringing. The Israeli ambassador, Avraham Harman, is over in Humphrey's office with [Israeli Embassy Minister Ephraim] Eppy Evron, who is practically in tears."

Humphrey was anxious and telephoned Roche. "What do you know about this?" Humphrey asked.

"It was very embarrassing, because I happened to know that what I had written the night before had already gone on speech cards, and [the President] was going on television," recalled Roche. "But I couldn't say this to Humphrey. I mean, Johnson once said about ways of getting information around Washington: 'Telephone, telegraph, or tell Hubert!'

"All day Johnson went on doing this. I called Rostow. I said, 'For God's sake, what is he doing?' Walt said, 'Oh, he's just getting a little therapy for all this pressure they put on.' "

Despite the worries of Israel's supporters, the fact was that the Israeli Embassy could find out almost anything it wanted about Administration policy.* Its officials, particularly Eppy Evron, the short, puckish Israeli minister who was one of the shrewdest diplomats Israel had ever produced, enjoyed extraordinary access to all levels of the government, including the President.

Although Johnson's top officials—the heads of the State Department, the Defense Department and the CIA—were all professionally objective, if sympathetic, toward Israel, as were most of the middle-level bureaucrats in those departments, the President himself was openly a supporter of Israel and he was surrounded by friends and advisers who also were supporters of Israel. These included such powerful figures—besides Abe Feinberg, Arthur

* The CIA's Helms, among others, believed that during this period there was no important secret in the U.S. government affecting Israel that Israel did not know about. As an example, he recalled one occasion when some Israeli arms requests had been filled with the wrong items; the list was resubmitted with all the top-secret code numbers attached and a note that said perhaps the Pentagon had not understood exactly which weapons had been sought in the original request. "It was a way for them to show me that they knew exactly what they wanted," said Helms.

Krim and John Roche—as Washington attorney Clark McA. Clifford, Associate Justice of the Supreme Court Abe Fortas, Ambassador to the United Nations Arthur Goldberg and Eugene V. Rostow, the under secretary of state for political affairs.

Of the two Rostow brothers, who occupied uniquely powerful posts, Walt, at fifty, was an economist who had served in the Office of Strategic Services, the forerunner of the CIA, during World War II. Walt Rostow was teaching at the Massachusetts Institute of Technology when he became close to John Kennedy and was appointed deputy special assistant for National Security Affairs in 1961. Johnson named him head of NSC in 1966. He kept close ties with the Jewish community, as anyone had to in his post, and his co-workers regarded him as fairly evenhanded in his attitudes toward the Middle East.

Gene Rostow, three years older than Walt, had been dean of the Yale law school before joining the Administration as the State Department's third-ranking officer in 1966, but his government service stretched back to World War II, when he first became an adviser to the State Department. He was a warm supporter of Israel.

The pressures did not let up on the President throughout the day. They had begun with a 7:55 A.M. telephone call from Secretary of State Dean Rusk and by 9:07 A.M. he had talked with U.N. Ambassador Arthur Goldberg, CIA Director Richard Helms, Walt Rostow and several others.

Rusk that May 23 briefed the Senate Foreign Relations Committee and later told Johnson that the senators believed "the Arabs should not be permitted to drive the Israelis into the sea." However, the legislators were against unilateral action by the United States and favored some sort of international effort through the United Nations.

Johnson found that a prudent course to adopt, especially since he was still under suspicion for the way he had handled the Gulf of Tonkin incident in 1964. At that time the alleged attack of North Vietnamese patrol boats against destroyers of the Seventh Fleet had allowed Johnson to take a small incident and use it to convince the Senate to pass a resolution significantly broadening his war powers. Later, however, he was charged with misleading the Congress and abusing his powers. Now, with antiwar sentiment reaching new heights of bitterness, he was careful not to repeat the Tonkin Gulf incident.

Israeli Ambassador Harman and his number two, Eppy Evron, used their open access to Walt Rostow that day to get an explanation of what the President was planning. They were informed that the course of action decided on was to go to the U.N. Security Council. Evron cabled Jerusalem that Rostow explained that "it was essential to use the U.N. platform before a unilateral position was adopted [and] . . . that we could rely on the President."

That evening at 6:11 o'clock, President Johnson went to the Fish Room accompanied by his daughter Lynda Bird and read the anxiously anticipated statement Roche had written about the blockade.

As was soon obvious, the pressure throughout the day had been unnecessary, the Jewish community's worries groundless.

"The United States considers the gulf to be an international waterway and feels that a blockade of Israeli shipping is illegal and potentially disastrous to the cause of peace," Johnson declared. He informed the nation that "our able ambassador" was now "pursuing the matter with great vigor" at the United Nations.

The favorable public mention of Arthur J. Goldberg was no doubt an effort to raise his morale, since he was feeling frustrated and unhappy in his U.N. post. Goldberg, a fifty-eight-year-old Chicagoan who had earned a liberal reputation as a labor attorney and John F. Kennedy's secretary of labor, had seemed to reach the peak of his career in 1962, when Kennedy appointed him to the U.S. Supreme Court. But at the strong urgings of Johnson he left his seat in 1965 to become the permanent representative at the United Nations, apparently with the understanding that in that role he could more forcefully exert influence to solve the conflict in Vietnam, which he opposed. However, Goldberg instead found himself increasingly cut off from the President and from formulating policy on the war.

By 1967, Goldberg's distinguished career appeared to be at a dead end, sidelined out of the main action in Vietnam and stifled by the rhetoric that passed for reality in the United Nations. Although the world body remained a prestigious and respected forum, it was hardly a substitute for the key role Goldberg had hoped to play.

Yet now Goldberg was soon to play a role far more significant and meaningful to him than any he could have confronted in distant Southeast Asia. Goldberg was a Zionist and, as he publicly professed while still on the Court, he was a friend and supporter of Israel just as had been Associate Justices Louis D. Brandeis and Felix Frankfurter before him. "I must frankly state," he said in a speech before the American Israel Public Affairs Committee in 1965, "that I do not understand the reasoning of those who question the support Americans and other free people, both Jewish and non-Jewish, extend to Israel and its people." He could see, he added, no incompatibility between remaining loyal to "the spiritual heritage of the Jewish people" and at the same time retaining "undivided allegiance" to America.

That proposition seemed unexceptionable in America's tradition of religious tolerance. But in practice, in the suspicious atmosphere endemic to the affairs of the Middle East, it proved difficult to establish and left many Arabs resentful and deeply distrustful of Goldberg's objectivity.

Now, along with many other strong supporters of Israel, Goldberg shared the fear that the Jewish state was in imminent peril. Only that day in his telephone call to Johnson he had expressed his concern about Israel's safety and was reassured by the President that he could look at intelligence estimates, all of which showed Israel to be far stronger than its neighbors.

Johnson's TV statement greatly heartened Israel and its supporters, who took it as an unequivocal endorsement of Israel's position. Minutes after Johnson finished speaking, Abe Feinberg telephoned him, saying, "Arthur Goldberg and I have just gotten through discussing your statement, which I think is very good."

Eppy Evron the next day telephoned Walt Rostow and told him, as Rostow reported to the President, that "he fully understands the 'terrible dilemma' which you faced yesterday in making a public statement—wanting both to reassure Israel and permit quiet diplomacy to work. He thought the final result was 'wonderful.' He wanted you to know that the Israeli Embassy in Washington was flooded with telephone calls from people we both would respect, who were deeply gratified by your statement. He wanted me to convey to you, if I felt it appropriate, his deep personal gratitude."

Moscow's reaction to the closure of the straits was released by the official government news service, Tass, on May 23. The statement condemned "aggressive" Israeli intentions and praised Egypt and other Arab states for honoring their "allied commitments for joint defense with Syria." It added threateningly: "But let no one have any doubt about the fact that should anyone try to unleash aggression in the Near East he would be met not only with the united strength of Arab countries, but also with strong opposition from the Soviet Union and all peace-loving states."

Despite the strong words, Washington and Moscow were trying to work together behind the scenes to calm the crisis. The day before the Tass announcement, before learning of the blockade, Johnson had sent another letter to Kosygin suggesting joint action to calm the atmosphere, adding: "The increasing harassment of Israel by elements based in Syria, with attendant reactions within Israel and within the Arab world, has brought the area close to major violence. Your and our ties to nations of the area could bring us into difficulties which I am confident neither of us seeks. It would appear a time for each of us to use our influence to the full in the cause of moderation, including our influence over action by the United Nations."

The Soviets tried to cooperate, but like America's limited ability to influence Israel, Russia's control over Egypt's actions did not extend far. The closure of the straits had been as much of a surprise in Moscow as it was in Washington. Nasser had taken the action without consulting or warning the Soviet Union.

———————

The reaction in Jordan was one of surprise and heightened apprehension. ". . . they seemed greatly appalled by the fact that hostilities in the area could engulf them," a later State Department history concluded. "Jordan's leadership saw itself faced with problems arising from Nasser's hostility to Jordan, the natural volatility of the Jordanian population, which was two-thirds [sic] Palestinian, and the belief of the populace that Jordan was so much under U.S. control that the regime in power would never make war on Israel.

"U.S. Embassy officials in Amman did not cease to importune the government of Jordan to exercise restraint."

But for Jordan, inexorably caught up in the whirlwind being sown by Egypt and Israel, it was not a question of restraint. It was a question of survival among its powerful neighbors.

———————

In Israel, the excited state of anxiety, the doubts and hesitations, the endless rounds of meetings, were beginning to take their toll. At the center of the storm was Chief of Staff Yitzhak Rabin. The same day that he heard of the Egyptian blockade, during Israel's greatest crisis in a decade, he had a momentary breakdown.

Rabin was a husky forty-five-year-old sabra, introverted, quiet, cautious, reflective—the complete opposite of the general image of the macho Israeli warrior. Though he had displayed courage and imagination in the 1948 war of Israel's independence, he had impatiently sat out the 1956 Suez war as commander of the quiescent Northern Command, bitterly referring to himself at the time as the "unemployed general."

He had achieved his high post as head of the IDF not because of his battlefield exploits or his charismatic leadership, of which he had almost none, but because of the clarity of his formidable analytic powers. He was appointed by Levi Eshkol to the highly prized top post of Israel's military forces on December 5, 1963, the seventh chief of staff in Israel's history.

From the start of the crisis, Rabin had felt the full weight of his position. He could get no clear guidance from Prime Minister Eshkol, who himself had become increasingly indecisive, and felt that the responsibility of war or peace rested solely on his shoulders. Rabin increased his cigarette smoking, now practically chain smoking, found it hard to sleep, and was noticeably tense and indecisive. Soon he found himself seeking advice, and perhaps consolation, from past leaders.

On the evening of May 21 he went to see former Prime Minister David Ben Gurion, though Ben Gurion harbored no good will toward him. The Old Man, as Ben Gurion had been called during his days of glory as Israel's founding father and longtime prime minister, was now truly old, in his eighty-first year, irascible and bitter toward his estranged old friend and successor Levi Eshkol. As it happened, Ben Gurion was meeting that same night with Dayan, Peres and other opposition leaders to discuss how to topple Eshkol and return Ben Gurion to the head of the government.

Ben Gurion left the meeting to see Rabin. The session was a disaster for Rabin. Instead of having his doubts dispelled by lucid advice, they were magnified under the lash of the Old Man's sharp tongue. As Rabin later wrote, "As soon as I opened the door—I didn't even have a chance to say hello—Ben Gurion launched into the attack."

Ben Gurion declared, according to Rabin's memoirs: "'We have been forced into a very grave situation. I very much doubt whether Nasser wanted to go to war, and now we are in serious trouble. Unlike in the past, we are totally isolated.'

"As Ben Gurion proceeded to pour scorn on the Cabinet and the Prime Minister, his words struck me like hammer blows," Rabin wrote. "Never have I experienced such a profound sense of disappointment and dismay. But Ben Gurion kept hammering away. 'You made a mistake,' he said, referring to our mobilization of the reserves. . . . 'You have led the state into a grave situation. We must not go to war. We are isolated. You bear the responsibility.' "

Rabin was crushed by the harangue. He had called on Ben Gurion for advice and sympathy; instead he had gotten abuse and scorn and, worse, he had been personally charged with placing the nation in peril. "Having come to Ben Gurion for encouragement, I left him feeling doubly despondent,"

Rabin continued. "I now felt the entire burden was resting on my shoulders. Many days were to pass before his words stopped ringing in my ears: 'You have led the state into a grave situation. You bear the responsibility.' "

Rabin called on Dayan at his Tel Aviv home the next night, May 22, to seek the advice of the famed former chief of staff. Again he found little solace. "He too was unsparing in his criticism of the Cabinet and the Army, although he refrained from personal recriminations," Rabin later wrote. "He felt we had erred in placing Nasser's leadership of the Arab world in jeopardy. The nature and scale of our reprisal actions against Syria and Jordan had left Nasser with no choice but to defend his image and prestige in his own country and throughout the Arab world, thereby setting off a train of escalation in the entire region."

For his part, Dayan was disturbed by Rabin's condition. "[He] seemed not only tired, which was natural, but also unsure of himself, perplexed, nervously chain smoking, with hardly the air of a man 'impatient for battle,' " Dayan stated in his autobiography. "He complained that instead of being allowed to do his work in the army, he was being rushed to Jerusalem each day to take part in government consultations, and that he was not getting from Eshkol a clear political-military line or definitive instructions."

Dayan found his "principal impression of the evening was that Rabin was in a state of dejection. . . ."

The next day brought new tensions for Rabin. His sleep was interrupted at 3:45 A.M. with the announcement of Nasser's blockade of the straits, and then he had a bruising, bitter argument with Interior Minister Moshe Chaim Shapira following the meeting of the Ministerial Committee on Defense. Shapira was adamantly opposed to Israel launching a war, and Rabin had called him aside to seek his reasons—only to find himself violently attacked by the minister.

"You're the one who owes an explanation," shot back Shapira. "Do you really believe that the Eshkol-Rabin team has to be more daring than the Ben Gurion-Dayan team? In 1950 and 1951 the straits were closed; did Israel rush into a war? The straits remained closed up to 1956; did that endanger Israel's security? . . . When *did* Ben Gurion strike? Only when Israel didn't have to go it alone! France and Britain were still world powers, and *they* undertook to destroy the Egyptian navy and air force. . . . French air squadrons were posted to Israel to safeguard us from Egyptian air raids. The British and French fleets defended Israel's shores. . . ."

Shapira's sentiments were shared by a number of Israel's political leaders, particularly of the religious parties, who seemed to be totally unaware of how strong the IDF had become since 1956. No longer were British and

French planes and ships needed to defend Israel. The generals appreciated this basic fact; the politicians did not. This rift helped explain the indecision that was racking the country, and the growing tensions developing between the politicians and the generals.

Although Rabin had been instrumental in helping to bring Israel's armed forces to their unprecedented strength, he nonetheless was a cautious—and modest—enough man to be stung by Shapira's words and to suffer doubts. Shapira's gibe about Eshkol and Rabin acting more daring than the legendary Ben Gurion-Dayan team had been well aimed. Ben Gurion and Dayan were national heroes, revered for their daring and charisma. Eshkol had been under virulent personal attack for years, particularly by Ben Gurion and his followers, as a bungler and indecisive leader; Rabin was young and untried. Who were they to outdo the leaders of 1956?

With his doubts stoked and his energies drained, Rabin returned to his Tel Aviv home from the May 23 meeting sparked by Nasser's blockade in "a state of mental and physical exhaustion." He later wrote, "The past few days had seemed endless. Meals were taken on the run and only when the occasion arose. I had hardly slept, and I was smoking like a steam engine. But it was more than nicotine that brought me down. The heavy sense of guilt that had been dogging me of late became unbearably strong.... I could not forget Ben Gurion's words—'*You* bear the responsibility'—and I was haunted by Shapira's harsh indictment."

He called Ezer Weizman, who arrived at Rabin's home shortly after 8 P.M. and found the chief of staff looking "broken and depressed."

What happened next is never likely to be adequately explained. Weizman, who had political ambitions and an airman's disdain for foot soldiers, claimed that Rabin wanted to resign. Rabin, who no less than Weizman had his own political ambitions, admits in his autobiography that he wanted to, and that he asked Weizman: "Am I to blame? Should I relinquish my post?" But then, according to Weizman, Rabin asked him to take over the duties of chief of staff. Given Rabin's agitation, his extremely tense condition, his doubts and concerns, this is perhaps credible. But as Rabin reasonably has noted, "I made him no such offer, nor was I empowered to 'bequeath' the job to him or anyone else. That is not a Chief of Staff's prerogative." Graciously, Rabin adds, "Be that as it may, Ezer talked me out of any thought of resignation."

Whatever the truth, there was no doubt that the leader of the military forces of Israel at this critical point in the nation's life was suffering a breakdown. Understandably, Weizman was distressed. He immediately pointed out the psychological advantage Nasser would gain, and the loss in morale

Israel would suffer, if at this dangerous moment the chief of staff resigned. He urged Rabin to get some rest and ordered that all telephone calls be routed to the Weizman home. That night, Weizman later wrote, "I couldn't shut my eyes. I didn't say a word to anyone, and at seven the next morning I returned to Rabin."

Again Rabin asked him to assume command, according to Weizman, but this time there was a doctor at the side of the chief of staff. He was given a tranquilizing injection and dozed off into a much needed deep sleep.

Weizman was now temporarily in charge of the IDF.

VIII
U THANT MEETS NASSER

Abba Eban, though deeply fatigued, spent his time on the flight to Paris reading some of President Charles de Gaulle's writings. He was excited about meeting the legendary Frenchman and a bit anxious too. He was more than aware that a certain coolness had crept into the Franco-Israeli relationship in recent years.

Although France's extraordinary military aid, most of it secret, and diplomatic support of Israel continued, there was no longer the warmth that had marked their relations in the 1950s before de Gaulle's return to power. No Israeli minister had ever been formally invited to France (though many had gone there on secret missions over the years), and no French minister had visited Israel while in office. The secretary-general of the French Foreign Ministry, Hervé Alphand, had traveled to Arab capitals in mid-May but not to Israel. Further, France had taken until May 23, a full week, to react without excitement to Egypt's request for the withdrawal of UNEF. When Eban had sent notes seeking reaffirmation of the American, British and French declarations of 1957 designating the Straits of Tiran an international waterway, the United States and Britain had quickly replied in the affirmative. France had remained silent. In fact, Quai d'Orsay officials were expressing some doubts about Israel's legal right to use the straits and wondering aloud about whether the economic value of Elath was worth the risk of war. Finally, just hours before Nasser's blockade speech on May 22, both Britain and France, publicly signaling their impotency to influence the Middle East, had renounced the Tripartite Declaration, which had served as the basis of the big powers' guarantee against aggression in the region. Since 1950 the declaration had been the official foundation for the Middle East policies of Britain, France and the United States, supposedly guaranteeing the status quo in the region and controlling arms shipments.

With these disturbing thoughts in mind, Eban reached the Elysée Palace shortly before noon on May 24. De Gaulle, now in his seventy-seventh year, was everything Eban expected—and feared. "Authority flowed from him like a steady tide," Eban observed in his memoirs. The old general was, as usual, charting his own independent course. He was outspokenly critical of America's involvement in Vietnam, where barely a decade earlier French colonial ambitions had been paid for by a humiliating and bloody defeat. He had extricated his torn country from Algeria in 1962, after eight brutal years of fighting; he had withdrawn from the military arm of NATO; and he insisted on developing France's own nuclear deterrent. Although he was a friend of Israel's, he was suspicious of Israeli expansionism, and thought it could bring only more conflict in the Middle East.

Seven years before Eban's visit, Ben Gurion had called on de Gaulle and, wrote de Gaulle in his memoirs, "revealed to me his intention of extending [Israel's] frontiers at the earliest opportunity. . . . I urged him not to do so. 'France,' I said, 'will help you to survive in the future as she has helped you in the past, whatever happens. But she is not prepared to provide you with the means of conquering new territory.' "

De Gaulle put a stop to the irregular arrangements that had developed between Tel Aviv and Paris since the Suez war, whereby Israelis had become permanently attached at all levels to French military staffs and services. But although the Israeli officials were henceforth banned from their quasi-governmental roles, the secret arms shipments continued.

In their meeting, de Gaulle had warned Ben Gurion that he believed "a great deal of caution was called for in her handling of the Arabs. The latter were her neighbors, and would always remain so. It was at their expense and on their lands that Israel had set herself up as a sovereign state. In doing so, she had wounded them in their religion and their pride."

Now in the final years of his life, de Gaulle was more than ever determined to try to repair France's relations with the Arab states. The ending of the Algerian war had freed him of the anti-Arab tilt France had endured for eight long years and he was pursuing an evenhanded course in the Middle East.

Before Eban could even be introduced, de Gaulle imperially declared: *"Ne faites pas la guerre."*

De Gaulle was sitting behind an imposing desk uncluttered by papers or a telephone. After the introduction was performed, he continued: "At any rate, don't shoot first. It would be catastrophic if Israel were to attack. The Four Powers must be left to resolve the dispute. France will influence the Soviet Union toward an attitude favorable to peace."

Eban explained Israel's position—that the straits' blockade was an act of aggression—and then, remembering some of de Gaulle's own lofty rhetoric ("France is only herself when at the highest rank"), he put Israel's case in similar terms: "Israel without honor is not Israel."

De Gaulle seemed unimpressed. He repeated to Eban that Israel would be ill-advised to engage in a war and that certainly it should not start one. Eban countered with Israel's view that hostilities had already begun with the imposition of the blockade. Anything Israel now did, he argued, would be a reaction. But de Gaulle did not accept Eban's argument. When Eban then contended that inaction could be more dangerous than action, the French president closed the interview as he had begun it. Referring to himself in the third person, he said: "De Gaulle understands the dangers which arise from inaction, but I advise you now not to be precipitate. Do not make war."

Eban was disappointed by the interview. He realized that "there was not the slightest room for any conclusion except that France was disengaging herself from any responsibility for helping us if we chose early resistance. The expressions of friendship were general; the advice to us not to act was specific and almost brutally direct."

His next stop, a quickly improvised visit to London, was considerably more satisfying. He had an interview with Labour Prime Minister Harold Wilson, an ardent admirer of Israel and its ruling socialist Mapai Party. They met at No. 10 Downing Street, where Eban found "a current of unembarrassed sympathy" for Israel. Wilson revealed that the Cabinet had met that morning and had concluded that Egypt's blockade "must not be allowed to triumph; Britain would join with others in an effort to open the straits." Wilson informed him that the British were working with Washington to form an international convoy to sail through the Straits of Tiran to emphasize their international character.

Aside from such unequivocal support, Eban was delighted that Wilson, unlike de Gaulle, refrained from lecturing him. "I found this lack of exhortation realistic and mature," recalled Eban. "I thought that Wilson was showing a distinguished statesmanship."

His mood considerably improved and his tentative appointment with President Johnson at least twenty-four hours away, Eban decided to have a leisurely dinner in London. Midway through the meal, exhaustion finally caught up with him and he returned to the Hotel Savoy for a good night's rest. But there was no escaping the crisis. Even in the hotel he found "the war atmosphere in the Middle East was evident from the heavy security guard outside my door. . . . The British radio and television, which I turned on briefly before retiring, were full of sympathy for Israel, but they had a distinctly funereal air."

Although he had not slept for more than forty hours, Eban's apprehensions about the coming crucial talks in Washington were so great that he tossed and turned the night away, anxious about whether Israel would receive the support it absolutely needed from the United States.

The period of waiting and indecision was also proving frustrating for Moshe Dayan. He had just celebrated his fifty-second birthday on May 4, yet he already seemed something of a relic in Israel. His four-year term as chief of staff had expired on January 28, 1958, and he had found nothing better to do than brush up on his limited formal education* by enrolling at Hebrew University in Jerusalem to study political science, although he probably knew more about the real world of politics and diplomacy than any of his teachers. The next year he was elected to parliament and became minister of agriculture when his idol, David Ben Gurion, formed his new government on December 16, 1959.

Ben Gurion finally resigned on July 16, 1963, after ruling the young country for almost thirteen of its fifteen years, and eight days later was replaced by his old friend Levi Eshkol.

Ben Gurion apparently had expected Eshkol to act as a caretaker prime minister until the Old Man's protégé Moshe Dayan could take over the government. The energetic Dayan was far more popular than Eshkol among the voters, and comparisons between the two men usually ended at Eshkol's expense. His friend Yigal Allon, one of the young war heroes of 1948 and a competitor with Dayan for political power, once observed: "When Dayan is hesitating, his admirers say that he is thinking; but when Eshkol is thinking, his critics say that he is hesitating."

Once in power as both prime minister and minister of defense, an arrangement made traditional by Ben Gurion, Eshkol had no intention of surrendering his high offices. What he lacked as a flashy vote-getter among the people he more than made up for by his mastery of Israel's intricate party politics. Repeatedly Ben Gurion challenged his leadership, and repeatedly Eshkol displayed his political adroitness by hanging on to power. Ben

* He had completed only two years of secondary education before his duties in the Haganah, the Jewish underground army in Palestine before the establishment of Israel, began to take up most of his time.

Gurion's attacks, and those of his two young activist protégés, Dayan and Shimon Peres, were soon joined by those of activists and native-born Israelis who disdained Eshkol's Diaspora diffidence and doubted his boldness.

Dayan finally recognized by 1964 that he was going to go nowhere in Eshkol's government and he resigned on November 3, citing the "stifling atmosphere" of the government. Ben Gurion continued his attacks but without noticeable effect. Frustrated and angered, he deserted the Mapai Party that he had for so long led and, with Dayan and Peres, established on July 12, 1965, a splinter party, Reshimat Poalei Israel, the Israel Labor List, known as Rafi. National elections were held that same year in November, pitting Rafi against Mapai for the socialist vote. The campaign became known as "the longest, the bitterest, the dirtiest, and the most expensive in the state's history," in the words of the *Jewish Chronicle*. Nonetheless, when the votes were counted, Eshkol's group held on to forty-five seats in parliament. Ben Gurion's new party managed to garner only ten seats, not even equaling his old enemy Menachem Begin's far-right Gahal Party, which won an impressive twenty-six seats in the 120-seat body.

From then on Dayan whiled away his days serving unenthusiastically in the parliament, writing a book on the Suez war, reconstructed as his *Diary of the Sinai Campaign,* and tending to the affairs of a small fishing company which he served as a director. Except for a trip to South Vietnam in August 1966 to write a series of articles on the war for *The Washington Post,* Dayan's life by the eve of the 1967 crisis had become mundane and unexciting, completely divorced from military affairs and his beloved Israel Defense Forces. That was soon to change.

Dayan, a sabra, born in 1915 in Deganiah, the first kibbutz in Palestine, fully shared the apprehension gripping the country that spring. "I knew in my bones that [the threats facing Israel] were basically historical Jewish problems which were rooted in our past," he later wrote. "How we tackled them would determine our future. I also knew that war was inevitable."

Dayan itched to participate in the war he saw coming. "Rather than hang around the parliamentary or other cafés in Jerusalem," he confessed in his autobiography, "I preferred, as long as I was physically able, to take part in the fighting, even just as a private." With his reputation, it was exceedingly unlikely, impossible really, that he would be called to arms as a private. But the assertion was indicative of his desire to get back in uniform, even under his old foe Eshkol, who remained minister of defense. Dayan spent much of the last week of May touring on his own as a civilian the Israeli military positions in the Southern Command along the Sinai.

On the night of May 24, he was wandering alone around the Negev city of

Beersheva, not far from Egyptian forces in the Sinai. As he walked along the streets, sidewalk café patrons began noticing the former general with the distinctive patch over his left eye, the result of a Vichy French bullet that jammed a binocular casting into his eye in Lebanon on June 8, 1941, while he was fighting with British forces.

The patrons, caught up like the rest of the nation in the fever of the crisis, began calling Dayan's name. Soon he was being followed by a procession of worshipers. "Moshe Dayan! Moshe Dayan!" they shouted. A drunk with tears in his eyes tried to kiss him. Adoring Israelis crowded around him.

Police tried vainly to extricate him from the excited crowd milling around him, peppering him with questions, chanting his name. He was finally freed by a driver he had known at the Ministry of Agriculture and taken to the privacy of his hotel.

———————

That same night U Thant finally met with Gamal Abdel Nasser. Accompanied by Rikhye, he went to the modest military-camp home Nasser had occupied as a colonel before the 1952 coup that had brought him to power. Nasser was a big and husky man, his smile easy, his shrewdness obvious, his black hair graying at the temples, his demeanor confident. Nasser sat down with his guests in a reception room furnished with French period pieces, popular at the time in Cairo, and with typical candor he revealed why he had announced closure of the Straits of Tiran while U Thant was still flying to Cairo.

"When we knew you were coming to Cairo, we decided to do it before you arrived here," said Nasser. "Had we not done so until after your arrival here you would have asked us not to blockade the Gulf. It would then have been impossible for us to refuse a request from the Secretary-General of the United Nations. . . . So we did it before you reached Cairo."

Nasser spent considerable time explaining that his actions had merely restored the situation to the way it had been before the Suez war eleven years earlier. He said now that UNEF was leaving and Sharm el Sheikh was under Egyptian control again, Arab dignity and honor had been restored. He had not, he pointed out, taken any illegal action or violated the General Armistice Agreements signed by Egypt, Jordan, Syria and Israel in 1949. In fact, he observed, it was Israel that was violating the agreements by stationing troops in the demilitarized zone at El Auja in the Sinai and by farming Arab land in the demilitarized zone under the Syrian Golan Heights.

Despite this, Nasser added, the friends of Israel—and particularly the United States—accused only the Arabs of violations and aggression. Relations between Cairo and Washington were now at a nadir, he noted, largely because of American delays in providing Egypt with $150 million in badly needed food aid.

"They say that they are our friends, and yet they don't give us food," Nasser said with emotion. "We waited and waited for them to come to our aid, and when they didn't, we had reached such a stage of exasperation that if we saw any American wheat baked into bread in our Cairo bakeries, it seemed like poison. We therefore withdrew our request for food as we felt that the United States was embarked on a war of starvation against us."

Nasser added pointedly: "Talk about double standards. It is the United States that has double standards—one for the Israelis and another for us."

Now the United States was opposing his actions because Israel objected to them, Nasser charged. Even though his troops in the Sinai were on Egyptian territory within internationally recognized frontiers and the navigation channel of the Straits of Tiran was within the three-mile limit of Egyptian territorial waters, still the United States remained on Israel's side and disputed these facts, Nasser protested. He told U Thant that he was ready to go into international arbitration or to the International Court in order to determine the legality of his position. But he complained that all he heard from Washington was its public declarations of support for Israel.

Turning to the specific causes of the current crisis, Nasser said that Israel had become noticeably more aggressive since the Samu attack the previous year. Then had come the April 7 battle with Syria and the spectacle of Israeli Mirages chasing Syrian MiGs to Damascus, of Israeli warplanes flying near an Arab capital.

It was against this background, Nasser explained, that he had acted. He contended it was impossible now for him to rescind any of his moves, all of which, after all, had merely restored the Middle East to its position prior to Israel's conquests in the Suez war. But, he volunteered, he would be willing to agree to U Thant's request for a two-week period of calm. During that time he would not talk about his blockade if Israel did not try to run it.

U Thant was delighted. He promised he would cable New York that very night to begin negotiations with Israel. Cautiously, he told Nasser that he hoped that during the next few tense days Egyptian troops would take no aggressive actions that might worsen the crisis. Nasser replied that in recent days diplomats from both the American and Russian embassies had sought the same assurances.

"I told them that we will not attack," said Nasser. "We have no intention of attacking unless we are attacked first, and then we will defend ourselves. And we [can] give you the same assurance. We will not attack first."

Highly satisfied with the meeting and Nasser's assurances, U Thant returned to New York immediately to report to the world community.

————————————

On the same day as U Thant's interview with Nasser, President Johnson presided over a meeting of the National Security Council attended by former ambassador to Egypt Luke Battle, now installed in his position as assistant secretary of state for the Near East; Director of Central Intelligence Richard Helms; Secretary of Defense Robert McNamara, Walt Rostow, Rusk, Chairman of the Joint Chiefs of Staff Earle G. Wheeler and others. For a change, the meeting was not devoted to Vietnam. Instead, it was on the Middle East. Dean Rusk briefed the group by opening with his judgment that the crisis was "serious but not yet desperate." He said he had a report that Nasser was ready to return to the General Armistice Agreement with Israel, meaning a return to the pre-Suez war status of the Straits of Tiran, "but the Israelis might not be in the mood to make that kind of concession."

Thus establishing the likelihood that the crisis would not soon abate, Rusk gave the group a rundown on how matters stood from Washington's view. "We are in touch with the U.S.S.R.," he said. "Privately we find the Russians playing a generally moderate game, but publicly they have taken a harsh view of the facts and have laid responsibility at Israel's door—and by inference at ours. Syria and Cairo say publicly they have Soviet support; but our general impression is that this is somewhat less than complete."

He reported that in his talk the previous day with the Senate Foreign Relations Committee he had found unanimity that the U.S. should not act unilaterally. Also, Israeli Foreign Minister Abba Eban was due to arrive the next day. "We have insisted on consultation, and he is here to consult." In summary, he said, he could not promise that the crisis would be over in twenty-four hours, but he had the impression that "no government wants war."

President Johnson observed with a touch of Texan hyperbole that "I want to play every card in the U.N., but I've never relied on it to save me when I'm going down for the third time." Referring to the British idea of an international convoy, he added: "I want to see Wilson and de Gaulle out there with their ships all lined up too." But he expressed concern about how "these things have a way of falling apart" and skepticism about the effectiveness of an international maritime convoy breaking the blockade. He noted how quickly early enthusiasm can evaporate, mentioning how Congress had strongly backed him in the early days in Vietnam. "We have to figure out what we can do if all these other courses fail," warned the President.

Then, his thoughts obviously still occupied by Vietnam, Johnson "alluded to statements by Senators Stuart Symington and J. William Fulbright to the effect that the U.S. could not manage two crises at once," according to the notes of the meeting. "They see it as a choice between Israel and Vietnam and believe we ought to withdraw from Vietnam. He told Secretary Rusk to let Senator Mansfield know that this kind of music in the Senate is just what Kosygin wants to hear."

Rusk commented: "We are witnessing an interesting reversal of role— doves have become hawks, and vice versa."

McNamara challenged the statements by Fulbright and Symington, and asked General Wheeler to comment on U.S. resources in the Mediterranean and the Pentagon's estimate of the military situation in the Middle East.

Wheeler admitted that "it would be harder to open the Gulf of Aqaba than we had at first thought. Because of the two Egyptian submarines in the Red Sea, we would need an ASW [antisubmarine warfare] unit, the nearest of which is now in Singapore—weeks away."

The chairman of the Joint Chiefs speculated that "if Israel does try to open the Gulf, it will attack first by air, striking initially the UAR's naval forces in the Red Sea and the air bases in the Sinai. Only after establishing air superiority would the Israelis try to take out the battery at Sharm el Sheikh. Therefore if the Israelis move, it might not be possible to localize a strike designed simply to open the Straits."

Wheeler tried to rebut the Fulbright-Symington charge about the U.S. not being powerful enough to handle two crises, but the facts told a different story. As he informed the meeting, "We have a powerful naval force in the Mediterranean but our land forces are few, limited to about 1,400 Marines now ashore at Naples, three days away.... Our nearest ASW unit is two weeks away.... The UAR coastal battery and naval and air forces in the Red Sea will be the units employed to blockade the Gulf of Aqaba.... We will have trouble with overflight and staging rights in Turkey, Libya and Spain if we have to introduce our own ground forces."

Although no one apparently mentioned it, the substance of what Wheeler had said amounted to an admission that Fulbright and Symington were essentially right in the short term. The U.S. did not have the forces in the area or the ability to get them there immediately. True, the ships of the Sixth Fleet represented a powerful force with their two aircraft carriers, but they were loaded with nuclear weapons. This crisis did not call for a nuclear sledgehammer and, short of that, there was little in the immediate days ahead that the United States could do to provide a physical presence in the region.

Wheeler concluded his remarks by observing that the "Israelis can hold their own."

This provoked a challenge from the President. Notes of the meeting report that "Johnson said Ambassador Goldberg is less certain about Israeli superiority. Mr. Helms noted that he had sent a recent assessment to Ambassador Goldberg but had had no response yet. Both Mr. Helms and General Wheeler promised to review this estimate."

Disagreement about Israel's military capabilities between the U.S. intelligence community and Israel and its supporters was to plague Washington up to the time that U.S. intelligence was proved decisively correct on the field of battle. Israel's army and air force were every bit as strong as the CIA claimed.

Johnson let the matter drop and asked about Soviet motives. Had the Soviets staged this crisis? "Neither General Wheeler nor Mr. Helms saw any sign of Soviet calculation behind these crises, though of course both admitted that the Soviets would view them as a godsend."

The discussion returned to speculation about the outbreak of hostilities. McNamara thought the "initial exchange would be a fierce air battle for air superiority which would deplete aircraft inventories on both sides. Then both the U.S. and U.S.S.R. would be faced with requests for air support. He felt that the U.S.S.R. might supply Soviet-piloted aircraft."

The President, according to the notes, "returned to Soviet motives. Mr. Helms said that he felt the U.S.S.R. likes the situation as it is now but is not ready to rush in. The Soviets would like to bring off a propaganda victory as in the 1950s with them as the peacemakers and saviors of the Arabs, while we end up fully blackballed in the Arab world as Israel's supporter."

Helms proved to have a better appreciation of the realities than McNamara when he added that he was not "as bearish as Secretary McNamara on Israeli air capability. He said that Israelis had taken the MiG that defected from Iraq last year through all kinds of maneuvers in Israel and had demonstrated in the 7 April air battle with Syria that they had learned their lessons well."

Helms was referring to a spectacular intelligence coup Israel had recently pulled off. Around August 15, 1966, an Iraqi Christian pilot, Munir Redfa, whose family was desperate to get its fortune out of socialist Iraq, defected by flying a MiG-21D to Israel after being paid a large sum of money by Israel's intelligence agency, Mossad. The MiG-21D at the time was considered Russia's hottest export combat plane and little was known about it in the West. The Soviets had supplied it to Egypt, Iraq and Syria, so the Israeli Air Force was especially anxious to learn its capabilities and limitations.

Israeli pilots proved decisively that, as Helms noted, they had indeed learned the MiG's weaknesses in the ten months they had to test the plane before war erupted. In fact, Israel's knowledge of the jet's limitations may well have contributed to the aggressiveness of some Israeli generals, particularly in the Air Force.

At the NSC meeting, Johnson turned the discussion to the question of Nasser's motives. Helms shrewdly speculated that Nasser had already achieved his objective by returning the situation to its pre-Suez war status. Gene Rostow opined that Nasser "was looking for someone to hold the Israelis back."

Luke Battle said he would have agreed with Helms's assessment that the Egyptian leader sought a limited propaganda victory—up to the time that Nasser actually blockaded the straits. But that dire step made Battle wonder whether "Nasser either has more Soviet support than we know about, or had gone slightly insane. . . . It is uncharacteristic for Nasser not to leave a door open behind him, and that is exactly what he appears to have done."

The President, noting that Abba Eban was going to arrive in Washington the following day, asked the group whether it thought he should meet with the Israeli foreign minister. According to the notes of the meeting, Gene Rostow replied "he felt we had held the Israelis back from a strike yesterday and that the President would undoubtedly have to see Eban."

Later that day there was a brief scare when an unidentified "sensitive New York source" informed Washington that Jordan had declared war on Israel. The State Department sent a flash cable to Amman seeking clarification. The answer came in a return flash cable in less than a half hour addressed to both the State Department and the White House: "This report not repeat not true."

The report on its face was completely implausible since Jordan was far too weak to make such a drastic move. Yet its circulation was indicative of how taut nerves were being drawn as the crisis deepened and the Johnson Administration thrashed around seeking a way to avoid another war.

One of the actions the Defense Department took that day was to order the U.S.S. *Liberty* to leave its patrol area off the west coast of Africa and proceed to the eastern Mediterranean via Rota, Spain. The *Liberty* was officially known by the Navy as AGTR 5, an auxiliary general technical research ship. It was in fact a SIGINT ship, a signals intelligence vessel that could eavesdrop on every sort of electronic communications from telephone to microwave to teletype. It had been on its fifth cruise of Africa, listening in on communications from all over the western part of the continent. Now, on May 24, it headed north at full steam to listen in to what was happening in the Middle East.

IX
ISRAEL DEMANDS A U.S. COMMITMENT

Foreign Minister Abba Eban arrived in the United States at about the same time President Johnson was leaving for a day trip to Canada. Johnson had been scheduled to visit Expo '67 on May 25 but had put off his final decision until that morning to be sure that the Middle East crisis was not about to explode into war. Assured by the CIA that hostilities were not imminent, he flew off from the South Lawn of the White House at 9:24 A.M. for a whirlwind tour of Canada. Had he known the contents of a message Eban was about to receive, he might have remained.

Eban was met in Washington by Ambassador Harman, who carried with him a personal, top-secret cable from Prime Minister Eshkol. On the drive to the Mayflower Hotel, Eban read the cable at a glance. He said nothing but his agitation was obvious to U.N. Ambassador Gideon Rafael, who had accompanied him from New York. When he was finally settled in his suite, Eban nervously paced up and down, reread the cable and then, according to Rafael, "flung it on a table, as he used to do with papers which utterly displeased him, and in a tone of command completely unnatural for him he snapped: 'Read it.'"

Eban's perturbation was understandable. The cable was an extraordinary communication. It warned:

Israel faces a grave danger of general attack by Egypt and Syria. In this situation, implementation of the American commitment is vital—in declaration and action—immediately, repeat, immediately, meaning a declaration by the U.S. government that any attack on Israel is equivalent to an attack on the United States. The concrete expression of this declaration will be specific orders to U.S. forces in the region that they are to combine operations with the IDF against any possible Arab attack on Israel. Whatever reply you get from the United States, limit yourself to stating that you will report to your government. In view of the gravity of the situation, this notification is to be delivered without delay to the highest American authority. In the absence of the President, deliver it to Secretary of State Rusk. . . . We stress the top secrecy of all dealings arising from this cable. Under no circumstances are you to phone us on this matter.

Eban was not only stunned but confused. The urgency and near hysterical tone of the cable and the grim picture it implied of Israel's peril contrasted sharply with the way the situation had been less than forty-eight hours earlier when he left the country.

Whatever the cause for this sudden and frightening change, Eban realized immediately that Eshkol was asking him to secure a commitment that no President "had [the] constitutional power to promise. . . . I found it hard to understand how such an extreme change could have come over our military positions since I heard our generals report in Tel Aviv on May 23. . . . At this point another cable reached me from Jerusalem reinforcing the first in even more emphatic terms. The issue was so grave that I felt no capacity to argue."

Eban, a South African whose original name was Aubrey Solomon, was well informed about U.S. constitutional restraints. He had lived in the United States during the decade of the 1950s and had a deep understanding of America, its democratic system and many of its leaders. He had first moved to Israel during World War II and entered the Jewish Agency (Israel's prestate government) in 1946, and in 1948 he was appointed Israel's representative to the United Nations in New York. In 1950 he was made ambassador to the United States as well. He retained those two high positions until May 1959, spending more time during the 1950s in the United States than in the rough-and-tumble of Israeli politics.

In his dual and demanding posts he became Israel's eloquent voice and symbol for a decade, persuasively arguing Israel's case in the international forum of the United Nations and privately in America's corridors of power. More than any single individual in the 1950s, Eban articulated for Americans the moral and legal case for Israel's existence. He was a gifted speaker, his accent that of his education at Cambridge, his words those of a juridical poet.

When he finally resigned at the age of forty-four to return to the hurly-burly of the political arena in Israel, Americans great and anonymous indulged in an outpouring of well wishes unique for a foreign official. A National Testimonial Committee was established to give Eban a festive send-off. Sponsors of the committee were a roll of America's political leaders, headed by the Vice President of the United States, Richard M. Nixon. Others included Herbert C. Hoover, Lyndon B. Johnson, John F. Kennedy, Adlai Stevenson, Harry S. Truman, Chief Justice of the Supreme Court Earl Warren and a host of senators, governors, judges and leaders of the intellectual community. *The New York Times* and *The Washington Post* as well as many smaller newspapers throughout the country published editorials praising his performance. Democratic Senator Paul H. Douglas of Illinois even went so far as to say before an audience of thousands in the Chicago Opera House that he wished Eban would be the Democratic presidential candidate in the 1960 campaign.

Eban probably would have done better had he taken Douglas' advice than he did back in Israel. The fact was that Israelis did not share Americans' enthusiasm for Eban. His pudgy, nervous appearance, his refined manners and sophisticated semantics, the faint odor of effeteness and elitism that clung to him, all evoked little admiration in Israel's cacophonous society of pioneers, political infighters and warriors. Any hopes he might have had about becoming Israel's prime minister were quickly dashed. Despite his stellar performance in the United States, it took him seven years to become Israel's foreign minister, the highest post he was ever likely to achieve.

The urgent cables Abba Eban received under Eshkol's name on May 25 in Washington represented in part the suspicions of Israel's hardliners that Eban was not tough enough. They wanted to prod him by exaggerating the threat facing Israel in order to elicit the maximum from Washington. More than that, the cables were a ploy to smoke out just how committed Washington was to Israel's position and how far it was ready to go to back the Jewish state in a war.

Eban wasted no time when he and his party of Rafael and others met with Rusk and several top State Department officials in Foggy Bottom. He read directly from the cables. Rusk gasped. He asked Eban to read slower, then personally took down the messages word for word. Without speaking, he stood up, opened his private bar and poured a drink for Eban and himself. Rusk gulped his silently and then wrote a note for Eugene Rostow, who left the room. Turning to Eban, Rusk slowly and emphatically informed him that none of the U.S. intelligence services was reporting similar warnings.

Staring directly into Eban's eye, his face humorless, Rusk voiced the suspicion that was to grip the Administration over the next few hours: "I do not wish to assume that your information is meant to give us advance notice of a planned Israeli preemptive strike. This would be a horrendous error."

Eban, despite his own sense of bewilderment about the cables, assured him that the messages, which after all were under the signature of Prime Minister Eshkol, were to be taken at their word.

The cables injected an unexpected new urgency and a dramatic different course to the talks, and the two sides agreed to adjourn their meetings and regroup for an early dinner.

There now ensued a frantic scramble throughout the government's national security apparatus—the CIA, the National Security Council, the Pentagon, the State Department—for some explanation of the Israeli cables. Had U.S. intelligence been so lax that it had missed this sudden shift to offensiveness by the Egyptian and Syrian armies? Was Israel under imminent assault, as the cables contended? Was war only hours away?

President Johnson arrived back at the South Lawn aboard a helicopter at 5:36 P.M., apparently already alerted to the contents of the Israeli cables. His favorite beagles were waiting for him but he hurried past them and went directly to the White House Oval Office. He emerged seven minutes later to clean up some of the routine business that crowds in on a President at all times, crisis or not.

This occasion was a presentation in the Flower Garden by David Rockefeller of "A Report to the President of the United States" by a high-level business group of executive volunteers to government service called the International Executive Service Corps. Johnson briefly addressed the group and was back in the Oval Office by 5:58 P.M. where he just had time to make a couple of telephone calls, including one to Walt Rostow, before performing a couple of other ceremonial functions that took twenty-five minutes.

At the end of the ceremonies, Johnson received a memorandum from Walt Rostow informing him that the Israeli government had not only sent the urgent telegrams to Eban, but had also called on the CIA station chief in Israel and given him a similar hair-raising account of Israeli fears. "Attached is a CIA appraisal of this estimate which throws a great deal of cold water on the Israeli estimate," Rostow wrote. The attachment remains classified but Rostow added by hand on the memorandum: "The two estimates—Israeli and CIA—both show how explosive are:

"—Israeli anxieties;

"—Nasser's hopes of picking up prestige;

"—U.S.S.R. desires for gaining prestige, short of a war."

By 7 P.M., Johnson was complaining that his United Press International teletype printer in his office was on the blink and asked someone to fix it. He was a news buff and constantly watched the wires of the news agencies and had three television sets in his office as well as his bedroom so he could simultaneously monitor the networks' news shows.

At 7:02, the top foreign affairs officials of the Administration began arriving for a meeting on the alarming content of the Israeli cables. For the next hour Johnson heard the views of former ambassador to Egypt Luke Battle, Dick Helms of the CIA, Gene and Walt Rostow, Cyrus Vance, the deputy secretary of defense sitting in for McNamara, and General Wheeler of the Joint Chiefs. Vice President Humphrey arrived halfway through the meeting after Johnson ordered that he be asked to join, "quickly and quietly."

Rusk meanwhile was entertaining Eban and his associates at an early working dinner at the State Department trying to comprehend what the Israelis were up to. The secretary of state was no stranger to the convoluted affairs of the Middle East. After a boyhood of poverty in Georgia, he had won a Rhodes scholarship, risen to the rank of colonel in the Army during World War II, and in 1947, at the age of thirty-eight, he had joined the State Department as Alger Hiss's replacement as head of the Office of Special Political Affairs. His position directly involved him in the tempest engulfing the United Nations and the Truman Administration over Palestine.

A character trait that marked Rusk's career emerged vividly during the heated and often acrimonious bureaucratic battles surrounding the Palestine question. He was totally loyal to his superiors. Whatever his personal feelings, once policy was decided by the President, Rusk hewed the line. Thus, although he sided with the State and War departments in opposing immediate recognition of the state of Israel on the grounds that a Jewish state imposed on the Arabs would perpetuate the Palestine conflict, he acted unhesitatingly when Truman ordered immediate recognition. He maintained his unquestioning loyalty and sense of modesty after being appointed secretary of state by President-elect Kennedy in 1960. He was just as loyal—to a fault, some of his critics thought—under Johnson.

Eban had known Rusk since those early days at the United Nations and found him unsympathetic but honest. At their dinner meeting, Rusk explained to Eban that there was absolutely no evidence that the Egyptian Army had gone into an offensive posture or that an attack on Israel was imminent. Quite the reverse, the evidence indicated it was the Israeli Army that was deployed in an order of battle that implied an aggressive intent.

The secretary of state used the dinner to emphasize to Eban that the Administration was determined to go through the United Nations, where an emergency meeting of the Security Council had begun the previous day, to seek a solution to the crisis. For both domestic political and international legal reasons, Rusk explained, it was important that the United States show that all efforts to find a multinational solution to the crisis be exhausted before any precipitate action. In other words, whatever Israel's game was, Rusk wanted to make clear that the Administration did not approve of the Jewish state launching a surprise attack.

Eban, under the prod of the scare cables, warned that time was short and that Israel's right of free navigation had to be upheld. The implication was clear that Israel was ready to go to war. Necessarily left unclear, since Eban himself did not know the answer, was the reason for the Israeli blitz of warnings about an imminent Egyptian attack.

After the dinner, Eban and Rusk went to the secretary of state's seventh-floor office. Rusk in the meantime had spoken with Johnson on the telephone and he relayed the President's determination that the United Nations must first be given a chance to try to solve the crisis.

In reporting his talks to Jerusalem at 1:30 A.M., Eban cabled that if the U.N. route failed, then "the President is likely to discuss a program for opening the straits by the maritime powers led by the United States, Britain and perhaps others." He added that Johnson might publicly pledge that the convoy, already dubbed the "Red Sea regatta" by Gene Rostow, would insist on sailing through the straits even if there was resistance by Egypt.

This had been welcome news to Eban, but he had not been able to receive the extraordinary commitment that Israel desperately sought—a pledge that an attack on Israel would be considered an attack on the United States.

Although the United States did not believe Israel's claim that Egypt was about to attack, the State Department that night took the precaution of calling the Egyptian ambassador to the building to warn him that Egypt should not be the first to open hostilities. While Eban and others had been having drinks on the terrace of the State Department building, Ambassador Mustapha Kemal waited alone in Gene Rostow's office. Rostow left the terrace and went down to his office for the meeting with Kemal.

"President Johnson has requested me by telephone to transmit through you a warning to your government," Rostow said. "We have heard rumors that Egypt may soon attack Israel. If such should occur, we wish to inform you that the United States will act in accordance with the Charter of the United Nations and also in accordance with its guarantee of the independence and integrity of Israel. The President's words to me were: 'We will be against whoever fires the first shot. We will honor our pledges. . . .' An attack on Israel would be suicide on your part."

In diplomatic practice, this warning implicitly carried with it a promise. If Egypt did not attack, then the United States would restrain Israel from attacking. But that the Johnson Administration did not have the will or cunning to do.

X
ABBA EBAN MEETS JOHNSON

Gamal Abdel Nasser was exultant. He seemed to be getting away with his risky gamble. Without firing a shot or suffering a single casualty, he had regained his leadership role in the Arab world and reversed the losses of 1956. It was an immensely significant achievement in Arab eyes, restoring to Egyptian sovereignty what had been taken from it by Israel, replacing the humiliation of the Arabs with pride.

Nasser did not try to conceal his glee and refound confidence. On May 26, while Eban was still in Washington waiting to see the President, Nasser delivered an inflammatory speech to the General Council of the International Confederation of Arab Trade Unions that practically amounted to a declaration of war. The harshly militant speech was broadcast in Arabic by Cairo Radio's Voice of the Arabs and was immediately translated by the CIA and delivered to the White House. Presumably the KGB (Komitet Gosudarstvennoi Bezopasnosti, the Committeee of State Security) performed the same function for Moscow.

"Taking over Sharm el Sheikh meant confrontation with Israel," Nasser boasted, heedlessly adding that it "also meant that we were ready to enter a general war with Israel."

Then he declared recklessly: "The battle will be a general one and our basic objective will be to destroy Israel.

"I probably could not have said such things five or even three years ago. If I had said such things and had been unable to carry them out, my words would have been empty and valueless. . . . Today, some eleven years after

1956, I say such things because I am confident. I know what we have here in Egypt and what Syria has. I also know that other states—Iraq, for instance—have sent . . . troops to Syria; Algeria will send troops; Kuwait also will send troops.

"This is Arab power. This is the true resurrection of the Arab nation. Today people must know the reality of the Arab world."

The whole world was soon to know the reality, but it was not what Nasser so euphorically thought it was.

Another inflammatory diatribe was made in Cairo that day which received as much attention in Israel and world capitals as Nasser's speech. It was contained in an article in the government-guided daily newspaper *Al Ahram*. Written by Mohamed Heikal, Nasser's close friend, it declared that war was "inevitable." The article was chilling in its acute objectiveness and its aggressive tone. Heikal perceptively wrote that the closing of the Straits of Tiran had put Israel in a position where it had to react. ". . . for many reasons, chiefly the psychological, Israel cannot accept or remain indifferent to what has taken place. . . . Israel has to reply now. It has to deal a blow. . . . Then it will be our turn to deal the second blow, which we will deliver with the utmost possible effectiveness. . . . Let Israel begin! Let our second blow then be ready! Let it be a knockout!"

Heikal's analysis was frighteningly correct. In Israeli eyes, the crisis no longer was centering on the blockade of the straits. The important thing now was Israeli prestige. It had to demonstrate to the world, particularly to the Arabs, that it could not be pushed around.

Although the Egyptians could see the inevitable logic leading to war, they apparently were so dazzled by their successes so far that they seemed to forget how weak they were compared to Israel. Partly this delusion of strength came from the euphoria of the moment, from wishful thinking, and partly from the encouragement of Egypt's military leaders. As in Israel, they were eager for a fight. Many officers had been openly disappointed when Nasser did not declare war during his speech announcing closure of the straits. To calm the restless officers, Field Marshal Abdel Hakim Amer, Egypt's highest military leader, said: "Don't worry, boys, you'll fight."

It was about 9:30 A.M. that May 26, Friday, when Rusk telephoned Eban and asked him if he would still be in Washington on Saturday. By that time, Rusk mentioned, U Thant would have arrived back in New York and reported to the Security Council on his talks with Nasser. "The leisurely implication of this question gave me great alarm," Eban later noted. He said he would have to check his schedule and would get back to Rusk.

Within fifteen minutes, he telephoned Rusk and told him flatly that he had to leave that evening in order to attend the regular Sunday Cabinet meeting in Jerusalem. "This could be one of the most crucial Cabinet meetings in our history," Eban wrote later. "Our decision would largely be based on what President Johnson conveyed to me today; U Thant's report was not the decisive factor in our eyes."

Eban warned Rusk that "frankly I thought we were in for hostilities next week. 'There is an act of blockade which will be resisted.' I doubted whether anything at this stage would change this outlook."

Eban told Rusk he was unhappy with the U.S. concern about the United Nations. This conjured up nothing but a vista of delay and procrastination, Eban said.

"I get you," replied Rusk as he hung up, promising to try to work out a meeting with the President that Friday.

The exaggerated claims from Israel about the country's imminent peril had caused a whirlwind of activity in U.S. intelligence circles. President Johnson had gone to the unusual length of ordering Helms and General Wheeler to "scrub down" the earlier report by the Board of National Estimates. The United Nations was also asked for information from its observers along Israel's frontiers. By Friday morning, all had come to the same conclusion: There was no immediate threat to Israel. The new Board of National Estimates report went even further this time. Israel could defeat any combination of Arab states or all of them at the same time and do it within a week. This intelligence was shared with Eban much as though he represented a formal military ally of the United States.

But when Eban arrived at the Pentagon that morning to take up the matter with Secretary of Defense McNamara and his top aides, including Joint Chiefs Chairman General Wheeler, there was yet another panicky-sounding cable delivered to him from Jerusalem. Once again he was warned that Israel believed an Egyptian attack was imminent, and that Israel might have to decide on war or peace as early as Sunday.

By now the puzzlement was as great as the different estimates of the military situation by the two countries. McNamara and his aides pointed out to Eban once again that Egyptian forces were not in an aggressive posture and that Israel was not opening itself to peril by not attacking immediately. The contrary was true, Eban was told. With each passing day the Egyptian Army was extending its vulnerability by lengthening its lines of communications deep into the Sinai. Reports indicated that the Egyptians were already experiencing confusion in their logistical system, and as the distances and complexities increased, the confusion was likely to get worse rather than better.

Israel, on the other hand, was getting stronger. Its mobilization was nearing peak effectiveness, its lines of supply and communications were short and efficient, and its army was strong and well equipped.

Said General Wheeler: "We have had the matter checked by our experts and we are all in agreement that you will win."

"But what if they attack our airfields?" asked Eban.

"No matter which of you strikes the first blow, you are the stronger to our minds," said Wheeler. "You will win in either case."

At the end of the meeting, Eban wrote in his autobiography, the U.S. officials told him that "the idea that Israel was being outmaneuvered in the military domain, and would have to act in a mood of 'now or never,' seemed to them so remote that they would be interested to know on what such appraisals were based."

Eban would have liked to know also, but all he had to rely on was the dire information in the stream of Cassandra cables he kept receiving from Jerusalem.

Rusk that day sent a long memorandum to the President reporting on his talks with Eban the previous night and outlining the State Department's recommendations for U.S. policy. "As you know," wrote Rusk, "the Israelis have told us their intelligence indicates that an Egyptian and Syrian attack is imminent. They have therefore requested a U.S. public statement of assurance and support to Israel against such aggression. Our intelligence does not confirm this Israeli estimate."

Rusk informed Johnson that Eban had "made clear that Ambassador Barbour's intervention on May 23 held off a preemptive strike by Israel. Barbour at that time had been authorized to float the British idea of a maritime convoy, which could pressure Nasser to protect maritime rights in the Gulf of Aqaba if U.N. action failed.

"Eban is here to find out whether this alternative is feasible. You have two basic options now:

"(1) to let the Israelis decide how best to protect their own national interests, in the light of the advice we have given them: i.e., to 'unleash' them.

"We recommend strongly against this option.

"(2) to take a positive position, but not as a final commitment, on the British proposal for forming a group of maritime powers to defy the blockade.

"We recommend this policy as our best hope of preventing a war which could gravely damage many American national interests."

Rusk told the President that "we put the case against preemptive strikes to Eban very hard." Now he urged Johnson to assure the foreign minister that "we will consult with the Israeli Government at every step of the way, and we expect the Israelis to reciprocate. . . . Nonetheless, we can proceed only on the assumption that Israel will make no military move that would precipitate hostilities in the area. Preemptive action by Israel would cause extreme difficulty for the United States. . . . The American people would do what has to be done if 'the fault is on the other side and there is no alternative.' Therefore, the question of responsibility for the initiation of hostilities is a major problem for us."

Rusk noted that the economic strain on Israel of keeping its reservists on active duty was severe and that the United States would try to alleviate it with additional aid. He was saying, in effect, that Israel should not use its economic distress as a motive to go to war.

At 1:33 P.M., Johnson went to the Cabinet Room for a full-scale review of the crisis and America's options. Walt Rostow had written a memorandum for the President outlining the areas of discussion he thought should be covered.

Under a heading of "elements to be checked" about Israel, Rostow had written:

"—belief that existence is threatened; this is their last chance in history; terrorism can only be stopped by force;

"—philosophy of pre-emptive strike due to their geography, and military role of tactical air supremacy over the battlefield;

"—consciousness of U.S. past commitments; their leverage over U.S.; and fact that, in the end, we are only power capable of maintaining continued existence of Israel;

"—fear that balance of political power in U.N. against them;

"—Arabs' consolidating military and diplomatic position with every passing day;

"—simple question to U.S.: what can you offer right now better than a pre-emptive strike?

"—second question: what will U.S. do over the longer term to guarantee

Israeli security if the Israelis do not now initiate war and exhaust diplomatic possibilities?"

The list of elements to be checked about the Egyptian position was considerably shorter. He advised the President to seek elucidation about the following areas:

"—reaction to 1956 defeat and prior real or believed humiliations, and deprivation of Arab rights;

"—serious domestic economic and political situation;

"—disarray in Arab world and Nasser's desire for prestige, leadership, and overthrow of moderates in Arab world;

"—desire to milk U.S.-U.S.S.R. rivalry to maximum, both ways, and deep suspicion of ultimate U.S. intent to get him."

All of Johnson's top officials were gathered for the meeting, including Helms, McNamara, the Rostow brothers, Rusk, General Wheeler and two close outside advisers, attorney Clark Clifford and Supreme Court Justice Abe Fortas, one of Johnson's closest advisers and a strong supporter of Israel. Although Fortas was sitting on the Court, he nonetheless frequently acted as an adviser to Johnson, as other justices had to other Presidents, and in the current crisis he took an active role on Israel's side.

Wheeler reviewed the military situation, saying that Israel could remain at its present level of mobilization for two months without endangering its security. Thus, militarily, there was no serious reason for the urgency to make a war-or-peace decision that Israel was demanding. Helms's report agreed, and again predicted that if Israel went to war it would easily win. Rusk reported on the diplomatic moves and coined a phrase that sounded more serious than it was: "Israel will not be alone unless it decides to go alone."

To Rusk and the President, the phrase seemed to mean that Israel was being put on warning that it should not start a war. But realistically it was an empty cliché. Israel was not likely to alert Washington if it planned to go to war, since then Johnson would probably try to exert pressure to prevent it and tension would come between the two countries at a time when Israel most desperately needed Washington's backing. Nonetheless, the phrase sounded so good that it was used repeatedly by Rusk and Johnson during the next week.

For his part, Johnson told the meeting that he could not make a clear commitment to use force against the blockade because of congressional sentiment. Then, without elucidation, he wondered aloud whether he might regret not giving Eban more than he planned to. At that point he left the meeting.

By midafternoon there still was no word about Eban's appointment with the President. Eppy Evron, the Israeli Embassy minister with close White House ties, was dispatched to the White House to see if he could not get a firm commitment for the meeting. Evron went to see Walt Rostow and discovered part of the problem was that the President feared Eban might use the meeting to drum up favorable publicity for Israel when he talked with the press later. Rostow naïvely wondered if Eban could be persuaded to tell the press that he had just dropped by the White House to pay a courtesy call. Evron pointed out that in the current tense atmosphere it was not likely anyone would believe the foreign minister of Israel had flown six thousand miles, in the midst of a crisis, simply to pay a social visit to the President of the United States. Rostow grasped the force of this logic and it was agreed that the meeting would take place if Israel promised it would not "publish a word of the conversation."

While Evron was with Rostow, Johnson called the Israeli minister to his office. For the next half hour, the President told him what he planned to say later to the boss of Evron's boss, Eban.

In his detailed report on the conversation to Jerusalem, Evron wrote: "[The President] had taken counsel with some of his leading advisers." Unnecessarily, he added what was well known in Jerusalem: "All of them could be described as friends of Israel. They have expressed their support for the following formulation: 'The objective is to open the straits for navigation by all states including Israel and this objective shall be carried out.'

"Mr. Johnson made it clear that the appraisal in Jerusalem about an imminent Egyptian surprise attack was not shared by the United States.

"Israel was a sovereign government, and if it decided to act alone, it could of course do so; but in that case everything that happened before and afterwards would be upon its responsibility and the United States would have no obligation for any consequences which might ensue. . . .

"He emphasized several times that Israel could depend on him. He said that he was not a coward, and did not renege on his promises, but he was not prepared to act in a manner which seemed to him to endanger the security of the United States, or to bring about the intervention of the Soviet Union simply because Israel has decided that Sunday is an ultimate date."

The meeting between Johnson and Eban was set for 7 P.M. To avoid publicity, Evron had agreed with Rostow that Eban would arrive at the White

House at a side gate. But his long conversation with the President had prevented him from getting word of this arrangement to Eban. So at the appointed time Evron waited at the side entrance with McNamara and others while Eban and Ambassador Harman tried to enter through the front gate. After about fifteen minutes the confusion was cleared up when a guard called a presidential aide and said: "Some guy out here by the name of Eban says he is supposed to see the President."

Eban met Johnson with tension "gripping my heart. It was clear that Israel faced a hard choice. But it was no less clear that her success would depend not only on her own valor, but also on the understanding that we could now achieve with our strongest friend."

Eban had first met Johnson when the then senator Johnson had come to his Washington home to hear Eban explain Israel's problems, and since then Eban found that Johnson had displayed "interest in Israel's destiny. When he became President," Eban wrote later, Johnson "established with Prime Minister Eshkol the kind of intimate confidence that had never before existed between heads of American and Israeli governments. We no longer had to use the back door for access to the center of American policy."

Eban's message to his old acquaintance that Friday evening was filled with foreboding and urgency. The President listened to Eban with concentration. There was a pause before he spoke.

"What a President says and thinks is not worth five cents unless he has the people and Congress behind him," Johnson said. "Without the Congress I'm just a six-foot-four Texan. With the Congress I'm President of the United States.

"Therefore we must see what comes out of the statement of the Secretary-General and the Security Council meeting [scheduled for the next day]. We should get busy to talk to those nations who have come out in support of freedom of navigation. If your Cabinet decides to do anything immediately and to do it on their own, that is for them. The United States is not going to do any retreating."

Johnson quickly quashed any expectation that he would publicly endorse the wild idea that an attack on Israel should be construed as an attack on the United States. That was beyond his constitutional authority, he said. But he added: "I know that Israel's life and blood are at stake. My own life and blood are at stake in many places and may be in others. . . . All I can tell you is what you have heard—friendship. . . . What you can tell your Cabinet is that the President, the Congress and the country will vigorously support a plan to use any or all measures to open the straits."

Johnson then said three times: "Israel will not be alone unless it decides to go alone."

Presumably to reassure Eban, Johnson added: "I am not a feeble mouse or a coward."

Eban asked if he could tell the Israeli Cabinet that "you are going to use all efforts in your power to get the Gulf of Aqaba open to all shipping, including that of Israel?"

"Yes," said Johnson.

At this point Eban returned to the scare cables from Israel and the possibility of an imminent Egyptian attack. Johnson declared, "All of our intelligence people are unanimous that if the UAR attacks you will whip hell out of them."

Johnson and his top advisers spent an hour and twenty-five minutes with the Israelis in a second-story office of the White House. At the end of the meeting, Eban was handed an aide-mémoire:

". . . regarding the straits we plan to pursue vigorously the measures which can be taken by maritime nations to assure that the straits and the Gulf remain open to free and innocent passage of all nations.

". . . I must emphasize the necessity for Israel not to make itself responsible for the initiation of hostilities. Israel will not be alone unless it decides to do it alone. We cannot imagine that Israel will make this decision."

Johnson walked Eban to the White House elevator.

"What do you reckon will be the result in Israel of what I have said?" Johnson asked.

"I replied that things were moving so quickly at home that my intuitions of yesterday had no real relevance."

Eban again asked whether he could assure the Cabinet that Johnson would do everything to assure the opening of the straits to Israeli shipping.

"Yes," said Johnson, taking Eban's hand in such a "paralyzing grip that I doubted that I would ever regain the use of it."

As Eban departed, Johnson returned to his advisers and, according to Gene Rostow's recollection, remarked: "I've failed. They'll go."

Johnson's mood apparently had improved a couple of hours later. By then he was bragging at a small White House dinner for several friends that the Israelis "came loaded for bear, but so was I! I let them talk for the first hour, and I just listened, and then I finished it up the last fifteen minutes. Secretary McNamara said he just wanted to throw his cap up in the air, and George Christian said it was the best meeting of the kind he had ever sat in on."

Eban went straight to National Airport, where he boarded a plane to New York and there met with another old American friend, U.N. Ambassador Arthur Goldberg. Eban later wrote that Goldberg told him that attempts to find a solution through the Security Council were already proving, as widely expected, ineffective. The only thing U Thant had brought back from his Cairo trip, said Goldberg, had been a promise not to initiate war.

"I found this assurance convincing," recalled Eban. "Nasser did not want war; he wanted victory without war."

After Eban had briefed Goldberg in detail about his talk with the President, Goldberg said, according to Eban's memoirs, that the essence of the matter was whether Eban had helped to convince President Johnson of Egypt's culpability and of Israel's innocence. "This was of crucial importance," wrote Eban. "If it was established in the American mind that Egypt's action was illicit, then Israel could hardly lose. Either she would gain international support against the blockade or if she acted alone, she would have the United States committed to the doctrine of Israel's rectitude and Cairo's guilt."

Eban left Goldberg to return to Israel, having accomplished in less than twenty-four hours what few world leaders would have been able to during a far longer period. He had met on brief notice with all of the top security leaders of the Administration, had received a sympathetic, if at times skeptical, ear, and had conveyed in stark terms of urgency and nervousness what Israel felt, as communicated by the series of Eshkol cables. It was only after he returned to Israel that he discovered the anxious wording of the cables was largely the result of the intercession of Chief of Staff Rabin.

The general had returned on May 25 from his illness to find his officers, particularly Weizman and Yariv, demanding that Israel go to war immediately—even before Eban's meeting with Lyndon Johnson. He now showed he could match their fervor by agreeing with them. This Eshkol refused to allow, and he did not change his mind even after Rabin and two of his generals sought a special meeting with him on the night of May 25 to impress how urgent they felt was the need to go on the offensive.

Impatient and unsatisfied with Eshkol's decision to exhaust the political avenues before going to war, and perhaps also still suffering under his critics' complaint about the country's lack of allies, Rabin sought permission to help write a cable to Eban. Working with officials of the Prime Minister's Office and the Foreign Ministry, Rabin used extreme language in an attempt to get a clear response from Washington. As he explained in his memoirs, his purpose was to elicit a statement that "either the United States explicitly committed itself to removing the blockade—not of the straits but of our borders, which were swarming with Arab troops—or the Americans must tell us frankly, 'You're on your own.'

"If we received the latter reply, I assumed that the Cabinet would shoulder full responsibility for the risks engendered by further delay and give the go-ahead for military action."

The purpose of the cables, in other words, had been to seek a nearly impossible commitment from the United States, and failing to achieve it, give the generals ammunition to pressure the politicians to approve the initiation of hostilities.

Washington's adroit handling of the incident thwarted Rabin's plan, but it had the effect of heightening Israel's sense of isolation by exaggerating the dangers that Israelis perceived were facing them and of increasing the urgency felt by both the generals and the politicians. The cable incident contributed to that elusive but significant combination of events and misperceptions that were feeding the region's rush to war.

RUSSIA GETS NERVOUS

By now, the threatening signs of war were so numerous that the Soviet Union finally decided to act decisively. Russian concerns were more than justified.

From Moscow's perspective, Abba Eban's high-level meetings in Washington had all the earmarks of collusion between Israel and the United States on how to defeat Russia's main allies in the Middle East. The statements and actions by the Johnson Administration all had the effect of lining up Washington behind Israel and against the Soviet Arab surrogates. At the very least, war would mean another proxy confrontation, carrying with it the inherent danger of escalation toward a direct conflict at a time when the war in Vietnam was already pushing both superpowers closer to a conflagration than either side wanted.

At the same time, reports from Israel reflected a determined militancy. Front-page stories in America, such as the one in the Washington *Star* on May 26, the same day Eban met with Johnson, were reporting that war seemed inevitable to Israelis. "Israel Reconciled to War," said the headline. The story reported that Tel Aviv's streets were empty and that there was an atmosphere of excitement about the "war which most Israelis seem to accept is coming. . . . The Israelis are ready."

Worse, in Moscow's view, was the nearly hysterical outpouring of braggadocio and threats from Arab capitals. Though Moscow had been generous in supplying Egypt and Syria with arsenals of its sophisticated weapons, it was by no means clear that the Arabs could defeat Israel, or if they could, that the United States would not then intervene and thereby face the Soviet

Union with a war-or-humiliation decision. There was no doubt, even with the debilitating war in Vietnam, that the United States remained a formidable power.

Finally, Moscow itself had badly erred in its campaign to try to forge unity among the Arab socialist states. Its repeated warnings of Israel's aggressive intentions, its constant urging that Egypt draw closer to Syria, had contributed to the dangerous atmosphere and perhaps even misled Nasser into believing he could go further than Israel was willing to allow him or the Soviets were willing to support him.

Moscow's actions had been miscalculated and resulted, in the eyes of the U.S. intelligence community, from a major intelligence failure. "They misread the Arabs, failing to realize how reckless they would become, and they failed to appreciate how threatening and provocative Nasser's moves were to Israel," said the CIA's Middle East clandestine operations chief James Critchfield years later. "This was nothing less than a massive intelligence catastrophe for Moscow, a great intelligence fiasco. They wanted unity so they could exert increased influence, but they ended up helping to push their friends to war and the worst defeat they ever suffered."

Russia now belatedly tried to avert the crisis it had helped create. On the same day that Nasser made his reckless speech, urgent cables under the signature of Premier Kosygin were sent to the Russian embassies in Tel Aviv and Cairo, arriving early in the morning of May 27.

At 3 A.M. that day the Soviet ambassador to Egypt, Dmitri Pozhidaev, arrived unannounced at Nasser's home and sought an interview. When Nasser was finally awakened, Pozhidaev told him that Moscow had warnings from Washington that Egypt was about to attack Israel. As friends, the ambassador said, the Soviets were urging him not to fire the first shot because the side that did would be in an untenable political position. Nasser, baffled by the Washington claim, insisted that he had given no orders for an attack nor were any planned.

At about the same time in Jerusalem, Soviet Ambassador Dmitri S. Chuvakhin had awakened a disgruntled Levi Eshkol to issue a similar warning, though he had a different version to deliver. Chuvakhin claimed Moscow had information it was Israel that was about to attack. Despite its urgency, the Soviet message was moderate in tone, urging merely that "it is essential to find means to settle the conflict by nonmilitary means." But Eshkol was not disposed to be lectured in even these mild terms. Israelis considered Chuvakhin arrogant, rude and hostile and he was widely disliked, so Eshkol was less than happy at being routed out of bed by him and having to pull a suit over his pajamas to receive him. He told Chuvakhin that the only reason Israel had mobilized was because of actions by Egypt and Syria. It was to those countries, he declared, that the Soviet representations should be made.

Chuvakhin countered that he was concerned only with Israel and asked directly whether the Jewish state planned an attack. When Eshkol refused to answer directly, Chuvakhin persisted. He asked the question three more times. Each time Eshkol evaded. Then in exasperation, he finally exclaimed that it was the Egyptians who had blockaded the straits and that it was Egyptian airplanes that were flying reconnaissance flights over Israeli territory. Weren't these the "first shots"? Eshkol asked irritably.

The prime minister then dressed down the Soviet envoy by pointing out to him that the "function of an ambassador . . . was to promote friendly relations . . . with the country to which he was accredited," according to notes of his comments. "It did not seem to [Eshkol] that Chuvakhin has cared or tried to do this. Since this was the case, he would be pleased to welcome a Soviet ambassador who held this conception of his role."

The various buffeting forces working on Eshkol were taking their toll. During the period when Eban was traveling to the capitals of the West, Eshkol had undergone an excruciating and humiliating ordeal at home. He was placed under extraordinary pressure by his political foes, particularly Ben Gurion and his colleagues, who felt he was too weak, and the generals, the majority of whom felt he was endangering the nation by delaying in launching war immediately.

The pressure had become acute several days earlier, on May 24, the same day Eban left on his odyssey. At that time the most controversial man in Israeli politics, former terrorist Menachem Begin, met with Eshkol and audaciously asked him to step aside as prime minister.

Begin was the scourge of Eshkol's majority Mapai Party. He was the leader of the ultranationalist Herut (Freedom) opposition party, which in 1965 had merged with the rightest Liberal Party to form Gahal, an acronym for the names of the two parties. He was also head of the Revisionist Zionists, who believed in a mystical Jewish militancy that was best expressed by Begin's motto: "I fight, therefore I am."

Now fifty-three years of age, small, slim, and intense, a passionate believer in the Jews' right to *Eretz Yisrael,* the historic land of the Jews, which he considered to extend to both sides of the Jordan River, Begin was a Polish immigrant who was generally dismissed by most Labor officials and many Israelis as a dangerous fanatic. Ben Gurion despised him, refused, when he was prime minister, to mention him by his name during the long years of Knesset debates, often ostentatiously walking out of the hall when Begin spoke, and even compared him to a Nazi.

As head of the Irgun Zvai Leumi (National Military Organization), the largest Jewish terrorist group in Palestine during the last years of the British Mandate, Begin had led the men and women responsible for the worst outrages of violence: the blowing up of the King David Hotel with the loss of ninety-one lives; the hanging of two British soldiers and the booby-trapping of their bodies; the indiscriminate bombings of Arab and British soldiers and civilians; the massacre at the Arab village of Deir Yassin, in which 240 men, women and children were killed, their bodies mutilated and stacked like cordwood on the barren earth or dumped down a well. All of this was done in the name of the biblical promise to the Jews of a homeland in Palestine.

So intent on having all of *Eretz Yisrael* were Begin and his followers that they vehemently fought adoption of the United Nations' 1947 Partition Plan as being "illegal. . . . It will never be recognized. . . . It will not bind the Jewish people," the Irgun warned. "Jerusalem was and will forever be our capital. *Eretz Yisrael* will be restored to the people of Israel. All of it."

When the plan was adopted, an Irgun Order of the Day declared: "We who have offered our lives for the day of redemption are not rejoicing. For the Homeland has not been liberated but mutilated."

Begin's militant and expansionist views did not change with the creation of Israel. In a radio address to the new nation on May 15, 1948, Begin said: "It is Hebrew arms which decide the boundaries of the Hebrew state. So it is now in battle; so it will be in the future." And so it was, at least for Begin.

He remained the uncompromising hardlining leader of the opposition throughout the 1950s and into the 1960s, preaching a litany of blood and sacrifice, an emotional, quasi-religious message that the Jewish people were the "God-covenanted owners" of the "whole land of Israel" and that it was the "fighting Jew" who had to protect it. With such fiery mysticism he had influenced a generation of young Israelis, many of them like Ezer Weizman who were now in leadership positions in the nation's security services and strong believers in Begin's fire and brimstone vision.

Begin's proposition to Eshkol that Wednesday afternoon was surprising and was made at considerable cost to the old terrorist's pride. He wanted the prime minister to step aside in order to allow Begin's old nemesis, David Ben Gurion, to become head of a national unity government. Under Begin's scheme, Eshkol would become deputy prime minister. To drive home his point, Begin reminded Eshkol of his stormy relations with Ben Gurion and said he was willing to forget them in order to form a strong government to meet the external threat. He also questioned Eshkol's grasp of military matters and the worth of trying to secure Washington's help.

Eshkol, not unnaturally, refused Begin's request and disputed his charges. But with typical humility he promised to put the proposal to his Labor Party colleagues. If they approved it, he vowed, then he would resign not only the prime ministership but also his post as defense minister.

In frustration, Eshkol then explained to Begin: "One of these days I may prove to you what I have done to equip the Army. As to my understanding of military matters, it is not what they have been thinking for many years. I have learned something in the meanwhile. And as to Johnson, I think I can obtain more from him. Believe me, I have the basis to say this."

As for working with his old friend and fellow pioneer David Ben Gurion, Eshkol said that was no longer possible. "These two horses . . . can no longer pull the same cart. This pair can no longer live together."

Begin, whose persistence was already as legendary as his fanaticism, then asked Eshkol if he would surrender the defense ministry to Ben Gurion. Again Eshkol refused.

The meeting ended on that negative note.

But to Eshkol the meaning was clear, and threatening. It meant that the suspicion that he was not capable of leading both the government and the defense ministry too in this perilous period of crisis was becoming more acute. Among concerned Israelis there was a belief spreading that Eshkol had to share power, that he was too weak and inexperienced in military affairs to hold both portfolios. If he would not surrender to Ben Gurion, then the least he should do was appoint one of Israel's many young war heroes to become defense minister.

Two names were increasingly being heard as potential defense ministers: Moshe Dayan and Yigal Allon, the latter also a native-born Israeli, now forty-eight years old and considered by many the ablest field commander in the 1948 war, even above Dayan. On the same day as Begin's confrontation with Eshkol, Allon returned from a visit to Moscow where he had attended an international conference as Israel's minister of labor. Allon retained close ties with the Israel Defense Forces and he immediately went to the General Staff Headquarters in Tel Aviv and received a two-hour briefing.

Like Dayan and most of the generals, he already was convinced that war was inevitable. But first the internal war between Eshkol and the hawks had to be concluded.

The next day, May 25, brought additional strain for Eshkol. Interior Minister Moshe Shapira, still determined to rein in the generals and hawks from rushing into war but also worried that Eshkol was in over his head, met with the prime minister. As spokesman for the powerful National Religious Party, an important faction in the government's coalition, he urged Eshkol to release the Defense Ministry portfolio to Ben Gurion. Again Eshkol refused.

But he then took a momentous step, one that would have far-reaching repercussions. He agreed to widen the membership of the Ministerial Committee on Defense to include two opposition parties, Begin's Gahal and Ben Gurion's Rafi, the first concrete step toward aligning all of the country's fractious political parties into a government of national unity. This agreement was tantamount to bestowing legitimacy on Begin and his views, and gave him a potent platform to influence the government.

Eshkol, slowly being beaten down, humiliated and scorned, doggedly carried on his duties. He went to the southern front on May 25 to inspect Israel's war preparations and meet with the local commanders. The meeting brought him more grief in the form of severe criticism by the young sabra commanders. The officers were unanimous in urging an immediate attack, and they sharply questioned Eshkol's wisdom in refusing to allow them to go to war at once. In particular, the fiery, impulsive commander of the Third Division, Brigadier General Ariel Sharon, already a legendary warrior though he was only thirty-nine, openly upbraided Eshkol for his hesitation. Sharon bluntly warned that the longer Israel waited to fight the greater its casualties would be.

His warnings had to be taken seriously since Sharon had fought in every previous war and was much admired for his courage and daring—although his hotheaded impulsiveness brought frequent criticism from his superiors. He was a professional soldier, the fighter who had turned the paratroopers into an elite strike force and who had commanded most of Israel's devastating retaliatory raids against Arab villages over the years, including the bloody Qibya raid in 1953, which took the lives of sixty-six Arab civilians. Dayan and Ben Gurion both admired his fighting talents enormously. Eshkol was less impressed. He refused to authorize an immediate attack.

The pressures on Eshkol continued to mount the next day as politicians and generals met among themselves and with each other to argue over and hash and rehash the burning questions of leadership and war. Some of Eshkol's colleagues, concerned about the demoralizing effects of the mounting political disputes, urged Eshkol to still the clamor by appointing Yigal Allon as minister of defense. The prime minister declined, but he met later that day with Allon to talk over the situation. By now Allon was not only convinced that war was inevitable and that Israel would win but that the country should strike immediately. He strongly urged Eshkol to approve a surprise attack.

"This is one of the great issues in Jewish history," Allon told Eshkol. "I believe you can go down in Jewish history as another King David—if you decide to act now."

Eshkol refused. But by now the old prime minister was beginning to realize that war was unavoidable. Allon later said he believed it was his meeting that day with Eshkol that convinced the prime minister to go to war.

The next day, Saturday, May 27, brought no relief for the fatigued and battered Eshkol. The sense of crisis was palpable. Newspaper headlines were shrill with foreboding: Egyptian units continuing to move into the Sinai, reports of Egypt's mining of the straits, the war cries of Nasser, Heikal and other Arab leaders, questions about the effectiveness of Eban's desperate mission to Washington, the indecisive discussions in the U.N. Security Council and U Thant's return to New York from Cairo.

Israelis were showing their concern by pouring into the Negev in search of husbands and relatives who had been mobilized. Civilians drove from camp to camp seeking their relatives. When they found them they embraced, chatted excitedly, and then left behind drinks, sandwiches and sweaters.

The mass Negev visitation had about it a festive air, but underneath it all, disrupting, irritating and demoralizing, was the constant drumbeat of doubts about Eshkol's ability to lead Israel in this time of national peril. Except for the generals, who were aware of the overwhelming strength of their forces, nearly everyone seemed to believe that the young Jewish state's very existence was in jeopardy—including, to their peril, the excited and impetuous Arab nations.

Though Eshkol had had little sleep because of the Soviet ambassador's early visit, he attended a briefing that Saturday by Chief of Staff Rabin at 9 A.M. Rabin by this time had dropped his moderate tone and insisted openly that time was pressing for Israel to go to war. During a series of meetings later in the morning, Eshkol met with hardlining Golda Meir. Since giving up the Foreign Ministry in January 1966, she had been serving as secretary-general of the Mapai Party. At sixty-nine years of age, she was still the dominant old lady of Israeli politics, tough and persistent. She applied still more pressure on Eshkol by urging him to appoint Allon defense minister. He again refused. But events were now accelerating.

That afternoon the factions headed by Ben Gurion and Begin agreed among themselves that they would insist that Eshkol give the Defense Ministry to Dayan.

In the evening, with nerves raw and tensions high throughout the country,

Israel's Cabinet came close to authorizing war. But still there were hesitations.

———————

Lyndon Johnson began May 27 in a far more leisurely manner than his counterparts in Cairo and Jerusalem. Vietnam was for the moment no more urgent than a dull headache and Johnson's attention was now focused on the Middle East. His first order of business was a telephone call to Arthur Goldberg at his residence in New York City at 8:15. Only the day before, columnist Drew Pearson had reported that Goldberg was unhappy in his U.N. post and wanted to return to the Supreme Court, but neither man mentioned the column. More pressing was the fact that U Thant was going to give his formal report on his emergency trip to Cairo to the Security Council that morning.

An hour later the President spoke with Walt Rostow. The previous day he had sent along to Johnson a letter from Washington attorney David Ginsburg, an avid supporter of Israel. He had written to Rostow warning that "it would be unwise for the U.S. to refrain from exercising its . . . rights at a time when the UAR is taking hostile action." He suggested that he was not sure that was what Israel wanted. "I've not seen or spoken with Eban, nor have I spoken about this with anyone in the Israeli Embassy," Ginsburg wrote. "I don't know therefore what their reaction would be."

Despite his close Israeli contacts, Rostow was unaware of just how close Israel was to deciding on war. Johnson decided after talking with Rostow that war was not imminent and he left the White House around 10:30 A.M. on his way to his Texas ranch for a long Memorial Day weekend. His plane stopped first at Newport News, Virginia, so Johnson could attend the commissioning ceremonies for the nation's newest aircraft carrier, the U.S.S. *John F. Kennedy*. The late President's nine-year-old daughter, Caroline, christened the ship while members of the Kennedy clan looked on, including Kennedy's widow, Jacqueline, and his brothers Edward and Robert, the latter having long been seen as the natural challenger to Johnson for the presidency in 1968. Johnson had never got on with the Kennedys and he spent only an hour at the ceremonies.

Accompanying the President to the ranch were Arthur B. Krim and his attractive wife, Mathilde. The Krims had become so friendly with Johnson that they were about to build a house on Lake Lyndon B. Johnson near the President's ranch on the Pedernales River in the Texas hill country west of Austin. The Johnsons and the Krims frequently spent weekends together in the hill country, the President visited the couple in their New York apartment when he was in Manhattan, and they occasionally stayed at the White House when they were in Washington.

Krim's wife, an ardent supporter of Israel, had a particularly intriguing background. Born Mathilde Galland in Italy in 1927, the same year Krim had graduated from Mount Vernon High School in New York, she was a striking blonde. She had been reared first as a Roman Catholic in Italy and then, when the family returned to her father's birthplace in Switzerland, as a Lutheran. Like many Westerners, she recalled years later, she suffered a profound shock of moral revulsion at the end of World War II when as a student she first saw newsreels of the Jewish victims of the concentration camps. Galvanized by the experience, she decided to learn more about the Jewish plight and sought out Jewish friends.

She soon fell in love with a student at the University of Geneva, David Danon, a young Bulgarian Jew who had been brought up in Palestine and exiled by the British for his association with the Jewish terrorist group led by Menachem Begin. Danon was studying to become a medical doctor, but, according to Mathilde, he spent most of his time recruiting and carrying out secret Irgun operations throughout Western Europe. The teenage Mathilde saw Danon as a dashing and heroic figure, an activist dedicating his life to the noble cause of the founding of a Jewish state in Palestine. He was a personal friend of the terrorists who killed British resident minister Lord Walter Moyne in Cairo in 1944 and who blew up the King David Hotel in Jerusalem in 1946 with heavy loss of life. To Mathilde these actions, bloody though they were, represented the depth of the convictions of Danon and the Irgunists, the measure of both their commitment and their despair.

Mathilde became so enamored of the Jewish struggle and of Danon's romantic undercover operations in Europe that she threw herself wholeheartedly into the Jewish cause. She converted to Judaism, married Danon and eventually found herself acting as an Irgun agent involved in highly dangerous underground activities herself. These included the transportation across international boundaries of explosives destined for Irgun cells in Europe and Palestine. As a seemingly innocent petite and pretty blonde out for a bicycle ride along Switzerland's borders, she in reality was taking messages and explosives into neighboring France and Italy.

In 1953, she received a Ph.D. in genetics at the University of Geneva and she and Danon finally moved to Israel, where Mathilde became a cancer researcher at the Weizmann Institute. After the birth of a daughter, she and Danon separated, but Mathilde's love of Israel did not wane. She remained at Weizmann, enthralled by the pioneering spirit of Israelis and the great effort at building a nation. While at Weizmann, she met Arthur Krim during one of his visits to Israel. They soon married and moved to the United States, where Mrs. Krim became a widely known researcher at the Memorial Sloan-Kettering Cancer Center in New York and a celebrated hostess in Hollywood and Manhattan.

Although her enthusiasm for Israel in later years became tempered under the policies of Menachem Begin, during the 1960s she remained an avid and vocal supporter of the Jewish state, freely and frequently expressing opinions to President Johnson. In the unfolding crisis now taking place in the Middle East, she and her husband spent nearly every day either visiting with the President or talking to him over the telephone.

"We talked with him all the time about Israel," Mathilde Krim recalled fifteen years later. "He admired Israel as a rancher who knew about making dry land bloom and what the Jews had done. Also, I think he had an entirely emotional liking for Jews, for what they had suffered, for the way they had been discriminated against, as he felt he had been discriminated against by the Eastern Establishment."

Thus, at this critical time, a strong and enthusiastic supporter of Israel was one of the Johnson family's closest friends and one whom the President listened to frequently and took seriously. As President, Johnson left himself more open to a passionately partisan voice than was prudent or even healthy during the accelerating crisis.

The Johnson party, including the Krims, arrived at the ranch at 2:45 P.M., and six minutes later the President was on the telephone with Dean Rusk to hear the latest on the Middle East. U Thant had already made his report but, as Johnson and his top officials expected, it had little in the way of practical import.

U Thant had used his report to justify his controversial decision to withdraw UNEF troops, arguing that just as Israel had the right not to accept the force, Egypt had the right to order its departure. He reported that he had the personal word of Nasser that Egypt would not initiate hostilities and that Nasser's aim was merely to return to the situation prevailing before the Suez war a decade earlier. He concluded by urging restraint and a breathing spell to allow tensions to subside. His words had no positive effect.

More important, an urgent message from Soviet Premier Kosygin had arrived during the day, warning that Russia would not sit by idly if Israel started a war. The State Department now alerted Johnson that it was working on a presidential message to relay the Soviet message to Israel.

Johnson did not sit around waiting for it. Instead he got behind the wheel of a Lincoln Continental convertible and drove the Krims around his spacious ranch, looking at the wild flowers and herds of deer, and on to a series of visits to his neighbors. At 6:20 P.M., while they were at a neighbor's house, an aide brought Johnson the State Department draft message for Eshkol. He made a small change and ordered it sent on to Jerusalem.

The message relayed Moscow's warning that "if Israel starts military action the Soviet Union will extend help to the attacked party." After reassuring Eshkol of America's interest in Israel's safety, the message cautioned: "As your friend, I repeat even more strongly what I said yesterday to Mr. Eban. It is essential that Israel not take any preemptive military action and thereby make itself responsible for the initiation of hostilities." The President strengthened the warning by writing two words so that the sentence read, "It is essential that Israel JUST MUST not take any preemptive military action . . ."

That presidential duty taken care of, Johnson and the Krims continued their sightseeing around the picturesque hill country, then had dinner at the ranch and retired before midnight, apparently secure that war again had been prevented.

The President's sleep would have been less sound if he had known how determined the Israeli generals had become to launch a war in the soonest time possible.

XII
ESHKOL STAMMERS A SPEECH

Abba Eban arrived back in Israel only on the night of May 27 and went directly to an emergency meeting of the Cabinet. He found the mood in the country "even more dramatic" than when he had departed three days earlier.

The sense of alarm and urgency in Israel was so pervasive that, as the newspapers were reporting, war seemed inevitable. In that wordless way in which societies facing peril and suffering deep anxiety occasionally draw together in a spirit of national unity and shared perceptions, Israel's leaders by now had begun operating on the assumption that the Jewish state would have to fight to survive. Even Levi Eshkol by now felt openly that way. He had finally completely succumbed to the hawks. The question no longer was whether there would be a war; it was when.

The fact that many officials in many countries, including the United States, still thought that the crisis could be resolved peacefully, that Israel was not imperiled by the Egyptian forces, which were either in defensive positions or in total disarray, that the CIA and military experts familiar with the region believed Israel would prevail in any conflict with any combination of Arab enemies, had little to do with the Israeli outlook. The sense of danger and isolation was complete, the belief total that the strategic tide was running against Israel and that only a violent response could break it. The issue was Israel's credibility. The defense forces were ready to attack. All that was needed was the political decision by the government to approve the time of war.

As Eban observed in his autobiography: "The issue that the ministers were deliberating was, in essence, one of political timing."

Eban was met at the airport and taken immediately to a crucial Cabinet meeting that had been under way in Tel Aviv since 8 P.M. The meeting was still going strong when Eban joined the sixteen ministers and Eshkol after 10 P.M. It went on for another seven hours, the room filled with clouds of smoke, piles of stained coffee cups, bleary eyes and occasional flares of temper. The arguments, by now familiar on both sides, washed back and forth over whether Israel should go to war immediately or give more time to cement the support of the United States, whether the passage of time would mean more or fewer casualties.

No one, however, seemed to believe that whatever the timing that Israel would be defeated. The Army's victory was assumed. What essentially was in doubt was what the passage of time would mean to Israel's economy, to its military posture, to the number of its casualties, and whether a surprise attack would injure its crucial relations with the United States.

Although Eban had just performed a dramatic feat of international diplomacy, his stock was not high in Israel. His political foes like Dayan and other hawks remained suspicious about his toughness, the accuracy of his reporting and even the worth of his mission. Some ministers suspected that Eban had been too conciliatory in Washington, had bowed to Johnson and failed to achieve any commitment that could be relied upon. Allon was one of these and three times he presented his case for going to war instantly.

Eban, stung by the doubts and implied criticisms, argued strongly for a postponement. It was obvious to him now that the series of scare cables that had deluged him in Washington had been fabrications. Egypt was not ready to attack, nor was Israel's security under instant threat. Yet Eban had been put in the awkward position of personally declaring to President Johnson that Israel faced an immediate Egyptian attack, in effect trading on his good reputation, giving his personal word. He had done so only reluctantly, he declared, but since he had, the least the Cabinet could do was give Washington another forty-eight hours in order to have a further round of consultations.

If Israel wanted to attack now, he declared, it should not have asked Washington to restrain Cairo two days earlier. An attack now by Israel would put the United States in an extremely embarrassing position, for which it would correctly blame Israel and Eban personally.

Rabin, sitting in as a consultant, opposed him, contending that the more time that passed the stronger Egypt would become. Egyptian troops, tanks and airplanes were continuing to pour into the Sinai. The greater Egypt's troop concentrations became, the higher would be Israel's casualties, an extremely sensitive issue in the small country. It was a persuasive argument, especially in the context that war was inevitable, that every day that passed was a serious drain on the economy and, in the end, only the timing was at stake anyway.

But still the ministers could not agree. As the arguments continued, Rabin gloomily observed, "the more evident it became that the IDF would not attack on the morning of Sunday, May 28."

Eshkol too was convinced that Israel would win if it acted now. But still he hesitated. He did not want to browbeat his colleagues into arriving at such a momentous decision. He wanted their considered support, not their thoughtless submission. Further, he had already been threatened by the National Religious Party faction that if war was decided on it would quit the coalition, bringing down the government.

Despite his fatigue, he kept the occasionally heated meeting in session through the long early-morning hours, listening, explaining, intervening between factions. Shrewdly, at the conclusion of the long meeting he did not insist on a formal vote. Instead, he received an informal expression of each minister's position. The result was nine for war and nine for delay. As the meeting adjourned with the coming of Sunday's dawn at 5 A.M., Eshkol set 3 P.M. for the tired and disheveled group to meet again.

While the Israeli leadership caught up on its rest, Gamal Abdel Nasser was preparing for his first press conference since the crisis erupted. Reporters from around the world had descended on the region following his dramatic closing of the straits. Now, in the afternoon of May 28, Nasser met with several hundred of them to try to explain his position and seek world understanding for his impetuous and provocative actions.

From Nasser's viewpoint, his maneuvering continued to be enormously successful, a view he no doubt would have modified had he been aware of how desperately determined the Israelis were to retain their gains from the 1956 war. But, blinded by satisfaction with his achievements and basking in the glory of his rewon leadership of the Arab world, he now attempted to cement his diplomatic victory by announcing to the world that there could be no turning back of the clock, no return to the humiliation of the presence of foreign troops on Egyptian soil.

Dressed in a business suit and a white shirt with a patterned tie, Nasser appeared relaxed and confident as he sat on a dais in front of a large eagle, Egypt's national emblem, amid the faded splendor of the presidential palace in the Cairo suburb of Heliopolis. He was considerably cooler than in his speech two days earlier, and his remarks were for the most part lacking in militant bombast. He made clear that he did not plan to go to war. He had, after all, already achieved what he had sought. But he left no doubt during the hour-and-a-half session that he intended to retain what he had regained and that Egypt would fight if Israel attacked. There would be no negotiations, he said. There was nothing to negotiate about since his actions had affected only Egyptian territory.

Although he enjoyed the support of the Arab and Third worlds and all of the Communist Bloc, Nasser expressed his disillusionment and frustration with the lack of backing from the United States and other Western countries, except France, which was remaining conspicuously neutral.

"We used to believe at the beginning of the revolution in 1952 that the United States is the country which would stand with the states and their freedom and independence—the state which emerged to help all people and not the state which emerged to dominate and take sides. But the United States sides with Israel.... We regard the United States as biased toward and taking the side of Israel one hundred percent. What concerns the United States in this matter? It is a direct problem between us and Israel. But the United States ... has been completely biased toward Israel and has totally ignored the rights of the Arabs."

He also bitterly criticized Britain and Canada for their pro-Israeli stances and repeatedly asked why the Western powers were so insensitive to Arab rights.

"The existence of Israel in itself is an aggression," he declared provocatively. "... what happened in 1948 was an aggression—an aggression against the Palestinian people. Israel expelled the Palestinians from their country and robbed them of their property. Today there are one million homeless Palestinians.... Where are the rights of the Arabs? There is no one who is talking about the rights of the Arabs.... All the states we see today—the United States, Britain, the Western powers—are talking about the rights of Israel and are siding with Israel. There is not one man who is talking about the Arabs or the rights of the Arabs or the rights of the Palestinian people in their own country and homeland."

Nasser explained that the crisis had developed because "Eshkol threatened to march on Damascus, occupy Syria and overthrow the national Syrian regime. It was our duty to come to the rescue of our Arab brother. It was

163

our duty to ask for the withdrawal of UNEF. When UNEF went, we had to go to the Gulf of Aqaba and restore things to what they were when we were in Aqaba in 1956."

Then Nasser upped the stakes in Western eyes by alluding to an oil boycott if war erupted. He reported that Kuwait had already promised to suspend shipments to the West "in the event of aggression to us or of the intervention of the West or the United States. I am waiting for the opinion of Saudi Arabia; I am waiting for the opinion of the other Arab countries."

He darkly hinted that if the Arab countries did not boycott the West then the masses might rise up and destroy their oil installations. "I believe the destruction of these interests and installations to be a dishonorable action," he said, adding disingenuously: "But of course if the Arab governments fail to take the patriotic steps and the necessary steps, then the Arab peoples will have to carry out their duty."

The boycott threat was more serious to Europe, which depended on Arab oil, than to the United States, which was still essentially self-sufficient.

The press conference concluded with a question about whether Nasser had considered the possibility of U.S. armed intervention on the side of Israel.

"I do not take the United States into account because if I do I shall never be able to do anything or to move," admitted Nasser.

He had every reason to be satisfied with his performance. He had made clear his determination to retain what was his and also that he did not want war. But the question of war was no longer his to decide.

A transcript of Nasser's remarks was received at Johnson's ranch at 6:25 P.M., but it is doubtful that the President read it. He was spending that Sunday touring his beloved hill country with the Krims to look at wildlife, herds of buffalo and deer, and to visit with neighbors. That night he talked by telephone with Justice Abe Fortas, who was reportedly becoming disillusioned with the way Rusk and the State Department were handling the Middle East crisis, fearing they were not being sympathetic enough toward Israel. The President finally went to bed shortly after 11 P.M., the Middle East and its problems half a world away.

Levi Eshkol and his ministers were back in session at three o'clock in the afternoon that Sunday still anguishing over the question of when to go to war. In the few short hours since they had met, there had been important developments that affected that question. Johnson's message urging restraint, sent the previous day, had arrived during the morning along with messages from Britain and France.

The message from Prime Minister Wilson was sympathetic: ". . . we strongly urge you to continue a policy of restraint, as long as diplomatic efforts are under way to find a satisfactory solution."

De Gaulle's message was less friendly. He urged Israel to show restraint and informed the government that he was still attempting to get the "four Great Powers"—Britain, France, the Soviet Union and the United States—to coordinate their actions. "The need is above all to ensure . . . that none of them undertakes any action or gesture which could be interpreted as taking sides." De Gaulle could hardly have chosen a less welcome formula, as far as Israel was concerned. With the United States and Britain both standing close by the Jewish state, the last thing Eshkol and his ministers wanted to see occur was a decision by those two countries actually to behave neutrally.

In addition to the messages from the three Western leaders, Dean Rusk had also sent a résumé of Eban's Washington talks. The résumé assured Israel that the United States was prepared to follow three actions: discussions in the United Nations, signing a declaration by the maritime powers reaffirming freedom of passage through the straits and preparing a plan to sail through the straits.

Rusk had appended a note of his own assuring Israel that the United States was proceeding urgently "to prepare the military aspects of the international naval escort plan." But he added forcefully: ". . . unilateral action on the part of Israel would be irresponsible and catastrophic."

Rusk's and Johnson's combination of promises and warnings had their intended effect. After Eban had read them aloud at the reconvened Cabinet meeting, Eshkol announced that he had earlier been prepared to propose immediate war. But on the basis of the U.S. assurances he was now ready to recommend a two-week delay before deciding when to go to war.

The Cabinet discussed the new situation exhaustively. It was clear to Israel's leaders that the Russian threat received via Washington the previous day could be ignored only as long as America stood by Israel's side. It was that consideration, the retention of U.S. support, that in the end carried the day. One by one, the hardliners joined Eshkol in approving a two-week delay. Only Transportation Minister Moshe Carmel, an old firebrand, voted against. Yigal Allon also thought delay was wrong but he merely abstained with the announcement that he reserved the right to recall the Cabinet to reconsider the decision if circumstances changed.

The Cabinet meeting lasted for nearly five hours and in the end Eshkol had his way. But his day was far from over.

The Prime Minister's Office had announced to the anxious and expectant nation that Eshkol would report on radio the state of the crisis that Sunday night and Israelis were now waiting in a mood of high excitement. Probably more than any people in the world, Israelis even in normal times followed the ebb and flow of news with the passion and intensity that others devote to sporting statistics. They devoured news, commented on it, argued about it and anticipated new developments with the keenness born of suffering and the varied backgrounds of their pasts.

Israelis on that tense Sunday night were huddled around their radios (there was still no television in the country) everywhere in the small nation waiting for Levi Eshkol's report, the latest news flash on their destiny. Emotions were high, anxieties in full bloom. Though there was no immediate threat to the country's security since Egypt's troops remained in defensive positions, Israelis perceived their situation as dire, a "live or perish" predicament.

Eshkol was by now bone tired. He was nearly sleepless and suffering a bad cold, his hectic schedule for the past few days crowded by a blur of meetings, messages, arguments and indecision, and the enervating attacks of his political opponents.

Though the Cabinet meeting had not ended until around 8 P.M., his radio speech was scheduled to be aired live at 8:30 P.M., which barely gave him time to read the script drafted for him by his harried aides. When he did finally get a chance to scan it, he did not like several passages and one of the aides hurriedly typed in revisions. The prime minister had no time to reread the speech before he went before the anxious nation.

Eshkol had never been a spellbinding orator, but that Sunday night he was even less inspiring than usual. He spoke with a noticeable stammer, sounding fatigued and insecure, and stumbled over parts of the revisions which he either could not decipher or now disagreed with. As he came to a part of the text concerning the Egyptian buildup of troops in the Sinai, he suddenly stopped. In the electric silence, the national radio audience could hear his labored breathing over the sensitive microphone, then Eshkol whispering: "What's this?" The sentence he was reading had included the word "removal" in connection with what Israel would do about the concentration of the Egyptian troops in the Sinai. He did not like the wording. He started reading again, improvising, saying this time that the government had decided on actions for the "movement" of the Egyptian forces.

The rest of the speech was no more satisfying to the feverish nation. Eshkol described the dangers facing Israel as unabated and the closing of the straits as "tantamount to an act of aggression against Israel." He added that the "government announces and declares that the Israel Defense Forces are strong enough to defeat any aggressor. . . ."

It was all disappointing to the waiting Israeli audience, which had expected some dramatic proclamation or development as a result of Eban's highly publicized tour of Western capitals. Instead, there was just Eshkol's dry and indecisive report. There were no ringing exhortations, no patriotic slogans, no inspired rhetoric, only the unsettling stammered utterances of an obviously tired old man and the realization that the frustrating period of no war, no peace was to continue. It was a vague, weak, quavering and unsatisfying performance. The nation was appalled.

Eshkol, in one six-minute speech, seemed to confirm the hardliners' charge that the old immigrant generation no longer represented the tough and forceful leadership that Israel now needed. Snapped one disgusted reserve officer who had listened to the speech at his post in the Negev: "Our real problem is not Nasser, but the second *aliyah,*" i.e., the immigrants who arrived shortly after the turn of the century and were the nation's founding fathers.

The speech was a disaster for Eshkol. It was now only a question of time before his critics would triumph.

But still the weary Eshkol's day was not over. Before he could finally find some rest he had to brief restive senior military officers about the nearly unanimous Cabinet decision to wait two more weeks. Chief of Staff Rabin had been upset and disappointed by the Cabinet's action and he had insisted that Eshkol at the least owed it to the headquarters' staff to explain the reasons behind it, a duty Rabin apparently felt he himself could not credibly carry out since he was so opposed to the Cabinet's action. When he had heard that there was to be a two-week delay, Rabin wrote in his memoirs, "My reaction bordered on disbelief, and I could already anticipate the hue and cry when I broke the news to the general staff."

The unfortunate Eshkol no doubt did have some idea how resentful his military commanders would be, but he dutifully confronted them nonetheless late Sunday night. "You can and you should say anything you like to me," he told the officers. "Talk as if you were out of uniform."

They did. It was a stormy, heated session.

"Your shilly-shallying will cost us thousands of deaths," warned Ariel Sharon.

"If you go on begging protection from Paris and Washington we shall be lost," shouted Brigadier General Abraham Yoffe.

Ezer Weizman grumbled: "Our leaders cannot get together to confront the Arab menace."

Even Yitzhak Rabin joined the criticism. "It looks as if the only strength the country can rely on is the Army," he said.

Eshkol patiently tried to explain to them that no matter how spectacular might be their victory, Israel could not spurn the United States and its few other friends and then expect international support after the war. This had been Ben Gurion's lesson from the 1956 war and Eshkol did not intend to undergo a similar humiliation at the hands of the United States.

Beyond that, Eshkol was convinced that his military officers were exaggerating, as warriors are wont to do, the dangers involved in waiting. It already was becoming known to ministers that the rapid buildup of what was now an estimated eighty thousand Egyptian forces in the Sinai was causing chaos among the Arab troops. Early U.S. estimates were proving correct: As Egyptian lines of communication lengthened, troops were encountering confusion and dislocation. Also, as each day passed, Israel was secretly receiving additional military equipment from Europe, mainly France, and the United States to strengthen its forces.

At the end of the generals' lecture, Eshkol shrugged his weary shoulders and said simply: "You are exaggerating quite a lot."

He left the meeting extremely depressed, particularly by the taunt: "Why are we always begging protection from others?"

Nonetheless, he had stuck by his decision. There would be no war immediately. Reason and restraint seemed to be prevailing that Sunday night. But, as usual in the Middle East, appearances were deceiving.

Eshkol's announcement that Israel would give diplomacy a two-week chance was greeted with relief in the West. It appeared that Washington's efforts were paying off. Nasser had publicly vowed that he would not initiate a war and now Eshkol had vowed he would not go to war immediately.

This welcome news reached Lyndon Johnson on his Texas ranch where he was still enjoying a typical long Memorial Day weekend, his time taken up with his ranch and the countryside he loved. Although he was on the telephone ten times that Monday, May 29, only three of the conversations were with Washington officials. Yet the Middle East had a way of intruding on his pleasures.

A powerful wave of pro-Israel sentiment was already building up in parts of the country over that Memorial Day weekend, particularly in the heavily Jewish New York area. Israel's supporters, both Jews and Gentiles, were issuing statements, holding special meetings and sermonizing. Eight church leaders, Roman Catholic, Protestant and Greek Orthodox, signed a statement calling on "our fellow Americans of all persuasions and groupings and on the administration to support the independence, integrity and freedom of Israel." Among the signers were Martin Luther King and Dr. Franklin Littell, president of Iowa Wesleyan College.

The Zionist Organization of America held a special meeting that was attended by New York area congressmen and Zionists. Representative Leonard Farbstein, a New York Democrat, told the group that the United States "must not permit the economically and morally bankrupt dictator . . . to destroy the only democracy in the Middle East—Israel." Synagogues rang with pro-Israel sermons that weekend too. Rabbi Edward T. Sandrow, president of the New York Board of Rabbis, declared that Egypt, Syria and other Arab nations were intent to carry out a "nefarious plan to destroy Israel." A "Salute to Israel" parade was held in Manhattan on Sunday and was attended by thousands.

Lyndon Johnson, the compleat politician, was not likely surprised by this powerful outpouring of pro-Israel sentiments, but he certainly had to be impressed. The contrast was stark with the lack of support for his Vietnam policies. The latest casualty figures showed 2,929 Americans killed and wounded the previous week. And only that week, two senior senators, Republican Thruston B. Morton of Kentucky and Democrat Claiborne Pell of Rhode Island, had publicly criticized him, Pell going so far as to worry about the possible "start of a domestic clamor to use nuclear weapons. . . ."

One of Johnson's speech writers, Ben J. Wattenberg, whose parents had moved to the United States from Palestine, was a strong supporter of the Jewish state and encouraged him in a memorandum to profit by the connection between the Middle East and Vietnam. "It is an irony, but a fact, that many of the Vietnam doves are hawks on Aqaba," Wattenberg wrote. "As your position in the Mideast has been firm and resolute, you stand to be cheered now by those who were jeering last week. To some extent . . . the Mideast crisis can help turn around the 'other war'—the domestic dissatisfaction about Vietnam. It seems to me as if the Mideast situation brings Vietnam into true perspective and that there is a great bonus to you if that relation becomes clearer. I have discussed this with Walt Rostow and he agrees."

Congressmen were also letting their pro-Israel feelings become known by using the inside track to the President via Walt Rostow. Senator Jacob Javits, a Republican from New York, had called on Rostow during the weekend to seek news about the Middle East and to offer some advice. He suggested to the national security adviser that it would be "reassuring to the U.S. Jewish community" if Johnson would "have in some members of Congress with special interests in Israel for a briefing." In sending along Javits' request to the ranch, Rostow added: "There is great concern. Such a meeting might ease that concern."

Javits also called on Defense Secretary McNamara that weekend, seeking assurances that the United States had "forces available to deal with both Vietnam and whatever might be needed to be done in the Middle East." Javits received the assurances and then went to Rostow's office at the White House and made another pitch for a congressional meeting with the President.

Reporting these events to Johnson, Rostow wrote: "Javits believes it would stabilize the U.S. Jewish community in the protracted emotional crisis we face in the days ahead. As for himself he wishes you to know that he believes politics has no place in this crisis; that you have put the issue precisely right in your May 23 statement; it is not a question of supporting Israel but of supporting certain principles which go to the national interest."

While Javits' idea was a worthwhile one, a fastidious concern for American national interests would have dictated that persons be included in the presidential meeting who could speak for the Moslem side as well. It also would have involved the inclusion of nonpartisans who could transcend an emotional commitment to one side or the other and view the crisis with a cooler eye toward where lay justice and legitimate U.S. interests. But so pervasive was the pro-Israel, anti-Arab atmosphere in the United States, and the influence of that atmosphere on Johnson, that the President unhesitatingly agreed to Javits' suggestion. "We'll set a date as soon as we get back," the President messaged Rostow.

HUSSEIN EMBRACES NASSER

On the same day, May 30, that Lyndon Johnson was returning to Washington, King Hussein of Jordan was on his way to Cairo to see his longtime enemy Gamal Abdel Nasser.

Hussein had decided that the time had come to invoke an Arab proverb: "I and my brother will fight our cousin but I, my brother and our cousin will fight the outsider." Hussein's decision had been motivated by a speech that Nasser gave before the National Assembly in Cairo on May 29 in which, while ruling out the initiation of war, he said: "Now, eleven years after 1956 we are restoring things to what they were in 1956. . . . The issue now at hand is not the Gulf of Aqaba, the Straits of Tiran or the withdrawal of UNEF, but the rights of the Palestinian people."

Increasingly, as Israel's hardliners had feared, Nasser was turning the crisis away from the narrow issue of the straits and toward the question of the legitimacy of the Jewish state itself. It was an issue far graver and more threatening to Israel than all of Nasser's troops in the Sinai. For if the grievances caused the Palestinians by the creation of Israel were to be redressed, the integrity of Israel would be in doubt. As Abba Eban later commented in his memoirs, Nasser's speech "took the conflict far back beyond the maritime context to place the question mark squarely on Israel's survival." From Israel's viewpoint, it was an attack on its jugular.

After listening to Nasser's speech, Hussein had summoned the Egyptian ambassador and told him that the time had come for Jordan and Egypt to set aside their differences and "coordinate means of defense against the Israeli threat." The next day the king, dressed in a slate-blue pilot's uniform, flew his own airplane to Cairo and was embraced by Nasser as "great brother." The two rulers wasted no time. They immediately signed a mutual-defense treaty like the one existing between Egypt and Syria. Its Article 1 declared that "any attack on either state" would be considered "an attack on both." Article 7 stipulated that "in the event of military operations starting, the Chief of Staff of the Armed Forces of the United Arab Republic shall assume command of operations in both states."

At a stroke, Nasser had added to his military machine, at least on paper, an elite force of fifty-five thousand soldiers and a small air force made up mainly of British-made subsonic Hawker Hunter fighter-bombers and a few U.S. F-104 interceptor jets. More important was the psychological victory. An old enemy had swallowed his pride and joined what was clearly becoming the winning side.

Hussein later explained that he had joined Nasser because "from every point of view we had no right nor could we decently justify a decision to stand aside in a cause in which the entire Arab world was determined unanimously to engage itself." That was another way of admitting the tremendous pressures he was being subjected to by other Arab states and, especially, the militant Palestinians who made up about half of his kingdom. Though he badly needed the Palestinians' support for the stability of his regime, he had continued to oppose guerrilla operations from his territory and he refused to accept units of the Palestine Liberation Army, the military arm of the PLO. PLA units were attached to the regular armies of Egypt, Iraq and Syria—but still not in Jordan. Hussein feared that PLA troops might be used to overthrow him so that Jordan could be turned into a Palestinian state.

Although Hussein's concern was a serious one, the fact was that the Palestine Liberation Army remained so ineffective as a fighting force against Israel that nearly two years after it had been formed National Security Adviser Rostow had still not heard of it. It was only on September 14, 1966, that the organization came to Rostow's attention when Representative Herbert Tenzer, the only Orthodox Jew in Congress, mentioned the "Palestine Liberation Front" in a memorandum. Rostow underlined the name and scrawled at the bottom of the memorandum: "What the hell is it?"

Five days later the CIA was able to tell him that it was called the Palestine Liberation Army and that "thus far this 'army' essentially exists only on paper." The intelligence agency reported that the PLA had an estimated eight thousand men attached to Arab armies. But, it added, "The PLA does not presently threaten Israel . . . and has not been involved in incidents along the Israeli border. . . ."

Congressman Tenzer's purpose in mentioning the PLA had been to equate it with the Viet Cong and thereby earn support among Jewish Americans for Johnson's policies in Vietnam. But Rostow discouraged this comparison. In an internal memorandum, he wrote: "I assume Tenzer's line would be that the PLA is a potential Middle Eastern Viet Cong and that friends of Israel should back the U.S. in Vietnam because Israel may face a similar threat one day. The analogy . . . is inaccurate. It's now largely a paper organization struggling for status. . . . It is not now a threat to Israel.

"We and the Israelis have tried to block recognition, hoping the PLO will die from lack of support. To have any group, even domestically in the U.S., repeatedly referring to the PLA as a going concern and a serious threat gives it status which it doesn't deserve and shouldn't achieve. . . . Strictly from the viewpoint of persuading American Jews to back us in Vietnam, there might be some virtue in privately taking the line Congressman Tenzer proposes. Moreover, any thoughtful friend of Israel might reasonably worry about the potential of the PLO. However, on balance, I don't think it helps either from Israel's viewpoint or ours to play up this angle."

King Hussein left Cairo on May 30, the same day he signed the mutual-defense pact. With him was PLO chieftain Ahmed Shukairy, who had attended the ceremony in Nasser's office at the ornate Qubba Palace, a former residence of deposed King Farouk. All through the year, Shukairy had been calling for Hussein's overthrow, saying, for instance: "The primary struggle is against the tyrant of Amman, Hussein, who has betrayed God, the Prophet, and the Palestine cause." Now they were brothers in the struggle against a common enemy.

The pact, and his reconciliation with Shukairy, brought instant popularity to Hussein.* When he and the PLO chieftain arrived in Amman that Tuesday afternoon they were greeted by large crowds of cheering supporters. The Cairo ceremony had been broadcast on Jordan's official radio and the announcer had expressed the emotions of many Jordanians when he declared: "This is an historic moment. The Arab nation today marches under the leadership of Hussein and Nasser."

From being a pariah, the object of assassination attempts and plots to overthrow him, Hussein in an instant had become a hero. Once again he had

* It also brought him the assurance that shipping to Jordan's only port at Aqaba, adjacent to Israel's Elath harbor, would be able to transit the Egyptian-controlled Straits of Tiran. If he had remained in conflict with Nasser, the Egyptians were perfectly capable of closing the straits to Jordanian as well as Israeli shipping.

demonstrated the political agility that had kept him in power for fourteen years. But this time he was going to pay dearly for his cleverness.

Hussein's unexpected alliance with Nasser came as another stunning triumph for the Egyptian leader. Everything seemed to be going his way. He not only had regained his high prestige and what he had lost in 1956 but even old enemies like Hussein were joining his cause and he again was the leader of that elusive entity called the Arab nation. Beyond that, he had just had assurances that the Soviet Union stood solidly by Egypt and the Arabs. This was a significant development and he had openly bragged about it in his National Assembly speech on May 29. "The Soviet Union stands with us in this battle and will not allow any country to interfere. This is the stand we have been hoping for."

Nasser's announcement meant that Egypt could count on Russia as a counterbalance to America's support for Israel, that Egypt too had a powerful friend ready to help. In the precarious equation of the balance of forces in the Middle East, that represented an assurance that Egypt could not be destroyed.

The only problem was that Moscow had given no such pledge, although Nasser did not know that yet.

The misunderstanding had resulted from a report by his defense minister, Shamseddin Badran. Badran had returned to Cairo the day before Nasser's boast to the National Assembly from a three-day visit to Moscow and had reported that the Russians were ready to back Egypt the whole way. In fact, the Soviets had been extremely careful in urging restraint. Premier Kosygin had told Badran during the visit that "you have achieved your point of view, so it is time now to compromise, to work politically." The message should have been clear. The Russians did not want a war.

But at the airport, as Badran was about to fly back to Cairo, he and Defense Minister Marshal Andrei A. Grechko were chatting when Grechko remarked: "Stand firm. Whatever you have to face, you will find us with you. Don't let yourselves be blackmailed by the Americans or anyone else."

Badran, a militant who was as anxious for war as the Israeli generals and who had been urging that Egypt attack first, preferred to report Grechko's remarks back to Nasser rather than the considered and cautious advice given by Kosygin.

The Egyptian ambassador to the Soviet Union, Murad Ghaleb, had been standing with the two men when Grechko made his remarks. After Badran's plane took off, Ghaleb turned to the defense minister and said: "That was very reassuring, Marshal." With a laugh, Grechko replied: "I just wanted to give him one for the road."

Ghaleb, realizing that Badran may have been misled by Grechko's spontaneous remarks, reported the exchange and his reservations about its seriousness to Nasser. But his report became snagged in Egypt's stifling bureaucracy and Nasser did not receive it until after war had erupted. By then it was too late.

The Egyptian-Jordanian mutual-defense pact caused another spasm of anxiety in Israel and tended to undermine the government's decision to postpone war. The country was already like a "coiled spring," Eban had remarked Tuesday morning before Hussein's arrival in Cairo. Now it was wound up so tight it was near snapping.

There was talk among Israelis about Egypt's bombers and even poison gas. Casualties in Israel alone, it was feared, might reach forty thousand. Rabbis were consecrating parks and gardens so they could be used as emergency cemeteries. Miles of nylon sheeting for wrapping bodies were being stockpiled, two yards for each, along with coffin boards, shovels and plaques.

As soon as Levi Eshkol learned of Hussein's action, he met with Eban and together they decided the new situation demanded prompt action. Their foremost concern remained nailing down Washington's intentions and the depth of its support.

Their confusion about U.S. policy was understandable. It resulted not from a lack of access to the Administration but from an excess. Despite the imposition by Johnson of a tight veil of secrecy over the Administration's deliberations since the start of the crisis, there were so many friends of Israel now counseling the embassy in Washington that it was getting too much information. It had become almost impossible to separate official policy from the private ideas and wishful thinking of Israel's numerous supporters. These included such officials as Associate Supreme Court Justice Abe Fortas, who was acting as a back channel between the White House and the Israeli Embassy.

Confusion was sown by conflicting messages. Walt Rostow only two days earlier had told Ambassador Avraham Harman that President Johnson could see no resolution of the crisis. And on the same morning that Hussein flew to Cairo, a cable from Harman arrived in Jerusalem saying he had been informed by some unidentified source that the State Department was drafting a declaration for eighty maritime powers to sign but that it would contain no mention of the use of force to open the straits. Instead, Israel would be offered compensation in order to pay for the heavy costs of keeping its reserve army mobilized.

In addition, *The New York Times* in its May 30 edition reported on its front page a story by John Finney that Washington was ready to compromise at Israel's expense by backing a plan to allow all ships to pass through the straits except those flying the Israeli flag. The report brought charges from Israel's supporters that the Administration was deserting Israel. In the event it turned out to be false and prompted both Dean Rusk and Walt Rostow to lodge complaints with the *Times* about the "injustice and inaccuracy of the story." The next day rumors began spreading in Washington that a U.S. warship was about to be sent through the straits, causing Defense Secretary McNamara publicly to deny it.

These stories may have been innocently based on bad information or they may have been planted by any of the various contenders in the crisis in order to smoke out the Administration's real intentions. Whatever their source, they succeeded in adding to the confusion about Administration policy.

Eshkol and Eban decided that the only way to penetrate this cloud of confusion was to send spymaster Meir Amit, the head of the Mossad, to Washington for a personal evaluation of U.S. policy. Using an assumed name, Amit left Israel by commercial airline on May 30, just hours after Hussein's Cairo visit.

Amit, a sabra and a retired army officer, was extremely close to Eshkol and on occasion saw him several times a day. The day before leaving for Washington he met with the prime minister three times. He was also one of the leading hardliners who believed that Israel's security was gravely threatened by Soviet plans to move into the southwest section of the Arabian Peninsula and greatly feared the possibility that Moscow would succeed in forging unity among the socialist Arab states. It had been essentially his views that were reflected in the alarming intelligence estimates to Washington about Soviet intentions over the past year.

Amit later explained the purpose of his trip. "The American intentions were not clear. . . . I believed that I could fathom their real intentions, and I succeeded in this."

Eshkol and Eban also drafted an urgent letter under Eshkol's name that day to Johnson. They warned that "a point is being approached at which counsels to Israel will lack any moral or logical basis. . . . President Nasser's rising prestige has already had serious effects in Jordan. . . . The time is ripe for confronting Nasser with a more intense and effective policy of resistance.

"I feel that I must make it clear in all candor that the continuation of this position for any considerable time is out of the question. . . . It is crucial that the international naval escort should move through the straits within a week or two."

President Johnson and his top aides grasped at the phrase "a week or two" and optimistically interpreted it to mean that Washington had two more weeks in which to seek a solution before Israel would attack. "This judgment was strengthened by information from other diplomatic sources," Johnson later admitted in his memoirs, though he did not identify those sources.

By now, however, the Israelis were not only confused about Washington's policy but they were becoming suspicious that Johnson was softening his stand and getting ready to accept a compromise solution. This suspicion was reinforced on May 31 when the President received Eshkol's letter and became angry at the wording of one of its sentences, which claimed that the United States had given assurances to open the straits by "any and all measures." This was beyond the President's constitutional authority and he ordered Walt Rostow to call in Eppy Evron and inform him that Israel did not have a blank check from the Administration. When Evron heard Rostow's complaint, he warned that his government would consider Johnson's caveat a weakening of American resolve.

But it was about as much as Johnson could pledge. His problem remained the widespread opposition to the escalating violence of the war in Vietnam, where day after day the slaughter continued with numbing monotony. His weakness was implicitly acknowledged in a memorandum from Bob McNamara: "While it is true that many congressional Vietnam doves may be in the process of conversion to [Israeli] hawks . . . an effort to get a meaningful resolution from the Congress runs the risk of becoming bogged down in acrimonious dispute." That Johnson was well aware of.

The Israelis were also made suspicious by the sudden dispatch to Cairo of an old Middle East hand. Charles W. Yost had retired from the State Department the previous year after a distinguished career that had included postings as ambassador to both Morocco and Syria and now he was called on to fly to Egypt as a special presidential envoy. With Ambassador-designate Nolte essentially sidelined because he had still not been able to present his credentials, and the Egyptians showing no urgency in accrediting him, Luke Battle felt that Washington badly needed someone who could have diplomatic access. Yost was an old friend of Egyptian Foreign Minister Mahmoud Riad and he was given the assignment.

In addition to Yost, Robert B. Anderson, secretary of the treasury during

177

the Eisenhower Administration, was also in Cairo working behind the scenes on Nasser. He was well suited for this clandestine role. It was Anderson who had undertaken a highly secret peace mission for Eisenhower in 1956 in the Middle East. He had shuttled between Egypt and Israel conferring with Nasser and Ben Gurion to try to find a solution to the conflict, but neither leader was willing to make serious compromises and nothing came of the ambitious scheme. Now in private business, Anderson had better entrée to Nasser than any of the U.S. diplomats on the scene and the State Department used him to get to the Egyptian leader.

Working with the belief that both sides would take no violent action for the next two weeks, Anderson seemed to be making significant headway in Cairo. He met secretly with Nasser on June 1 for a long review of the crisis. Anderson found the Egyptian leader dressed in sports clothes, relaxed, friendly and confident.

In a long EYES ONLY cable to the President and the secretary of state, Anderson reported that "Nasser expressed keen desire to have friendship of American people and American govt, explaining that under no circumstances was he a Communist.... He felt that U.S. policy was motivated largely by the large Jewish vote in U.S. and that American govt would be reluctant to oppose this voting strength."

Anderson wrote that Nasser had pointed out that the Arab countries stretched from Morocco to the Persian Gulf, and that in the present crisis he had the support of all these countries plus Pakistan, India and other nations. "He did not see how a minority in the U.S. could influence U.S. policy to oppose what such a vast region and such large numbers of people believed proper," Anderson wrote.

He added that he had replied by explaining that "U.S. govt was not motivated by political considerations but was concerned essentially in maintaining peace and the integrity of countries." Anderson did not report Nasser's reaction to this statement. Instead, Anderson went on to report that Nasser said he found American actions "oriented toward Israel and not toward the Arab point of view. He kept reassuring me that he was not going to start a war. ..."

Nonetheless, Nasser made it clear that he was determined to maintain the blockade of the Straits of Tiran to Israeli shipping. "He proposed merely to return to the status of 1956 which had been at least tolerated by all the nations for eight years," Anderson wrote.

He reported he had asked Nasser what types of shipping would be blockaded and the Egyptian had replied, "'Israeli ships, oil or any refined products and arms for Israel.' Here he stated that all countries claimed territorial waters to a greater distance offshore than he was asserting and further that he was at war with Israel and had been since 1948. . . ." When asked whether he would accept adjudication of the dispute by the World Court, Nasser said he would consult his legal advisers. Anderson added: "He did not rule out completely possibility of a World Court review if it could be done speedily."

Anderson summarized his impressions of Nasser's position by noting that any effort to open the straits would be regarded by the Egyptian leader as an act of aggression. "He stated that his target system was prepared and that this time he would be ready. . . . He seemed confident . . . of his military capability."

In a personal aside, Anderson informed Lyndon Johnson that before traveling to Cairo he had spent three days in Beirut where he had met a wide spectrum of Arabs. "They are people who are generally moderate and have a tendency to oppose Nasser. At this time they were all applauding Nasser's actions, insisting on the closing of the Gulf of Aqaba and taking a position that the U.S. was supporting a minority for political purposes. I am impressed more because of the quality of the people who made these assertions than the fact that they were made." He recommended that Washington avoid taking actions that "could be construed as favoring Israeli cause."

Anderson's amiable meeting with Nasser signaled to Washington that a breakthrough had been achieved in the crisis. This impression was strongly reinforced by Nasser's agreement to send his vice president, Zacharia Mohieddin, to Washington for talks on ways to resolve the dispute.

Anderson noted in his report that Nasser "seemed anxious to have Mohieddin explain his position directly to U.S. govt and said he hoped we would take the long view. . . ." It was agreed that Mohieddin would discuss the issues with President Johnson in Washington on June 7.

Thus, with the Israeli indication that it would not attack for two weeks, the Administration now thought it had maneuvered both sides in such a way that there would be abundant time to try to find a peaceful solution. From Washington's viewpoint, its diplomacy was working.

But neither Egypt nor Israel was as sanguine as Washington. From Israel's viewpoint, the last thing officials there wanted to see was a compromise solution worked out between Cairo and Washington. Compromise could only mean to Israel losing at least some fraction of the gains it had achieved in the 1956 war. Thus Israel was disturbed to get notification of Mohieddin's pending trip from Luke Battle. He realized the danger in sharing this information but believed that there were so many Israeli supporters in the government that Tel Aviv would learn of it in any case. Battle calculated that the State Department might as well demonstrate its openness by officially informing Tel Aviv. But he worried that Israel might take action to preempt the trip which, if successful, would greatly add to Nasser's prestige.

On his side, Nasser was made even more suspicious of U.S. intentions on the same day he agreed to Mohieddin's trip when the U.S. aircraft carrier *Intrepid* sailed through the Suez Canal with its planes lined on deck.*

The *Intrepid*'s passage was interpreted in Egypt as American muscle flexing and small crowds of Egyptians lined the canal cursing the ship and angrily waving shoes at it. In fact, both McNamara and Rusk had agreed three days earlier that the carrier should get out of the Mediterranean and in a position to go to Vietnam in case the canal became blocked. In their haste to get the carrier east of Suez they apparently gave no thought to how provocative the warship's passage through Egypt's canal would appear to the Egyptians.

Despite his suspicions of U.S. policy, Nasser replied on June 2 to Johnson's May 22 letter. It was a long message rehashing much of what he had told Anderson the day before, adding that "I am convinced that any joint endeavor on our part to establish communication of thought might at least contribute to dissipate part of the artificial clouds intended to depict the exercise of right as a sin and the right of defense as aggression." After a review of the history of the Arab-Israeli conflict, Nasser observed: "Whatever our attempts to divide the aspects of the problem, it is imperative in the end that we return to the origin and fundamentals, namely the right of the Palestinian people to return to their homeland, and the responsibility of the international community in securing the exercise of this right."

He concluded by warmly accepting Johnson's offer, long since apparently forgotten in Washington, to send Hubert Humphrey to the region and said the Vice President would be "welcome at any time."

Fateful events were also taking place during this period inside Israel. On June 1, Abba Eban, who had exercised a strong restraining influence on the impatient generals, finally gave in to the war mood and the political opposition building up against him. He held a meeting in the morning in Tel Aviv with Rabin and Yariv and told them, according to his memoirs, that "I no

* It may have been whispers about the *Intrepid*'s passage through the canal that had sparked the rumors at the end of the month that a warship was about to penetrate the Straits of Tiran.

longer had any political inhibitions to such military resistance as was deemed feasible, necessary and effective. . . ." His agreement to wage war removed a major obstacle that had been holding back the generals. "I had lived with the knowledge that if I withdrew my inhibiting hand, military resistance . . . would become certain."

Eban's conversion had resulted from a number of factors, not the least of them being Nasser's soaring prestige and Anderson's meeting in Cairo with Nasser. Although the meeting had been held in the utmost secrecy, the Israeli government had learned of it even before Battle's notification of its result.

As Eban recalled in his memoirs: "It was probable that this initiative would aim at a face-saving compromise—and that the face to be saved would be Nasser's, not Israel's. For us the importance of denying Nasser political and psychological victory had become no less important than the concrete interest involved in the issue of navigation."

Further, the mutual-defense treaty between Amman and Cairo not only heightened Nasser's prestige but it was widely perceived as a grave threat to Israel, though in reality it would take months of coordination and training for the pact's unified command to become a serious military factor. But it was words and symbols as much as actions that were now guiding the policies of the Arabs and Israel, and the one thing the Arabs were not short of was verbiage. Typical of their heated rhetoric in this period were the words of Iraqi President Abdel Rahman Aref, who declared in a radio address on June 1: "Brethren and sons, this is the day of the battle to avenge our martyred brethren who fell in 1948. It is the day to wash away the stigma. We shall, God willing, meet in Tel Aviv and Haifa."

On the same day, the PLO's Shukairy gave a news interview in Jordanian Jerusalem and was asked what would happen to the Israelis if there was a war and the Arabs won. He replied:

"Those who survive will remain in Palestine. I estimate that none of them will survive."

Beyond such Arab bombast, heightened by the war nerves gripping the country, Eban was now receiving reports that Meir Amit began sending back from Washington on May 31. His first report, received June 1, said that "there is a growing chance for American political backing if we act on our own." How he came to that conclusion is not certain since he held no meetings at the State Department and apparently confined himself to sessions at the Pentagon and the CIA as well as with Israel's friends. In Israel it was assumed that he had privately been given the go-ahead during his talks with Helms and McNamara, but both men later strongly denied that.

Amit also reported: "From hints and scattered facts that I have heard, I get the impression that the maritime force project is running into heavier water every hour." Nonetheless, he urged that Israel wait for several days before launching war in order to give the maritime plan a chance to force the straits. But increasingly the nations of the world were showing little interest in the idea.

Amit's report was reinforced by a high-level intelligence assessment that Eban received in the late afternoon on June 1. The mysterious report came from what Eban described as "an American, known for his close contact with government thinking." The person has never been further identified, but his comments brought optimism to Eban. The American source had concluded that because of Israel's earlier show of caution that "if the measures being taken by the United States prove ineffective, the United States would now back Israel."

The report had a "decisive effect on my attitude," Eban wrote later. He thought that it was particularly interesting because it contained no "exhortation to us to stay our hand much longer. Our restraint in the past was strongly praised; its continuation in the future was not suggested."

Eban was intrigued. Was the United States now resigned to seeing Israel go it alone? He ordered a meticulous scrutiny of all cables and records of conversations that had taken place with U.S. officials over the past forty-eight hours. "It emerged that [during that period] no responsible American leader had assumed the authority to urge Israel to wait for any length of time or to place excessive reliance on international action. . . ."

Finally, Eban was as susceptible to the country's war emotions and the aggressive desires of the generals as was Eshkol. The pressures were intense, particularly from Ezer Weizman and other activists.

Weizman lost no chance to press his excited belief that Israel should attack immediately. In the last days of May he repeatedly urged action. In one meeting with Eshkol he declared: "The strongest army since King David's is at your command. Order that army to march and you will become known as the conqueror in the war for the survival of Israel. If you do not . . . you will bring the total annihilation of the Third Jewish State." Such forceful words with their emotional appeal to tribal history strongly contributed to the sense of urgency gripping Israeli leaders.

At another time, after attending one of the endless and inconclusive Cabinet meetings, Weizman became so frustrated at the ministers' indecisiveness that he stormed out of the room and went into an anteroom where he tore his general's insignia from his left shoulder and threw them on a table. The scene was witnessed by several officials and the story of Weizman's gesture quickly circulated around the country, adding to the by now widely held impression that Eshkol was dithering and incapable of taking decisive action.

Weizman's views closely reflected those at Central Command headquarters in Tel Aviv. One day Weizman found the commander, Brigadier General Uzi Narkiss, walking around "in a constant state of excitement." Narkiss and Amos Horev, a professional soldier who later became quartermaster-general and head of Technion, the prestigious Institute of Technology in Haifa, were anxious for war. Weizman later wrote that both men " 'worked' on me: 'This is the great opportunity to do something terrific to the Jordanians! We mustn't miss it!' I asked Amos, 'What do you think is the best break-through route in Sinai?' He replied, 'The solution to reopening the straits is . . . to liberate Jerusalem and the West Bank.' "

On Thursday evening, June 1, Levi Eshkol, worn down by the unrelenting arguments, threats of resignation, biting personal attacks about his indecisive leadership and his lack of military experience, finally bowed to his growing list of critics and surrendered the Ministry of Defense to Moshe Dayan. It was one of the most difficult and humiliating moments of his life and he had not succumbed easily.

No doubt bearing strongly on his decision was the unhappiness of the generals. He was fully aware that his military leaders were impatient to the point of despair—if not yet open revolt, which some observers believed was close. British journalist and BBC commentator Jon Kimche wrote: ". . . there was no doubt at the time that a number of leading army commanders and staff officers would not have stood by idly if the composition of the Eshkol Government had not been changed and if no action had been taken in the face of the gathering Arab storm. . . . In the case of Dayan, it was the fear of an army coup, however formulated, that forced [Eshkol's] hand."

A White House worker with close ties to Israel also later reported in a memorandum that reached Walt Rostow that "a senior [Israeli] general told me that army discontent with Eshkol's leadership was so strong that it might have become overt in some form had Dayan not been appointed."

Weizman later touched on the issue, denying the possibility of a coup but at the same time confirming that the generals had not been ready to sit by idly too much longer. "There were disagreements in the General Staff about how long to 'give' the government to try out all the possibilities of a political settlement for the crisis," he later wrote. "Not that anyone thought of acting in defiance of the government. . . ."

In his desperation to retain the defense post, Eshkol had first offered Dayan the largely empty position of deputy prime minister, and then, when the one-eyed general had turned that down, the command of the southern forces in the Negev. Dayan promptly accepted but by now his popularity was so high and the mood of the country so extreme that demonstrations broke out in Tel Aviv protesting Eshkol's self-serving move. A petition to make Dayan defense minister, aimed at getting a thousand signatures, quickly garnered twenty thousand. It was clear that for Eshkol's government to survive the prime minister could make no lesser gesture than handing over the defense post to Dayan.

At the same time, Eshkol officially broadened his coalition by making it a government of national unity. Menachem Begin and another nationalist, Yosef Saphir, were brought into the Cabinet as ministers without portfolio. It was a momentous move in terms of Israeli domestic politics. For the first time Begin, who had spent his career in the political wilderness, had been accepted as a legitimate member of the government. In the crucial days and months ahead, Begin's uncompromising views would lend powerful support to the nation's hardliners.

Now the internal fighting within Israel was finally resolved. Attention could focus exclusively on the war Israel was about to launch.

The spy ship U.S.S. *Liberty* by now was in Rota, Spain, taking on fuel and provisions for an extended tour along the coastlines of the Middle East. It had arrived on May 31. On June 2, it left, passing three Soviet ships at the Strait of Gibraltar, and sailed toward the eastern Mediterranean. Its mission was obvious to any experienced eye because of the extraordinary number of antennas sticking out from its superstructure. There were forty-five antennas, giving the ship the ability to pick up any kind of electronic communication within many miles.

Less impressive were its armaments, only four .50-caliber Browning machine guns and a scattering of small arms. The reason for the light armaments was that the Navy considered *Liberty* a noncombatant. Its 292-man crew was made up largely of technicians assigned to the Naval Security Group, the cryptologic arm of the Navy. The *Liberty*'s only function was to listen in on foreign communications and send them back to Fort George G.

Meade, Maryland, the headquarters of the National Security Agency, America's highly secret communications spying organization.

Apparently unanticipated by the Navy was the possibility that some nations might take extreme exception to having their communications monitored. They might consider the *Liberty* very much a combatant.

XIV
ISRAEL DECIDES ON WAR

At about 11 A.M. Friday, June 2, Israeli Embassy Minister Eppy Evron called on his friend Walt Rostow in the White House. He said he was not speaking officially and merely wanted to pose some hypothetical questions. Left unsaid was that they were questions designed to determine the true attitude of the Administration toward a first strike by Israel.

What, he asked, would the United States do if Israel tried to force the straits' blockade, was fired upon and then attacked Sharm el Sheikh? Would the United States consider this a legitimate act of self-defense? He emphasized that the 1957 U.S. commitment on the straits, and Israel's understanding of it, consisted of not one but two parts: first, a U.S. pledge to assert the rights of free passage through the straits; and second, an explicit acknowledgment of Israel's right to use force to protect its free passage.

He offered the intriguing opinion that it might be better for U.S. interests in the region and in its relations with the Soviet Union if Israel acted on its own without involving the United States. He asked what would be the U.S. reaction if the Soviets intervened? Rostow said he would check with Johnson, an answer that may have implied to Evron U.S. acquiescence in an Israeli first strike.

What Evron was seeking was confirmation of the report of Eban's unidentified American source that Washington would not protest too much if Israel went to war. It was a crucial question for the Israeli government, the only issue that by now was still holding the country back from launching a war. Realistically, it could do that only with the knowledge that it had

America's backing. U.S. support was essential, both during the war to counterbalance the Soviet Union and after the war to support its diplomatic position to retain whatever gains it achieved.

To determine the depth and nature of U.S. support, the Israeli Embassy that June 2 had deployed its formidable resources. In addition to Evron's "unofficial" meeting with Rostow and spymaster Meir Amit's clandestine circulating around Washington, Ambassador Harman was active too in probing the U.S. government.

Harman was returning to Israel that day for urgent consultations, which no one could doubt involved the basic question of war or peace, and before leaving he met with Dean Rusk. The secretary of state had little outwardly to offer. The Administration was so involved in Vietnam, so weak domestically, and so preoccupied with how to gain political support that it had no serious new ideas how to resolve the dispute in the far-off Middle East. In American eyes, compromise increasingly seemed to be the only way out.

This view was reinforced by a study of the Joint Chiefs of Staff which showed that critics like Senators Fulbright and Symington after all were right: the U.S. could not fight two wars. The study observed that there would be enormous problems involved in trying to force open the straits. A memorandum written June 2 for the secretary of defense noted that if Egypt resisted "we must be prepared to conduct strikes against the UAR ranging from discriminating air and naval attacks against selected military targets to full-scale airstrikes against all UAR military targets." Yet, the memo conceded, it would take a month to get adequate forces to the area and then it would be at the expense of other commands. U.S. forces east of Suez could be used, the study concluded, but they were limited and "the capability of these forces to prevail, if attacked by major UAR forces, is doubtful." It was not a bright outlook and made the idea of a compromise all the more attractive.

Rusk had received further encouragement for compromise from Charles Yost. The veteran diplomat had sent a somber report on his findings in Cairo on the same day as the secretary of state's meeting with Harman. It offered little hope that there could be a U.S. resolution of the crisis.

"There is unanimity among observers I have seen here that UARG [United Arab Republic Government] at this point cannot and will not relax position on closure Tiran Straits except as result overwhelming application of military force," Yost had cabled. "Opinion in other Arab countries seems practically unanimous in backing UAR on this issue. While this may appear in U.S. as 'aggression,' it is seen here as entirely legitimate restoration 1956 status quo which was upset by Israeli aggression. . . . Moreover, legal case is at least open to doubt.

"I have reluctantly come to conclusion that there is no prospect for success our present tactic of mobilizing maritime powers to reopen straits, except by exercise military force which would be out of proportion to real U.S. interests at stake. . . . If we pursue this tactic much further, I am afraid we may find ourselves in the same dead end as British and French in 1956."

This was a message of vital importance to Israel. And, if the network of supporters of Israel was working as efficiently as U.S. officials suspected, then the Israeli government probably soon saw a copy of Yost's cable, even though it was classified secret. Yost's conclusions were extremely alarming to Israel's cause, since they confirmed Israeli fears that some U.S. officials were starting to believe that a compromise was needed to achieve a solution to the crisis. That would leave Nasser with his prestige at an all-time high and, worse, it would leave Israel shorn of its 1956 gains and seeming weak and irresolute. Under no circumstances could that be allowed.

"While I realize very great importance Israel attaches to keeping straits open, I cannot believe this is vital to Israel's existence, especially recalling that straits were closed prior to 1957," Yost wrote. "Gain to Nasser's prestige resulting from this victory will be unfortunate and troublesome but post facto attempts by either great powers or Israel to reverse it are more likely to prolong than to curtail his currently resurrected leadership of Arab world."

The best Yost could suggest, which in the circumstances was an objective reading of how to protect U.S. interests—but not Israeli interests—was to propose that Washington should "concentrate on limiting damage. . . ." This emerging line of thinking made it all the more urgent for Israel to determine the worth of the U.S. commitment and to move quickly.

As Ambassador Harman subtly probed this sensitive issue that Friday, the best that Rusk could offer was to review for him U.S. policy and the status of current U.S. efforts. It was not an inspiring litany. America was seeking international support in the United Nations, so far unsuccessfully. It was having only limited success in acquiring backing in the world community to form a multinational armada to test the blockade; the legal issue of the straits was too cloudy, the emotional grievances of the Palestinians and the Jews too compelling and contradictory, and the political issue too explosive for most countries to do more than procrastinate while the superpowers postured and tried to sort out their interests. Nothing had been firmly decided, Rusk reportedly admitted to Harman at the end of their meeting.

There could have been no doubt to the observant ambassador that U.S policy was essentially bankrupt from Israel's viewpoint. More than that, it could turn inimical if the pending visit of Egyptian Vice President Mohieddin should achieve the unlikely by resulting in a compromise solution. Even if that did not happen, none of the American projects, in fact, was showing any serious promise to resolve the crisis in a way advantageous to Israel, certainly not in a manner tolerable either to Israel's anxieties or its ambitions.

Before the end of June 2, Harman and his two colleagues, Evron and Amit, had managed to accomplish, like Eban only the week before, what representatives of probably no other country, not NATO allies and certainly no Arab country, could have done during a similar period. With almost no advance scheduling, they had personal audiences with all of America's top security and foreign affairs officials in a matter of hours. They had personally talked with the secretary of state, the secretary of defense, the head of the Central Intelligence Agency, the President's national security adviser and many others.

At the end of their heroic efforts, the Israelis could not have failed to realize, even if they somehow remained unaware of Yost's cable, that Israeli and U.S. interests had reached a divide. No matter how discreet and diplomatic the comments of U.S. officials, they finally had to reveal, explicitly or implicitly, that the Johnson Administration had no solution beyond a compromise. At the least it wanted a resolution that would not further erode its ebbing support in Congress and in the Arab world. It did not want a war. Yet it had no serious idea how to make Nasser back down.

This was intolerable for Israel. It urgently needed a release from its apprehensions and a halt to the drain on its economy and its own self-image as a strong and independent nation.

Harman and Amit flew back to Israel immediately after the ambassador's meeting with Rusk to report personally their findings. Eshkol, Allon, Dayan and Rabin had secretly agreed among themselves on that same day that Israel would not go to war before Monday, June 5. This was a convoluted way of saying it was likely to go to war on that day. But by phrasing the decision negatively, Eshkol assured that no action would be taken before hearing from Harman and Amit and yet pacified his impatient generals. As Rabin later wrote: "If we were really down to two days before H hour, there was little cause for complaint."

The waiting period would give time for the Cabinet to meet on June 4 and receive a full briefing about what Amit and Harman had learned of the mood in Washington. Largely on the basis of the Cabinet's reading of America's real intentions—as opposed to what Johnson and Rusk were saying officially in public—would the formal determination be made on setting the exact time for war.

With Amit's departure, and other information at his disposal, the CIA's Helms wrote a letter to President Johnson warning him that Israel would probably start a war in several days. Helms sent the letter as a personal EYES ONLY message, thereby avoiding normal official channels, which were less secure. Helms felt comfortable with his prediction because Amit had confided in him that his instant return to Israel would mean the decision for war had been taken. The plumbing of information worked for both sides.

On June 3, Rusk sent a circular telegram to the U.S. ambassadors in Arab capitals saying the situation was "as complex and as dangerous as any we have faced." He then warned that no one "should assume the United States could hold back Israel," in the words of the State Department's administrative history of the crisis. It added:

"[Rusk] commented that the 'holy war' psychology of the Arabs was matched by an apocalyptic psychology within Israel, and the United States should not assume Israel could be ordered not to fight in defense of its interests."

Also on Saturday, the day after Amit and Harman flew off to Israel, Lyndon Johnson traveled to New York to deliver a speech at a Democratic Party fund-raising dinner. Drafting of the speech had caused some problems within the White House. John Roche had worked on it and when Hal Saunders saw the result he fired off a letter of protest to Walt Rostow.

"As now written, it is a 100% pro-Israel speech," Saunders wrote. "I share Roche's emotional commitment to Israel, but I do not think we have to drop all our interests in the rest of the Middle East to fulfill it. It's not even in Israel's interest that we do that. Every step we take closer to Israel boosts Nasser one step higher on the Arab ladder."

Saunders' points were well taken, as usual, and in the end the Middle East section was dropped from the speech. But Johnson could not resist alluding to the crisis in extemporaneous remarks that June 3 Saturday night in the ballroom of the Americana Hotel in Manhattan. "America's determination is to preserve the peace," he said. "It is determined to preserve the territorial integrity of the nations involved in that area."

Although his comments were general and seemingly neutral, the audience was sure enough about his support for Israel that the phrase about territorial integrity was broadly interpreted as referring to Israel's security. His remarks were received with enthusiasm by the 1,650 diners, who included many members of New York's large and influential Jewish community. Such support was welcome to the President, who outside the hotel was being picketed by about fourteen hundred protesters of his Vietnam policy.

Johnson went from the Americana to the Waldorf-Astoria where he attended a $1,000-a-plate dinner dance closed to the press. It was sponsored by the President's Club of New York, the most potent source of LBJ's campaign funds. His close friend Arthur Krim was chairman of the club and got the proceedings under way by introducing Vice President Humphrey, who in turn introduced the President.

While at the table, Johnson was approached by Abe Feinberg, the wealthy fund raiser.* Leaning over the shoulder of Mathilde Krim, seated next to the President, Feinberg, who was close enough to the Israelis to know, whispered to Johnson: "Mr. President, it [Israel's attack] can't be held any longer. It's going to be within the next twenty-four hours." With Helms's warning still fresh, Johnson by now must have been getting the message. But it was information that was largely useless from a policy viewpoint. He had already done everything he could think of to deter Israel. Now he could only wait.

The President, his standing enhanced in the Jewish community by his New York appearances, returned to Washington that same night and was back in the White House by 1:30 A.M. It was, in his view, a day well spent. True, there had been anti-Vietnam war pickets. But there had also been strong applause for his Middle East policy.

Amit and Harman had arrived back in Israel on Saturday and that night they went to Prime Minister Eshkol's Jerusalem home. Also there were

* So powerful was Feinberg in national politics that his help and advice were sought by representatives of all factions of the Democratic Party, including Senator Robert Kennedy, no friend of Johnson's—and a potential rival for the Democratic presidential nomination in 1968. Kennedy was also attending the dinner dance that night and approached Feinberg for assistance. He asked him to get together a group of contributors and politicians at Feinberg's apartment for the following day. Feinberg replied: "Bobby, the President of the United States is running this operation."

Kennedy said: "Well, I could go over your head and get them myself."

"And you can also go fuck yourself," replied Feinberg. "I'm going to listen to the President of the United States and not to you."

Allon, Dayan, Eban and several others. The reports of Amit and Harman were in accord with the intelligence report from the unnamed American that Eban had received earlier. It appeared that America would not oppose an Israeli first strike.

"We were unanimous in our interpretation of the position in Washington," Eban later wrote. "It was now clear that the United States was not going to be able to involve itself unilaterally or multilaterally in any enforcement action within a period relevant to our plight. But we all felt that if Israel found means of breaking out of the siege and blockade, the United States would not now take a hostile position."

The small but powerful group decided that night to recommend formally to the Cabinet the next day that Israel go to war.

A letter from Johnson, sent that Saturday and perhaps prompted by Helms's warning of imminent war, apparently had no influence on their decision. Johnson once again had pledged his support, but he also cautioned that "our leadership is unanimous that the United States should not move in isolation." He also warned once again: "I must emphasize the necessity for Israel not to make itself responsible for the initiation of hostilities. Israel will not be alone unless it decides to go alone."

But by now the Israeli leadership already knew that that was not true. It could go alone and still not remain alone.

Nor did a warning that same day from Charles de Gaulle impress the determined officials. De Gaulle had bluntly told Israeli Ambassador Walter Eytan that if Israel went to war it would suffer large losses, its diplomatic standing would be threatened and the United States could not be counted on in the long run because of its oil interests. Further, said de Gaulle, if Israel fired the first shot, he would cut off France's massive arms supplies. In the meantime French weapons were already being held up at ports until it was determined whether Israel was going to war. If it refrained, the weapons shipments would be resumed, de Gaulle promised. He urged Israel to wait for his Four Power plan to have a chance to work, though in fact the Soviet Union by this time had shown no interest in it.

"Don't make war," de Gaulle urged. "I know that the other party does not want war. . . . If you are attacked, you will not be abandoned to destruction."

Eban dismissed de Gaulle's advice with the remark that "he seemed to be living in a previous world—the world of his youth."

A Soviet warning was also brushed aside. Only two days before, Foreign Minister Andrei A. Gromyko had called in Israel's ambassador and given him a communiqué for Tel Aviv: "The Soviet Government wishes to repeat and make clear that it will do everything to prevent the possibility of military conflict. Its efforts are now concentrated on this aim, but should the government of Israel take upon itself the responsibility of an outbreak of war, it will have to pay the full price for the results."

Eban concluded that there was nothing in the Soviet warning, or its earlier warning to Washington, "to indicate the eventuality of armed interventions [by the Soviet Union]." This was true, of course, as long as Israel retained U.S. support. As for Britain, it was fully behind Israel and coordinating its policy with the United States.

Finally, the path was clear for war.

That Saturday Dayan held his first press conference since becoming defense minister. He attempted to give the impression that war was not imminent, and he succeeded. When asked about the time being consumed by diplomacy, he replied: "I accept the situation as it is. . . . The point, I should think just now, is that it is more or less a situation of being too late or too early—too late to react regarding our chances in the military field . . . and too early to draw conclusions as to the diplomatic way of handling the matter."

To further create the illusion that war was not near, Dayan repeated a ruse he had used on the eve of the 1956 war. He had thousands of soldiers released for the weekend. Their appearance back in their homes and on the beaches and in the cafés seemed to confirm that tensions were relaxing. Some reporters gave up their vigil and left Israel in search of more pressing stories.

One who remained was young Winston Churchill, grandson of the British statesman. At lunch in Dayan's house that Saturday, Churchill observed: "My grandfather needed Hitler so that he could get into power."

Cracked Dayan in return: "It took eighty thousand Egyptian soldiers in the Sinai Peninsula for me to get to be defense minister."

Indeed, Arab forces arrayed against Israel amounted to a great many more than 80,000. Egypt alone had 210,000 troops ready for deployment against Israel, and 100,000 of them with 930 battle tanks were ready in the Sinai. Syria had 63,000 troops and Jordan 55,000. Altogether, the Arab armies had 328,000 troops to fling against Israel. This was not a great number in terms of the large Arab populations, but it represented a significant force nonetheless. In addition, the Arabs were well armed with heavy artillery, battle tanks, fighter jets and, in the case of Egypt, thirty Russian-made Tu-16 bombers, which were a threat to Israel's cities. In total, the Arabs had more than twice as many tanks (2,330 to 1,000) as the Israelis and 682 combat aircraft compared to Israel's 286. Only in armored personnel carriers did Israel come close to the Arabs, 1,500 to 1,845.

Little appreciated, however, was the enormous size of Israel's armed forces in comparison to its small population. With full mobilization, Israel's largely civilian army numbered 250,000 men, highly trained and motivated. It was the quality of these fighting troops that Israel depended on to overcome the numerical superiority of the Arabs in both manpower and weapons.

The official decision to go to war came on Sunday, June 4. The Cabinet sat for seven hours, once again going over all the arguments, by now familiar, for and against war. At the end, Eshkol asked for a show of hands. The vote was unanimous.

It was not fear of Egypt or the closure of the Straits of Tiran that motivated the Cabinet's decision. It was the generals' confidence that victory would be theirs and the need to prove to the Arabs that Israel could not be intimidated.

In order to mask their real intentions, the ministers issued a dull statement reporting that they had merely reviewed the security situation and then gone on to routine business.

The communiqué achieved its purpose. Its bland recital of routine business convinced more people that war had once again been averted. Several more foreign correspondents left the country convinced the crisis had abated.

They would have remained had they been aware of the secret resolution the Cabinet had passed that June 4 evening. It read:

> After hearing a report on the military and political situation from the Prime Minister, the Foreign Minister, the Defense Minister, the Chief of Staff and the head of military intelligence, the Government ascertained that the armies of Egypt, Syria and Jordan are deployed for immediate multifront aggression, threatening the very existence of the State.
>
> The Government resolves to take military action in order to liberate Israel from the stranglehold of aggression which is progressively being tightened around Israel.

The Government authorizes the Prime Minister and the Defense Minister to confirm to the General Staff of the IDF the time for action.

Members of the Cabinet will receive as soon as possible the information concerning the military operation to be carried out.

The Government charges the Foreign Minister with the task of exhausting all possibilities of political action in order to explain Israel's stand to obtain the support of the powers.

The resolution gave to Eshkol and Dayan the power to decide by themselves the time of the attack. They did not wait long.

War was scheduled to start the next day, Monday, June 5, at 7:45 A.M.

———————

Eshkol that Sunday evening drove to his Tel Aviv home with his wife, Miriam. He was restless. He paced the floor talking about the war that was about to begin, about the casualties, about what would justify the blood that was soon to start flowing.

"You know," he said, "tomorrow there will be widows and orphans, and it's my responsibility." He paused and then added: "We will have to take it back."

"What do you have to take back?" asked his wife.

"We have to take back Jerusalem."

The veteran politician had expressed what no doubt many other Israelis were already experiencing. If the opportunity came to capture beloved Jerusalem, there would be almost no force, certainly no political force, that could hold Israel back from reoccupying its ancient capital.

———————

In Egypt that weekend, the atmosphere, according to a later report by diplomat Charlie Yost, was an "odd mixture of exaltation and fatalism, exaltation over what had been achieved, fatalism before the inescapable realization that Israel might prefer war to a political defeat of this magnitude. There was a clear understanding that Israel might attack at any time, no overwhelming confidence as to the outcome, but a determination to defend, whatever the costs, the intoxicating gains which had been won."

Columnist James Reston was also in Cairo that weekend. He found the Nile Hilton deserted. "Doormen and even telephone operators are not only civil but genial and prompt, and quiet flows the Nile. This is trouble? . . . Yet Cairo is anxious, nonetheless. It is applying its military pressure on the installment plan. It has made its moves and is now making its arguments and is counting on the assumption that Washington, embroiled in Vietnam, will not think the challenge is worth the price. On this, Nasser may be right in the short run, but he cannot be sure about Israel."

In a story datelined Sunday, June 4, the eve of Israel's attack, Reston wrote: "Cairo does not want war and it is certainly not ready for war."

Anthony Nutting, the high-ranking British diplomat who quit the Eden government in disgust over London's collusion with Paris and Tel Aviv to attack Nasser in 1956, also was in Cairo around the same time. He had become friendly with Nasser over the years and now met with him for a discussion of the crisis. Nutting found the Egyptian leader believing that unless Israel had Western allies participating in an attack on Egypt, as it had in 1956, then war would not break out.

"Living as he then was in the atmosphere of 1956, Nasser refused to believe that he was seriously threatened by an Israeli attack," Nutting later wrote in his biography of Nasser. "In my own talks with him during those last critical days he seemed convinced that he could ride out the storm, provided he offered Israel no further provocation. . . . While he had no doubt that some Israelis were itching to fight Egypt over the Gulf, he firmly believed that discretion would prevail in Tel Aviv. Without the active cooperation of either American or British bomber squadrons, he was convinced that Israel could not destroy Egypt's air force. . . ."

In addition, Nasser believed that even if Israel attacked, the United Nations would quickly stop the fighting and make Israel withdraw as it had done in 1956. Laughing, Nasser told Nutting that since Israel had the straits open for the past eleven years, "it was Egypt's turn to close it for the next eleven years, after which the two parties could discuss what should be done."

Imprudently, Nasser expressed his confidence that Sunday in another boastful speech. "They [Israelis] speak about the Sinai war of 1956 and their victories," Nasser declared. "Today we tell them: We are facing you in battle and are burning with desire for it to start in order to get revenge for the 1956 treachery."

Nasser's desire, if not his expectation, was about to be fulfilled sooner than he dreamed.

Correspondent Flora Lewis was in Amman that weekend. In a story filed to *The Washington Post* on June 4, she reported that "Jordan is continuing to take a cautious and defensive position. . . . The king has maneuvered carefully and, in the view of western diplomats here, with much courage.

But no one is offering bets on how long these efforts will succeed in holding up his throne. If there is war and Jordan is not aggressive enough for Palestinian taste he will be in trouble."

Aboard the *Liberty*, the crew was given holiday routine that Sunday. Wind and rain battered the old converted World War II freighter and its crew stayed indoors. For those technicians off duty, about the most exciting pastime was to wander into the coordination center on the third deck and glance at the chart showing the ship's track as it headed toward its assigned patrol area in the Middle East, still nearly three days' sail away.

Walt Rostow that night invited Eppy Evron to dinner. His advice to the Israeli minister: "Wait until the end of next week before you decide to act."

Lyndon Johnson that Sunday had a lazy day. He slept late and did not have breakfast in the White House until 10 A.M. Then he tried to call Arthur Krim but missed him. The afternoon was spent on a boat ride on the Potomac. That evening he talked with Krim, who had returned his call, and then whiled away a quiet evening at the home of his close adviser and friend Justice Abe Fortas. He was back at the White House before 11 P.M.

There had been only one contact with his top officials that day. It was with Defense Secretary McNamara, but the subject obviously had not been Israel's war decision since there was no further communication with security or foreign affairs officials.

At 11:45 P.M., Lyndon Johnson went to bed. At that moment in Israel, the coiled might of the Air Force was about to unleash a devastating attack.

PART TWO
WAR

June 5 to June 10, 1967

XV
JUNE 5: ISRAEL ATTACKS

The Israeli warplanes popped up from their wave-skimming dash across the Mediterranean into attack formation over Egypt with stunning suddenness. The early-morning sky was empty of clouds—and Egyptian planes.

There, across the Sinai and the length of Egypt, sat the Soviet-supplied air force of the Arabs' largest nation. Israeli reconnaissance had been precise. Every airfield with real planes had been identified; so too had those with decoys, empty models set out to draw futile attack. The Israelis were not fooled.

The warplanes of the Israeli Air Force roared high into the crystalline sky, their jets and engines straining, the pilots searching frantically on the sere landscape for the dots that represented their targets. Then they began diving, their speed accelerating wildly through the sand-moted air, the G forces pulling on their bodies as they zeroed in on Egypt's sitting and vulnerable air force.

In the underground headquarters in Tel Aviv, Generals Dayan, Rabin and Weizman were huddled around Brigadier General Mordechai ("Motti") Hod, the stolid commander of the Air Force. Sitting silently by a war table, Hod appeared calm and composed. Only one thing gave away his extreme tension. He was gulping gallons of water. "There was an enormous water jug beside him," recalled Weizman in his memoirs, "and he picked it up with both hands, put it to his lips, and . . . you heard a kind of prolonged gurgling, and then ... it was empty.... The jug was replenished for him and, without blinking an eyelid, without even going away for a drain, he gulped it down once more."

Hod had told his pilots that morning: "Again enemies have joined together against us on every side. The spirit of the heroes of Israel through all the generations will accompany you into battle. The immortal heroism of the warriors of Joshua Ben-Nun, the heroes of King David, the Maccabees and the fighters of the War of Independence and Sinai will serve you as a source from which to take strength and will power to strike the Egyptian enemy that threatens our security, independence and future.

"By his overwhelming defeat, we will guarantee peace and security for ourselves, our children and the generations to come."

Now, in tense silence, Hod and Israel's high command waited expectantly as they gambled the bulk of their air force on a surprise attack. They had planned well. They knew that every morning at dawn, the traditional attack time, the Egyptian Air Force was put on alert, ready to repulse raiders. By 7:45 each day, 8:45 A.M. in Egypt, which was on daylight saving time, when the desert morning mists cleared and the merciless Middle East sun was already hot, the alert was over. At this time the Egyptian pilots took their coffee break and senior officers were finishing their breakfasts and were on their way to the air bases, where they usually arrived at 9 A.M. With luck, the Israeli attack would both achieve complete surprise and commence during the Egyptian Air Force's period of maximum vulnerability.

Unknown to the Israeli planners, fate too was on their side. The commander of the Egyptian armed forces, Field Marshal Abdel Hakim Amer, had chosen that morning to fly to the Sinai to inspect an air base. To ensure the safe passage of Amer's plane, the air defense system had been shut down.

Tension was palpable at the Israeli command post. Ezer Weizman, the man who had preceded Hod as commander and who had devoted his life to modernizing and perfecting the Air Force, was anxious and taut. "For five years I had been talking of this operation, explaining it, hatching it, dreaming of it, manufacturing it link by link, training men to carry it out," he wrote later. "Now, in another quarter of an hour, we would know if it was only a dream, or whether it would come true...."

The gathered generals waited with their ears tuned to the silent communications equipment. The breaking of radio silence would be the announcement that the attack had begun.

"At 7:45 it was hard to live with the suspense any longer," recalled Weizman in his memoirs. "Breathing was uneven, faces pale. And then the first reports came in."

They were stunning. Over the radio came reports that five Egyptian planes had been destroyed, then another four, another two, another three, another four planes blasted—all while they sat defenseless on the ground. Surprise had been total.

Weizman was ecstatic—and suspicious. The reports were too good to be true. "No one said it, but there was a terrible fear in our hearts: 'Have the fellows picked up the Arab habit of exaggeration?' Even those who believed in this operation, recommended it and fought for it to be put into action suddenly found it too big and inconceivable. But it was a fact."

One hundred eighty-three Israeli planes took part in the first attack. Flights of four planes each roared in low over the airfields and radar stations using their cannons for devastating strafing runs against the parked Egyptian planes and their bombs to crater runways so the Egyptians could not fly up to challenge them. The flights stayed over their targets for about seven minutes, enough time for a bombing run and three or four strafing passes, and then three minutes later were replaced by other attackers. The initial assault lasted eighty minutes and accounted for 189 planes destroyed on the ground, sixteen radar stations smashed, and six airfields rendered inoperable, four in the Sinai and two west of the Suez Canal.

Almost immediately afterward, a second wave of 164 planes, some of which had already taken part in the first strike, hit Egyptian targets with crushing ferocity for another eighty minutes of hellish bombings and cannon fire.

Before 11 A.M. Israeli time, 5 A.M. in Washington, the war was essentially won. Egypt had lost 309 of its 340 serviceable airplanes, including all thirty of the long-range Tu-16 bombers that Israel had feared would be used to bomb its civilian population in the cities. Just as serious, from Egypt's viewpoint, was the loss of about 100 pilots, most of them while still on the ground, out of a total of only 350. Nearly all of its airfields lay in ruins, including those as far away as Luxor.

Israel's loss was nineteen planes, two of them shot down by Egyptian MiGs and the rest lost to antiaircraft fire or malfunctions.

Before noon, Jordanian planes strafed a small Israeli airfield near Kfar Sirkin. Hearing of the attack, Motti Hod coolly ordered: "Do the Jordanians."

Israeli planes attacked Jordanian airfields, catching thirty aircraft on the ground, which wiped out Jordan's air force. A short time later Syrian planes bombed near the oil refinery at Haifa and attacked Israeli positions at the Sea of Galilee and an air base at Megiddo. Hod promptly launched massive attacks against Syrian airfields. Fifty-seven Syrian planes were destroyed, most of them on the ground, effectively leaving Syria too without an air force. Two hours later, Iraqi planes attacked the seaside city of Natanya. In retaliation, Hod ordered Israeli planes to fly five hundred miles across Jordan and into Iraq where they attacked the military base at Habbaniyah near the Kirkuk oil pipeline, destroying ten planes on the ground.

Israel had for all practical purposes eliminated the air forces of the confrontation Arab states in the first day of fighting. As a General Staff officer remarked: "Israel is now the only air power in the Middle East." The Israeli Air Force was now turned with devastating effect against Egypt's hopelessly trapped ground forces in the Sinai, where three Israeli armored units were already attacking.

Even before the raids on the Arab air forces had stopped, excitable Ezer Weizman telephoned his wife, Reuma, from the command post and exclaimed: "We've won the war!"

"Ezer," said his patient wife, "are you crazy? At ten o'clock in the morning? You've gone and finished the war?"

With its main forces involved against Egypt, Israel did not want to have to contend with a second front, at least not that morning. Realistically, however, there was no way King Hussein could sit idly by once war erupted, no matter what his private hesitations. Emotions in the Arab world and among the Palestinians were too inflamed for him to survive if he did not enter the war. It had become a *jihad,* a holy war, and it was Hussein's troops who were on the front line face-to-face with Israeli forces along their common long frontier and in the divided city of Jerusalem. He was now a member of a formal mutual-defense pact with Egypt, half of his citizens were Palestinians, the war was being called by the Arab states a struggle for Palestine, and he was the official custodian of the Moslem shrines in Jerusalem. "He had no alternative," Anwar Khatib, governor of the West Bank, observed later. "If he didn't take part all the people would blame him that because he didn't take an active part they lost the war. He couldn't behave otherwise."

Stoically, Hussein later said: "I had no choice. Passions were too high."

The imperative dynamics propelling Hussein were no doubt not lost on Israel's strategists, but still they made an effort to keep the king pacified while they pressed their attack against Egypt. At 8:30 A.M. that Monday, the United Nations' Lieutenant General Odd Bull, the Norwegian in charge of the U.N. Truce Supervision Organization, received a telephone call from Israel's Foreign Ministry asking him to come to the ministry immediately. When he arrived, the U.N. official was told, falsely, by Arthur Lourie, the deputy director-general of the ministry, that the war had started when Egyptian planes had taken off against Israel and were intercepted by Israeli aircraft.

Lourie then asked Bull to relay a message to Hussein: "We shall not initiate any action whatsoever against Jordan. However, should Jordan open hostilities, we shall react with all our might, and the King will have to bear the full responsibility for all the consequences."

Bull was reluctant. "This was a threat, pure and simple," he wrote later, "and it is not the normal practice of the U.N. to pass on threats from one government to another. But this message seemed so important that we quickly sent it . . . and King Hussein received the message before 10:30 the same morning."

Hussein was not impressed. He had been told by Nasser that morning that the Israelis had lost dozens of planes in their attack, and Iraq claimed to have bombed downtown Tel Aviv with devastating effect. In addition, Moshe Dayan had shrewdly ordered that no mention be made by Israeli officials of the country's victories in order "to keep the enemy camps confused." Thus while Israel was silent about the course of the war, Cairo Radio was reporting imaginary victories. One report it broadcast was that forty Israeli planes had been shot down by the Egyptian Air Force. Recalled Dayan: "There was, of course, no substance to this claim, but Arab vanity and extravagance now served us well."

Under the combination of these imperatives and misperceptions, Hussein haughtily replied to the Eshkol plea for restraint: "They started the battle. Well, they are receiving our reply by air."*

Jordanian guns opened fire into Israel that morning. They lobbed shells into Tel Aviv, Jerusalem and other areas. Israeli civilians dashed for cover in impromptu shelters, inside closets, anywhere that offered protection against the random rain of artillery fire. Israel responded with a heavy counterfire of artillery and mortars and blazing aircraft attacks. And, in a brutal display of Israel's power, one of its planes flew over Amman and fired two rockets and machine-gun bursts directly into Hussein's Basman Palace in the downtown area, causing considerable damage to the administration building. Both rockets hit close enough to the king's office that if he had been there

---

* As he later admitted: "We were misinformed about what had happened in Egypt . . . These reports . . . had much to do with our confusion and false interpretation of the situation."

rather than at the general command headquarters, he likely would have been killed. Hussein now was soon to lose something far dearer and more precious to him and the Arab world than his air force.

He was going to lose the revered city of Jerusalem.

Jordanian firing into western Jerusalem where 200,000 Jews lived became intense. Shells rained down near the Knesset (parliament), the Israel Museum and Hebrew University. At 1:30 P.M., Jordanian troops occupied Government House, General Odd Bull's headquarters in no-man's-land atop a ridge called the Hill of Evil Counsel. Legend had it that the hill was the site where Judas betrayed Jesus, where Judas hanged himself from a hackberry tree and where the high priest Caiaphas gave counsel that led to Christ's crucifixion. Now it was the area of the first advance by Jordanian troops toward Israeli territory in Jewish Jerusalem, which lay only yards away.

With considerable courage, Odd Bull refused to allow the Jordanian soldiers to remain in the magnificent yellow-stone building. But he could not get them to leave the gardens, from where they fired into Israeli territory and provoked a violent Israeli response. At 3:52 P.M., Israeli troops shot their way through the headquarters' solid doors. One bullet lodged in the right thigh of a U.N. observer, Major Keith Howard, an Australian volunteer who had arrived only two days earlier.

Women and children, administrative employees and dependents of U.N. officials, were lying in the smoke-filled corridors for safety as Israeli troopers ran through the building lobbing hand grenades into various rooms. Fearful of a massacre, Howard and another U.N. official, Jack Bellwood, exposed themselves by standing up and yelling, "U.N.! U.N.!" An Israeli major running through the building nearly collided with them, then swung his Tommy gun at them and said, somewhat to their surprise: "Please be very careful as I'm rather nervous."

Soon all the U.N. people were running out of the building. Before Howard knew it, he was alone, unfamiliar with the city, unable to speak Arabic or Hebrew, not sure which forces controlled what areas. Walking outside, he found the gardens wrecked, vehicles burning, and smoke and debris everywhere. By a stroke of luck, one jeep had ignition keys still in it, although its radiator had been shot through and one tire was flat. Despite his wound, Howard climbed in and drove through the streets of Jerusalem. More by chance than calculation he came across some of the survivors of Government House at the Office of the Chief Israeli Liaison Officer to the United Nations. By that time, the jeep's punctured radiator was belching clouds of steam and its flattened tire was in shreds.

"Almost immediately I was confronted by an irate Dutchman whom I subsequently learned was Hoffmeyer, the chief of U.N. transport," recalled Howard. " 'What do you think you are doing, driving that car with an over-heated engine—and flat tire! You should be ashamed of yourself! Give me the keys at once!' "

Unknown to Howard was that despite Bull's vehement protests about the headquarters being in neutral territory and the property of the United Nations, the Israelis had demanded that he and his staff evacuate the installation, which housed UNTSO's major communication network with New York. With resentment, they moved into the President Hotel in Jewish Jerusalem and Bull for the second time that day visited Arthur Lourie at the Foreign Ministry to protest his expulsion from Government House. But it was in vain.*

While Bull was complaining, a special session of the parliament and an emergency meeting of the Cabinet were taking place not far from Government House. There was already a euphoric mood of victory among the parliament members, and a growing realization that a historic opportunity lay at hand. With Israeli forces triumphant everywhere, the grandest, the almost unthinkable goal of all was now possible: the capture of the Old City of Jerusalem. To capture the Old City with its sacred Western (Wailing) Wall, the last remnant of the ancient Jewish empire, was an idea almost intoxicating in its grandeur to the Israelis.

It was obvious by now to the parliament and Cabinet members that the deed could be accomplished by the Israel Defense Forces. The only inhibition was world opinion. Would the rest of the world sit idly by while the tiny Jewish nation took control of the holy places revered not only by Jews but by Christians and Moslems?

Interior Minister Shapira wondered aloud: "Should we do it? Do we dare do it?" Ben Gurion openly urged the Old City's capture. Justice Minister Yaacov Shimshon Shapiro recalled later: "There wasn't anyone ... who didn't want Jerusalem united. It was a question of whether it could be done—what would be the outcome?"

The question was tantalizing and perplexing. After all, Israel had not been allowed to retain the barren Sinai Peninsula in 1956. Could it hope in its wildest dreams that it would be allowed to retain the storied Old City of Jerusalem, so rich in history and legend and so symbolic to so many peoples? It was a dizzying thought, and a disturbing one too. For it would be

---

* Bull and his staff were not allowed to return until August 24, only to find the Israelis had built a new fence around the installation, reducing its area to a third of the original size.

emotionally wrenching, traumatic and profoundly demoralizing if once the Old City was theirs the Israeli people would then be forced to surrender it.

While Jordanian shells burst nearby, the Cabinet members met in a cramped air-raid shelter in the basement of the Knesset building weighing these heavy considerations. In the end, shortly before 11 P.M., Eshkol finally expressed the yearnings they all shared and gave rationalization to the historic course they were about to embark on.

"We are going to take the Old City of Jerusalem," he declared, adding, "in order to remove the danger of the bombardment and the shelling incessantly being carried out by Jordan." Most of Jordan's shelling was coming from the ridges around Jerusalem and not from the cramped and crowded Old City. But that did not matter in this emotional and charged moment.

As Justice Minister Shapiro said: "Jerusalem is so deeply rooted in every one of us that it is beyond discussion."

"There was no formal vote on this," Josef Burg, minister of social welfare, recounted later. "It was, so to say, an atmosphere of consensus."

No minutes were taken of the historic meeting. The Cabinet's record says merely: "Fifth of June 1967. Eshkol said that the Cabinet wants Old Jerusalem. . . ."

Abba Eban realized that Eshkol's decision again placed heavy duties on him, for it was as important for him to gain international—and particularly American—support for Israel to retain its gains as it was for the Army to achieve the gains in the first place. "The prospect that we might lose at the conference table what was being gained on the battlefield . . . [was] an obsessive Israeli anxiety," he later wrote. "That there would be a call for cease-fire was inevitable. . . . But a unanimous international policy for restoring the previous lines was a far graver matter.

"If such a resolution was adopted, Israel would either be pried loose of her gains without peace or, at best, be left to possess them in a situation of international isolation, boycott and political blockade."

Eban now devoted all of his impressive intellectual and linguistic resources toward the effort to prevent the United Nations from adopting a cease-fire resolution that would also call for a return to previous lines.

New York Times correspondent Eric Pace that Monday morning was leaving his Cairo hotel and walking along Kasr Nil Street when he sensed something was wrong. The street, Cairo's bedraggled equivalent of Madison Avenue, was unnaturally hushed. Traffic was nearly stopped; shoppers and pedestrians were huddled around radios listening to news reports. Pace rushed on to the Reuter office where he found a reporter frantically typing. The reporter looked up and said simply: "War has begun."

Cairo Radio had announced the Israeli attacks on the airfields, but it gave no hint of how destructive the raids had been. Then cheers rang out in the street. The radio had just announced that two dozen Israeli planes had been shot down. Youths happily chanted "Nas-ser, Nas-ser" as they ran through the streets fruitlessly searching for the wreckage of downed Israeli planes. Air-raid sirens wailed intermittently and there was the boom of antiaircraft fire from the suburbs, but no Israeli planes were visible.

"Every Egyptian I talked to seemed confident of victory over Israel," reported Pace. "Nasser had said it was assured. The Cairo Radio announcer barked, 'Now is the day and hour to conquer,' and reported that Egyptian land forces had 'wiped out two enemy attacks' in the Sinai Peninsula."

It was impossible to check out the Egyptian claims. Reporters were forbidden to approach the Israeli frontier. All that Pace and other reporters in Cairo could be sure of was that the war had finally begun.

Foreign Minister Mahmoud Riad had been awakened by a shattering explosion that seemed to have occurred west of Cairo. "I realized that Israel had begun its attack," he later recorded. "I hastened to my office . . . and was soon to receive the shock of my life. Nasser telephoned to inform me that all Egyptian military airfields had been hit and that our air force had been paralyzed."

Riad sought to get reliable information from the general command on which to base Egypt's political moves, but he could find no one who knew what was going on. Panic and confusion were rife.

Israel's forces were triumphant everywhere. The 100,000 men and 930 tanks in the Egyptian units now in the Sinai were in panicky retreat before the might of more than 70,000 Israeli troops thrusting forward with about 800 tanks. Israel's smaller force was more than compensated by its total air superiority. Egyptian troops were being incinerated in pools of burning napalm dropped on them by the swarming Israeli planes.

The crew of the *Liberty*, operating on its own without armed escort or armaments, heard of the outbreak of war with apprehension. The ship was sailing straight toward the area of hostilities, vulnerable to any force that wanted to challenge it. The ship, under skipper Commander William L. McGonagle, decided to request of Vice Admiral William I. Martin, commander of the Sixth Fleet, a destroyer escort that could both protect the *Liberty* and serve as an auxiliary communications station. McGonagle that day placed the crew on a modified alert with two men added to the forecastle as lookout-gun crews. In terms of the firepower being employed in the Middle East, it was a pitiful gesture.

Washington's first official notification that war had erupted came at 2:38 A.M. (8:38 A.M. in Israel). An announcement by Israel's Defense Ministry said: "Since the early hours of this morning, heavy fighting has been taking place on the southern front between Egyptian armored and aerial forces which moved against Israel and our forces which went into action in order to check them."

The announcement caused a flurry of telephone calls, routing officials out of their beds and sending them on to their offices at the Pentagon, the State Department and the White House.

Less than two hours later, at 4:05 o'clock in Washington, the U.S. Embassy in Tel Aviv sent a flash cable to Washington relaying another announcement from the Defense Ministry.

The ministry again blamed Egypt for the opening of hostilities. "Egyptian armored forces advanced at dawn toward the Negev. Our own forces advanced to repel them. At the same time a large number of radar tracks of Egyptian jets were observed on the screen. The tracks were directed towards the Israeli shoreline.... IDF air force craft took to the air against enemy aircraft. Air battle [*sic*] are still going on. The prime minister has called an urgent meeting with a number of ministers."

The announcements were totally untrue, but they had the effect of confusing the touchy issue of who had fired the first shot. The confusion was spread when Eban personally misinformed Ambassador Wally Barbour. Within minutes of issuance of the second communiqué, Barbour was called to Eban's office and told that "early this morning Israelis observed Egyptian units moving in large numbers toward Israel and in fact considerable force penetrated Israeli territory and clashed with Israeli ground forces."

Barbour cabled Washington that "consequently, GOI [Government of Israel] gave order to attack. Military situation somewhat clear. Only fighting so far is with Egypt. GOI believes its attack on Egyptian airfields has been a success. Also Eban thinks Egyptian ground movement from Gaza probably stopped."

Eban informed Barbour that he had consulted with Eshkol and was going to draft a message to President Johnson explaining the reasons for the Israeli actions and expressing the belief that the "world understands Israel is victim of Nasser's aggression."

Significantly, Barbour reported to Washington that Eban had told him that the Eshkol message would contain assurances that Israel was not interested in retaining captured territory. The letter, he cabled, "will add that GOI has no rpt no intention taking advantage of situation to enlarge its territory, that hopes peace can be restored within present boundaries. . . ."

Lyndon Johnson was first informed of the war in a telephone call by Walt Rostow at 4:30 A.M. "War has broken out in the Middle East," he said.

"How did it start?" asked Johnson. "Who fired first?"

"We're not quite sure right now," Rostow replied. He promised to find out.

Rostow and Hal Saunders had arrived at the White House Situation Room shortly after the first notification of war. Rostow now turned to Saunders and said: "Find out at once how it started. I want to know who began the fighting."

Saunders worked on the question briefly but as the hours passed the answer seemed less important. Whatever Johnson's public statements, the fact was that he and the country generally were so committed to Israel that it seemed a moot question. Nearly every official assumed it was Israel which started the war, though at this time there was no proof. But America was with Israel under any circumstances. Saunders and Rostow finally let the matter drop, concluding, in Saunders' words, that "we were asking the wrong question. It was like asking who started the battle instead of who started the war."

Other calls to the President that morning quickly followed: from Rusk at 5:09, Rostow again at 6:15, Press secretary George Christian at 6:35 A.M. Rusk had wanted permission to send a cable to Moscow to express "our dismay and surprise at the reports of conflict." The cable said that "we feel it is very important that the United Nations Security Council succeed in bringing this fighting to an end as quickly as possible and are ready to cooperate with all members of the Council to that end." Johnson gave his approval.

When Sergeant Paul Glynn reported for duty at the White House at 7:30 A.M., he found the President sitting in his bedroom quietly watching television. Glynn noted that the "President gave no indications of it being anything but a normal day—showered, shaved, and dressed and left the bedroom. Breakfast of chipped beef, grapefruit and tea."

Before he could get to his downstairs office, the President talked on the telephone with Goldberg, McNamara and twice more with Rostow.

He also took time to drop by the third-story bedroom where Mathilde

Krim had been staying as a houseguest since her return from Texas after the Memorial Day weekend.

"I was still in bed," she recalled years later. "He was accompanied by a couple of aides. He came in and said, 'The war has started.' We both knew who had started it."

McNamara's message to Johnson had been dramatic. "Mr. President," he had said, "the hot line is up." Communist Premier Aleksei Kosygin had activated the top-level communications link at 7:47 A.M. to exchange views on the fighting. It was the first time the leaders of the Soviet Union and the United States had ever used the "hot line," the direct telex link between Washington and Moscow that had been installed on August 30, 1963.*

Kosygin was at the Kremlin end of the line, and he agreed to stay by the machine until Johnson could get to the White House Situation Room where McNamara, Rostow and Rusk were already waiting. Rusk's message was sent at 8:15 A.M. Johnson entered the room at 8:17 A.M. Kosygin's message referred to the explosiveness of the Middle East and the need for Moscow and Washington to cooperate. He also assured Johnson that the Soviet Union was determined to work for a quick cease-fire and expressed the hope that the United States would work to restrain Israel.

After carefully studying Kosygin's remarks, Johnson reactivated the hot line at 8:47 to report that he would be taking actions to stop the fighting and to express his appreciation that the Soviets were also interested in seeing the war contained.

Meanwhile, the public efforts of the government were devoted to assuming a calm, coherent and fair posture. Press secretary Christian, after consultations with Johnson, Rostow and Rusk, had issued at 7:05 A.M. a statement that the Administration was "deeply distressed" about the outbreak of war. He added that although it was unclear who had begun hostilities, "the United States will devote all of its energies to bring about an end to the fighting." His words were general and received little attention.

His counterpart at the State Department was not so lucky. Shortly before 1 P.M., the department's press secretary, Robert J. McCloskey, made a seemingly innocuous statement that caused more of a furor, more outrage in

---

* Although Johnson did not know it at the time, there had been a problem in getting the hot line piped into the White House. As the President recalled in his memoirs, "To [McNamara's] amazement, [his communications people] advised him that it could not be done—that the hot line ended at the Pentagon. McNamara said sharply that with all the money we had invested in military communications there must be some way to send Moscow's message directly to the White House Situation Room, and they had better figure it out. They quickly found a way."

the Jewish community and more headache for the President than anything else said during the war.

It occurred during the regular State Department daily news briefing when reporters were particularly interested in hearing about violent demonstrations that had broken out against American embassies and installations in Arab countries, including Iraq, Libya, Sudan, Syria, Tunisia and Yemen. There had been no injuries, but still the news was worrisome and the reporters pursued their questions.

"These demonstrations obviously are linking the U.S. with Israel," observed one reporter at the briefing. "The U.S. position in the U.N. had been stated as being neutral. Would you reaffirm that?"

"Indeed I would—I would be more than happy to," answered McCloskey as he innocently uttered the most controversial statement of his distinguished career. "We have tried to steer an evenhanded course through this. Our position is neutral in thought, word and deed."

McCloskey had remembered the phrase from earlier in the morning when he was seated in the State Department Operations Room. Several officials had shown satisfaction with continuing reports of Israeli successes, and Gene Rostow had turned to them with a broad smile and admonished: "Gentlemen, gentlemen, do not forget that we are neutral in word, thought and deed."

The reporters were intrigued by the phrase, which as used by McCloskey did not carry the same undertone of irony that it did when uttered by Rostow.

"Do you feel we can continue to maintain a neutral position, no matter what happens in the Middle East?" one asked.

"That will be the effort," said McCloskey.

"Bob," asked another reporter, "would the financing of one of the belligerents through U.S. [Israeli] bonds be a violation of our position of neutrality?"

The other reporters laughed. It was well known that Israel received significant money contributions in the form of bonds purchased by Americans.

"Well that presumes something that I am, first of all, not familiar with, and therefore may draw an inappropriate answer," McCloskey said carefully. "I would, for background, say that politically the answer is no."

Under the rules of the briefing, McCloskey's putting his answer on background meant that it could not be attributed to him by name. By now the reporters had scented that they were on to something important.

"What do you mean 'politically'?" one asked.

McCloskey, realizing he was getting deeper into a sensitive area than he had planned, remained silent. The skeptical reporters moved on to other questions, but as the briefing came to an end one of them asked: "Bob, how do you make sure that all officials are neutral in thought?"

"If that's the last question," said a wary McCloskey, "let's go."

On that note, the briefing broke up. Several minutes later the Associated Press sent a bulletin around the world: "The United States is neutral in the present Middle East war, the State Department's spokesman announced today."

On the surface, the U.S. position as enunciated by McCloskey was a forthright and unexceptional statement of American policy. Yet the Johnson Administration, despite its denials, had become so closely allied with Israel—indeed by thought, word and deed—that the mere utterance of neutrality was considered by Israel's supporters and others to be an abandonment of the Jewish state.

The reaction was instantaneous and ferocious. Members of Congress outdid one another during the afternoon pledging their unswerving support to Israel. By the time of George Christian's afternoon press briefing at the White House the reporters wanted to know just what McCloskey had meant. That left Christian in a difficult position since the President wanted to dissociate himself from McCloskey's statement but at the same time did not want Christian to repudiate the State Department in public, thereby giving the impression of disarray in the Administration.

The President himself was maintaining a studied silence, but behind the scenes he was anxiously monitoring the comments of his Administration's spokesmen. Earlier in the day he had ordered Christian to bring him "page by page [of transcript], as each page becomes available, of any briefing" Christian gave. Thus caution had become the word around the White House and Christian was extremely circumspect in handling the neutrality issue. But the more diplomatic he was, the more the correspondents became suspicious. It did not take them long to sense that they had caught the Administration in an embarrassing position.

After a great deal of verbal fencing, a reporter asked if the neutrality statement "had been cleared with the White House before it was issued?"

That was one question Christian was anxious to answer. "No," he said.

"Were you aware of it?"

"No, I was not," said Christian.

The questioning drifted on to other areas but still the reporters were curious and they returned repeatedly to the neutrality issue.

"George, respectfully, I am confused," confessed a reporter. "A spokesman for the State Department says this country's policy is one of neutrality, we are neutral. In questioning here it seems to me, and perhaps I misunderstand, you don't confirm that. Is our policy one of neutrality or not?"

Christian stonewalled.

Exasperated, a reporter asked: "George, do you reaffirm the State Department's statement that this country is neutral in thought, word and deed? Would you reaffirm it or not reaffirm it?"

In desperation, Christian threw the ball back to the State Department, which had created the flap.

"For interpretations . . . I would have to refer you over to Secretary Rusk. Let him interpret it for you," Christian said.

Less than an hour later, the Secretary of State found it necessary to hold a background meeting with the press to try to clarify the matter. Dean Rusk advised the correspondents that they should attribute their stories to "official sources—not high official sources but official sources." He continued: "I might just say a word on a good deal of discussion during the day on this word 'neutral.' It's a word that carries both a technical and a general connotation. Now, the fact is that we're not a belligerent. . . . Our citizens in the area are entitled to be treated as citizens of a country which is not belligerent.

"That does not in any way imply a lack of deep concern about the situation," Rusk added. "Any notion that 'neutral' means disinterest is just very far beside the point."

Rusk's remarks hardly clarified the issue. The commotion grew so great that later that day he had to issue a formal release under the imprimatur of the White House clarifying whether the United States was neutral or not in the Middle East war.

By a feat of diplomatic prestidigitation, his prepared statement managed to avoid using the word "neutral" in describing the government's policy but at the same time did not openly repudiate McCloskey's statement. It reaffirmed Johnson's May 23 statement and the country's commitment to the territorial integrity of all states in the region. As for neutrality, it merely noted that "neutrality does not mean indifference."

The Administration thought that it had finally quieted the flap. But it was to continue to plague Johnson during the days to come and bring great pressure on him from Israel's supporters.

In the White House, Lyndon Johnson kept up a dizzying round of meetings and telephone conversations with his top officials throughout the day.

He also received a message from his friend Arthur Krim. A memorandum to the President that day read: "Arthur Krim reports that many arms shipments are packed and ready to go to Israel, but are being held up. He thinks it would be most helpful if these could be released."

Under the message the President had scribbled: "1,000 rounds of 105mm artillery shells cleared. 2,000 fuses—availability, Gas masks. New requests: A-4 jet fighter-bombers Hawk antiaircraft missiles."

Before the day was out, Krim was informed that gas masks had already been dispatched to Israel and he left a message for Johnson expressing his appreciation.

The President also received a personal message from his intellectual-in-residence John Roche. "I don't believe in bothering busy people," Roche wrote. "But if there is anything I can do, I am here. I think you know that I have a very close relationship with both the American Jewish community and the Israelis. If you want to send anyone to Israel, I am available." The least of the President's problems was to find friends of Israel, and Roche remained in Washington.

As a breather from his chores, Johnson drank diet root beer and sat from time to time in his personal small lounge, watching all three television sets at the same time. At one point he asked that "the top television man come into my office and work on the sound on these sets. I like a clear, sharp sound," he said, illustrating with a staccato voice. "But what I'm getting is a mumbly, foggy sound," which he imitated by thumbing his lips and humming.

In addition to monitoring television, the President also kept track of the latest developments coming over the news services' teletype machines in the Oval Office. At one point he was observed "bent down on his hindquarters . . . to read the material as it came off the ticker."

He had lunch with George Christian and Tom Jones, his top press aides, and later observed that his suit was too tight. He explained that when he "got a bit upset his appetite increased—and right now he was starving, just couldn't get enough to eat." One of the causes of his current upset was McCloskey's neutrality remark. He told Christian he thought the statement had been a mistake. His food that lunch consisted of four grilled pimento-cheese sandwiches and two helpings of fruit Jell-O with custard sauce.

Johnson worked into the night. He had approved a letter to Britain's Harold Wilson about the Middle East, but later Walt Rostow had sent it back saying he had changed a sentence that had read: "We had feared that the Israelis might feel compelled to strike, but we had had no advance indication from them that they had actually taken a decision to do so. . . ." Rostow changed the sentence so that the blame was removed from Israel as the attacker. He explained to Johnson: "I changed the first paragraph so that we did not put flatly into the record a judgment that Israel had kicked this off from a standing start." Israel at the time was still denying that it had started the war.

But it already was more than obvious to White House officials that the Israelis were scoring stunning victories. At about the same time he returned Wilson's letter, Rostow also sent the President a memorandum reporting on the fighting in which he jocularly referred to the results as "the first day's turkey shoot."

It was 9:53 P.M. before Johnson left his chores and went upstairs to his living quarters. At 10:35 P.M., Justice Abe Fortas called to discuss the Middle East. During their conversation the President put Fortas on hold and said to a secretary: "Bring me the folder I just gave you on the statistics on the airplanes downed in the Middle East today."

Johnson finally went to bed at 11:15 P.M. By that time Israel's triumph over Egypt was nearly complete in the Sinai Peninsula and Israelis were eyeing a bigger prize: the Old City of Jerusalem.

XVI
JUNE 6: NASSER
SEVERS RELATIONS

"**W**ill His Majesty make an announcement on the participation of Americans and British?"

It was the voice of Gamal Abdel Nasser talking by radio to King Hussein. The time was 4:50 A.M. Tuesday, the dawning of the second day of the war. It had already been lost, essentially, but the two Arab leaders had not yet reconciled themselves to that harsh fact. Perhaps, in their despair, they could not even bring themselves to recognize it yet.

Hussein's answer was unintelligible so Nasser asked again: "Will we say the U.S. and England or just the U.S.?"

"The U.S. and Britain," replied Hussein.

"Does Britain have aircraft carriers?" asked Nasser.

Hussein's answer was again unclear.

"By God, I will make an announcement and you will make an announcement . . . that American and British airplanes are taking part against us from aircraft carriers. We will stress the matter and we will drive the point home."

"Good," Hussein answered, "all right."

"A thousand thanks," said Nasser. "Do not give up. We are with you with all our heart and we are flying our planes over Israel today, our planes are striking at Israel's airfields since morning."

Nasser, in his urgency to encourage Hussein to continue fighting, was again misleading him. He had no air force left.

Listening to the two men talk were Israeli radiomen. Israel, which released a text of the conversation two days later, and many others claimed it proved that Hussein and Nasser had made up the story of Anglo-American involvement as a way to explain to their masses Israel's victories. That may have been the case, but the conversation was ambiguous enough to lend itself to another interpretation: the two Arab leaders might actually have believed there was Anglo-American collusion and were trying to coordinate their policies as allies.

Chief of Staff Yitzhak Rabin admitted later that it was possible that Hussein might have thought there was such collusion because he found it implausible that Israel could have accomplished its victories without outside help. The same may have been true for Nasser. Both leaders had lived through the 1956 war when Britain and France actually had colluded with Israel. With that background, it was not farfetched for them to suspect that something similar had happened. But as the days went by and it became clear that U.S. planes had not been involved, Hussein stopped making the charge, and later so too did Nasser.

Another possibility was that Israel had pulled off one of the most effective ruses of the war by putting U.S. markings on several planes to deceive and demoralize Nasser. The Egyptian leader's excessive suspicions about big-power intrigue with Israel were well known. If he could be fooled into believing that the United States was openly helping Israel in the war, then his resolve would be undermined and his temper ignited, setting him up to act rashly, which he did.

The possibility that the Israelis had pulled off such a ploy was raised two days after the start of the war in a CIA report that quoted a person who was extremely knowledgeable, presumably a high Soviet official.* The unidentified person insisted that Russians had personally seen U.S.-manufactured aircraft with U.S. Air Force markings flying over Ismailia in the first days of the war. If the Israelis were responsible for this deception, it paid them enormous dividends in terms of further alienating Egypt and Jordan from the United States.

The interception of the Nasser-Hussein conversation was the kind of feat of electronic wizardry that the *Liberty* was so well equipped to perform. But it was still another day's sail away, still sailing by itself into the combat zone.

---

* All names in the report, declassified 11/7/80, have been censored. The report appears based on an electronic intercept of some sort, perhaps of a telephone conversation or a listening device, between a Soviet official and an unidentified person. The Soviet is obviously well informed because he mentions the Johnson-Kosygin hot-line exchanges even though these were held as a closely guarded secret at this time, in Moscow as well as in Washington.

219

To the ship's request for an armed escort, Sixth Fleet commander Admiral Martin had replied: "LIBERTY IS A CLEARLY MARKED UNITED STATES SHIP IN INTERNATIONAL WATERS, NOT A PARTICIPANT IN THE CONFLICT AND NOT A REASONABLE SUBJECT FOR ATTACK BY ANY NATION." In the unlikely event of an attack, Admiral Martin promised, jet aircraft could be over the ship within ten minutes. The request was denied.

Nasser made another call early that morning. He telephoned Foreign Minister Mahmoud Riad at home and informed him that he had no doubt that U.S. planes had been involved because the Air Force had been devastated. To protest this U.S. collusion, he said, he had decided to sever diplomatic relations with the United States.

Riad noted later: "I argued that such a decision was not beneficial to us, although I was equally convinced that collusion had taken place."

Nasser was adamant. "The U.S. must be made to feel the brunt of its collusion with Israel. We must bring the weight of mobilized Arab anger to bear on her. The severing of relations is imperative."

"Granted," said Riad, "but we shall need to deal politically with the U.S. within the near future."

"Never," declared Nasser. "Collusion between the U.S. and Israel at this level means that the U.S. has something up its sleeve, a price we have to pay for Israeli withdrawal. . . . The U.S. leaves us no choice."

Nasser's anger was heightened by a remark Dean Rusk had made the previous day during his briefing for the press. Rusk had been asked who had fired the first shot and he had tried to duck the question. The secretary of state had claimed it was still too early to tell. But the Egyptians knew full well who had started the war and there can be little doubt that U.S. intelligence also knew, as Johnson's original letter to Wilson indicated before it was changed by Rostow. In fact, there had been little doubt in the minds of most officials right from the start that it was Israel that had fired the first shot. But, as Hal Saunders had explained, it seemed a moot point after the event.

Riad immediately went to his office and summoned Ambassador-designate Dick Nolte, though Nolte still had not been accredited. He had been scheduled to present his credentials the day before, but with the bad luck that had dogged him since his appointment, the event was overtaken by the outbreak of war. Riad told Nolte of Egypt's suspicions about U.S. collusion and that Cairo was breaking relations with Washington. Nolte insisted that no U.S. planes had taken part and urged Riad to reconsider, but the foreign minister was not swayed.

The crux of the problem, said Riad, was not whether U.S. planes had attacked with Israel but that President Johnson had given his personal assurances that Israel would not attack if Egypt refrained from war. "Now that Israel has started the war by attacking us, the least we could expect, in the light of these assurances, was that President Johnson would demand the immediate withdrawal of Israeli forces to their original positions," said Riad. He added: "Dean Rusk's statement that the U.S. was not aware who had started hostilities did not augur well. . . ."

Cairo Radio reported the severing of relations and the collusion accusation that same morning, causing anger in Washington, even among State Department Arabists, and further polarizing U.S. public opinion against the Arabs and for Israel. Secretary of State Rusk publicly condemned the charge of U.S. airplane involvement that morning. "These charges are utterly and wholly false," said the usually mild-speaking Georgian. "We can only conclude that this was a malicious charge, known to be false, and, therefore, obviously was invented for some purpose not fully disclosed."

On instructions from Washington, the U.S. Embassy in Cairo lodged a strong protest late that Tuesday morning. After talking with Foreign Minister Riad again, Nolte cabled: "I pointed out the danger that these assertions might lead to violence against Americans here. The foreign minister used the occasion to say that they had ample proof unfortunately of Anglo-American aircraft and carriers being involved in the fighting."

Riad also had other things to say to Nolte.

"You say you are against aggression but when you have aggression of Israel against Egypt you do nothing," Riad said. "You say you don't know who is the aggressor. It is perfectly clear who is the aggressor and there are ninety or at least eighty ambassadors in Cairo who know this to be true.

"You are not neutral at all. If Egypt had been the aggressor, the Sixth Fleet would now be on the shore of Egypt."

––––––––––––––

The McCloskey statement was still causing Johnson headaches. In a message to the President, John Roche wrote: "Listening to McCloskey yesterday, and reading the State Department's staff summary today [Tuesday], I was appalled to realize that there is a real underground sentiment for kissing some Arab backsides. This is, in my judgment, worse than unprincipled—it is stupid. (And my pro-Israeli convictions are irrelevant to this point. . . .)

The Arabs have to hate us. . . . They must create the myth that the United States, not *Israel singlehanded,* clobbered them.

"The net consequence of trying to 'sweet talk' the Arabs is that they have contempt for us—and we alienate Jewish support in the United States.

"I am not suggesting for one second that our Middle Eastern policy should be determined in terms of domestic political considerations. But there is no reason why we shouldn't collect the domestic bonus that will fall in our lap for following a sound policy. Which brings us back to a question once (perhaps erroneously) attributed to you: 'Whose State Department is it?' "

Telegrams protesting McCloskey's statement were pouring into the White House. Typical was one signed by Charles E. Silberman of New York, director of the Carnegie Study of the Education of Educators: "State Department declaration of neutrality an act of dishonor and cowardice that defames my country's honor and weakens its most vital interests, namely, the credibility of U.S. commitments. How can any nation now trust our word? I plead with you . . . to now with force, if necessary, to uphold our commitments to Israel."

Democratic and Republican members of Congress were deluged with protests. Senator Javits said Israel's supporters were "dismayed" and "confused" by McCloskey's statement and urged the President personally to disavow it. He added that Johnson should make it clear that any cease-fire must guarantee "a permanent peace." This was a phrase that was to be used increasingly over the following days and soon was to become the code formulation for opposing any call for Israel to withdraw.

Senator Charles H. Percy, a Republican from Illinois, issued a statement saying, "I cannot feel neutral when a dictator threatens to drive a free people into the sea." Senator Wayne Morse of Oregon, a Democrat who was loudly critical of the Vietnam war, said he found the McCloskey remark "incomprehensible" and demanded that the United States assure Israel "the equivalent of the weapons we have made available to her enemies," which in itself was a bit incomprehensible since Israel already was getting far more weapons than any Arab state.

David S. Broder reported in *The Washington Post* that "Senators and Representatives from states with large Jewish populations have reported exceptionally heavy mail. The office of Sen. Robert F. Kennedy of New York said it had opened and counted over 12,000 letters and telegrams on the Middle East last week and had 'at least as much more' in the past two days. There were comparable reports from Senators from Pennsylvania, Illinois and California."

In a memorandum to the President that Tuesday, the State Department's number two man, Nick Katzenbach, suggested that the "neutrality problem" be handled again by George Christian. He proposed that Christian say McCloskey had meant nothing more than what Johnson had "repeatedly said. We support the territorial integrity and independence of all states in the Middle East."

Somewhat wistfully, he added: "While all of us agree that it is necessary to get something more on the record, we are inclined to believe other events of the day will swallow this particular point in new events."

In that he was wrong.

Lyndon Johnson had more to worry about that Tuesday than the "neutrality problem." He had been awakened at 4:29 A.M. by the White House Situation Room reporting on the progress of the war. At 5:34 o'clock, the hot line was activated for the fourth time in the crisis. Premier Kosygin was sending a message urging that the two superpowers work harder to achieve a cease-fire. Kosygin added that the Soviet Union also wanted a withdrawal back to the lines existing before the war. In the rush of Middle East events, the far more important war for America, Vietnam, was by now being practically ignored by the Administration.

Johnson met with McNamara, Walt Rostow, Rusk and others to study Kosygin's message and then, after several other appointments, at 10:03 A.M. he ordered the hot line activated to send his answer. He firmly denied Egyptian charges that U.S. planes had been involved in Israel's attack and urged that the U.S.S.R. and the United States both support in the United Nations a simple cease-fire resolution—with no withdrawal provision.

This was the position that Israel was already strongly pushing. The argument for a simple cease-fire by this time was that the continuing slaughter of Arabs was so great that any formula to stop the fighting was better than the prolongation of the war. Once the carnage had stopped, lesser questions— like withdrawal—could be discussed. From Israel's position, a cease-fire without withdrawal would mean that it could use the captured territories to barter for peace—or to keep them. To that end, its supporters were already active in promoting a cease-fire without a withdrawal clause.

Even by the second day of the war, it was obvious that Israel would have a great deal to barter with. In the Sinai, Egyptian forces were reduced to trying to move at night in order to escape the devastating attacks from Israel's air force. Egyptian resistance was effectively broken. Israel's mighty armored force sliced on three axes through the Sinai wastes, one force charging along the coastal road, another to its south and the third across the middle of the peninsula in a mad rush toward the Suez Canal a hundred miles to the west.

Israeli troops also were fanning throughout the West Bank. Jordanian troops suffered the same fiery fate as the Egyptians at the hands of the free-flying Israeli Air Force. Palestinian towns fell one after the other. The noose around the Old City of Jerusalem was drawing tighter.

Everywhere Israel's forces attacked in the Sinai and the West Bank they were succeeding spectacularly, just as the CIA had predicted. But would international opinion allow the Jewish state to keep its gains?

It was this issue—of whether the cease-fire being sought by the United Nations would be a simple halt to combat, with the forces staying in place at the time of cease-fire, or whether there would be a withdrawal to the lines on the eve of the war—that was now consuming Abba Eban. Although the fighting continued, it already had become clear that the most crucial issue now was whether Israel would be allowed to profit from the fruits of its conquest. Eban, with his consummate diplomatic skills, was determined to see that it would. His memories of 1956 were still vivid. He did not want a repeat of Israel's humiliating withdrawal.

On the day of the eruption of war he had issued orders that his U.N. ambassador, Gideon Rafael, was to delay a vote in the Security Council for at least a half day to give Israeli forces more time for conquest before being confronted by a cease-fire demand. In addition, Rafael was told, when a vote on a cease-fire finally could no longer be avoided, he should attempt to see that it did not include the usual U.N. formulation linking it with a demand for withdrawal.

"I promise you at least two days before a cease-fire," replied Rafael.

He had sympathetic support from Arthur Goldberg, Rafael wrote in his memoirs. During the first day of combat, the American representative to the United Nations had telephoned Rafael and, according to the Israeli diplomat, "Goldberg was frightfully worried about Israel and the military equation." Later at the United Nations that day Goldberg asked Rafael, "Gideon, what do you want me to do?"

"I said, 'I want time, nothing else.' He apparently understood that and it apparently fitted American objectives. So we got our time."

As it turned out, Israel would have gotten its desired time even without

Rafael's efforts. As usual, the Council delegates were split among themselves and could not agree on a resolution. An emergency meeting of the Security Council had been convened on the first day of war at 9:30 A.M. Monday to hear Israeli and Egyptian charges that the other had begun the war. Then at 11:15 o'clock, a recess—that was supposed to be short—was called. But as the delegates milled around the Council chamber sounding one another out, it became apparent that no resolution on a cease-fire at this point could win approval.

The problem was in finding the precise formulation. India, a supporter of the Arab side, favored a resolution calling for a cease-fire and a return to the positions both sides held on June 4, the day before the war. But this would leave Egypt with its blockade of the Straits of Tiran intact and was strongly opposed by Israel and other nations. France suggested a clever compromise calling for withdrawal to positions held "before hostilities broke out." But when did hostilities begin? Israel had claimed all along that imposition of the blockade was itself an act of aggression. Egypt countered by contending that it was impossible for a country to commit a hostile act on its own territory.

Complicating the consultations were the different positions of the Soviet Union and the United States. The Soviets wanted not only a cease-fire and withdrawal but also a Council condemnation of Israel as the aggressor. The United States favored the Israeli position, a simple resolution calling for a cease-fire with no mention of condemnation or withdrawal. Since both America and Russia were permanent members of the Council with veto power, no resolution could hope to pass unless it had the backing of both.

Rafael recalled in his memoirs that during the first part of Monday, while it was still unclear in New York which side was winning, the Soviet ambassador, Nikolai Fedorenko, had remained unavailable. "If the Egyptians were approaching the gates of Tel Aviv, there was no hurry to stop them," observed Rafael. "Certainly not to adopt a resolution of withdrawal to the original lines. By five o'clock in the evening, Fedorenko popped up as though he were stung by a hornet and looked for Arthur Goldberg." It was by then generally known that Israel was scoring a historic triumph on the battlefield.

According to Rafael: "I told Arthur Goldberg, 'You are not so available for the next few hours.'"

Even if it is true that America's ambassador to the U.N. engaged in delaying tactics at Israel's behest, it hardly mattered whether Goldberg was available or not because the Council members remained deeply divided.

Although the Council president, Hans Tabor of Denmark, had told the delegates he had hoped for a brief recess, it was not until 10:20 P.M. that he recalled the members to the Council table. They were still so divided that he announced there was no point in reconvening that day. No resolution was put forward at all and the Council disbanded without taking any action. The next meeting was scheduled for 11:30 A.M. Tuesday.

Despite this delay, so important to Israel was the withdrawal issue that, after Eshkol had given approval for the capture of the Old City of Jerusalem, Eban left for New York to carry personally the battle in the Council chambers he knew so well. It was not an easy journey. The airlines had canceled all flights into and out of Israel. It was after 3 A.M. Tuesday before Eban and his aide, Moshe Raviv, managed to hire a small two-engine plane to fly to Athens where they hoped they could find a commercial flight that would get them to New York in time for Tuesday's Council debate. Time was running out. It was already dawn when Eban sighted the Acropolis from the tiny plane, and, once landed in Athens, it took more precious minutes to find a flight to New York.

Eban was over the Atlantic in a KLM airliner and still three hours from New York when a radiogram reached him through the pilot's cabin. It was from Ambassador Rafael and informed him that a worldwide audience would be following the debate on that crucial day and that no resolution had yet been adopted.

Eban and Raviv finally landed at Kennedy Airport in the late afternoon Tuesday and went immediately to the Israeli mission in New York. The Security Council session that had been scheduled for 11:30 that morning had still not begun because the delegates remained in deadlocked disagreement about the contents of a resolution.

Goldberg and Fedorenko had been meeting for hours trying to work out a compromise. While they were conferring, Rafael sent Goldberg a note: "I appeal to you not to agree to any withdrawal clause that would establish an Egyptian claim for Israeli withdrawal before belligerence including Tiran blockade is terminated. Nasser should never again reap a political victory from a military defeat."

Rafael was getting powerful support. Walt Rostow that morning had passed on a message to the President informing him that "Arthur Goldberg called this morning to tell me he had received a telephone call from Jerusalem from Chief Justice Agranat. (They entered the Chicago bar the same year.) The message is via Goldberg to you from Prime Minister Eshkol. There are two points:

"1. Eshkol 'hopes you understand' the action taken by Israel. . . .

"2. Eshkol strongly hopes that we will take no action that would limit Israeli action in achieving freedom of passage through the Gulf of Aqaba. . . .

"We should be back with a recommendation about the second point later in the day."

Implicit in the second point, of course, was the withdrawal issue.

A few hours later, at 4 P.M., Rostow sent his recommendations to the President. "If the Israelis go fast enough, and the Soviets get worried enough, a simple cease-fire might be the best answer. This would mean that we could use the de facto situation on the ground to try to negotiate not a return to armistice lines but a definitive peace in the Middle East." The phrase "definitive peace" was a variation of "permanent peace," both meaning that Israel should not be asked to withdraw short of peace treaties.

By 5:15 P.M., Goldberg and Fedorenko had met again and agreed on a resolution calling for a simple cease-fire with no mention of withdrawal. The Russians by now apparently were so worried by the extent of Egyptian losses that they believed it more important to stop the slaughter than to worry about the future.

Less than an hour later, at 6:06 P.M., Kosygin activated the hot line again, the third time that day, and confirmed that the Kremlin agreed to the wording of the proposed resolution. (The hot line was used once more that Tuesday when Johnson responded to Kosygin's message and activated the line to assure him that the resolution had passed.)

Eban's first act when he had arrived in New York was to telephone Goldberg. Unaware that the superpowers had agreed on a resolution, the foreign minister launched into a passionate lecture, arguing that the resolution should contain nothing but a call for a cease-fire. After patiently hearing him out, Goldberg said:

"Abba, you don't have to rush over to see me. It's all finished, draft resolution and everything. You don't have to worry. . . . Send Gideon over; I'll give him a draft. He deserves it. He's been on my back for the last thirty-six hours." Goldberg added that it had been the Russians who in the end had compromised. "If anyone broke, it was Fedorenko. He has yielded all along the line."

The Council finally convened at 6:30 P.M. Tuesday and unanimously adopted Resolution 233. It said simply that the Council "calls upon the governments concerned as a first step to take forthwith all measures for an immediate cease-fire and for a cessation of all military activities in the area."

Israel had won the first diplomatic battle. But a phrase in the resolution was disturbing to Eban. It called the cease-fire "a first step." The Council would be considering more resolutions in the days ahead, resolutions that still could jeopardize Israel's gains. As Eban noted: "I felt that Israel had gained an important first round, but no more. The danger of international pressure for restoring the Egyptian troop concentrations and blockade had been averted for the moment. But it was clear that once the cease-fire was in effect, the Arabs and Soviets would return to the matter of withdrawal."

With the world press scrutinizing their every word, the representatives of the Middle Eastern nations then explained their positions before the Security Council. When Eban's turn came, he electrified the audience by declaring: "I have just come from Jerusalem to tell the Security Council that Israel, by its independent effort and sacrifice, has passed from serious danger to successful and glorious resistance."

His speech, somber and dignified, said Israel "is now willing to demonstrate its instinct for peace. Let us build a new system of relationships from the wreckage of the old. Let us discern across the darkness the vision of a better and a brighter dawn."

The speech was listened to by millions and won important support for Israel. The Chicago *Tribune* called it "one of the great speeches of modern times." Columnist Ralph McGill wrote that Eban "had cut up the Egyptian delegates with the sword of truth." So popular was it that Columbia Records made a recording of the speech and sold tens of thousands of copies.

But the diplomatic war was not won yet. At the urgent request of the Soviet delegation, President Tabor scheduled the Council to reconvene at 1 P.M. Wednesday to consider a Russian proposal.

Jordan immediately accepted the cease-fire. It had been trying to get a halt to the fighting since early Tuesday morning. Its efforts were ignored by Israel despite a plea from the State Department sent through the U.S. Embassy in Tel Aviv.

"You should inform GOI of Jordanian desire for immediate cease-fire and urge GOI that it would be in their interest to make necessary arrangements immediately and directly rather than through UN," said the message. "This would split Jordan off from other Arab states. It may be preferable that cease-fire remain secret temporarily if king is to maintain control."

Despite King Hussein's offer, Israel pressed its attacks on the West Bank and against the Old City of Jerusalem. Jordanian losses were already staggering in the second day of the war. The Israeli Air Force was using napalm liberally and great numbers of Jordanians and Palestinians were being incinerated. A cable from the U.S. Embassy in Amman reported that by noon on Tuesday "most Jordanian units fighting isolated battles without central control. Jordanian Air Force destroyed; all runways out commission along with . . . radar . . . losing tanks at the rate of one every ten minutes. IDF Air Force yesterday and again today hit many civilian targets on West Bank where there absolutely no military emplacements. . . . Street fighting continues in Old City Jerusalem. . . . Army casualties 'unbearably high.' "

The cable added that "Iraqis have done their best to help. However, Israeli Air Force has been attacking them before they even arrived in Jordan. . . . Syrians have done bare minimum to help out since beginning of conflict."

In fact, Syria had not even begun yet to feel the full brunt of Israeli power. Israel was waiting to clean up its battles with Egypt and Jordan before turning its attention to the hated Syrians.

Egypt found the cease-fire unacceptable without a provision for withdrawal, although Israeli forces were triumphing everywhere. Instead Egypt had another kind of withdrawal in mind. It formally informed the ill-starred Dick Nolte of its "withdrawal of recognition" of Washington. He cabled Washington: "Basis of withdrawal is U.S. air support for Israel in current hostilities, not only initially, but 'replacing Israeli losses as they occur,' according to Cairo Radio.

"Thus endeth my meteoric mission to Cairo. Nolte."*

Egypt's charges of U.S. involvement and its severing of diplomatic relations were followed that day by the breaking of relations with Washington by five other Arab nations: Algeria, Iraq, Sudan, Syria and Yemen, and later by Mauritius.

Perhaps more than Nasser realized, Egypt right now badly needed a cease-fire. By the end of the second day of fighting Israeli forces had overrun the main Egyptian defenses protected by elements of three divisions in the Sinai and were advancing toward the major armored concentrations in the center of the peninsula, the only remaining obstacle before the Suez Canal. On the West Bank, Israeli troops were spread throughout, overwhelming Jordanian troops with a combination of armor and close air support. The Old City of Jerusalem stood surrounded and ready for assault. The only quiet areas were the frontiers with Lebanon and Syria. Lebanon

* Nolte never was officially accredited as ambassador to Cairo, though he is often identified as the last U.S. chief of mission in 1967. That honor officially belongs to Luke Battle. Nolte later resumed his old job as executive director of the Institute of Current World Affairs, a post he held until retiring in 1978.

had consistently refrained from any hostile actions; the Syrian government, since its air force had been destroyed, was still showing no appetite for war.

Under such conditions, Israel, despite Eban's ringing U.N. speech about a better and brighter dawn, demonstrated no interest in a cease-fire.

A CIA appraisal of Israeli objectives prepared that Tuesday concluded that the "immediate and primary GOI war aim is destruction of the center of power of the radical Arab Socialist movement, i.e., the Nasser regime. . . . If the arms of the radical Arabs can be destroyed, the GOI assumes, Turkey, Iran and Israel will represent an overwhelming balance of military power in the area. Thus the maximum destruction of Soviet weapons in the hands of the Arabs is the second major GOI objective. Israel will attempt to destroy the Syrian regime and to eliminate both Syria and Jordan as modern states. . . . Hussein's trip to Cairo marked Jordan, in Israeli eyes, for elimination."

It was not a bright outlook for the Arab nations. But it did not take into account Soviet determination.

In Washington, the President spent much of his day, as he had the day before, in an endless round of meetings and discussions about the war in the Middle East. Just before 11 P.M., after a late dinner, the President rose and said, "I was one of the four o'clockers this morning—so I'm going to bed."

At that time in the eastern Mediterranean, the U.S.S. *Liberty* was finally approaching the war zone. In another day it would be on station, listening in on the communications of all the combatants.

XVII
JUNE 7: THE CAPTURE OF JERUSALEM

I t was 4 A.M. Wednesday in Washington when the age-old dream of
Jews was realized. At that hour the Old City of Jerusalem was captured by Israeli troops. For the first time since 135 A.D., Jerusalem, ancient,
golden Jerusalem, the City of David, the city of peace, the city that Jews for
centuries had expressed their longing to return to "next year," was at last in
the hands of the Jews.

The end had come suddenly and, in terms of the profligate slaughter of
past battles, almost bloodlessly. The Old City with its forty thousand Arab
residents had been completely surrounded since the previous evening. Only
a few stragglers remained from the small contingent of Jordanian soldiers
who had been there; the rest had slipped away during the night undetected
by the Israeli forces. The Moslem notables of the Old City had already decided that they would not, could not, resist an Israeli attack. They were prepared to surrender the fabled city to spare its civilian population and its
precious shrines.

Shortly before 10 A.M. local time, on the third day of the war, the half-
track vehicle of Colonel Mordechai ("Motta") Gur, commander of the
Fifty-fifth Paratrooper Brigade, burst through the shattered heavy doors of
St. Stephen's Gate, also known as Lion's Gate, in the crenellated eastern
wall of the Old City and entered the Via Dolorosa. The Temple Mount was
only a short distance away.

Gur and his group sped toward it, the tracks of their vehicle skidding and
setting off sparks on the ancient stone streets. Except for minor sniper fire,
they reached without incident the Temple Mount with its magnificent Dome

of the Rock, the golden octagonal mosque built by the Ommayad Caliph Abdel Malek between 687 and 691. For more than a thousand years it had served as a holy place of Islam. Briefly, during the Crusades, it was converted into a Christian church, Templum Domini. Now the blue-and-white Star of David, Israel's flag, the banner of the modern Jewish state, was about to flutter from it.

At 10 A.M., Motta Gur exultantly radioed the Israeli Central Command and announced: "Temple Mount is in our hands. Temple Mount is ours. Temple Mount is ours!"

It was an awesome moment of rapturous emotion for the Israeli troopers. They quickly descended to the Western Wall, the Wailing Wall where no Jew had been permitted to pray for the past nineteen years, and kissed and caressed the great Herodian slabs of golden Jerusalem limestone that made up its base. Here in these huge ashlars was the last remnant of the Second Temple, the last temple of the Jewish people. It had been constructed millennia earlier, destroyed in 70 A.D. and then the site was briefly recaptured in 134 A.D. by the Jewish warrior Bar Kochba. Since then it had been controlled by Rome, Christians and, mainly, Moslems. Now for the first time in 1,833 years it was back in Jewish hands.

Within minutes the small area in front of the towering sixty-foot wall studded with some wild flowers and the patina of the ages was filled with joyous Israeli soldiers. Still dressed in their combat gear, with rifles over their shoulders, many with *kippas* (skullcaps) on their heads, dusty and unshaven, they were laughing and crying, delirious and disbelieving in their happiness and wonderment. They chanted ancient prayers—thus the name Wailing Wall—bowing up and down, their combat equipment clinking and rattling as their rifles swayed and bobbed with their genuflections. Within a half hour Shlomo Goren, the chief Ashkenazi rabbi of Israel, carrying a Torah scroll and a shofar, which he blew from time to time, led a group of his followers worshipfully to the wall. On reaching it, he solemnly declared:

"I, General Shlomo Goren, chief rabbi of the Israel Defense Forces, have come to this place never to leave again."

No one could doubt that the rabbi meant what he said, and many others felt the same way. When Colonel Gur told a radio reporter simply that "the holy city is ours," he was interrupted by Major General Haim Barlev: "Forever." Gur continued: "Ours forever, as Haim Barlev says. For always and always."

A short while later, a delegation of somber Arabs approached Gur and formally surrendered the city.

Dayan, Rabin and Central Command commander Uzi Narkiss arrived at the wall by 2 P.M. The moment was sweet for each of them, but particularly for Narkiss and Rabin. Narkiss had been the commander of the Fourth Battalion of the Harel Brigade, which had been involved in the final unsuccessful effort to defend the Jewish Quarter of the Old City in 1948. Rabin had been the commander of the brigade. Both had watched as their forces failed and the Old City remained in Arab control. Now, finally, after nineteen years, in their own lifetime, it was theirs.

"I felt this was the height of my life," Rabin later said. ". . . for me, as one who was born in Jerusalem and fought in forty-eight in the besieged Jerusalem—trying to take the Old City and not succeeding—and now as chief of staff to bring about the unification of the city and visiting the Western Wall—it's fulfillment of a dream."

At a press conference, Moshe Dayan declared unequivocally: "This morning the Israel Defense Forces liberated Jerusalem. We have united Jerusalem, the divided capital of Israel. We have returned to the holiest of our holy places, never to part from it again."

Eshkol arrived at the wall later that afternoon. When the soldiers saw him they broke out in a chorus of "Jerusalem of Gold," a popular new Hebrew ballad they had been singing off and on since capturing the Old City. Its evocative and prophetic lyrics, vibrant with longing and nostalgia, communicated better than any of the official statements the emotional pull of the Old City and the lands of the ancient Jewish kingdom. For Israelis, the song became the anthem of war.

> We have come back to the deep wells
> To the marketplace again.
> The trumpet sounds on the Mount of
> the Temple
> In the Old City.
> In the caverns of the cliff
> Glitter a thousand suns.
> We shall go down to the Dead Sea again
> By the road to Jericho.

The prime minister slipped a piece of paper with a prayer written by his wife between the massive stones of the wall, a traditional gesture of the Jews. He was pale and visibly upset when he returned home. His wife, Miriam, asked what was wrong.

"I have had such a palpitation of the heart," he replied. "I cannot remember anything like it for years—maybe once when I cheated and I was afraid my father would find out."

Later that day Eshkol experienced the discomfiture of the conqueror. Much as the Romans had summoned the ancient Hebrews, he summoned the leaders of the various Christian communities, Armenian, Greek Orthodox, Protestant, Roman Catholic. He formally told them that Israel now controlled all of Jerusalem and all its holy places. Shrines and churches would be respected and protected, he promised, and they would be open to all denominations for worship.

That night Eshkol said he could sense the hatred of the churchmen. They apparently could not believe that they, "the lords of two thousand years," would now have to come to the Jews.

He asked his wife: "Were the Jews, when we had to meet with all sorts of Gentiles who were oppressing us, who were conquering us, as miserable as they were when they had to face me?"

Apparently the fall of the Old City was not considered important enough to awaken the President. He slept undisturbed that morning until he awoke at 6:15 o'clock.

But to Israel and its U.S. supporters, the capture of all of Jerusalem made it all the more imperative that Johnson be convinced that opposition to withdrawal should be the official policy of the United States. Loyalists to Israel were divided, as were Israelis themselves. Some sincerely believed the captured territories should be used as bargaining chips for a permanent peace; others believed that under no circumstances should any parts of the territories be returned. One thing was certain: most, if not all, Jews desperately longed to retain a united Jerusalem as Israel's capital.

To that end, Israel's many supporters surrounding the President now exerted themselves with unprecedented energy. Seldom, if ever, had a President been subjected, or allowed himself to be subjected, to such a concerted campaign as Lyndon Johnson that Wednesday. It was all pro-Israel; Arabs seemed to have no advocates.

Two of his earliest telephone calls were from Abe Fortas, who followed them up with a message recommending that the United States avoid taking any immediate position. "Once there is a cease-fire, the United States should not try and draw up blueprints for restructuring the Middle East," suggested the associate justice of the Supreme Court. "... we should let the Israelis and Arabs negotiate this out, and save ourselves until the last half of the ninth inning in the negotiations."

Fortas' recommendation meant, in effect, that Washington should back Israel and not call for an immediate withdrawal. It was not on its face an absurd position, and it was one appreciated by the President. After all, Eisenhower had forced Israel to give up its conquests and what had it achieved? In addition, Johnson had strongly opposed Ike at the time. He was not likely to do now what he had thought wrong nearly eleven years earlier.

Mathilde Krim also had advice for the President. She was going to New York for a few days and not returning to the White House, where she was still a houseguest, until Friday. Before departing she had tried to reach the President and failed. (He was in a meeting of the National Security Council.) So she dictated a long note to Johnson urging him to come out more strongly for Israel. She suggested this was necessary to prevent a rally scheduled for the next day by thousands of Jews in Lafayette Square, across from the White House, from turning into an anti-Johnson demonstration. Jewish Americans, she said, were still upset by McCloskey's neutrality statement. The memorandum added: "She thinks she has a way to help regain the President's position. . . . She suggested that another speech or statement be made today or tonight calling for a permanent peace settlement." Again that phrase "permanent peace." It was already well established as meaning "no withdrawal."

Mrs. Krim then dictated a statement that she thought the President should deliver verbatim to the American people:

"The United States will not resume relations with a government headed by Nasser because he is responsible for useless and deplorable bloodshed and because of his cynical and irresponsible accusations of the United States and his attempt to provoke a major conflagration. . . ."

The President was so impressed with her comments that later in the day he personally read some of them to Secretary of State Rusk. But he did not, as she suggested, read them to the American people.

Abe Feinberg also made his views known that day, and at the same time took the occasion to convey a back-channel message from Abba Eban. This was done through Walt Rostow, who left a National Security Council meeting of the Administration's top officials to accept an "urgent" call about the "topic you are now talking about" from Bill D. Moyers, Johnson's former press spokesman. Rostow went to an anteroom and did little talking. Instead, he hastily made notes, then said: "Thank you, Bill, you're not bothering me, you're being helpful."

When he returned to the Cabinet meeting, Rostow passed to the President the notes he had written: "Bill Moyers reports via Fineberg* from Eban:

* Rostow's spelling; the typed version has it spelled correctly.

"1. When USSR asks withdrawal from cease-fire lines, Eban will say: NO DRAW-BACK WITHOUT DEFINITIVE PEACE.

"2. Eban will be seeing Goldberg to ask US support.

"3. Fineberg says this is route for the President totally to *retrieve* position after 'neutrality' and all that."

Later in the day Rostow also passed along another long dictated message from Mrs. Krim. It was essentially a repeat of her morning message, but longer and in starker terms.

"She doesn't believe the President evaluates correctly the resentment still lingering after the McCloskey statement several days ago. There are reports of very strong anti-American feelings in Israel—that Israelis feel they have won the war not with the U.S., but despite the U.S. In the Jewish community it is very difficult to explain the coincidence of the statement and the beginning of hostilities. The Jews are a people with a persecution complex and they understood the statement of the State Dept. to mean that in an hour of gravest danger to them . . . that this country disengaged itself. . . . That is why they reacted so violently when the neutrality statement came out. . . .

"There is great danger that the Jewish rally to be held tomorrow in Lafayette Square here will be anti-Johnson, rather than a pro-Israel, demonstration. Even Minister Evron says things are going out of hand. . . .

"Mrs. Krim, her husband and other people they have talked to feel the situation can still be salvaged for the President provided he makes very soon—possibly even today—a very strong statement. . . ."

That concern seemed to be eradicated later in the day when David Ginsburg, the Washington attorney, sent a message to the President through Joe Califano. "David Ginsburg reported to me that he thinks the meeting of the one thousand Jewish leaders tonight at the Sheraton-Carlton and the rally of thousands of Jews tomorrow in Lafayette Square at 2:30 P.M. is under control," Califano wrote in a memorandum to Johnson. "Tomorrow the main speaker is Morris Abrams, head of the American-Jewish Committee. David has been over his speech and rewritten it and assures me it will be o.k.

"David says the theme will be solidarity with Israel, combined with declarations that the President is doing a magnificent job in the Israel crisis."

Even two junior members of Johnson's own staff took the occasion to fire off a confidential memorandum to the President. Speech writer Ben Wattenberg and Lawrence Levinson, a domestic affairs aide, wrote Johnson what he already knew: The neutrality statement had caused "sharp disillusion and dismay" in the Jewish American community. "The major concern today among Jewish leaders now is this: that Israel, apparently having won the war, may be forced to lose the peace—again (as in 1956). They were concerned that the U.N. would attempt to sell Israel down the river—and that only the U.S. could prevent that. Today, that is what American Jews are looking to the President for: assurances of a real, guaranteed, meaningful peace in the Middle East, and that Israel not be forced to a roll-back as they were by the Dulles-Eisenhower position in 1956."

They had employed the speech writers' variation of the permanent peace theme: real, guaranteed, meaningful peace. By whatever flourish, it meant there should be no Israeli withdrawal, as in 1956.

By now, the Soviet Union was desperate. It was obvious that the most urgent need of its Middle Eastern allies, armed with Soviet weapons and being humiliated on the battlefield, was an immediate cease-fire. The importance of withdrawal and similar questions of the future paled in comparison to the slaughter of Arab troops taking place in the Sinai and the West Bank, on the third day of the war.

Premier Kosygin that Wednesday reactivated the hot line again to complain to President Johnson that Israel had still not accepted a cease-fire as called for in the previous day's Security Council resolution. In a cool response, unencumbered by any salutation beyond "Mr. Chairman," Johnson urged Kosygin "to counsel moderation where it is needed."

Kosygin obviously thought that the subject for the counseling of moderation was Israel. That same Wednesday he sent a threatening oral message via his Tel Aviv ambassador to Israel warning that the Soviet Union might break diplomatic relations. If the fighting does not stop, he warned, the Soviet Union will "1) reconsider its attitude toward Israel and decide on the future of the diplomatic relations with Israel which by its actions has placed itself in opposition to all peace-loving states, 2) it is obvious that the Soviet government will also examine and implement other necessary steps which emanate from the aggressive policy of Israel."

Ambassador Barbour cabled the State Department that the Israelis "are not repeat not inclined to take this as serious ultimatum, pointing out that it contains internal evidence of Soviet intention reserve considerable room for maneuver."

The Soviets also pressed their case at the United Nations. At 1 P.M., the Security Council meeting they had requested opened with most members expecting to hear a Russian demand that Israel cease fire and withdraw. But the Soviets by now had become so concerned that Ambassador Fedorenko did not even raise the issues. He angrily condemned Israel in his remarks to the Council, accusing it of "marching in the bloody footsteps of Hitler's executioners." But, surprisingly, he then introduced a resolution much along the lines of Tuesday's. It neither condemned Israel nor called for withdrawal. Instead, in order to retrieve as much as possible from a disastrous situation, the Soviet resolution "demanded" a cease-fire by 2000 hours GMT (10 P.M. in Israel).

Abba Eban repeated to the Council that "we favor, we support, we accept the resolution calling for immediate measures to institute a cease-fire." But the Israeli acceptance was not as firm as it appeared. It was conditional on Arab acceptance, even though it was the Israelis who were attacking throughout the region. Nonetheless, Eban was able to point out that he could not find a single sentence in any speech by any Arab official saying " 'we Syria, we Iraq, we UAR, welcome and accept the cease-fire resolution.' " (Of course, Syria and Iraq were not in the war.) On the contrary, he said, media reports from Cairo indicated that Egypt rejected a cease-fire. True, he added, Jordan had agreed to stop the fighting but what did that mean when the Egyptian command now controlled its armed forces as a result of Jordan's defense treaty with Egypt?

The fact was Israel had no desire for a cease-fire yet, and the Egyptians, stunned and humiliated, seemed too mortified to be able to admit the dimensions of their horrendous defeat.

Despite Eban's claim, King Hussein, not Egypt, retained control of his troops, at least as much control as anyone could exercise over a routed and retreating mass of men fleeing for their lives. He was still desperately trying, without success, to get Israel to stop fighting. Over the past twenty-four hours, Israel had rebuffed his overtures by claiming that he was attempting to deceive it. But the deception was not Hussein's, as the U.S. ambassador to Amman, Findley Burns, Jr., had been trying to convey to the State Department.

"For past several hours Radio Amman has been announcing GOJ acceptance of cease-fire," Burns cabled. "Israeli suggestion that king deliberately following tactic of deception hardly supportable. Israeli military intelligence well aware Jordanian losses. IDF briefings . . . have covered losses in detail."

Indeed, Hussein's losses by midafternoon Wednesday were staggering. His forces had been chased from all of Jerusalem, the holy city he had been sworn to protect for all of Islam, and from all the biblical cities of Judea and Samaria: Bethlehem, Hebron, Jericho and Nablus (ancient Shechem). Israeli troops controlled the entire West Bank, from Jenin in the north to

Samu in the south, from the Dead Sea in the east to Qalqilya in the west. They also held all three bridges across the River Jordan, assuring their ability to defend the area against the unlikely event of counterattacks from the East Bank.

As the Israeli forces advanced, the Palestinian population was seized with panic. Many gathered what few possessions they could carry and fled for their lives.

Another pitiful wave of men, women and children was soon to turn into a Palestinian flood of homeless refugees for the second time in nineteen years.

Ambassador Burns in Amman was so worried about the repercussions of the humiliating rout of Hussein's army and the explosive bitterness of the new refugees that he feared the king might be overthrown by his furious subjects. He was also worried about the safety of Americans in the region. A virulent wave of anti-Americanism was sweeping the Arab world. Mobs had been attacking and demonstrating against U.S. installations throughout the region since the claim the previous day by Hussein and Nasser that U.S. planes had helped Israel. When the devastating dimensions of Hussein's defeat became known, Burns realized, the mob could turn its violent passions against Americans personally and the king too.

"I recognize IDF goal may well be total destruction of Jordanian army," Burns cabled Washington. "I consider that . . . would have disastrous effects on this regime and on area stability as whole. I am gravely concerned about resultant effects on public order and on safety large American community still in kingdom. For all these considerations I consider it imperative we spare no effort to arrange this cease-fire."

He was so concerned that he made a highly unusual suggestion for an ambassador. "I respectfully urge," cabled Burns, "that President telephone Primin [Prime Minister] Eshkol to bring cease-fire into effect soonest."

Without a telephone call from Johnson, Israel finally accepted the Soviet-sponsored 10 P.M. cease-fire, although the fighting continued for three more hours. Then, except for the crack of a sporadic sniper's bullet, silence descended on Jordan.

Inexplicably, Washington failed to learn that the cease-fire had taken hold. As late as 10:40 P.M. EDT (4:40 A.M. Thursday in Israel) Secretary of State Rusk rushed off a flash cable to the U.S. Embassy in Tel Aviv: "You should make strongest representation of dangerous situation to highest available level GOI. You should stress influx refugees to East Bank and rapid disintegration Jordan security forces now constitute real threat to regime and to large American and foreign community in Jordan. We are taking action with Eban but you should make most vigorous plea for Israeli acceptance cease-fire offer and immediate public notice this action."

Five minutes after his cable was dispatched, the White House Situation Room reported that "we have just received information that a cease-fire was effected between Jordan and Israeli forces at 5 P.M. EDT today. At present, both sides appear to be observing the cease-fire."

Israel's conquest of the West Bank was now complete.

Another U.S. diplomat, hapless Dick Nolte in Cairo, was beginning to have fears similar to Burns's in Amman. Though he had earlier bid his official adieu, Nolte was still in the embassy preparing for evacuation and worrying about the repercussions of what was clearly becoming one of the most humiliating defeats in warfare. The desert was an inferno of burning tanks, of thousands of desperate Egyptian soldiers, stunned and shelterless and often shoeless, fleeing across the hot sands toward the safety of the Suez Canal, of advancing Israeli armored units racing toward the canal to trap the remnants of the Egyptian Army.

"... many Egyptian wounded lay along the road, under collapsed or overturned vehicles, or among corpses in the fields, trying to attract attention with the little strength they had left," wrote Israeli reporter Amos Elon as he accompanied Israeli troops across the Sinai. "Their dark faces, above their torn and bloody bodies, were terrible to look at. . . . Even worse was the feeling that one was powerless to do anything for them at the moment. The army was rushing to prevent the escape of the Egyptian Army through passes to the canal and it was impossible to render any useful assistance."

In Cairo, Nolte sent a cable to Washington saying a general revulsion against Nasser was likely to emerge as a result of Egypt's awful losses. "Survival of Nasser regime at home is in question as well as the allegiance of other Arab states," Nolte wrote. Regardless of what happened to Nasser, he added, the United States should be ready to supply medical assistance to the war casualties in order to restore some U.S. influence in the country.

Nolte, looking ahead, presciently warned that the current fighting was doing nothing to redress the major problem between Israel and the Arabs—the Palestinians. "Necessary to recognize very real passion mobilized in whole area by Nasser on Palestine issue," he wrote. "Present defeat would only make that 'anger of inferiority' all the more ready a few years hence for the next hero. . . . Maybe now, on basis of new security, Israel can be made to see wisdom of settlement along less one-sided lines. Impartial and constructive U.S. role here could go far toward reversing universal loss of respect for and influence of U.S. in whole Arab world."

While Nolte worried about the future, there was an atmosphere of unreality in the Egyptian capital. Trucks with loudspeakers rolled through Cairo's streets blaring out slogans: "We shall win!" The daily newspaper *Al Akhbar* carried a headline that third day of the war crying "Our Forces, in Strength and Heroism, Give Chase to American and British Fighters."

Times reporter Eric Pace found that every Egyptian he talked with believed that there had been intervention by American and British aircraft at the beginning of the war. But, Pace observed, "They remained polite. 'Why do you help the Israelis?' one asked gently, as though to an errant child."

The news got worse as the day progressed. Egyptian troops took up positions along the Suez Canal, one hundred miles inside Egyptian territory. Cairo Radio announced in the afternoon that Egyptian forces had fallen back to "secondary positions" in the Sinai but were "fighting fiercely."

Then came a dramatic admission. The radio tersely announced the garrison at Sharm el Sheikh had joined other units "now concentrated in the Sinai Peninsula." Translated, that was a clear admission that Egypt had abandoned its hold on the Straits of Tiran, the putative cause of the fighting. Israeli troops occupied the strategic base at the scenic tip of the Sinai Peninsula that same day, without firing a shot.

Pace reported: "The propaganda about United States and British involvement seemed to have prepared the people to accept the idea of losing—and the military communiqués gave no idea of the size of Egypt's losses in arms and men."

With diplomatic relations severed, American news correspondents were ordered to move to the Nile Hilton. When Pace arrived there he discovered that the staff would not let him out again. "I demanded to see the officer in charge, who turned out to be an amiable captain. He asked if the Ministry of Interior had ordered me to leave the country. I said no, with emphasis (the order had come from the Ministry of Information), and he let me go. I never went back, particularly when it developed that all the other American newspapermen were being interned in the hotel until their transportation out of the country could be arranged."

Pace checked into the old colonial vintage Semiramis Hotel and that night took a walk around Cairo. "Guards and bystanders shouted at me in Arabic, but I didn't know what they were saying so I just waved a hand (would they think I was throwing a grenade?) and walked on. It was difficult in the darkness not to stumble against brick blast walls that had been built outside the entrances of important buildings like banks to protect them against air raids. In the silence of an earlier blackout I had heard a cat mewing. But tonight Cairo's cats were still."

There was no stillness in the Sinai. There, under silvery stars blinking in the pure desert air, the night was filled with sounds. The cries of the wounded and the frightened, of the thirsty and the dying, wafted across the churned sands as the mighty Israeli juggernaut relentlessly advanced toward the banks of the Suez Canal, threatening Cairo itself.

That night the U.S.S. *Liberty* approached within sight of the Gaza Strip to begin its spying duties. Aboard the electronic interception ship the sailors had listened to a news broadcast which included a report that Arthur Goldberg, in rebutting Egyptian charges of U.S. involvement, had assured the United Nations that "no American ship is within three hundred miles of the fighting." The assertion gave the *Liberty*'s crew a hearty chuckle.

But there was no humor in Washington. Chairman of the Joint Chiefs of Staff Buz Wheeler was worried about the political repercussions that would result if the *Liberty*'s position was discovered. The Sixth Fleet was indeed staying out of the eastern Mediterranean to avoid any appearance of colluding with Israel as well as to stay away from the Russian ships operating in the area. But the *Liberty* had been ordered to patrol within twelve and a half nautical miles of Egypt and six and a half miles of Israel, a half mile out from the distances each country claimed for its territorial waters.

A Joint Chiefs of Staff committee shortly before midnight in the Middle East ordered the ship to conduct its patrol farther out to sea, staying twenty nautical miles from Egypt and fifteen from Israel. An hour later, the Pentagon staff, mindful of Wheeler's concern, decided to be safe. It ordered the *Liberty* to conduct its patrol at a distance of one hundred miles from the shoreline of any of the belligerents.

By bureaucratic blunder, both messages failed to reach the *Liberty*. The Army Communication Center serving the Joint Chiefs sent the first message to the Naval Communication Station in the Philippines. The second message became ensnared in a series of misroutings and delays, including a vital four-and-half-hour period where it languished unrelayed aboard the aircraft carrier U.S.S. *America* in the Mediterranean because of priority preparations for a press conference to rebut Nasser's charge of U.S. involvement.

Although unaware of the messages, the *Liberty*'s skipper, Commander McGonagle, was having his own doubts about operating so close to a combat zone. As captain, he had the prerogative to sail his ship away from danger. But when he asked an electronics expert how a withdrawal to a patrol zone fifty miles at sea would affect the ship's mission, he was told that it would reduce its effectiveness by 80 percent.

McGonagle thought for a minute and then said: "Okay. We'll go all the way in."

That night he added to his overnight orders to the officer of the deck: "Keep gun crews/lookouts alert. Call me for all challenges received, or in the event air or surface contacts approach in a suspicious manner."

In Washington, Wednesday had been another harried day for Lyndon Johnson. In addition to two exchanges on the hot line with the Kremlin, a bipartisan breakfast with the congressional leadership and numerous other routine chores, ranging from the continuing agony of Vietnam, where 214 Americans had been killed and 1,161 wounded the previous week, to receiving an engraved gold lifetime pass to National Football League games, there had been a meeting of the National Security Council.

Johnson took the occasion to establish a Special Committee to coordinate Middle East policy. McGeorge Bundy, the supremely well organized former head of the NSC under President John F. Kennedy and during the early years of Johnson's presidency and now president of the Ford Foundation, was appointed executive secretary of the committee and special consultant to the President. The purpose of the appointment, the President told the NSC meeting, was to "ensure coordination of the work of our government" to "help build a new peace" in the Middle East.

Actually, there was unhappiness with Gene Rostow's managerial talents, which were considered so weak by some of his colleagues that his style was labeled a "floating crap game." Also, there was some sensitivity to rising talk that Rostow and the Administration in general were too pro-Israel. In a memorandum to Johnson that day, Press secretary George Christian noted that "there is a definite ripple of speculation that Bundy was brought in to save the situation, that Rostow is Jewish and can't be effective in this, etc. . . . I have emphasized in talks with reporters that in the situation like this, it is necessary to coordinate programs in the White House, and that it requires full-time attention."

But it was not only Rostow who was reflecting the pro-Israel emotions sweeping the country. Wally Barbour, the ambassador in Tel Aviv, also weighed in that day with a brief on Israel's behalf.

"It is quite clear that current success of Israeli military effort has had fundamental and lasting effect of convincing Israelis of all walks of life that this is opportunity for them to move from restricted status of semi- and temporary acceptance which has characterized the first 19 years of Israel's existence to a condition of complete and entire nationhood enjoying all the attributes of other independent states. Translated into specifics and objectives which they will seek in the political sphere this means that they will insist on moving from a cease-fire position directly to the conclusion of final peace treaties with their neighbors. . . ."

Barbour prophesied, incorrectly, that "despite the heady atmosphere of victory and the temptation this may provide for territorial expansion, the voice of wisdom will prevent them from changing fundamentally the assurances given at the outset that they will remain within their present borders."

He concluded by observing that Israelis believed their war "had been so successful as to have created an opportunity for Israel to achieve full unrestricted statehood and to reshape the situation in the Arab world at least sufficiently to safe-guard Israel future security concerns."

Concluded Barbour: ". . . I believe the Israelis can be expected to accept nothing less."

Although there was a happy mood of celebration around the United States at Israel's stunning victories and the defeat of Russian arms in the hands of Arabs, Johnson was somber. In one of his more thoughtful moods, he wisely warned the NSC meeting that he was "not sure we were out of our troubles." According to notes of the meeting, "He could not visualize the USSR saying it had miscalculated, and then walking away. Our objective should be to 'develop as few heroes and as few heels as we can.' It is important for everybody to know we are not for aggression. We are sorry this has taken place.

"The President said that by the time we get through with all the festering problems we are going to wish the war had not happened."

Those were the wisest words uttered that day, for what was now unfolding in the Middle East would set the region on a course of hatred and war far worse than ever before.

The President did not get to his living quarters until 9:18 P.M. that Wednesday. Despite the length of his day, the evening took on a relaxed, homey atmosphere when Lady Bird joined him in the West Hall. But the outside world soon intruded on the relaxed atmosphere of the mansion. Johnson's domestic political adviser called at 11:17 P.M. and, although the

President finally retired at 11:30, his rest was disturbed by one more call at 11:59 P.M. It was from Mrs. Krim, who was still in New York.

In the eastern Mediterranean, where it was already the dawn of June 8, the watch officer aboard the U.S.S. *Liberty*, Ensign John D. Scott, noticed something suspicious. When he was relieved a short time later, he told his replacement, Lieutenant James M. Ennes, Jr., about it.

"About an hour ago we were circled by a flying boxcar. Real slow and easy." He had no idea of the nationality of the plane or the nature of its mission. But he told Ennes that all four of the ship's .50-caliber Browning machine guns now had ammunition and two of the forward gun mounts were manned by gunners in battle dress.

At the moment Ennes was more worried about navigation in the shallow waters than the mysterious plane. The shoreline at that point was undistinguished by landmarks and, fearful of causing an international incident by accidentally drifting into Egyptian waters, Ennes took unusual care to keep the ship on course twelve and a half miles off the Sinai coast.

He also took the precaution to have a new five-by-eight-foot American flag hoisted on the mast for easy identification. Washington might have trouble in proclaiming neutrality, but here in the battle zone the *Liberty* wanted it understood that it was a neutral ship.

Meanwhile in Washington, it was unknown that the orders to move the ship farther out to sea had still not been delivered. It was assumed the *Liberty* was well away from harm's way. All attention was on Israel's lightning attacks and on the question of when the war might finally end.

XVIII
JUNE 8:
U.S.S. *LIBERTY*
ATTACKED

King Hussein normally reflected the stoic dignity and impecca-
ble dress traditional of his Sandhurst training, usually manag-
ing to make even army fatigues look like a dress uniform. But on Thursday
when he appeared before about fifty foreign and Jordanian correspondents
at the army headquarters in Amman, he was unshaven, haggard, emotional
and near tears.

"Our losses were tremendous," he explained. "But we are proud of the
fact we fought honorably. We are proud of our men and of the fact that, despite all odds, we were able to stand like men, not only in the front line but
also at home. The battle was waged against us almost exclusively from the
air with overwhelming strength and continual, sustained air attacks on every
single unit of our armed forces, day and night, right until last night when the
cease-fire took effect."

The young monarch valiantly tried to put as good a face on his humiliating loss as possible. He said his haggardness resulted from lack of sleep, not
a lack of morale. "Needless to say we have been continuously awake since
the hostilities started. Do not attribute what you see to any other factor. . . .
Our morale is high."

But he was a beaten, dispirited man. He had not slept for three days, existing on adrenalin and endless cups of tea and countless cigarettes. He was
filled with a sense of shame and despair, burdened by his enormous losses in
men and matériel and especially by a sense of failure, his personal failure to
defend the holy places, Jerusalem with its holy mosques and Hebron with its

venerated Cave of Machpelah, the burial place of the patriarchs, Abraham, Isaac and Jacob, worshiped by Jews and Moslems alike. In an emotional radio address to his subjects that day, Hussein's deep voice nearly broke as he spoke of his and the nation's disaster.

"What is done is done," he said stoically. But he added: "My heart breaks when I think of the loss of all our fallen soldiers. They were dearer to me than my own self."

Then no doubt thinking of his assassinated grandfather and his grandfather's father, Hussein ibn Ali, the grand sharif and emir of Mecca, hereditary custodian of the Moslem holy places, who in 1925 lost his Arabian domain to the House of Saud (thus *Saudi* Arabia), Hussein spoke of the misfortune that had plagued his family.

"My brothers, I seem to belong to a family which, according to the will of Allah, must suffer and make sacrifices for its country without end. Our calamity is greater than anyone could have imagined."

Indeed, in men alone, his losses were staggering. His forces had fought more tenaciously than any other, and the toll in casualties was, as Hussein said, heartbreaking. Estimated Jordanian losses were at first put at 6,094 dead and missing. But many of those reported missing were West Bankers who had simply returned to their homes or became refugees when the fighting stopped. A later, more accurate, estimate was that 696 had been killed in less than three days of fighting.

Israeli casualties were about 550 killed and 2,400 wounded, a higher casualty toll than on any other front, a testament to the ferocity of the West Bank fighting.

There were other casualties too, in their way even more heartbreaking than the dead because they were destined to perpetuate their own misery through later generations. They were the new wave of refugees, mainly women and children and old people, innocent, helpless and bereft of home and hope. An estimated twenty to thirty thousand of the newly dispossessed had already fled across the Jordan to the East Bank by Thursday.

They were only the beginning of a human flood tide of destitution and despair. Many of them had been made refugees by the 1948 war. Now, nineteen years later, they were homeless again.

Economically, Hussein's losses matched the dimensions of the human tragedy. As much as 50 percent of his country's best agricultural land and its main religious and tourist attractions had been lost with the fall of the West Bank. Resentment and anger were high among the two million Jordanians. They felt cheated, humiliated and deserted. They suspected U.S. and British collusion with Israel, incompetence in the government, weakness in Hussein. They were embittered and frustrated, and their seething passions threatened to explode against the king.

With the atmosphere so charged, Jordanian officials warned Americans and Britons to stay off the streets in downtown Amman. Wherever Americans and Britons went they drew angry looks from Arabs. In addition to newsmen, there were three hundred U.S. civilians in Jordan and a concerted effort was now made to evacuate them before the fury of the mob exploded. Washington arranged for the mass evacuation to take place the next day. Meanwhile, U.S. diplomats were sleeping in the embassy and other Americans were staying in their homes or hotels to secure their safety. Suddenly, "neutrality" had become a precious word for the frightened and imperiled Americans in Jordan.

There were other Americans that Thursday morning experiencing unease, if not yet fright. They were the crew of the U.S.S. *Liberty*, which was conducting its leisurely five-knot patrol along the Egyptian coast still unaware that the ship had been ordered away from the area of hostilities. Shortly after the minaret in the Sinai town of El Arish came into view at 9:30 A.M., a lookout shouted: "Airplane passing astern, sir!"

A single jet flew past on the starboard side too far away for its markings to be discerned. It made only one pass and disappeared.

The appearance of an unknown airplane in a war zone was worrisome, but this morning it was not unduly so to the men of the *Liberty*. After all, the new U.S. flag was flying from the tripod-shaped foremast standing nearly one hundred feet tall. A light nine-to-twelve-knot breeze ruffled the ensign, making it clearly visible. The sea was calm, the sky so clear that lookouts could see the curvature of the earth. The ship's identification letters, AGTR 5, were painted in white on both sides of the bow and the stern. On the stern also was the *Liberty*'s name. Beyond these easily identifiable features, the *Liberty*'s unique profile was like almost no other in the world. Its many antennas and distinctive microwave moon-bounce communication dish told even a nonprofessional that this was no ordinary ship.

It was generally agreed among the crew that the only possible threat to the American ship would come from Egypt or the Soviet squadron operating in the eastern Mediterranean. But Egypt's air force was already destroyed and the Soviet Union had shown no inclination to get involved. That left only the Israelis, and they were America's best friend in the region, so the dangers seemed minimal.

That was a comforting thought to many in the crew. As one of the civilian electronics experts aboard concluded, the jet "must be Israeli because what else is flying out here at this point in the war and also it's coming from the direction of Israel and it's going back to Israel, so it was obvious it was Israeli. I didn't think much of it. They were just out there checking us out. That's what I'd do too."

Obviously the gunners at the four machine-gun mounts shared that relaxed view. They continued to lounge about and chat with shipmates. Off-duty men were lying around the deck in swimsuits on blankets and lounge chairs, soaking up a Mediterranean suntan. They were not bothered by the unidentified jet either.

Shortly before 10 A.M., the bridge lookouts reported jet fighters approaching from astern. The gunners were still lounging about. Lieutenant Ennes ordered them to be alert. Unidentified aircraft were in the area, he warned. Then off to starboard, high in the azure sky, two sleek jets with the distinctive delta wings of French-built Mirage III fighter-bombers flew in tight formation paralleling the *Liberty*'s course to starboard. They flew past the ship, turned and flew back down the port side. They circled the ship three times, keeping a prudent distance.

Ennes glanced at the flag atop the tall mast. It was standing straight out in the light breeze, its colors crisp in the morning light. Through binoculars he could see clusters of rockets hanging under the Mirages' wings and the outlines of the pilots in their cockpits. But he could discern no markings, perhaps because of the planes' position. Still, he was not overly worried. ". . . if I could see the pilots in their cockpits," he figured, "the pilots could certainly see our flag and no doubt our ship's name and number."

Like Ennes, the crew remained relaxed. Sailors continued sunbathing. The sea continued calm, the sky cloudlessly bright, the breeze cooling. The Stars and Stripes fluttered in the gentle wind.

At about 10:30 A.M., the flying boxcar returned. It was a French-built Nord 2501 Noratlas transport that Israel had converted to a SIGINT ferret and reconnaissance snooper equipped with lens openings for photo coverage. Like the Mirages, it approached from astern, flew past to starboard, banked and flew back to port. It was a lazy pattern, becoming no more threatening than the gentle white bow wave that washed alongside the ship. In fact, the close scrutiny was leading to a certain sense of security.

"Well, they certainly know who we are by now, don't they?" commented Commander McGonagle to Ennes on the bridge. He added reassuringly: "It's good that they are checking us out this carefully. This way there won't be any mistakes."

Suddenly, the lumbering plane banked sharply and headed directly toward the ship, skimming the waves at around two hundred feet. It roared over the *Liberty* so close that the portholes for its reconnaissance cameras were clearly visible. On its wings were Israel's insignia, the Star of David.

In Cairo that Thursday, the Stars and Stripes was hauled down from the U.S. Embassy flagpole and replaced with the yellow-and-red Spanish flag. Spain had agreed to act on behalf of American interests while diplomatic relations between the United States and Egypt remained severed.

Reporter Eric Pace had wandered onto the embassy grounds while Marine guard Sergeant Gary Applegate was raising the Spanish flag. "There was much joking and exclaiming of '*Sí, señor*' and the like among the embassy staff," Pace reported, "but Sergeant Applegate, a real Marine, was glum. 'I'd much rather see Old Glory up there,' he said."

The embassy's few remaining officers also took part in the banter. Ambassador Dick Nolte was overseeing the destruction of sensitive papers and codes, preparing for evacuation. Political officer Richard Parker, glancing at the Spanish flag, turned to Nolte and said: "I guess this really does end the Spanish-American war."

Despite the light tone, the moments of humor were few and strained. The situation for Americans was perilous. The awful truth—that some great national disaster was taking place—was finally sinking in on the Egyptian masses. Although Cairo Radio continued broadcasting reports of various victories, they all were taking place in the Sinai, on Egyptian territory. When Egypt's thirty-one million people finally realized the dimensions of their humiliation, which they already believed was being visited on them with the aid of America and Britain, they could turn into an angry mob. It had happened before, as many people remembered vividly. Fifteen years earlier, Cairenes had gone berserk against British occupation and turned downtown Cairo into an inferno of destruction of British property. Seventeen Europeans were killed in the January 26, 1952, rampage that became known as Black Saturday. It could happen again.

This fear lay behind a flurry of messages exchanged between the embassy and the State Department throughout the day.

"Almost total defeat UAR armed forces is beginning to sink in on populace, as are reports of demonstrations against U.S. installations throughout the area," cabled Nolte. "We think there is danger situation here may deteriorate rapidly and that even if UARG [United Arab Republic Government] willing protect us it may be unable to do so. We therefore want option evacuate all Americans official and unofficial from Cairo."

There were by now only four hundred U.S. citizens, mainly businessmen and reporters, and seventy-five officials left in Cairo. Washington quickly gave its approval for Nolte to order an evacuation at his discretion. The State Department cable added: "Since situation suggests possible danger European community as whole, suggest you consult friendly embassies (French, Italian) with idea arranging joint diplomatic action prevent major attacks on westerners." But Washington's reading was wrong. It was specifically Americans, and to a lesser extent the British, who were the targets of Egyptian anger.

There was much to fuel that anger, though most Egyptians did not yet know it. In the Sinai, the 100,000-man Egyptian Army had been decimated. Israeli reporter Amos Elon that day drove through the Mitla Pass, the strategic defile leading from central Sinai to the Suez Canal. He arrived a few hours after its capture and found it a "shocking valley of death, littered with corpses and hundreds of burning tanks and trucks in the now familiar cloud of smoke and the disgusting sweet smell of burning human flesh."

The retreating Egyptians, Elon reported, "had left behind them in the desert an immense array of equipment—some of it destroyed, but much of it abandoned, unused.... No one has yet counted the captured equipment. But it already appeared that more than half the Egyptian armor had been captured or hit. Still lying in the desert were Russian-made T-34, T-54 and T-55 tanks, some brand-new and without a scratch, straight from the factory: amphibious tanks, cannon of all sorts, some with their barrels still protected against the dust by airtight plastic covers. Large parts of Sinai looked like enormous junkyards."

But still Egypt refused to agree to a cease-fire. To an urgent request from Moscow that Nasser bow to the U.N. Security Council, the Egyptian president had replied: "... how could we terminate our military operations when enemy forces continued to launch ground and air attacks against us? ... We were determined to continue the fight until Israeli withdrawal was achieved, and we expected the serious and instant support of the Soviet Union in this venture."

An official of the Foreign Ministry was more candid when he told one of Nolte's officers that Egypt could not accept a cease-fire because the repercussions would be too serious. "What would we tell the people?" he asked.

Throughout that Thursday, Cairo Radio announced to the accompaniment of martial music that the day's fighting would be decisive. It too apparently was still unaware of the horrific dimensions of Egypt's losses, or perhaps it was under orders to ignore them.

The fact was that there were no more major battles to be fought. Egypt's army was smashed and scattered, many of its bravest soldiers dead and thousands of others wandering the scorching sands, waterless and in a daze. Egypt's defeat was total.

Though the bodies of fallen Arabs still littered the streets of Jerusalem ("It's a little grim," Brigadier General Chaim Herzog admitted to Washington *Post* reporter Bernard D. Nossiter, "but now we are finding them by smell"), jubilation reigned in Israel. Ambassador Wally Barbour reported to Washington that "emotional reaction to unexpected windfall of access to Jewish holy places has been unequaled since 1948 proclamation of independence."

Israelis were already referring to the "liberation" of the Old City, though that was not the way Arabs who had been living there for many centuries saw it. Barbour reported the visits by Israel's leaders to the Wailing Wall and inaccurately observed: "In their several remarks Israeli leaders made clear their intention retain access Jewish shrines Old City. . . ." Israeli leaders were making clear more than that. They had already said they planned to retain all of Jerusalem, but Barbour apparently did not report that.

The Hebrew press was filled with stories about the joy Israelis were experiencing, especially the ecstasy over the capture of the Old City. *Davar,* the Labor Party's semi-official daily, rhapsodized: "The people has returned to its capital and the capital has returned to its people. They will not be separated again."

Haaretz, an influential daily, demanded that the armed forces now turn their attention to Syria. "Finish the job," prodded *Haaretz.* "Everything started with Syria. The time has come to add up and settle accounts."

The victorious generals needed no prodding. The U.S. Consulate in Jerusalem advised by flash cable that U.N. observers reported that Israelis at 10 A.M. local time Thursday "have just launched intensive air and artillery bombardment of Syrian positions opposite central demilitarized zone as apparent prelude to large-scale attack in effort to seize heights overlooking border kibbutzim."

Secretary of State Rusk immediately replied by flash cable that the report was "deeply disturbing. You should urgently approach foreign office at highest level to express deep concern this new indication military action by

GOI. If reported bombardment correct, we should assume it prelude to military action against Syrian positions on Syrian soil. Such a development, following on heels Israeli acceptance of Security Council cease-fire resolution would cast doubts on Israeli intentions and create gravest problem for USG representatives in Arab countries.

"You should stress we must at all costs have complete cessation Israeli military action except in cases where clearly some replying fire is necessary in self-defense."

This strongly worded cable no doubt contributed to Israel's decision to delay its attack by one day—and at the same time perhaps also to increase its interest in the eavesdropping activities of the U.S.S. *Liberty*. If the ship could listen in on Israeli military communications, as it could, then the United States could discover Israel's plans to attack Syria. Foreknowledge of the attack might bring an ultimatum from the United States, an ultimatum that could not be ignored because Israel desperately still needed Washington's support both in the United Nations and to fend off any threats from the Soviet Union. Without the United States, the Soviet Union might directly intervene if Israel took on its last, comparatively unscathed client, Syria.

But as with the launching of the war itself, there was no question about not attacking Syria. It was merely a question of timing. The mood in the country was not only one of jubilation but also of revenge. Israelis blamed Syria as much as Egypt for the current crisis, and farmers in the north who had experienced Syrian bombardments from the Golan Heights over the years were crying for blood. A delegation of the farmers visited Northern Commander Major General David ("Dado") Elazar and later Prime Minister Eshkol to press their demands for an attack on Syria. Elazar needed no encouragement. As Ezer Weizman later wrote, "Never was Dado so tiresome in demanding that he be allowed to attack Syria. He continually bombarded General Staff with phone calls."

Elazar was preaching to the converted. The senior officers were already in favor of more conquest, Weizman recalled. "With almost our whole air force available, and the Egyptian, Jordanian and Syrian air forces practically eliminated, our strength was enormous. . . . For years we have awaited such an opportunity for settling accounts with our most bitter foes."

Ambassador Barbour, closely identifying with Israel's aims, advised Washington in response to Rusk's cable that "I would point out that Syrian shelling of kibbutzim and settlements in Israel below the Syrian heights has been continuous and incessant up to the present time with enormous damage; some kibbutzim, etc., have been completely leveled above ground, and with continuous threat to populations . . . after nineteen years under Syrian guns.

"In circumstances I would not repeat not be surprised if reported Israeli attack does take place or has already done so."

In fact, Barbour was reflecting the Israeli line, not reality. The Syrians had made no major move throughout the war and the front had been the quietest of all. With Israel enjoying total air superiority, the Syrians were reduced to firing artillery attacks against Israeli troop concentrations and against fortified kibbutzim, as Dayan later admitted.

Despite the mood for revenge, Israel for the moment held off any major attack. Perhaps a combination of Rusk's toughly worded cable, fear of the Russians and possibly concern about how much the *Liberty* was learning about Israel's plans combined to make Israel reconsider for the moment.

At 1:10 P.M. (7:10 A.M. in Washington) aboard the *Liberty*, Skipper McGonagle held a general quarters drill. A news report had mentioned use of poison gas in the Sinai fighting, which was false, and the skipper took the occasion to train the crew in chemical-attack procedures. The drill was soon over and the crew returned to its patrol routine, the sunbathers back to their deck chairs and towels.

"It's good that we have sunbathers on deck," McGonagle said to Ennes. "It helps to show that we're peaceful."

Over the ship's loudspeaker system, McGonagle reminded the men that they were in a war zone and the next call to arms could be a genuine one. He mentioned a huge cloud of smoke off to the left that threatened to obscure El Arish as evidence of the heavy fighting still going on. But, he added, local forces knew the *Liberty* was in the area since there had been repeated aerial reconnaissances.

McGonagle had barely ended his comments at 2 P.M. when radar reported three airplanes approaching the ship. Ennes was the first to see one of the planes, a delta-winged Mirage that was flying to starboard about five to six miles away. While he, McGonagle and the rest of the men on the bridge stared at the jet, expecting it to settle in to what had become a familiar reconnaissance pattern, a second plane swooped in from port and fired rockets directly at the bridge.

Pandemonium erupted. A terrible heat and noise shot through the ship. Rocket fragments and 30mm bullets punched through the heavy deck plating, through the thin skin of the bulkheads, through the flesh of the stunned crewmen. Ennes was hit in the first attack, his left leg broken above the knee and two dozen rocket fragments buried in his body.

The planes attacked again and again. They hit the *Liberty* with everything they had: rockets and 30mm armor-piercing shells. The pilothouse quickly became a charnel, blood flowing so thickly over the metal floor that men slipped and fell in it. The wounded and the dying were scattered about, helplessly adding to the red slush.

Then came more planes, Mystères with rockets, cannon and, most dreaded of all, napalm. The jets fired their rockets on their approach, and then as they swooped over the stricken ship, they released their silvery canisters of jellied gasoline that exploded into flames on contact, slopping along the decks and through the doors and the large holes gouged out by the rockets and cannon fire. The *Liberty* was now a floating hell of flames and screaming men. The wounded and the dead were everywhere.

Skipper McGonagle was wounded by shrapnel in the right leg and was suffering a loss of blood, but he remained on station, directing the frantic fire-fighting efforts against three major blazes topside.

There already were eight men dead. All the ship's antennas had been damaged or destroyed, which may have been the attackers' prime target in order to prevent *Liberty* from calling for help or transmitting the communications that it had intercepted during the morning.

Despite the loss of antennas, the crew was able to patch up its high-command radio-circuit antenna to send off flash messages. Crouching on the desk to get away from the heavy, acrid smoke enveloping the ship, Radiomen James Halman and Joseph Ward attempted to send off a voice message requesting assistance. But they discovered that all frequencies were being jammed. A loud buzz-saw sound drowned out their words. It was only in the brief seconds when the planes launched their rockets that the jamming stopped. Apparently the jamming came from the aircraft and could not be performed at the same time that the rockets were in the air. It was during one of these lulls that the radiomen finally got off their message: "Any station, this is Rockstar [*Liberty*'s voice radio call sign]. We are under attack by unidentified jet aircraft and require immediate assistance."

The message was picked up by the aircraft carrier U.S.S. *Saratoga*, which was sailing with the Sixth Fleet south of Crete about 450 miles west of the *Liberty*. It immediately relayed the message to all regional commands, including the commander of the Sixth Fleet, Vice Admiral Martin, aboard his flagship, the guided-missile light cruiser U.S.S. *Little Rock*.

But the *Liberty*'s ordeal was far from over.

The air attacks had no sooner ceased than the second blow of the well-

255

coordinated attack hit the *Liberty*. At 2:24 P.M., nearly a half hour after the assault had begun, lookouts sighted three high-speed boats approaching the ship in torpedo-launch formation.

At this point Skipper McGonagle noticed that the American flag had been shot down during the air attacks and he ordered that the largest flag aboard, the eight-by-twelve-foot holiday ensign, be hoisted on the yardarm. The center boat flashed a signal light, but because of fire and smoke aboard the ship McGonagle could not read it. The *Liberty*'s own signal light had been destroyed during the air attacks and the skipper attempted to signal with a hand-held Aldis lamp. But the boats kept coming in attack formation. McGonagle thought he saw an Israeli flag on one of the boats.

"Stand by for torpedo attack, starboard side!" yelled the wounded McGonagle into the announcing system.

The boats, skimming across the waves at twenty-seven to thirty knots, closed in with their 20mm and 40mm machine guns blazing. One bullet smashed through the chart house and hit a young sailor in the neck, killing him instantly. Then a torpedo passed astern of the ship at about twenty-five yards at 2:34 P.M. A minute later there was a huge explosion.

A torpedo with a thousand-pound warhead had slammed into the *Liberty*'s starboard side forward of the bridge and several feet under the waterline, tearing a thirty-nine-foot hole between frames 53 and 66. This was either extraordinary luck or extraordinary sharpshooting for that location was exactly where the ship's sophisticated SIGINT equipment was located. As the sea poured into the lower decks, trapping men below, many of them the most skilled electronics technicians in the Navy, the ship tipped over into a dangerous list. Radiomen managed to get off another message on the high-command voice net reporting the new attack. It also was received by the *Saratoga* and was relayed to various commands.

It was not until 3:45 P.M., an hour and forty-five minutes after the start of the first air attack, that the Sixth Fleet finally got itself together to begin launching planes from the carriers *America* and *Saratoga* with orders to "use force including destruction as necessary to control the situation." Because some of the planes were slow, propeller-driven Skyraiders, the estimated time of arrival at the *Liberty* was not until 5:15 P.M. Admiral Martin's earlier promise to provide air protection within ten minutes had been an empty one.

On the *Liberty*, the force of the torpedo had knocked out power and steering control, and the ship was now listing nine degrees to starboard and dead in the water. McGonagle was on the bridge surrounded by the dead and dying. His navigator and quartermaster were dead, his executive officer was dying, and his officer of the deck and junior officer of the deck were badly wounded. Blood from McGonagle's leg wound was filling his right shoe. Water was flooding the lower decks through the gap caused by the torpedo, the steam engines powering the propeller had stopped and small fires were raging seemingly everywhere. It appeared the ship had to be abandoned.

The three torpedo boats reduced their speed and drifted lazily around the ship, then sped up and began firing their machine guns at the waterline, apparently waiting for the *Liberty* to sink. When yells of "Prepare to abandon ship!" rang out and three *Liberty* rubber life rafts were lowered into the water, one of the Israeli boats shot two of them, deflating them; the third was hauled aboard as a war trophy.

Apparently tired of waiting for the *Liberty* to slip under the waves, the torpedo boats finally retired toward Israel at 3:05 P.M. They soon were replaced by two large troop-carrying helicopters that circled the ship several times and then departed without any effort at communicating with or boarding the stricken ship. The Star of David was clearly visible on both helicopters.

Miraculously, the crew was getting damage under control and it no longer appeared that the *Liberty* was about to sink. With great exertion, the flooding had been stopped and fires extinguished. The mess decks had been converted into a casualty collection station. The dead and missing now numbered more than thirty with well over one hundred wounded, many of them gravely.

At about the same time that the torpedo boats departed, about 3 P.M. *Liberty* time, the U.S. naval attaché in Tel Aviv, Commander Ernest Carl Castle, was called to the Defense Ministry and told that Israeli sea and air forces had attacked an American ship. By mistake, it was claimed. By this time, of course, the increased radio traffic of the Sixth Fleet as it prepared to launch the rescue effort would have alerted Israel that the fleet was aware *Liberty* had been attacked and a potential clash with U.S. forces was in the making. It was now in Israel's interests to get out the word as soon as possible that there had been an "accident" and avoid a direct confrontation.

It worked. Commander Castle flashed the Israeli admission to the White House, the State Department, the Joint Chiefs of Staff and others. On the basis of his message, the planes from the Sixth Fleet were recalled and two destroyers and a fleet tug were sent to help the *Liberty*.

An effort to keep the incident quiet began almost immediately. Wally Barbour cabled from Tel Aviv that since the *Liberty* was American, "its proximity to scene conflict could feed Arab suspicions of U.S.-Israeli collusion." It was a bizarre line of reasoning after all the carnage of U.S. sailors, but it contributed to the consensus that formed almost immediately within the Administration to play down the incident.

In Washington, President Johnson's morning was highlighted again—for the fourth straight morning—with a message from Premier Kosygin sent on the hot line at 9:48 o'clock. While the Russians were pressuring Egypt to stop fighting, they were also, with increased insistence, pushing the United States to get Israel to halt its attacks against Egypt and Syria. Kosygin complained that despite an agreement reached the previous day to achieve a cease-fire in place, the United States still had not managed to get Israel's cooperation. Johnson replied that "although we are trying, we doubt that the United States alone can effectively persuade both sides to cease fire. I instructed Ambassador Goldberg last night to present a resolution today. This resolution calls on all parties in the strongest terms to cease fire immediately.

"I am glad to have had your message and have instructed our ambassador in New York to maintain close contact with the ambassador of the Soviet Union and trust you will want to do likewise."

A minute after Kosygin's message, at 9:49 A.M., Walt Rostow telephoned Johnson about the attack on the *Liberty* and followed that with a quick note: "We have a flash report from the Joint Reconnaissance Center indicating the U.S. elint (electronics intelligence) ship, the LIBERTY, has been torpedoed in the Mediterranean. . . . Reconnaissance aircraft are out from the 6th Fleet. We have no knowledge of the submarine or surface vessel which committed this act."

While the hot line was still activated, Johnson sent an immediate report to Kosygin—perhaps partly to smoke out whether the Russians were responsible, intentionally or unintentionally—to explain the unusual Fleet activity in the area: "You should know that I have just received a report that a US ship off the Egyptian coast has been torpedoed. I have ordered aircraft from carriers in the Mediterranean and other US ships to proceed immediately to the scene to protect the ship, investigate the circumstances of the attack, and rescue survivors."

At 11:17 A.M., he sent a fuller report to the Soviets over the hot line. "We have just learned that U.S.S. *Liberty,* an auxiliary ship, has apparently been torpedoed by Israeli forces in error off Port Said. We have instructed our carrier *Saratoga,* now in the Mediterranean, to dispatch aircraft to the scene to investigate. We wish you to know that investigation is the sole purpose of this flight of aircraft, and hope that you will take appropriate steps to see that proper parties are informed."

While the Kremlin now knew about the Israeli attack on the *Liberty,* the American people did not. From the very beginning, the Johnson Administration gave every evidence of a determination to play down the attack.

At his regular daily press conference starting at 11:18 A.M., an hour and a half after Washington had learned of the assault and had informed Moscow of it, George Christian gave no hint to the press that it had occurred. The reporters sensed something was going on but they did not know what. They had been made suspicious a short time earlier by Dean Rusk's sudden departure from Capitol Hill where he was testifying before a congressional committee, but the wily Christian eluded all their snares.

"George," asked a reporter at the start of the press conference, "is Secretary Rusk in the building?"

"Yes."

"Seeing the President?"

"Yes."

"Senator Wayne Morse told reporters he was called away from the Hill for an 'emergency meeting.' I am quoting a reporter on the Hill. Is that true?"

"Secretary Rusk is here," said Christian.

"Can you say anything more?"

"No," said Christian, "I cannot."

Then he was directly asked if he was "aware of any emergency."

"I am not going to comment on it," said Christian.

Later in the seventeen-minute conference, the reporters came back to the question of why Rusk had hurried to the White House, but Christian would not budge.

Finally one reporter inquired: "Can we look for any new developments here today?"

"There is always a possibility," said the press secretary, who was sitting on one of the hottest stories of the war.

In fact, while Christian was holding his press conference, the President was meeting with his top advisers: Rusk, Bundy, McNamara, Walt Rostow, U.S. ambassador to the Soviet Union Llewellyn E. Thompson, Jr., on home leave, and political adviser Clark Clifford, who had been instrumental in persuading President Harry S. Truman to make the United States the first country to recognize Israel in 1948. Although there was reported skepticism that the attack was totally accidental, the inclination of the officials was to accept Israel's version since none of them could see why the Israelis would risk losing U.S. support by such a dangerous action. It may have been the result of a local trigger-happy commander, they agreed, though there was no evidence of that either. But even if that were the case, that did not amount to a hostile act ordered by the top echelons of the government.

Beyond the lack of evidence, the President and his advisers were aware that they needed all the influence they could bring to bear on Israel right now to get it to stop fighting. A direct, emotional confrontation at this time would only lessen Washington's ability to achieve a cease-fire. In the end, Clark Clifford was detailed to investigate the attack and everyone else was ordered to keep mum until his report was completed.*

Thus that afternoon, Deputy Secretary of Defense Cyrus Vance telephoned the commander in chief of the Navy, European command, to order that no news releases be made by any of the *Liberty*'s survivors or any naval source. All comments to the press would come from Washington.

If Johnson or any of his advisers needed any reminder of how sensitive politically the Israel-United States relationship was they had only to peek out of the White House that afternoon. There the pro-Israel rally that Mathilde Krim had been worried about was taking place with twenty to thirty thousand enthusiastic supporters of Israel jammed into Lafayette Park. What had been a rally to elicit support for Israel had turned into a euphoric victory celebration with the waving of Israeli flags and placards reading "End Arab Aggression" and "God Is on Our Side." Two senators, leading U.S. rabbis and others addressed the enthusiastic crowd for nearly two hours.

Across Pennsylvania Avenue, about two hundred Arab Americans marched on the White House sidewalk, separated from the pro-Israel rally by a cordon of police and tightly parked buses. They were considerably more subdued and carried placards saying "We want our land" and "Johnson, hands off the Middle East."

Under Secretary of State Nick Katzenbach appeared at a White House gate and talked separately for a couple of minutes with leaders of both groups. The Arab American leader, M. T. Mehdi, secretary-general of the Action Committee on American-Arab Relations, told Katzenbach that he thought U.S. policy was dominated by Zionists. He also said that the United

---

* Clifford's report concluded there was no evidence of a deliberate attack and that became the official attitude of the Administration.

States should make clear that it supports the territorial integrity of all the nations in the Middle East—not just that of Israel.

Afterward, Mehdi was exultant about the exchange. "This is a very significant day in the lives of Arabs in this country," he said. "It has given the American Arabs the same opportunity to influence policy in the Middle East that the American Zionists have had."

Despite the crises brewing around him, Johnson that Thursday was hosting the official visit to Washington of President Hastings Kamuza Banda of Malawi. Johnson was scheduled to entertain the African leader at a White House luncheon and one of his speech writers had written a brief toast for the President to deliver. But when he read it over shortly before lunch, he did not understand a sentence reading: "Gibbon called independence 'the first of earthly blessings.' "

Hurriedly, Johnson took the opportunity of a bathroom visit by Banda to call one of his secretaries to ask how to pronounce "Gibbon" and "also find out who he is." A speech writer soon explained that it rhymed with ribbon and had "come from *The Rise and Fall* [sic] *of the Roman Empire.*"

In the afternoon, Kosygin used the hot line again to inform Johnson that his 11:17 A.M. message had been passed on to Nasser. Johnson replied warmly later that day: "I deeply appreciate your transmitting the message to President Nasser. We lost 10 men, 16 critically wounded, and 65 wounded, as a result of Israeli attack, for which they have apologized. Respectfully, Lyndon B. Johnson."*

In Cairo, the full extent of Egypt's disastrous defeat was finally making itself known to Gamal Abdel Nasser. Despite the risks of an open revolt, he realized he soon had to accept a cease-fire. But first he had to explain to a powerful supporter the facts of life in the Middle East. Like Israel, Nasser had been in touch throughout the crisis with his friends, including Communist China.

Now, as the demands for a cease-fire grew louder, Chairman Mao Tse-tung strongly advised him against accepting one. When Nasser replied that he had lost his army the Chinese leader responded with a suggestion. He urged Nasser to break up his army into independent brigades that could lose

---

* These were preliminary casualty figures, nowhere near the real totals. But, oddly, Johnson in his memoirs repeats the number ten for those killed, although at the time he wrote (1971), the true figure, thirty-four, had long been known.

themselves among the civilian population. They then could continue the battle in a guerrilla war of national liberation, Mao explained.

Nasser wrote Mao: "[The Sinai] is a desert and we cannot conduct a people's liberation war in Sinai because there are no people there. There are no more than thirty thousand people in the whole of Sinai. The whole area is arid and you can see for thirty and forty miles. The independent brigades would stand no chance."

Not even his divisions had stood a chance. Egypt officially reported its casualties at ten thousand soldiers and fifteen hundred officers with an estimated half of them killed or wounded in battle and many of the rest dying in the desert. About five thousand soldiers and five hundred officers, nearly half of them wounded, fell into Israeli captivity. Other Egyptian losses included about seven hundred tanks, six hundred of which had been destroyed or damaged and the rest captured, four hundred field guns and ten thousand vehicles of various types. In all, Egyptian losses amounted to 80 percent of its military equipment in the brief war, Nasser later reported.

Israeli losses were about three hundred killed and one thousand wounded and sixty-one tanks destroyed in the Sinai.

Israel had spectacularly proved the overwhelming might of air superiority. With the Arab air forces destroyed, Israeli planes had been free to roam the skies unmolested, blasting any Arab ground forces that tried to move. Those that tried to stay put and hide were then grist for Israel's mobile ground forces that mopped them up at will.

At 5 P.M. Washington time, Nasser telephoned Foreign Minister Riad. "In a voice choking with grief and bitterness he told me that the collapse of the armed forces had been total, far beyond anything he had imagined and that we were no longer capable of continuing the fight," Riad later wrote. Nasser instructed Riad to have Egypt's U.N. ambassador inform the Security Council that Egypt accepted the cease-fire.

The war for Egypt was over.

Eight hours later Syria followed suit. But Israel was not about to let the country that had been taunting it for so long get off that easily.

The survivors aboard the *Liberty* somehow managed to stop up with rags and other plugs the worst of the 821 gaping shellfire holes riddling the ship, while also tending to the wounded and dying, and keeping the stricken ship afloat. Two thirds of its crew were casualties, the death toll eventually reaching 34 with 171 wounded; a quarter of the ship was flooded and its sophisticated electronics equipment, the reason for its existence, was destroyed.

Air and sea surveillance by Israeli craft had continued. At one point the torpedo boats had returned and asked: "Do you need any help?" Commander McGonagle, enraged, gave his new quartermaster a suitable earthy American answer to signal back. The boats withdrew to a safe distance and soon departed.

Around 6:35 P.M., as dusk gathered over the waters of the Mediterranean, another Israeli helicopter arrived at the *Liberty* and hovered near the mangled, combat-scarred bridge. The helicopter signaled that it wanted to land. McGonagle, in no mood for foreign visitors, gave them the finger. Frustrated, someone in the helicopter finally dropped a brown paper bag weighted with two oranges and enclosing the calling card of naval attaché Commander Ernest Carl Castle with a note on the back: "Have you casualties?" Since three bodies still had not been removed from the forecastle, the answer must have been obvious. But McGonagle spent some time trying to signal with the Aldis lamp that, yes, there were casualties. The helicopter finally had to depart with the gathering of dusk.

Only by extraordinary devotion by the crew and with luck had *Liberty* remained afloat. But its usefulness was finished. Israel was now free without fear of U.S. eavesdropping to pursue its final objective in the war: the capture of the Golan Heights.

XIX
JUNE 9:
ASSAULT AGAINST
SYRIA

Yitzhak Rabin was still sleeping Friday when he was called to the telephone at 7 A.M. It was Ezer Weizman with electrifying news. "Fifteen minutes ago, Dayan contacted Dado [General Elazar, commander of the Northern Command] and ordered him to attack the Syrians immediately," Weizman said.

Rabin, who had been enjoying his first rest at home since the war started, at once set off for General Headquarters to see what had happened. Dayan had opposed a renewal of Thursday's aborted attack the previous evening, yet now he had bypassed the chief of staff, whose duty it was to issue operational orders to regional commanders, and personally had told Elazar to attack.

Rabin discovered that Dayan had arrived at General Headquarters around 6 A.M., received a briefing about Egypt's total disintegration and still was opposed to hitting Syria. But then just before 7 o'clock he changed his mind and ordered the assault.

Both Rabin and Weizman expressed mystification at Dayan's decision, which itself was an extremely unusual state of affairs for senior officers in the closely knit Israeli Army, where everybody's actions were the fuel of a highly efficient rumor system. Few secrets long survived the lively curiosity of Israelis about one another, and certainly almost none about so important a subject as why Israel broke the cease-fire to attack Syria.

Yet Rabin years later claimed that Dayan's decision was made "for reasons I have never grasped." Weizman expressed equal bewilderment: "There is no explanation for what happened to Moshe Dayan ... why an absolute and total ban was replaced ... by a laconic order to Dado: 'Forward.' "

Dayan himself was seemingly matter-of-fact about the subject in his memoirs. In recounting Syria's war actions, Dayan wrote: ". . . the Syrians carried out two unsuccessful attacks on a northern kibbutz and a military post on June 6. Thereafter, they confined themselves to shelling our kibbutzim and a few of our army camps.

"At 11:30 A.M. on Friday, June 9, after Jordan was completely and Egypt almost out of the campaign, our forces attacked the Syrian fortified positions on the border. The cease-fire went into effect a day and a half later." He was referring to the cease-fire that Israel had agreed should go into effect that morning.

The reasons for his decision, Dayan wrote, were the total defeat of Egypt, Syria's acceptance of a cease-fire and an intelligence report that the Syrian front was collapsing. "These announcements and reports prompted me to change my mind."

Dayan added: "We were not forced to go to war with Syria because of the Syrian-initiated attacks during the week. The reasons we campaigned in Syria were primarily to save our settlements in northern Galilee from incessant Syrian shelling, and also to show the Syrians that they could not continue to harass us with impunity."

One possible additional reason for his change of mind was left unmentioned by Dayan. That was the destruction the previous day of the *Liberty*. Interestingly, though his memoirs are quite inclusive about the details of the war, he did not make a single reference to the attack on the *Liberty* in all of his 640-page autobiography.*

By Friday morning's renewed attack on Syria, it would have been clear to

---

* Dayan's silence may have been well advised. At least one CIA report identified him as the person who personally ordered the *Liberty* attack. The report related that confidential sources, presumably Israeli, ". . . said that Dayan personally ordered the attack on the ship and that one of his generals adamantly opposed the action and said, 'This is pure murder.' One of the admirals who was present also disapproved the action, and it was he who ordered it stopped and not Dayan." From CIA information report, "Attack on USS *Liberty* Ordered by Dayan," Nov. 7, 1967.

An earlier CIA information report, "Comment on Known Identity of USS *Liberty*," July 27, 1967, said: "[The source] implied that the ship's identity was known at least six hours before the attack but that Israeli headquarters was not sure as to how many people might have access to the information the LIBERTY was intercepting. He also implied that there was no certainty or control as to where the information was going and again reiterated that Israeli forces did not make mistakes in their campaign. He was emphatic in stating to me that they knew what kind of ship USS LIBERTY was and what it was doing offshore."

the Israeli high command that the *Liberty* was totally out of action and incapable of monitoring Israel's military moves. More significantly, it was also plain by then that the reaction in Washington had not been so violent as to endanger the crucially needed American support for Israel during its Syrian adventure. It may have been these factors that finally caused Dayan to change his mind about the attack on the Golan Heights.

The result was catastrophic for Syria. Israel claimed in a cable to the Security Council that Friday morning that sixteen Israeli villages had been subjected to Syrian artillery attacks and, with that as justification, launched a powerful assault on the steep heights. The information that the spy Eli Cohen had provided Israel from Damascus several years earlier now began paying dividends.

Apparently the attack did not come as a surprise to the United States. In his memoirs, Lyndon Johnson asserted that "we did know Israel's military intentions toward Syria." How? He did not elaborate and any papers relating to such information remain classified. In its brief patrol before the attack, could the *Liberty* have accomplished at least part of its task? Did its sensitive antennas pick up the orders for the Thursday attack on Syria and relay them to Washington before it was called off and Dayan's attention focused on the U.S. vessel? No answers have been forthcoming from the National Security Agency or the Navy.

The U.N. Security Council had been long on words but short on action during the past twenty-four hours. Both the United States and the Soviet Union had introduced additional resolutions but had been unable to muster support for them. Despite President Johnson's hot-line statement to Kosygin the previous day, the two ambassadors were not working together. The U.S. proposal was too complicated and too vague, mentioning withdrawal but not indicating to where, while the Soviet Union wanted the Council to say it "vigorously condemns Israel's aggressive activities" and "demands that Israel should immediately halt its military activities . . . and withdraw . . . beyond the armistice lines."

Israel's opening of a new front by breaking the cease-fire with Syria galvanized the fifteen delegates. By early Friday afternoon they unanimously agreed on a resolution submitted by Council President Tabor saying the Council "demands that hostilities should cease forthwith" and "requests the Secretary-General to make immediate contacts with the governments of Israel and Syria to arrange immediate compliance . . . and to report to the Security Council not later than two hours from now."

At 4 P.M., U Thant reported that both Syria and Israel were ready to stop immediately their military operations, though in fact Israel's thrust was at that time only gathering the momentum that it needed to take the heavily fortified Heights. Nonetheless, the Council had no way of knowing that and it appeared its action was having an effect. It was further encouraged at its evening meeting when it was reported that Syria had issued cease-fire orders to its troops at 5:30 P.M. (EDT), which was followed by a similar declaration by Israel thirty-five minutes later.

There then began a series of conflicting reports about what was actually going on in the war zone. Syrian messages at 6:50 and 7:05 o'clock complained of Israeli violations, which were vigorously denied by Israeli Ambassador Rafael. Despite his denials, the Israelis were actually pressing their attack. Their successes were so complete by the end of the day that Syrian forces all along the Heights were starting to withdraw, leaving the Heights open to Israeli occupation—and the Security Council befuddled about what was actually going on.

While Syria suffered its ordeal, Egypt's was at an end. By afternoon, Cairo Radio was telling the populace that the fighting had stopped. It did not say how far the Israelis had advanced or how great was the defeat. The announcement brought no change to Cairo's sullen calm. Everyone was waiting for a speech scheduled for television that Friday night by President Nasser.

Friday being the Moslem sabbath, the capital's streets were filled with Islamic clergymen giving sidewalk services, some of them ritualistically denouncing imperialism, by which they meant the United States. Still, many Egyptians were just as angry at the Soviet Union.

"Why didn't the Russians help us?" one Egyptian asked correspondent Eric Pace. "They give us only words."

When Nasser finally appeared on TV, he looked tired and dejected. No one knew what he would say. He had not appeared or spoken in public since the beginning of the war. Many people, influenced by the wildly optimistic reports broadcast by Cairo Radio, were angry with him for accepting the cease-fire, believing he had given up too easily.

For Nasser, it was his darkest hour. He was near a breakdown, haggard from worry, choked by emotion. He read from a text, something he seldom did, his voice quavering and hesitant. He accepted full responsibility for the "setback." He said the origins of the war were Israel's threats to Syria. He accused the United States and Britain of providing Israel air support.

When he finally got around to his purpose, in the middle of the speech, the news was stunning: "I have decided to give up completely and finally every official post and every political role and to return to the ranks of the public to do my duty with them like every other citizen. . . . The forces of imperialism imagine that Abdel Nasser is their enemy. I want it to be clear to them that it is the entire Arab nation and not Gamal Abdel Nasser."

The country briefly seemed frozen in stunned silence. Then yelling erupted in the streets. Pace found that "people sobbed. Tears ran down men's cheeks. . . . In the streets and alleys anguished shouting grew. Air raid sirens wailed, adding to the excitement . . . gangs of youths yelling, 'Nasser! Only Nasser!' . . . The shouted protests against Nasser's resignation continued on into the night."

In the gathering twilight, with Cairo still partially blacked out, tens of thousands, then hundreds of thousands, of Cairenes poured into the streets weeping and shouting, "Nasser, Nasser, don't leave us. We need you." Some men and women were in their nightclothes. They were of all ages, all classes, all stunned and grief-stricken. Tens of thousands gathered at the National Assembly shouting his name. A half million massed from Nasser's home at Manshief el Bakri to the center of Cairo in a night-long vigil to show their support when he traveled to the Assembly the next day. The noise of their mourning was like a growing storm.

The news of Nasser's resignation was greeted with despair in Arab capitals and joy in Israel. In the Arab sections of Beirut groups of demonstrators chanted "We want Nasser," and President Johnson was hanged in effigy above a street with the Star of David marked on his clothes. In Khartoum people wept openly in the streets. But in Israel, crowds cheered at the news, boys ran through Tel Aviv's streets beating on kettles, and the nonkosher cafés (kosher ones were closed for the start of the sabbath at sundown) were crowded with happy, joyous Israelis, celebrating the lightning victories, the successful assault still continuing against Syria and now the apparent end of the man they had perceived as their most formidable opponent for the past fifteen years.

In Washington, Dean Rusk held his regular weekly background briefing for State Department correspondents. His remarks could be attributed only to "American official sources," although any close reader of the newspapers was well aware of the source. Rusk had no better idea about Nasser's future than anyone else and he was quick to admit it.

"... we have nothing privately out of Cairo, or anywhere else, indicating anything more than you're getting on the tickers," he said in his opening statement. "So if you're wondering what about President Nasser, I don't know any more than you do."

Rusk insisted that the United States still did not know who had started the fighting. "We, quite frankly, don't know the final truth of some of those events of the first few hours preceding the events on which we can make real judgments."

Nor did he know what plans Israel had for the territories already captured and others it was capturing that moment in Syria. "Quite frankly, we don't know. We have had very little from them about their thinking about the shape of a future settlement here in this situation."

And he refused to get into a discussion on whether the United States was living up to its long-term pledge to protect the "territorial integrity" of all the nations in the Middle East.

A reporter asked him: "You wouldn't care to give a definition of this point, would you?"

Rusk: "No."

The assembled reporters broke up in laughter. Their amusement was understandable. The Administration was not being honest about its true policy, and it was amusing, in a black-humor sort of way, to watch as officials grotesquely twisted words in an attempt to make them seem what they were not. To any seasoned reporter, it had been obvious ever since the verbal acrobatics over "neutrality" that in fact the Administration was trying to have the best of both worlds—a public stance of fair objectivity and a private one of support for Israel.

Despite the Administration's repeated assertion that it was committed to the territorial integrity of all Middle Eastern nations, it was well understood by this time that what the statement actually meant was the territorial integrity of only one country, Israel.

Nonetheless, the reporters tried to get from the secretary of state an explanation that might clarify for them, much less their readers, the obvious difference between what Administration spokesmen said was U.S. policy and the policy as actually being practiced by the United States. How could the Administration say on the one hand that it was neutral and in favor of territorial integrity and on the other make no complaint about Israel's redrawing of the Middle Eastern map?

One reporter asked: "Is there a definition for territorial integrity, Mr. Secretary, or are you waiting to formulate your definition when you see what you are faced with?"

"No," answered Rusk impatiently. "It doesn't do any good for the United States, for me, to try to tell you that we are going to proscribe the answer in the area, when, in the last two or three weeks out there, none of the governments in the area have taken our advice. So why should I go down this trail?

"Let's let them sweat with their problems for a bit. Let the Arabs face the practical consequences of the attitudes they have taken in the past twenty years; and let the Israelis face the overwhelming necessity that they are going to have some sort of a relationship or reconciliation with the Arab world. Let's let some of these things ferment for a bit."

Although Rusk had remained remarkably evenhanded in the pro-Israel atmosphere of the Johnson White House and the country at large, he too was caught up in the national admiration of Israel's victories. For what he was now proposing could not have fitted better into Israel's strategy. If the Administration was content to let the contestants "sweat" and the situation "ferment," then Israel would not be faced with a repeat of 1956, would not have to return the captured territories if it chose not to even though conquest by force was against the Charter of the United Nations and contrary to the often enunciated national policy of the United States.

By Friday public opinion in the United States and Europe was so powerfully pro-Israel that it seemed almost unpatriotic not to support the Zionist state. Americans and Europeans were celebrating Israel's victories as fervently and passionately as though they were their own. Despite the attack on the *Liberty*, there was no public outcry against Israel. Indeed, the media had nothing but praise for the country.

A headline in the Chicago *Sun-Times* said: "Israel Reports a Victory Sweep: What a Great Day." Columnist Mary McGrory proclaimed: "We are all Israelis." *Time* magazine printed a two-page essay titled *Arabia Decepta: A People Self-Deluded* that was so scathing as to amount to labeling Arabs racially inferior.

Americans' love of the underdog made especially appealing the idea of one tiny nation taking on the combined might of the Arab states, and the public outpouring in favor of Israel was extraordinary. Demonstrations throughout the United States hailed Israel; donations of money and even volunteers to fight were offered with unprecedented generosity. Mayor John V. Lindsay of New York City was acting more like the mayor of Tel Aviv than of America's largest city. On the same day as Rusk's backgrounder, sixteen senior officials of Lindsay's Administration announced plans to assist the United Jewish Appeal in raising funds for Israel. Lindsay publicly supported the group and aided it by declaring the following week as "United Jewish Appeal Week."

He also agreed to appear as a special guest along with Senator Jacob Javits and former foreign minister Golda Meir at a "Stars for Israel" evening at Madison Square Garden on the coming Monday featuring some of the top names in show business. "In this time of danger for the people of Israel join in giving your support to this great cause," entreated a nearly full-page ad in *The New York Times*. Among the stars donating their talents were many Jewish American performers as well as such other popular entertainers as Marian Anderson, Tallulah Bankhead, Perry Como, Lena Horne, Ed McMahon, Melina Mercouri and Ed Sullivan.

Not only politicians and performers were caught up in the pro-Israel fever that was sweeping the United States. Many ordinary people were donating money to Israel in record numbers and amounts. Israel Bonds officials reported that Friday $5 million worth were bought, the largest amount paid for bonds in a single day since 1951. That brought to $25 million the sum of bonds bought since the beginning of the crisis.

Outright contributions were heavy too. UJA reported more than a dozen individual contributions of $1 million. New York alone had pledges totaling $20 million within the first three days of the war. An unidentified Gentile, who usually contributed $3,000 a year, gave $300,000. Nor was New York the only city where contributions were forthcoming. The United Jewish Appeal reported receiving before the war was over $3,500,000 from Chicago; $3,100,000 from Cleveland; $2,500,000 from Boston; $1,540,000 from Providence, Rhode Island; $1,250,000 from Newark, New Jersey; $1,200,000 from St. Louis; $1,132,000 from Atlanta, Georgia; $920,000 from Milwaukee, Wisconsin; $800,000 from both Cincinnati and Des Moines, Iowa; $462,000 from Harrisburg, Pennsylvania; and $310,000 from Seattle, Washington.

By the time the crisis ended, more than $100 million had been contributed. This was all the more remarkable because the UJA's regular fundraising drive had been completed in the spring just before the war and had raised $65 million. The contributions by awed and adoring Americans continued throughout the year. By the end of the year, they had given $180 million and bought $100 million in bonds for a grand total, counting the regular contributions, of $430 million.

Many also volunteered themselves. Several thousands of Americans volunteered to go to Israel to work the jobs of the reservists on the front lines, to serve in hospitals or even to fight themselves. Despite a State Department ban on travel to a war zone, so many volunteered that Israel officially discouraged such actions, saying they only complicated Israel's problems.

By coincidence, this was the first time that Americans could legally fight in another nation's army. On May 29, the Supreme Court, in *Afroyim* v. *Rusk,* had ruled in favor (5 to 4, with Abe Fortas casting the swing vote) of Beys Afroyim. He was a naturalized Jewish American from Poland, who had been denied his citizenship for voting in an Israeli election. The effect of the ruling was to grant dual citizenship to him and other Americans living in Israel, the first time large numbers of Americans had ever been granted the opportunity to carry two passports. It was a privilege unique to Americans moving to Israel, allowing them to reside in Israel but cast votes in U.S. elections.

Corporations contributed to the Israeli war effort too. TWA and KLM airlines both offered to transport goods without charge to Israel. Johnson & Johnson, the pharmaceutical firm, like many others, donated surgical dressings. S. Klein, a New York department store, offered linens and blankets.

There was a similar outpouring in Britain. UJA reported that Britons had contributed $24 million in special crisis donations. It said its French arm had set a goal of $10 million.

Israel's swift and convincing victories, so decisive and surgical compared to the enervating, endless war in Vietnam, were causing unexpected and unimagined results among Jews everywhere. There was a new pride, a new identification, a new feeling of brotherhood between Diaspora Jews and Israelis. So emotional and dramatic was the eruption of feelings by Jewish Americans that polls found an unprecedented level of identification at the height of the war with 99 percent of Jewish Americans expressing strong support for Israel.

The *Intermountain Jewish News* proclaimed, without undue exaggeration, that "the glorious fighters of Israel have made an automatic hero of every Jew in America, yea of the world."

An unidentified thirty-year-old Jewish woman told *The New York Times* that she was "absolutely overwhelmed" by Israel's victories. She was not, she said, a Zionist or a religious Jew, "but yesterday I felt very identified. I felt a pride in being Jewish that I've never felt. . . . It was a real change from seeing the Jews as the long-suffering victims."

Arthur Waskow, an activist in the peace movement, suddenly found war by Israel a different experience. He and other Jewish Americans "discovered a great attachment to Israel that was so deep that they surprised themselves."

Many Americans, Protestants, Catholics, flower children, atheists, shared in these discoveries of renewed pride and cheered Israel on.

———————

Lyndon Johnson that Friday had a comparatively quiet day. He slept until 7:45 A.M. and for the first time since the fighting broke out the Soviet Union did not activate the hot line. The day was taken up mainly with the routine chores of the presidency, receiving a new Department of Agriculture study on conservation, attending the swearing-in ceremony for a new head of the Equal Employment Opportunity Commission, returning his attention to the long, unwinnable war in Vietnam. He took time out to give Defense Secretary McNamara several birthday gifts, including an Accutron wristwatch, with the comment: "Bob, here are a few items honoring your day."

An aide noted: "The Secretary seemed somewhat surprised and said, 'My goodness, Mr. President, thank you—thank you!' " Later, Johnson remembered he had forgotten to have the watch engraved on the back and sent a secretary to McNamara's office to retrieve it. "The Secretary's secretary told her the Secretary came back to his cffice . . . and showed it off so proudly— with twinkles in his eyes—saying the one he had been wearing was a $20 one he had had about 20 years and he not only needed one but this was the greatest one to have," recorded an aide.

That evening Johnson attended a meeting of McGeorge Bundy's Special Committee for a late briefing on the diplomatic and military moves in the Middle East. Bundy too, though brought in to keep a level head, seemed caught up with pro-Israel fever. He suggested that the President make a speech to, among other things, "emphasize that this task to secure a strong Israel and a stable Middle East is in the first instance a task for the nations in the area. This is good LBJ doctrine and good Israeli doctrine, and therefore a good doctrine to get out in public."

Later in the evening Johnson met with *Time* magazine correspondent Hugh Sidey to give him a personal briefing on the week's dramatic events for the coming issue of the national newsweekly. Although the Administration was playing down the attack on the *Liberty*, Johnson commented: "Imagine what would happen if we had bombed an Israeli ship by mistake."

"Well," replied Sidey, "imagine what would've happened if the Soviets had bombed it."

Both men chuckled and went on to other matters.

———————

Although President Johnson had briefly mentioned the *Liberty* in his private talk with Hugh Sidey, the Administration's effort to keep the story under wraps was succeeding. The *Liberty* was already off the front pages of *The Washington Post* and *The New York Times* and, surprisingly, no one during Rusk's long background briefing in the afternoon had bothered asking him about it. Even the White House correspondents had displayed an untypical lack of concern. During the two daily briefings Friday by George Christian, the subject had been broached only once by reporters despite the fact that Christian that day had revealed that the death total was already at thirty-one. He also took the opportunity to read into the record an apologetic letter that Prime Minister Eshkol had sent the President earlier in the day.

"I was deeply grieved by the tragic loss of life on the U.S. naval ship *Liberty*. Please accept my deep condolences and convey my sympathy to all the bereaved families. May all bloodshed come to an end, and may our God grant us peace evermore."

There was still much shedding of blood aboard the *Liberty*. There were wounded everywhere, which the ship duly reported to headquarters. However, Ensign Malcomb Patrick O'Malley had listed the number as "wounded in action." Back came a message asking "What *action?*"

O'Malley was furious. "They say it wasn't 'action,' it was 'an accident.' I'd like to tell 'em to come out here and see the difference between 'action' and 'accident.' Stupid bastards!"

The hush-up was already in full gear.

The first ship to the scene was not American but Russian. Shortly after midnight the guided-missile destroyer 626/4 arrived and flashed by light signal in English: "Do you need help?"

"No, thank you," the *Liberty* answered.

"I will stand by in case you need me" came the reply.

The Soviet warship stayed by the stricken *Liberty* throughout the long night until a tug and the destroyers *Davis* and *Massey* arrived at dawn. During all this time the badly wounded Skipper McGonagle had stayed in command, occasionally lapsing into unconsciousness, fighting his weakness by sheer will and cups of black coffee. It was only after the arrival of the American destroyers that he finally allowed himself to seek some rest. When he got to his cabin, he found it a shambles caused by napalm and rockets. One rocket had exploded in his pillow. An unexploded cannon shell lay in his shower. He had it removed and then gave himself up to sleep.

Soon the wounded were being helicoptered to other ships of the Sixth Fleet and the *Liberty* began its limping voyage to dry dock at Valletta, Malta.

It had taken sixteen and a half hours for the Sixth Fleet to provide aid.

———————————————

On the Golan Heights, Israeli forces regrouped and rested, waiting for dawn and the last thrust of the war.

Throughout Friday, the Soviet Union had watched with mounting alarm Israel's violation of the cease-fire and its crushing blows against Syria. Now the Kremlin finally decided to get tough.

XX

JUNE 10:
RUSSIA THREATENS

On Saturday, Syria became panicky. It feared the relentless Israeli military machine was going to keep moving until it was in Damascus itself and had overthrown the government, as Israeli officials had threatened for so long. There was no natural physical obstruction to stop Israel's advance. The great Syrian plain stretched flat from the Golan Heights for forty miles straight to the Syrian capital. Nor was the Syrian Army capable of stopping the Israeli force. Already the Syrians were in total disarray and retreating under the crushing attacks by the Israeli Air Force and its advancing troops.

Syrian fears were so great that the government demanded after midnight an emergency meeting of the Security Council, which was finally scheduled for the unusual hour of 4:30 A.M. Saturday.

When the 1,354th meeting of the Security Council opened, Syria charged, prematurely as it turned out, that Israel had already occupied the provincial capital of Kuneitra, a city of about thirty thousand persons in the middle of the Heights, and that Israeli troops were pressing onward toward Damascus.

U Thant told the Council that U.N. General Odd Bull had reported air raids against Damascus airport and the suburbs of Damascus, and that fighting was continuing on the Golan Heights. Bull had added that the Israeli Foreign Ministry denied the bombing reports, contending that Israeli aircraft were over Syrian territory only to protect Israeli soldiers.

Soviet Ambassador Fedorenko was furious. He charged that Israeli Ambassador Rafael had sat "five hours among us and openly misled the Council and tried to divert the attention of the Security Council and play for time for the annexationist purposes of the Israeli hordes. . . . The criminal bandit activity against Syria must be condemned immediately and unreservedly."

Arthur Goldberg opposed condemnation. He pointed out that the meeting had been convened specifically on the question of Kuneitra. "Let us have General Bull's representative go to Kuneitra and report to this Council," Goldberg said. "Is Kuneitra in the possession of the Syrian forces or is it in the possession of the Israeli forces? When we get that information the Council will know what to do."

When a few minutes later another message from Odd Bull was received reporting another air attack near Damascus, Goldberg again felt more information was needed.

"It is not entirely clear to me whether this report is based on firsthand observation or not, but I say specifically that a bombing—if it is going on—is in violation of the orders," he said. "Any firing from gun emplacements into Israeli villages would be in violation of the cease-fire order and likewise could not be condoned.

"We need, it is perfectly obvious, a comprehensive report as to what is going on in the entire area."

Without reliable information, Goldberg contended, the United States was not prepared to pass judgment on which party was responsible for violating the cease-fire.

Although it may have not been his intent, the effect of Goldberg's remarks was to prevent the Council from taking any immediate action and thus gave Israel more time to achieve its conquest of the Golan Heights.

Rafael vehemently denied that any air attacks had taken place against Damascus. He told the Council that his government had contacted Bull and requested him "urgently to dispatch observers to the frontier line to verify the situation so that reliable reports can be transmitted to the Security Council." He also claimed, falsely, that Israel was abiding by the cease-fire. The only fighting by Israeli forces, he said, was to stop Syrian artillery bombardments of Israeli territory.

After a seventy-minute break starting at 7 A.M., the delegates reassembled to find another message reporting U.N. observers had witnessed three separate air attacks around Damascus, although "all attacks appeared to be outside the city of Damascus."

Soviet Ambassador Fedorenko, reflecting the growing rage of his government and its frustration at the delaying tactics of the United States, declared: "The perpetuation of the crime is proved. . . . We are compelled to note the inexplicable position adopted by . . . especially the representative of the United States."

By now, the Soviet Union was fed up, frustrated at its inability to make Israel stop fighting and piqued by snide remarks in the media and elsewhere on its impotence and the quality of its weapons in Arab hands. Israeli and Western officials were openly laughing at Russia and even the Arabs were accusing it of weakness. Its arch Communist foe, China, was taunting it with charges of perfidy. The Chinese Communist newspaper *Jenmin Jih Pao* exacerbated Moscow's discomfiture by writing that the Russians had "stabbed the Arab people in the back."*

At 7:30 A.M. EDT Saturday, June 10, the Soviet Union finally acted. It abruptly severed diplomatic relations with Israel.†

The Soviet government charged Israel with "gross violations" of the cease-fires and ominously warned: "Unless Israel halts immediately its military action," the Soviet Union "jointly with other peace-loving states will undertake sanctions against Israel, with all the consequences flowing therefrom."

The harsh Soviet action, one which it seldom employed in its diplomacy, was enough to jolt Israel into declaring it was ready to make arrangements for a cease-fire. Almost simultaneously with the Soviet action, Dayan asked to meet with General Bull to work out the details at 2 P.M. (8 A.M. EDT).

By that time, Israel had achieved all of its goals. Israeli troops had occupied Kuneitra and secured all of the Heights by noon. The earlier false Syrian report that Kuneitra had fallen during the night, apparently a ploy to draw the Security Council's attention to Syria's plight, had backfired. It completely demoralized the Syrian troops and shortly after its issuance they deserted all their positions and retreated toward Damascus, leaving Kuneitra and other fortified posts empty and free for the taking by Israeli troops.

---

* After an initial flirtation with Israel, during which Israel conferred *de jure* recognition on the Communist government in China on January 9, 1950, Peking, like Moscow, had become a champion of the Arab cause by the mid-1950s. The subsequent Sino-Soviet split did not weaken the two Communist powers' support of the Arabs. In fact, it tended to make them competitors in proving who was the better friend. The Chinese, having less to offer materially, outdid the Soviets in their support of the Palestinian guerrilla groups. Thus at a time when Moscow still ignored Fatah and the PLO, Peking warmly greeted a PLO delegation on March 16, 1965. Chairman Mao Tse-tung told the delegation, headed by Shukairy: "You are the front gate of the great continent [Asia], and we are the rear. [Western imperialists] created Israel for you, and Formosa for us. Their goal is the same. . . . Asia is the biggest continent in the world, and the West wants to continue exploiting it."

† Other East Bloc states soon followed: Bulgaria and Czechoslovakia that same day; Hungary and Poland on June 12; Yugoslavia on June 13.

Kosygin reinforced the message of the Kremlin's determination to halt the fighting by activating the hot line at 8:48 A.M. He requested that "the President come to the equipment as soon as possible."

Johnson was still in his bedroom. He had had a bad night, interrupted repeatedly by telephone calls about Israel's attacks on Syria. There had been five calls by 4:05 A.M., by which time he had such pain in his left shoulder that he telephoned for a doctor. He was examined immediately and pronounced in good shape. More telephone calls followed until he finally fell asleep at 6 A.M. He dozed until thirteen minutes before Kosygin's message.

Johnson got to the Situation Room nine minutes after the hot line's activation. Kosygin's message was a chilling one. He flatly informed Johnson that a "very crucial moment" had arrived, that there was the risk of a "grave catastrophe" and if Israel did not stop fighting within the next few hours the Soviet Union would take "necessary actions, including military."

The strong message sent a shock through Johnson and his advisers, who included Mac Bundy, Dick Helms, Nick Katzenbach, Bob McNamara, Walt Rostow and ambassador to the Soviet Union Llewellyn Thompson. The use of the term "military" was an open threat, never made lightly by the Soviets, and Thompson read back over the original Russian language message to be certain it had been correctly interpreted. It had.

"The room was deathly still as we carefully studied this grave communication," Johnson wrote in his memoirs.

"The atmosphere was tense," said Helms later. "The conversation was conducted in the lowest voices I have ever heard."

Once again, as in 1956, the United States and the Soviet Union were being dragged toward a superpower confrontation as a result of the Middle East.

Katzenbach excused himself to call in the Israeli ambassador and insist that Israel must stop its attacks. No one knew what else to do, how to respond to Kosygin's unveiled threat. But because the threat was so naked they felt it was necessary to react. But how?

Johnson, his appetite sharpened by tension, had been eating a breakfast of melon balls, cream chipped beef and hot tea. When he finished, he left the room briefly.

McNamara said in a low voice to Thompson: "Don't you think it might be useful if the Sixth Fleet, which is simply orbiting around Sicily . . . simply turn and head those two aircraft carriers and their accompanying ships to the eastern Mediterranean?"

Thompson liked the idea. So did Helms, who said, "The Soviets will get the message right away because . . . they're sure watching the Sixth Fleet like a hawk with their various electronic devices and others. Once the U.S. ships line up and start to go in that direction, the message is going to get back to Moscow in a hurry."

At this point the President returned.

"We've been talking about this and we'd like to recommend that we head the fleet toward the eastern Mediterranean," said McNamara.

Smiling, Johnson said, "Good idea. Where is the Sixth Fleet now?"

McNamara picked up the telephone, spoke and then said: "It is approximately three hundred miles west of the Syrian coast." Its orders were to stay at least one hundred miles away from the Soviet squadron in order to avoid any incidents.

The Russian force was impressive. It included about twenty warships with supporting vessels plus eight or nine submarines, but no aircraft carriers, which Russia at the time did not possess.

"How fast do these [American] carriers normally travel?" asked Johnson.

"About twenty-five knots," said McNamara. "Traveling normally, they are some ten or twelve hours away from the Syrian coast."

"There are times when the wisdom and rightness of a President's judgment are critically important," Johnson later wrote proudly. "We were at such a moment. The Soviets had made a decision. I had to respond."

The President ordered the Sixth Fleet to reduce its restricted distance from the Soviet squadron to fifty miles. Now the United States and the Soviet Union were on a direct collision course.

No one said a word. Thompson recalled the time as one of "great concern and utmost gravity."

"We all knew the Russians would get the message as soon as their monitors observed the change in the fleet's pattern," Johnson wrote in his memoirs with a touch of Texan machismo. "That message, which no translator would need to interpret to the Kremlin leadership, was that the United States was prepared to resist Soviet intrusion in the Middle East."

The Soviet Union was no longer the comparatively weak adversary that Dwight Eisenhower had faced down in the Middle East eleven years earlier. Now it too had a formidable missile force, an enlarged and powerful navy, and apparently the will to use these forces to defend its national interests. A period of intense suspense descended over the White House while the President and his senior officials waited to see how Moscow would respond to the American riposte.

Meantime, Johnson also had to go through the diplomatic formalities. He had to reply on the hot line to Kosygin's message. He kept his message moderate, saying simply that the United States was pressing Israel to cease fire and had received assurances that the Israelis would comply. He did not mention the movement of the Sixth Fleet.

Anxiety set in as the President and his aides awaited Moscow's reaction to their gambit.

Word of the Soviet threat was quickly relayed to Goldberg at the United Nations. He immediately asked Gideon Rafael to join him in the delegates' lounge and, without preliminaries, said to the Israeli diplomat: "The situation has reached a point where you must immediately make a statement that Israel has ceased all military operations on the Syrian front. Fedorenko any minute now is going to make a statement in the form of an ultimatum. He will declare that 'the Soviet government is prepared to use every available means to make Israel respect the cease-fire resolution.' "

Rafael realized the gravity of Goldberg's warning, but he pointed out, he was helpless to make such a declaration without the authorization of his government.

Goldberg was dismayed. "I speak to you on specific and urgent instructions from the President of the United States," he said. "We do not know whether and how the Soviets will materialize their threat.

"But what we do know is that the United States Government does not want the war to end as the result of a Soviet ultimatum. This would be disastrous for the future not only of Israel but of us all. It is your responsibility to act now."

This of course was the essence of the U.S. concern at the United Nations. It did not want the Soviet Union to receive credit for stopping the fighting.

Rafael again declined to make a statement. At that moment he was called away to the telephone. It was the Foreign Ministry in Jerusalem calling.

"Please write down the following statement which you are asked to make immediately," said Moshe Sasson, the ministry's director of military liaison.

General Dayan and General Bull have just concluded their meeting. Israel has accepted the proposals made by the UN representative for the implementation of the cease-fire resolution and the arrangements for the supervision of the cease-fire. General Dayan stated that on his part the cease-fire could enter into force at any hour. . . . It was agreed that General Bull will fix the hour for the cease-fire entering into force. . . .

Israel's capitulation in the face of the Soviet threat was complete. It was also convenient. Israel had already totally accomplished its war aims and

281

more. In six days of fighting, the Jewish state of under three million had vanquished Egypt, Jordan and Syria, with a combined population of nearly thirty-nine million persons, captured territory three times its size, placed under occupation a million Palestinians, and uprooted and turned into refugees hundreds of thousands of others.

Bull set the cease-fire for 12:30 P.M. EDT, five hours after Moscow severed relations with Tel Aviv and less than four hours after Kosygin's hot-line call to Johnson and the Administration's subsequent heavy pressure on Israel. For Syria, it was all too late.

It had lost the Heights; an estimated 107,000 of its population had been turned into refugees, 17,000 of them for the second time since 1948; and its casualties numbered about 600 killed and 700 wounded. Israel's losses were estimated at 127 killed and 625 wounded.

Sixteen hours after Nasser announced his resignation, the streets of Cairo were still so jammed by worried and tearful Egyptians that the president could not travel to the National Assembly. Instead, he sent a letter, which was read by Speaker Anwar Sadat to the 360 members of the legislative body and was relayed across the country by radio.

His voice charged with emotion, Sadat read: "I wished, if the nation had helped me, to stand by my decision to resign. No one can imagine my feelings at this moment in view of the people's determination to refuse my resignation. I feel that the people's will cannot be refused. Therefore, I have decided to stay where the people want me to stay until all the traces of aggression have been erased."

Pandemonium broke out in the streets. Hundreds of thousands of Egyptians, including many who had poured into the capital overnight from distant villages, screamed with joy, danced and sang and embraced one another in their delirium. Car horns blared, women screamed the ululating *zagrouta,* the traditional call Arab women yell in moments of great happiness, children shouted and jumped merrily, men cried in their relief and exultation. They were the young and the old, the rich and the poor, the educated and the illiterate. There was no question that the people of Egypt wanted Nasser to remain and continue as their leader, no matter what disasters his actions had brought them.

Many foreigners had dismissed Nasser's attempt at resignation as a stratagem, a calculated scheme to divert the people's attention away from their enormous losses in the Sinai in order to retain his power. That is probably crediting him with too much perspicacity. No doubt there was some element of calculation in his actions, but those who knew him and who witnessed the unbridled affection and joy of the people at his decision to remain believed he was sincere when he attempted to resign.

Certainly there was no doubt that his despair at his humiliating defeat at the hands of Israel was not only profound but deserved. He felt responsible and guilty. He suffered and he finally made his decision without consulting anyone. Nor had he done anything to organize the demonstrations. The eruption of support was spontaneous and was shared throughout the Arab world. At forty-nine years of age, he appeared to have many years of service left. There was no one of similar stature within Egypt or in any other Arab country. In these circumstances, he reversed his emotional decision of the previous evening with as much sincerity, it seemed, as that with which he had made his original decision.

Nasser was never quite the same afterward. Anwar Sadat spoke by telephone with him several times shortly after the withdrawal of his resignation. "Every time I felt he was worse," Sadat reported. "His voice was that of a man who belonged in the past—a dark, hollow, distant past. He must be in bed, I thought; he must be suffering very much. His pride, his most treasured asset, had been hurt as never before. Only a few days earlier the world had waited, tense and expectant, for every word he uttered at his famous press conference. Now people everywhere sneered at him and made him a laughingstock. The events of June 5 dealt him a fatal blow. They finished him off.

"That was how he looked at the time, and for a long time afterwards—a living corpse. The pallor of death was evident on his face and hands, although he still moved and walked, listened and talked."

During the early hours of Saturday morning, the Americans remaining in Cairo had been advised to leave because of the milling, anxious crowds awaiting Nasser's decision. There was fear they might vent their anger against foreigners. Ambassador Nolte and his aides traveled to Alexandria where they were to board a Greek ship late Saturday for evacuation to Athens. The American reporters interned in the Nile Hilton also were sent to Alexandria at the same time by the worried Egyptian government.

That left correspondent Eric Pace the lone American reporter in Cairo. He had planned to go with the other reporters, but the huge crowds had made him change his mind about pushing his way to the Hilton. As it turned out, there were no serious incidents and by midafternoon the crowds had dispersed. But Pace was now left behind as an illegal alien. When he telephoned the Information Ministry to advise officials of his presence, one official "gave the Egyptian equivalent of a harumph," wrote Pace. "And that was all."

Pace went about his reportorial chores. In terms of American coverage, he now had the story of postwar Egypt all to himself. It was not until three days later that the authorities got around to picking him up and gently loading him on a Italian cruise ship for a leisurely sail across the Mediterranean to Italy.

Israel was now trumpeting its triumphs, and making clear that it was determined to profit from the war. Yisrael Galili, the government's information minister, told reporters that Saturday that "Israel cannot return to the 1949 armistices and boundaries determined by those agreements."

Israel was unilaterally renouncing the arduously wrought armistice agreements that for eighteen years had defined the frontiers between the Jewish state and its neighbors, Egypt, Jordan, Lebanon and Syria. Now, victorious, Israel would draw its own frontiers.

In Washington, the hot line was activated four more times as Kosygin complained again that the fighting was continuing and Johnson tried to assure him that it was stopping. At 11:54 A.M. EDT, Johnson made the last use of the direct communications link to assure the Soviet leader that the fighting was truly ending. It did on schedule thirty-six minutes later.

Johnson had remained in the Situation Room during the tense morning. Now, after sending his last message to Kosygin, he finally departed. The crisis, quite suddenly, was over. The Soviets had not responded to the movements of the Sixth Fleet, which in any event had been overtaken by Israel's cease-fire, nor did they publicize their threats that contributed to the ending of the fighting. Shrewdly, they did not put Johnson in a position where he had to react to Soviet boasting in public. Instead, the use that Saturday of the hot line went unreported until emotions cooled and most Americans were unaware of how close their country had come to a confrontation with the Soviet Union.

It was 3:50 P.M. before the obviously relaxing President began getting ready for a well-deserved bit of fun. He had invited sixteen couples to take an overnight cruise on the Potomac in the presidential yacht *Sequoia*, and now, with the cease-fires in the Middle East holding and the crisis with Moscow defused, he drove to the Anacostia Naval Yard pier and boarded the graceful ship. His aides noticed he was "very relaxed."

That night President Johnson slept on the gentle waters of the Potomac, far away from the hot line, far from the Middle East, far, far from the U.S.S. *Liberty* with its cargo of dead and wounded, even farther from Vietnam, where other Americans were dying.

———

There was no rest for the Palestinians uprooted from their homes or those remaining in the conquered areas. Their ordeal was only beginning. Now the looting and destruction of Arab homes and in some cases whole villages by the victorious Israeli troops was about to begin as the long dark night of occupation descended on the region.

———

In New York, McGeorge Bundy conferred that weekend with Arthur Goldberg on ways to counter the Soviet Union at the United Nations. Moscow was still determined to have a resolution passed that would condemn Israel and call for its withdrawal from captured territory. Bundy was firmly with the majority in the White House who favored the Israeli position that the policy of the United States should be a passive one, that it not seek a withdrawal of Israel's troops except in return for some sort of peace settlement. A memorandum to the President that Sunday noted that "Bundy believes the line we should hold to for the next few days is 'let's have peace.' He says now is not the time for new policy statements."

The Security Council remained in session that weekend because of continued reports from Syria that Israel was improving its position by violating the cease-fire. Exchanges between the various sides were heated, particularly the comments of Fedorenko. He referred to a TV statement made that Sunday by Moshe Dayan denigrating the United Nations. "We hear insults," complained Fedorenko. "General Moshe Dayan . . . says that the map of the Middle East will be rearranged and that the Israeli State will have new frontiers. Moshe Dayan stated: 'I certainly cannot recall that any problem was ever settled by diplomacy or through the United Nations.' "

Fedorenko again demanded that the Council condemn Israel and take "decisive and immediate measures to ensure the implementation by Israel of the resolutions adopted by the Security Council."

Because of opposition led by the United States, the meeting continued indecisively into the early hours of Monday. Finally, as he had done before, Council President Tabor introduced a draft resolution of his own at 3 A.M. condemning "any and all violations of the cease-fire" and the "prompt return to the cease-fire positions of any troops which may have moved forward subsequent to 1630 GMT on 10 June 1967." It made no reference to condemnation of Israel, withdrawal or which side might have violated the cease-fire. The draft passed unanimously as Resolution 236, the fourth cease-fire resolution adopted by the Council. Its effect was to emphasize the Council's demand that the fighting stop completely, but it did not carry the Council's work any further in the direction of finding a solution to the crisis.

Yet there was an urgent need for such a resolution. Israel was already moving swiftly to consolidate its hold on the occupied territories.

PART THREE
AFTERMATH

June 11 to November 22, 1967

_____XXI_____
PALESTINIANS EVICTED

I n the occupied territories, Israel wasted no time. Under cover of darkness on Saturday night and into Sunday morning, the Israelis made their first move in the Old City of Jerusalem.

Floodlights were set up near the Wailing Wall and Israeli officers marched from door to door of the Moghrabi Quarter ordering out the pious Moslems who had lived there for many years near their revered mosques on the Temple Mount, which they called the Haram esh Sharef (the noble sanctuary). The residents were given three hours to leave their homes. Then a bulldozer moved in, knocking down residences one by one. Afterward, in one crushed house, an old woman, apparently uninjured, was found in the ruins. She died a short time later.

In all, the bulldozer wiped out the homes of 135 families. The 650 evicted Arabs lost most of their possessions in the swift operation. It was carried out with all haste in order to "create a fact," a tactic meant to conclude a controversial action before international opposition could materialize. The action was generally regarded as a violation of the Fourth Geneva Convention of 1949.*

* Israel was a signatory to the convention, officially known as the Geneva Convention Relative to the Protection of Civilian Persons in Time of War of August 12, 1949. International attorneys cite several articles of the convention as prohibiting such actions, most specially Article 49(6), which states: "The Occupying Power shall not deport or transfer parts of its own civilian population into the territory it occupies." Israel claimed the convention did not apply to the West Bank or the Gaza Strip because neither Jordan nor Egypt had clear sovereignty over those territories.

One reason publicly advanced for the swift destruction of the Moghrabi Quarter was made by Israeli Jerusalem's blustery mayor, Teddy Kollek, a native of Hungary who had emigrated to Palestine in 1935. It was to clear a large plaza in front of the Wailing Wall so Jews had more room to congregate at their sacred site. Urgency was needed, Kollek maintained, because the government had decided to open the wall to Israelis on the following Wednesday, the day of the Shavuot holiday, and room had to be made for all the expected Jewish worshipers. "But how would these hundreds of thousands reach the Wall through the dangerous narrow alleyways unless the quarter was torn down?" he asked.

More believably, he went on to admit in his 1978 autobiography that speed also was necessary because of expected opposition from the international community. "My overpowering feeling was: do it now; it may be impossible to do it later, and it *must* be done."

Other *faits accomplis* had already taken place in the occupied territories, and more were about to come. Three villages in the fertile Latrun Valley that had defied capture in 1948 had already been totally razed by Israeli bulldozers, their residents scattered without concern for their future. Beit Nuba, Imwas and Yalu lay just across the frontier on the West Bank, about fifteen miles northwest of Jerusalem, and obstructed a direct route from Jerusalem to Tel Aviv. The residents had been ordered out early in the predawn darkness of June 6 without explanation, given no chance to rescue their possessions except for what they could carry, left to wander without shelter or food or water. When the shooting finally ended, Israel Radio instructed the thousands of frightened and hiding Palestinians to return to their villages. But the villagers of Beit Nuba, Imwas and Yalu were kept out by Israeli troops. Reporters and other possible witnesses were also prevented from entering the area.

Some of the Israeli soldiers, most of them young civilian reservists, were appalled when they took up their stations at Beit Nuba and were ordered to shoot over the heads of any Arabs attempting to return. Then the bulldozers went to work.

"The homes in Beit Nuba are beautiful stone houses," wrote one of the Israeli soldiers, Amos Kenan. "Each house stands in an orchard of olives, apricots and grapevines. Each tree stands in its carefully watered bed. They

But W. T. Mallison, professor of international law at Georgetown University, and others maintained the Israeli argument was defective because its effect would be to deny protection of the convention's provisions to all those persons living in disputed territory, clearly not the intention of the framers of the convention.

are well kept. Between the trees lie neatly hoed and weeded rows of vegetables."

The bulldozers pushed over everything, houses with most of their contents still intact, trees, whatever was in their way. Dynamite was used on heavy obstructions. While the destruction continued, a group of villagers approached.

"There were old men hardly able to walk, old women murmuring to themselves, babies in their mother's arms, small children weeping, begging for water," Kenan wrote.

They carried white flags. The soldiers ordered them to go to another village, but they replied they had been driven out of every village they tried to enter. They said they had been wandering for four days without food, without water. Some of their relatives had already died on the road.

"On the horizon we spotted the next group approaching. A man carrying a fifty-kilogram sack of flour on his back, and that was how he walked, mile after mile," reported Kenan. "More old men, more women, more babies. They flopped down exhausted at the spot where they were told to sit. Some had brought along a cow or two, or a calf—all their earthly possessions. We did not allow them to go into the village to pick up their belongings, for the order was that they must not be allowed to see their houses being destroyed."

As the bulldozers roared and dynamite exploded and house after house fell into heaps, some of the children began crying. So too did some of the young Israeli soldiers. They gave what water and cigarettes and candy they had to the villagers. But the destruction continued and the agony of the villagers grew more acute.

"More of our soldiers wept," wrote Kenan. "We asked the officers why these refugees were being sent back and forth and driven away from everywhere they went. The officers said it would do them good to walk and asked, 'Why worry about them, they're only Arabs.'"

More villagers arrived. There were now hundreds of them watching their homes, the homes of their fathers and their fathers' fathers, their homes for generations, being blown up and ground into rubble. The soldiers did not know what to do with them. They were so needy and helpless.

Finally an officer went to headquarters and asked for orders on where to send the distressed villagers. "He came back and said there was no order, we were to drive them away," wrote Kenan.

The soldiers drove them away.

Arab sources later put the number of residents in the three villages at ten thousand; Israel insisted their number was only four thousand. Whatever the number their fate was the same, dispossession and homelessness.

Sister Marie-Thérèse, a French nun, eluded officials attempting to keep her away and visited the area shortly after the bulldozers departed. She found undamaged the gracious Trappist monastery, still serenely sitting on a small hillock at the head of the Latrun Valley. But Sister Marie-Thérèse discovered the villages were gone. "... there was what the Israelis did not want us to see: three villages systematically destroyed by dynamite and bulldozer," she recorded in her diary. "Alone in the deathly silence donkeys wandered about in the ruins. Here and there a crushed piece of furniture, or a torn pillow stuck out of the mass of plaster, stones and concrete. A cooking pan and its lid abandoned in the middle of the road."

Similar scenes occurred elsewhere, Kenan reported. "We also learned that it was not in our sector alone that areas were 'straightened out'; the same thing was going on in all sectors."

One of the other victims was the village of Qalqilya, west of Nablus. Its approximately fourteen thousand residents had taken to the nearby hills during the fighting, in which about twenty homes were destroyed or damaged, the mayor told U.N. officials. After the fighting stopped, and Israeli troops occupied the city, residents were kept out for an additional three days. When they returned they found 850 of the town's 2,000 homes had been destroyed. The Israeli officer in command of the town claimed the buildings were ruined during the fighting and that they and others had to be dynamited because they were so damaged they were unsafe.

In fact, Moshe Dayan later learned that "many houses had been damaged not as a result of battle but of punitive action by Israeli soldiers ... in reprisal for Arab sniping at our troops." Such reprisals were against official policy, Dayan said, and he ordered cement and other materials be given to the residents of Qalqilya so they could go about the task of rebuilding their homes.

Similar reprisals occurred at two villages near Hebron and Dayan took the same action. At Beit Awa, Israeli troops entered the village at 5:30 A.M. on Sunday, June 11, told the 2,500 villagers each to take two loaves of bread and ordered them to the hills. When they were allowed to return a week later 90 percent of their four hundred homes were completely destroyed and the rest were damaged. Even the groves around the village had been burned.

A nearby village, Beit Mersin, with a population of about five hundred, was completely destroyed. Deliberate destruction of homes was also reported at such other villages as Beit Illo, Edna, Kharas and Sourif.

In those few cases where Israeli officials publicly admitted responsibility for this systematic destruction, the reasons varied from security considerations to clearing out structures made unsafe by war damage. But already there was a chilling suggestion that a deeper, darker purpose lay behind Israel's actions: the dispersal of the Palestinian people from their land.

Indeed, while the government officially denied encouraging—or discouraging—the Palestinians to leave, its agents were prodding West Bankers to get out, to flee east across the desert into Jordan or north into Lebanon or west into Egypt. In the streets of Bethlehem Israeli soldiers drove around with loudspeakers shouting: "You have two hours to leave your homes and flee to Jericho and Amman. If you don't, your houses will be shelled." In a number of municipalities, Israeli buses and trucks were made available to carry any Palestinians wishing to go to Jordan.

The scene at the Allenby Bridge near Jericho was one of chaos and misery. The bridge had been demolished by Israel during the war, and now the refugees with their children and their few possessions had to clamber down the muddy banks into the shallow Jordan and wade across or balance on a makeshift span. Israeli soldiers seated in chairs along the bank watched the exodus silently. When one woman who had crossed to help fleeing relatives tried to return to her children in Bethlehem, she was barred. An Israeli officer seated in his armchair declared that once a Palestinian had crossed the river there could be no return.

Tens of thousands of Palestinians still had no idea what to do—flee for their lives or stay. And if they did remain they could not be sure they would find their homes still standing. Many were still living in the hills, under trees in the chill nights, waiting. They were like lost cattle. They descended on neighborhoods uninvited and helpless, a sudden visitation of a hungry and thirsty and unwanted horde.

Raymonda Tawil, a Palestinian writer and wife of a Nablus banker, had awoke one morning during the fighting to find a "human sea. I gaze out of the window at one of the most amazing, horrifying scenes I have ever beheld. Outside our house, in the road, in the olive groves, there are literally thousands of people—old, young, families with children, pregnant women, cripples. In their arms or on their backs they carry bundles with a few possessions. Young women clutch babies. Everywhere the same exhausted, broken figures, the stunned, desperate faces. It is like a nightmare." The refugees were from Qalqilya.*

* Dayan also visited a group of Qalqilya refugees and described their condition in different terms: "If there ruined houses had not been visible across the way, one

Some of the refugees did not wait for the heartbreak of returning to their shattered homes.

"The Israelis were sending buses for some of the refugees, taking them to the Allenby Bridge and dropping them off there, abandoned, bedraggled, with their few miserable possessions, whole families with men and women, old people, children in arms," wrote Raymonda Tawil. "Silent and dazed, the columns of refugees . . . were heading for an uncertain, homeless future; at best, they could hope to begin life again in yet another impoverished refugee camp."

There was nothing for the refugees who crossed into the East Bank. There were soon nearly 100,000 of them crowding the 300,000 residents of Amman, taking over schools, mosques and public buildings for their shelter. Thousands slept on the sidewalks and in doorways or on the city's rocky hillsides. Food was scarce and quickly became expensive. Many Palestinians were reduced to foraging in garbage cans.

For those who remained on the West Bank and were lucky enough to find their homes still standing, there was another heartbreak facing some of them: the theft of their belongings. Widespread looting was reported throughout the occupied areas, especially in Jerusalem. Stores and homes in Jerusalem were sacked, cars were stolen and even jewels from the Holy Sepulcher in the Old City were missing (but later restored).

Abdullah Schleifer, a Jew who had converted to Islam and lived in the Old City, was in his home when neighbors reported that Israelis were looting a religious school and mosque on the ground floor. Schleifer rushed down and stopped a soldier and two civilians with their arms full of plundered books. When he asked why they were taking the books, one replied in embarrassment that he was a student and he thought the Arabs did not "need" the books.

"His attitude was . . . part of that same consciousness that was to bring dozens of Israeli sightseers to our door and the doors of our neighbors in the coming days," observed Schleifer. "If the door was not firmly locked, they would walk in unannounced and suddenly we would discover a family of Israelis calming strolling about our apartment, looking out of the windows at the view or examining the rooms. If the door was locked, they would knock and demand entry 'to look around.' "

Looting in some places was thorough. All the equipment in the operating

---

might have thought that these people were out enjoying a mass picnic. Under each tree sat a family. The children cavorted on blankets spread on the ground and were having a great time unraveling bundles of clothing; the women were bent over the fire with their pots, while the men . . . dozed peacefully."

room of the hospital in Qalqilya was missing, right down to the operating table and the lights hanging above it.

The provincial capital of Kuneitra, on the Syrian Golan Heights, which fell without a fight, was stripped by Israeli soldiers. A U.N. special representative, Nils-Goran Gussing, visited the city and found that "nearly every shop and every house seemed to have been broken into and looted. A visit to one apartment building confirmed the thoroughness with which the looting had been done, and showed that in some cases dwellings had been set on fire after looting had occurred."

Gussing's report added: "Israeli spokesmen did not deny the looting but pointed out that looting is often associated with warfare."

Nearly all of the 115,000 residents of the Golan Heights except for 6,000 Druse, members of a minor Moslem sect, and all but about 200 of the population of Kuneitra had fled.

Sister Marie-Thérèse reported that the quality of the Israeli soldiers declined as the days passed. "The first wave of Israeli soldiers were decent, humane, and courageous, doing as little damage as possible, the second wave was made up of thieves, looters and sometimes killers, and the third was more disturbing still since it seemed to act from a resolute desire for systematic destruction," she wrote.

There were reports to the United Nations of torture, summary executions and other forms of brutality, but in the confusion and anger of the war they were nearly impossible to document. Nonetheless, many Palestinians were understandably frightened. They were fleeing their homes by the tens of thousands for the safety, if not the comfort, across the River Jordan.

Nor were the personnel of the United Nations safe from abuse and looting. In a report to the Security Council, U Thant confirmed that fourteen Indian members of UNEF and one Brazilian had been killed during the fighting in the Gaza Strip and seventeen others wounded. They had been killed by Israeli aircraft and shells, which had rained down on UNEF headquarters in Gaza near where Egypt had emplaced several mortar and artillery positions.

Israeli troops had occupied UNEF headquarters on the second day of the war, U Thant reported, and when the U.N. staff returned that night they found that radios, tape recorders and clocks had been looted, but office equipment and documents had gone untouched. Since there were a great number of Israeli soldiers in and around the compound, UNEF officers asked the IDF to provide security and then departed. When they returned on June 9, reported U Thant, they found that "most of the office furniture, typewriters, fans and other UNEF property had been removed by the Israel military personnel. In fact, UNEF representatives actually witnessed the removal of these items but were unable to secure any effective action by the responsible Israel authorities to prevent it. All of the United Nations vehicles in running condition had also been removed by Israel forces and were seen in use in the Gaza area."

U Thant reported similar pilfering at UNEF's camp at Rafah, southwest of Gaza, which Israeli forces occupied on the first afternoon of the war. ". . . by 1900 hours Israel Defense Forces tanks were inside the camp firing on the local UNEF civilian employes," reported U Thant. UNEF civilian and military personnel identified themselves, but they nonetheless were ordered to lie on the ground with their arms behind their backs. They were "forced to spend the night on the sand in the open without food or water."

Moshe Dayan later apologized to General Rikhye about the high number of Indian casualties. However, he coolly added "that there had been rumors that the Indian troops had helped the Arabs during . . . the war. This had created a certain amount of ill will amongst the Israeli forces towards the Indian troops."

———

Almost nothing of Israel's looting and destruction was reported in the press during those first euphoric days of victory. Partly this was because Israel was successful in hiding its actions. Israeli officials repeatedly denied that any Arabs had been displaced and made homeless by deliberate destruction of their houses. In addition to this official stonewalling, the government prohibited reporters from traveling in the occupied territories without an Israeli escort.

Beyond these practices, the world, especially Western Europe and the United States, was too exhilarated to think of the predictable dark underside of military occupation. Instead, there was cheering and approval nearly everywhere for the Israeli Army's gallant victories, for its dashing speed, its tactical brilliance, its handsome heroes.

More than cheering, there was a positive resistance to believe anything negative about the Israeli forces, to see them as less than superhuman warriors emerged from the biblical past, symbols for the righting of ancient wrongs. A British free-lance journalist, Michael Adams, an eloquent writer, was the first to report in detail for the British press the story of the obliteration of Beit Nuba, Imwas and Yalu. It was in early 1968, more than six months after their destruction, that he came across the story while on a trip to Israel under contract to the *Manchester Guardian*. He wrote the story and sent it to the *Guardian,* but the newspaper's editor found the story so shocking and unbelievable that he refused to print it.

With only a few notable exceptions, stories coming out of Israel and printed in the major U.S. dailies during this period were almost invariably focused on the glory of Israel's achievements and the humanity of its occupation policies. They were mute about the plight of a people suddenly rendered captive or homeless in their own land, silent now that victims of the past had suddenly become oppressors of the present.

This blindness to a whole people's suffering and the unrestrained glorification of Israel was widely shared and partly explained by the lingering Holocaust guilt of the West. The Christian West experienced a sense of relief, of expiation, with Israel's triumph. There was in the West an undercurrent of feeling that finally its guilt over the Nazi atrocities was at last exculpated.

The French daily *Le Monde* expressed what many were feeling that spring and summer: "In the past few days Europe has in a sense rid itself of the guilt it incurred in the drama of the Second World War and, before that, in the persecutions which, from the Russian pogroms to the Dreyfus affair, accompanied the birth of Zionism. In the continent of Europe the Jews were at last avenged—but alas, on the backs of Arabs—for the tragic and stupid accusation: 'They went like sheep to the slaughter.' "

That ovine specter had haunted Jews ever since World War II, particularly Israelis who had been in concentration camps. Repeatedly they asked themselves and each other how a people could walk meekly to its own destruction—if only they had fought, if only each of the six million victims had taken one German soldier with him to death. It was a lesson that incessantly occupied the thoughts of many Israelis and steeled them to fight.

For those Jews who had not experienced the crematoria, especially the Jewish Americans safe in the United States, there were also haunting and persistent parallel questions: Had they done enough, could they have stopped the Holocaust? Were they doing enough to support their brethren in Israel?

Suddenly, Israel's smashing victory seemed vindication, proof to themselves and the world that Jews would never again walk "like sheep to the slaughter."

Praise came from everywhere for Israel, in the press, in public speeches, from the pulpit. Senator Robert F. Kennedy described Israel that weekend of June 10–11 in a speech at New York's Fordham University as a "tiny outpost of western culture and ideals.... This gallant democracy, this nation of survivors from history's greatest example of man's capacity for senseless cruelty to his fellow man, cannot be allowed to succumb to the threats and assaults of her neighbors."

In a Gallup Poll released that Sunday, 55 percent of the Americans questioned said they strongly sympathized with Israel. Only 4 percent sided with the Arabs. President Johnson also earned high marks for his performance. Forty-seven percent said they approved of his actions during the war; only 14 percent disapproved.

A count of letters pouring into the State Department—5,241 pieces of mail processed in one day, 17,445 in four days—was overwhelmingly in support of Israel. Ninety-six to 98 percent favored Israel. The highest single-day pro-Arab mail equaled 1 percent.

It seemed that everyone was agog and admiring of the élan of the Israeli soldier. Harry C. McPherson, Jr., who served as Johnson's liaison with the Jewish community, had happened to arrive in Israel on the day the war erupted. In a report to the President on June 11 he wrote: "Incidentally, Israel at war destroys the prototype of the pale, scrawny Jew; the soldiers I saw were tough, muscular and sun-burned. There is also an extraordinary combination of discipline and democracy among officers and enlisted men; the latter rarely salute and frequently argue. . . .

"After the doubts, confusions and ambiguities of Vietnam it was deeply moving to see people whose commitment is total and unquestioning."

Although Washington officialdom was still maintaining publicly that it had not been able to figure out who had actually started the war, there was little doubt in McPherson's mind that it was Israel. He reported that while at the Gaza frontier on the second day of the war he had come across fatigued truck drivers. When he had asked his escort officer about them, he was told: "They've earned their sleep. They've been driving down here since Sunday afternoon." Observed McPherson: "The Israeli 'response' began Monday morning. . . . My feeling is that an Arab attack was not so imminent, but that the Israelis simply decided to hit first. . . ."

He also reported that the war had been won by mid-Monday and that Israel had been supremely confident of victory. While he was seated with Israel's intelligence chief outside Eshkol's office at noon on the first day of the war, the air raid sirens had gone off. McPherson asked the official if they should go to the shelter. "He looked at his watch and said, 'It won't be necessary.' "

He concluded by warning the President that "the Israelis do not intend to repeat 1956. . . . We would have to push them back by military force, in my opinion, to accomplish a repeat of 1956; the cutoff of aid would not do it."

Israel's supporters were making that message perfectly clear. At a pro-

Israel rally that Sunday in New York, Senator Javits declared that the United States "must not stand by as Israel is asked to pull back from positions gained through the expenditures of so much blood and heroism unless it is made certain that Israel's future security is guaranteed."

In Israel, Moshe Dayan was stressing the same point, only stronger. "I don't think we should in any way give back the Gaza strip to Egypt or the western part of Jordan to King Hussein," he said on CBS's *Face the Nation* program on Sunday. He added that Jerusalem was Israel's capital and was now reunited. If the Arabs did not want to enter direct talks, he said, "then there will be a new map, not of the Middle East, but of Israel."

Levi Eshkol reiterated the message the next day in a televised report on the war to the nation. "Let this be said: there should be no illusion that Israel is prepared to return to the conditions that existed a week ago. . . . We have fought alone for our existence and our security, and we are therefore justified in deciding for ourselves what are the genuine and indispensable interests of our state, and how to guarantee its future. We shall never return to the conditions prevailing before."

Although the top Administration officials attempted to maintain a cool objectivity toward Israel in this celebratory period, the political reality was that the international and financial injuries resulting from the war did not begin to match for Lyndon Johnson the domestic advantages accruing to him from his pro-Israel policies. Polls consistently continued to show that 99 percent of Jewish Americans wholeheartedly supported Israel during the war and, despite their feelings about Vietnam, that support was transferred to some considerable degree to Johnson.

The President was widely appreciated for his Middle East policies, not only in the United States but in Israel as well. If many Americans had trouble understanding whether the country really believed in neutrality and the territorial integrity of the Middle East states or not, there was no such confusion in Israel. In a poll taken right after the war, the President of the United States emerged as the most popular man in Israel, beating out even the war's two great heroes, Moshe Dayan and Yitzhak Rabin.

Democratic leaders attending a fourteen-state Midwest Democratic conference that weekend adopted a resolution hailing the Administration's "commendable policy" during the crisis. A poll of Congress by the Associated Press showed that none of the congressmen who responded thought Israel should withdraw without assurances of peace, which was essentially the Administration's policy as well as Israel's.

Johnson luxuriated that June 11 Sunday in what from his view was the highly successful conclusion to a dangerous crisis. He stayed aboard the *Sequoia,* lazily sunbathing during the day, napping in the afternoon, and chatting with his guests. It was not until 7:10 P.M. that the ship arrived back at Anacostia Naval Yard. He retired at 11:30 P.M., the crisis surmounted and his political capital greatly enhanced.

XXII
JOHNSON AND KOSYGIN MEET

Leaders of the Soviet Union had reason to feel they had been out-maneuvered by the United States and Israel. Their clients in the Middle East had been defeated humiliatingly, Israel now occupied vast stretches of Arab land and yet the United Nations had not once branded Israel an aggressor or condemned it for its occupation. They made a final effort to win acceptance of their case in the Security Council.

On Tuesday, June 13, Walt Rostow informed Johnson that "we learned from a sensitive source that the Russians are putting in a resolution to the Security Council which is a variant of the one they have had before the Council for some time. . . ." Rostow's information was that the Soviets again would demand condemnation of Israel and seek withdrawal. He added: "McGeorge Bundy's comment: 'This is one we think we can block easily.' "

That turned out to be an accurate assessment. The 1,358th session of the Security Council met in the afternoon of June 13 at Russia's request. The meeting was opened by a long and denunciatory speech by Russian Ambassador Fedorenko, who then introduced a toughly worded draft resolution that "vigorously" condemned Israel and called its territorial gains "unacceptable and unlawful." It accused Israel of defiance of the United Nations and demanded immediate and unconditional withdrawal.

Turning to Arthur Goldberg, Fedorenko questioned whether the United States remained "firmly committed to the support of the political independence and territorial integrity of all the nations in the area." Was the United States, he bluntly asked, "prepared to affirm that it is against the territorial claims of Tel Aviv?"

Only several hours earlier that day, at a noon press conference held fifteen minutes after Rostow had informed the President of the Soviet recourse to the Security Council, Johnson had once again repeated that the nation's policy remained committed to the political and territorial integrity of the nations of the Middle East. But when pressed by reporters, he refused to elaborate, insisting merely that "that is our policy. It will continue to be our policy."

In other words, if Israel could achieve peace by holding on to the territories as a bargaining chip, as Israel's supporters were assuring the President, then territorial integrity became academic in Johnson's view. If Eisenhower's policy of making Israel return its conquests did not work, then maybe this barter policy would.

Almost by a process of osmosis, the popular sentiment for using the territories as a bargaining chip had by now become the policy of the U.S. government. No formal decision was made, no searching exploration of the long-term implications of such a policy was conducted, according to Hal Saunders. "It was an attitude so widely shared that it simply became the underlying assumption of all the policymakers."

But the policy had a basic flaw, a misconception that was to lead to the reverse of what U.S. officials sought in the Middle East. This was its assumption that Eisenhower had been wrong in making Israel return its captured territory in 1957, and that this action in turn led to the current war. According to this view, insistently promulgated by Israeli officials, if Israel had been allowed to barter the captured territories for peace at that time the current crisis could have been avoided.

The fallacy in this was the expectation that the Arabs could be made to accept Israel's existence by being beaten into submission. That clearly could not occur, as the 1973 war was soon to prove. In fact, the reverse was probably true. If Eisenhower had allowed Israel to retain the Sinai, chances were high that the Arabs, under the goad of that humiliation, would have precipitated a crisis even earlier than 1967. As it was, the underlying causes of the war—the dispossession of the refugees, Israel's refusal to allow them to return to their homes or to compensate them for their losses, the antagonistic policies of hardliners on both sides, to name only a few—had nothing to do with the question of the 1957 withdrawal. But so powerful was this perception that Eisenhower had been mistaken that it now became the accepted wisdom of both Israeli and U.S. policymakers—with dire consequences.

At the United Nations that day, Goldberg denounced the Soviet draft resolution and defended the many facets of the U.S. draft with its vague withdrawal clause that had been submitted five days earlier in the Security

Council. Goldberg did not press for a vote, being content, as was Israel, to allow the Council to consider the matter at much greater length. But the Soviets were impatient. They wanted action, and they had a plan for getting it.

They had decided by this time that if they could not get a strong resolution passed in the Council, where the United States and Britain wielded enormous influence, then they had another route. They would take the matter to the General Assembly where the world's many small nations openly deplored the use of force by stronger neighbors and opposed Israel's continued occupation of Arab lands.

Fedorenko, to clear the way to go to the General Assembly, insisted that the Council vote on the Soviet draft resolution. But, as Bundy had predicted and the Kremlin no doubt anticipated, the Soviet draft failed to pass when the vote took place the next day. In two ballots, its greatest support equaled six votes, three short of the nine necessary for adoption.

The Council concluded its session that same June 14 by passing a humanitarian resolution introduced by Argentina, Brazil and Ethiopia calling on Israel to ensure the welfare of the people of the conquered territories and to allow the prompt return of the refugees; it also asked the Arab governments to respect the Geneva Convention.

Thus in its meetings, which began May 24, the Council had managed to pass four cease-fire resolutions and one humanitarian resolution, but it had failed to agree on a resolution setting out practical terms leading to peace or to the return of land captured by force. The inability of its members to agree left Israel free to go about strengthening its hold on the captured territories, and this Moscow was determined to stop. It called for an immediate convening of an emergency meeting of the General Assembly, only the fifth in its history.*

The meeting was set for 9:30 A.M. Saturday, June 17. As evidence of Soviet confidence in its Assembly gambit, Premier Kosygin personally led a high-level delegation to New York. Top delegations from other East Bloc countries also attended as well as high delegations from other countries. In all, ten premiers attended, nine of them from Communist countries (the tenth was Jens Otto Krag of Denmark), as well as nearly a score of foreign ministers.

Kosygin's purpose was nothing less than to turn the Assembly session into a world summit conference on the Middle East. It was a dramatic and bold

---

* Two of the previous emergency meetings involved the Middle East: the 1956 Suez crisis and the 1958 landing of U.S. Marines in Lebanon. The two others were on the 1956 Soviet invasion of Hungary and the 1960 crisis in the Belgian Congo.

move and, given the fact that a large majority of the members favored Israeli withdrawal, one for which the Soviets had a chance of receiving the backing of most nations. But Kosygin had not adequately assessed the natural divisiveness among the regions of the world, even if he did anticipate America's strong opposition.

At the first Assembly meeting, which Kosygin attended, having arrived at dawn on his first visit to the United States, Arthur Goldberg made the opening speech by declaring that "all proposals" for peace in the Middle East should be debated and not just the Soviets' proposal for the "liquidation of the consequences of aggression and the immediate withdrawal of Israeli forces behind the armistice lines."

Oddly, neither Kosygin nor his delegation raised an objection to Goldberg's move. They sat in silence. It was left to Jordan's ambassador, Mohammad H. Farra, to object that Goldberg was trying to widen the debate in order to divert the Assembly from the "real issue," withdrawal. But the Soviets did not intervene and the Assembly acquiesced in Goldberg's suggestion. The effect was to dilute the focus of the debate and allow the introduction of subjects extraneous to the question of withdrawal.

With that, the Assembly recessed until Monday, leaving an expectant world in suspense.

Convening of the General Assembly was perceived in Israel as a direct threat to the country's interests. The government leaked word that weekend that it was moving immediately to unite Jerusalem as the Jewish capital before the issue became a subject of the Assembly negotiations.

The next day, however, Israel did a complete turnabout. The Cabinet at its regular Sunday meeting declined to authorize unification. Nonetheless, Israeli officials left no doubt that Israel planned to do so eventually. As *The New York Times* reported, ". . . authoritative sources emphasized that there had been no weakening in Israel's determination to unite the two parts of Jerusalem as Israel's capital. A number of countries, including the United States and Britain, have made representations to Israel over the last few days. The intention now is to heed the advice of friendly countries and not rush in the Knesset the legal steps that would make one city of the two sectors."

Israel's public restraint was in line with the policy adopted by the White House, as outlined in a memorandum by Mac Bundy to Johnson at the end of the war. The Administration's tactics in the immediate postwar period, Bundy wrote, must include getting Israel to temper its public image. "A first priority action is to persuade the Israeli Government to make the most moderate public statement of their position that they can," advised Bundy. "Secretary Rusk will talk to Ambassador Harman about this."

The problem with this advice was that even the Administration seemed to get confused between Israel's fluid and evolving position and the one it presented in public. This flawed perception constantly plagued U.S. officials as they sought to find a solution acceptable to both Israel and the Arabs. The strength and popular support within Israel of Begin and other hardliners were consistently underestimated by Washington, with the result that U.S. negotiators repeatedly misread Israeli intentions.

The popularity of Begin's position should have been obvious when immediately after the war several organizations sprang up in Israel whose sole purpose was retention of the occupied territories. The most impressive of these was the Land of Israel Movement, which attracted members from across the political, social and economic spectrum of Israeli society and was dedicated solely to retaining the captured land. As its manifesto proclaimed, the purpose of the group was "to be loyal to the entirety of our country—for the sake of the people's past as well as its future, and no government in Israel is entitled to give up this entirety, which represents the inherent and inalienable right of our people from the beginnings of its history."

One of the Land of Israel Movement's leading members was the poet Uri Zvi Greenberg, a native of Poland who emigrated to Palestine in 1924 and whose nationalistic poetry expressed the yearnings of the hardliners and the religious passion shared by many Israelis toward all of the land of Palestine. In a 1938 work called *Book of Chastisement and Faith,* Greenberg had articulated these emotions by writing:

> And there will be a day when from the River
> of Egypt to the Euphrates
> And from the sea to beyond Moab my young warriors
> will ascend
> And they will call my enemies and haters to the
> last battle
> And blood will decide who is the only ruler here.

This mystical mixture of nationalism and religious fervor was shared by a number of members of the nonpartisan movement. Moshe Moskowitz, a native of Czechoslovakia who had emigrated to Palestine in 1935, expressed it to Israeli writer Rael Jean Isaac: "I believe this country is in one of the stages of redemption. The redemption of the land and people go together. We keep getting parts of the land; slowly more and more is added. . . . What guides Jewish people cannot be explained in terms of the general history of nations. The only question is how much suffering goes with this process. But I do not doubt that the land and the people will find their mutual redemption."

Beyond religious motivations, others who flocked to the Land of Israel Movement were inspired by security interests and territorial ambitions. Explained Zvi Shiloah, a native of Poland who emigrated in 1931: "I have not based my views on a historical conception of borders, because there have been many boundaries and all of them are historical. We need a geopolitical conception. We need a conception of a 'great Israel' extending from the Mediterranean to the Persian Gulf. . . . We must separate the Arab territories from one another. We must develop the geopolitical vision to recognize that it is essential to control large spaces, so that people cannot talk of Israel as a small obstacle in the Near East. The unity of Arab states is in any case a fiction, but once Israel becomes a big wedge between them, even the fiction disappears."

These were the authentic voices of many of the people of Israel after the war. But somehow their clear and unequivocal yearnings seemed not to be heard in Washington. Instead, the Johnson Administration preferred to listen to Abba Eban's dulcet voice of reason. This was understandable enough, since it offered the promise of compromise, but then it also assumed that his was the dominant voice, which was not a realistic assumption. True, there had also appeared after the war a peace movement, but it attracted no following of prominent members comparable to the Land of Israel Movement nor did it achieve unity of purpose. Nor, most importantly, was it capable of matching the feat of the anti-withdrawal advocates, who gathered 150,000 signatures on a petition opposing surrender of the West Bank and Golan Heights.

But it was moderate voices and Eban's that Washington preferred to hear, ignoring the significant and powerful group of Israelis totally opposed to any withdrawal on the West Bank. This self-imposed myopia repeatedly caused U.S. officials to confuse the moderate image they were urging Israel to display for the reality, which was considerably different.

Lyndon Johnson spent that weekend at Camp David entertaining Australian Prime Minister Harold E. Holt and a number of other guests, including Arthur and Mathilde Krim. Kosygin's presence in New York and what the Soviet premier was going to say to the emergency meeting of the General Assembly were much on Johnson's mind. Shortly before dinner Saturday night, June 17, he telephoned Walt Rostow and dictated a message to Kosygin: "The President deeply regrets that you are going to be engaged full time at the UN but he understands and he doesn't want to complicate in any way. And if you should desire to spend any time in discussing matters of great mutual interest, the President would have his helicopter ready to go to Camp David or some place near New York, like resort areas in Catskills and Ellenville, N.Y." Johnson instructed Rostow to discuss the message with McNamara, Rusk and others before sending it along to Kosygin.

The Soviet premier was scheduled to be the first speaker at the Assembly session opening at 10:30 A.M. Monday, and Johnson that weekend worked on a speech of his own. It was to be given an hour before the U.N. meeting, neatly commanding equal attention in the media with Kosygin's remarks.

The President read drafts of his speech Saturday night at dinner with Holt, the Krims and others, "inserting additions and making changes, also accepting comments and suggestions from all at the table," according to notes in the President's Daily Diary. This was the speech which was to establish the nation's official policy in the Middle East.

At 9:30 A.M. Monday, before live coverage by all three TV networks, the President of the United States read his speech to the National Foreign Policy Conference of Educators' meeting in the State Department. Johnson enunciated "five great principles of peace" for the Middle East, which from now on would become the pillars of U.S. policy. These, he said, were: 1) security for all nations in the region; 2) justice for the refugees; 3) respect for maritime rights; 4) limitation of the arms race; and 5) "respect for political independence and territorial integrity of all the states of the area. We reaffirmed that principle at the height of the crisis. We reaffirm it again today, on behalf of all."

Johnson added that "certainly troops must be withdrawn." But in the same sentence he linked withdrawal with attainment of all five principles he had just outlined. Like the draft resolution the United States had put before the Security Council, it was a prescription so broad and amorphous that its net effect was to practically assure that there would be no immediate withdrawal of Israeli troops.

Abe Feinberg telephoned the White House later that day and reported the Jewish community was delighted with the speech. A memorandum left for the President said Feinberg thought "the speech . . . was wonderful. 'He hit the nail right on the head.' Mr. Feinberg said he had visited with Israelis and Jewish leaders all over the country and they are high in their appreciation. He said he had never seen the President make a better delivery."

An hour after Johnson's speech, Premier Kosygin took the podium in the General Assembly. The President by that time was back in the White House. Saying he planned to get a short nap, he actually went to his bedroom and watched from his rubbing table Kosygin's speech on television. He told his aides not to inform the press that he was watching.

Kosygin's speech was an unemotional, detailed, forty-minute presentation of the events leading to the war and a reminder to the small nations that a fate similar to the Arabs' could overtake them: "If Israel's claims do not receive a rebuff today, tomorrow a new aggressor, big or small, may attempt to overrun lands of other peaceful countries. . . . If we here, in the United Nations, fail to take the necessary measures, even those states which are not parties to the conflict may draw the conclusion that they cannot expect protection from the United Nations."

His draft resolution called for condemnation of Israel and demanded its withdrawal and compensation for Arab war losses.

Arthur Goldberg answered Kosygin the next day by introducing a broad-gauged American draft resolution embodying Johnson's five principles. He charged that the Soviet draft was flawed because it was biased against Israel. "Israel alone is to be condemned as an aggressor—though surely in the light of all the events, both recent and long past, that led up to the fighting, it would be neither equitable nor constructive for this organization to issue a one-sided condemnation," Goldberg declared.

Goldberg's draft referred only marginally to withdrawal in the overall search for peace. The search was to be based on "mutual recognition of the political independence and territorial integrity of all countries in the area, encompassing recognized boundaries and other arrangements, including disengagement and withdrawal of forces, that will give them security against terror, destruction and war."

During the course of the far-ranging debate in following sessions, two more draft resolutions were introduced, one by the Latin countries and another by the neutral nations of Asia and Africa. Both these draft resolutions, like the Soviet one, unequivocally demanded Israeli withdrawal from captured territories. Thus the Soviet Union and its bloc members were now joined by nations in Latin America, Africa and Asia in demanding withdrawal. It appeared as though the Soviet Union was about to find victory for its position in the General Assembly.

————

While the 122 nations of the world organization maneuvered over the wording of a resolution that the necessary two thirds of them could approve, President Johnson finally persuaded Premier Kosygin to hold private talks. They and their senior aides met on Friday, June 23, in the New Jersey town of Glassboro in the twenty-two-room Victorian home of Dr. Thomas E. Robinson, the president of Glassboro State College. The discussions, lasting five hours, were wide-ranging and amiable, but they brought the two sides no nearer to agreement on the Middle East.

There was a sobering moment, however, that emphasized to the leaders how out of control the nuclear programs of their two countries had become. It came during luncheon when Johnson related to the gathered officials that he and Kosygin had talked at length about the costs of nuclear weapons, "and how money was going down the drain because the weapon was old by the time they were ready to use it," according to the notes of the President's Daily Diary. "I told him that we had the same hopes, but I hadn't found a way for us to all agree on it."

Kosygin asked to hear McNamara's views.

"We react to you and we must maintain a certain nuclear strength regardless of what is said around the table," said McNamara.

"And we react to you," interjected Kosygin, "so that's an agreed point."

"Yes, you are not different from us," replied McNamara. "You must react to us. What an insane road we are both following."

"How well you speak!" said Kosygin.

But that was all it amounted to—words. They made no progress on nuclear disarmament nor on the Middle East. Yet the talks had become friendly enough that the two sides agreed to reconvene on Sunday.

Johnson immediately flew to Philadelphia International Airport where he was joined by Arthur Krim and his wife for a flight to Los Angeles to attend a scheduled Democratic fund-raising dinner dance. Afterward, he left Los Angeles that same night and flew with the Krims back to the ranch, where they spent Saturday boating and driving around the hill country.

At 12:41 P.M. Sunday, Johnson was back in Glassboro. The second and final session with Kosygin was no more successful than the first. It lasted slightly more than four hours. There then followed an opéra bouffe.

The two sides had agreed that they would hold separate news conferences that evening, Johnson in Washington and Kosygin in New York. But since the Kosygin party was using a U.S. helicopter and Johnson the faster presidential jet, there was a chance that the White House party could fly back to the capital before Kosygin reached New York and thus upstage him by holding Johnson's press conference first. That is what the President and his party now tried to do.

The flight "was to be speeded up as much as possible for the President was in a race with time, for he wanted to make his statement on live television at the White House prior to Kosygin's televised press conference in New York," noted the President's Daily Diary. As *Air Force One* landed at Washington National Airport, "the President and his party quickly lined up at the back door of the plane so that they could go directly to the waiting helicopter with a minimum of time. However, as the door opened, it was discovered that the steps had been placed, by mistake, at the front of the plane, so as the President and party raced through the plane, it could be heard over the intercom, 'Make way for the President.' It looked almost like one of the old silent movies in which a comedy of errors occurred."

But it worked.

Johnson made his remarks on the South Lawn of the White House starting at 7:40 P.M. Kosygin did not begin his press conference in Conference Room 4 of the General Assembly Building until 8:04. What he had to say for the next hour and twenty minutes brought no cheer to Washington or Tel Aviv. He firmly stated that the first step toward peace in the Middle East must be withdrawal of Israeli forces from captured Arab territory.

But that, as it was about to demonstrate, Israel had no intention of doing.

XXIII
ISRAEL
ANNEXES JERUSALEM

While Israel basked in the West's adulation, it made its move to take over all of Jerusalem. Emotions were too high within Israel, political pressures too great and U.S. support now proven so dependable that delay of the monumental action was no longer possible. Unification of the city was universally desired by Israelis.

The first step was eradication of the fences, minefields and other remnants of the hated demarcation lines that divided Jerusalem as a result of the 1949 armistice agreement with Jordan. Israel was determined that Jerusalem would be not only its capital but its undivided capital.

Yet unification needed the framework of legality. Since no nation recognized Israel's claim to Jerusalem as its capital, not even Jewish Western Jerusalem, international opposition to unification of the city under Israeli sovereignty would be predictably strong. Nonetheless, so keen was the yearning among practically all Israelis to have Jerusalem their own that the government moved with dispatch.

On June 27, the Israeli parliament passed an apparently innocuous statute giving the government authority to apply Israeli law, justice and administration "in any area of Palestine, to be determined by its decree."

The next day, 20th Sivan 5727 of the Hebrew calendar, 21th Rabia El-Awal 1387 of the Moslem calendar, June 28, 1967, in the Christian calendar, Interior Minister Moshe Chaim Shapira issued a decree titled "Declaration of the Extension of the Boundaries of the Jerusalem Municipal Corporation." It sounded almost like another technical, routine municipal ordinance rather than the historic claim by Jews to the city holy to three religions. Its effect was immediate. Jewish administration was imposed on all aspects of municipal life and the Arabs living there became resident aliens in Israel.

The decree extended the city limits nine miles in the north to the edge of the Palestinian city of El Bireh and ten miles in the south to the outskirts of largely Christian Bethlehem. The boundaries had been chosen carefully. They more than doubled the size of Jerusalem, extending its limits from twenty-seven square miles to sixty-seven square miles, and ensured the perpetuation of a Jewish majority.* As Deputy Mayor of Jerusalem Meron Benvenisti later admitted: "When the city's boundaries were marked out, Arab-populated neighborhoods were excluded in order to ensure an overwhelming Jewish majority." Inside the new municipal limits were 200,000 Jews and 70,000 Arabs, now only 28,000 of them in the Old City.

That same night, Moshe Dayan, who as defense minister was responsible for administration of the occupied territories, met with Mayor Kollek and several others on the terrace of the King David Hotel overlooking the golden walls of the Old City that so recently had been a barrier to Israelis. Dayan was insistent that the more than one and a half miles of fences and other dividers had to come down the next day; there could be no waiting.

But Kollek and the others were worried and hesitant.

"I feared that the sudden removal of all restraints could be dangerous," Kollek wrote later. "Who knew what smoldering hatreds might flare up if you suddenly gave Jews access to the Old City and allowed Arabs to move freely in West Jerusalem? But this is just what Dayan proposed to do. . . .

"We argued strongly for taking things slowly, but Dayan just sat back with his feet on the table and would not be moved one inch," Kollek recalled in his 1978 book. "Gradually we saw that his behavior was not stubbornness; it was borne of conviction based on an entirely different concept of how the Arabs would act when faced with a *fait accompli*. When he explained why he thought there was little likelihood of vengeance on the part of the Arabs and retaliation by the Jews, his theory had considerable substance, and we were eventually convinced to take the risk."

* For example, the new municipal boundaries extended probelike northward to include the Arab Jerusalem Airport (Kalandia) but not the 10,000 Palestinians in the Kalandia refugee camp or the village of Ram. Similarly, the borders were drawn so that they included much of the land of abutting Palestinian villages but not their populations. Examples are, in the west, Beit Iksas and Beit Hanina and, in the east, Hizma, Anata, Bethany and Abu Dis. In the south, the new borders included sparsely populated areas of Beit Sahur and Bethlehem. In later years, major portions of all these lands were confiscated for "public purposes" and turned into housing projects open to Israelis only, thus effectively surrounding the Palestinian population while at the same time denying Palestinians any opportunity to develop new housing of their own.

At dawn on June 29, Israel acted. Check posts were dismantled, walls blown up, sniper nests destroyed. In all, fifty-five fortified emplacements, thirty-six Jordanian and nineteen Israeli, were destroyed and tens of thousands of land mines and ten miles of barbed wire removed. Curiously, cautiously at first, Arabs and Jews faced one another over the open spaces. A few of the more daring moved across the frontier line and began mingling freely for the first time since 1948. Then, as it became clear that the two peoples that morning were less filled with hatred than curiosity, there was a huge exchange of people as thousands of Arabs and Jews commingled, examining one another's living and working quarters, shopping and sightseeing.

"Many Jews were scared," wrote Kollek. "Some people said that families with teenage daughters would not go on living in Jerusalem for fear of the Arabs. Others made all sorts of dire predictions. None of these came true."

For their part, the Moslems were shocked by the bare arms and scanty dresses of the Israeli women and intimidated by the rifles carried openly by the men. But in general the atmosphere was friendly, if wary, and, both sides being ever willing to trade, shopkeepers did a brisk business with the new tourists.

Israeli officials were quick to assure the world that the Jerusalem decree was simply a legal formality. Abba Eban declared that Israel had no intention of actually annexing the holy city. The declaration, he said, "dealt solely with the municipal and administrative aspects" of unifying Jerusalem. Israel was not "annexing" Jerusalem as part of its land, he insisted. It was merely establishing a legal basis to extend Jewish Jerusalem's services to the Arab side.

Indeed, that was done with alacrity. Within days, East Jerusalem was inextricably tied by umbilicals of public service to Jewish Jerusalem—another *fait accompli*. The Arabs' electrical system was integrated into Israel's electrical grid, its water supply was attached to Israel's, and so were its telephone system and other services. Israeli emergency regulations were imposed. Income tax offices were opened in the Old City and taxes collected. The Jordanian banking system was closed and replaced by Israel's. Israeli identification cards were issued to the Arabs, giving their name, age and religion. The two cities were soon completely fused physically and, in Israel's eyes if not in anyone else's, legally.

The United States and most other nations deplored the Israeli action, correctly seeing it as de facto annexation no matter what Israel called it. "The hasty administrative action . . . cannot be regarded as determining the future of the holy places or the status of Jerusalem in relation to them," said a White House spokesman on the same day of the issuance of the municipal decree. "The United States has never recognized such unilateral action by any state in the area as governing the international status of Jerusalem."

Despite this straightforward stance, whenever the issue came before the United Nations that July the United States managed to abstain from supporting resolutions declaring Israel's claim to Jerusalem invalid. Not surprisingly, with that kind of support from Washington, Tel Aviv ignored protests from around the world and calmly went about turning Jerusalem into the united capital of the state of Israel.

Regardless of its setbacks in the United Nations, the Soviet Union was by no means idle in the Middle East. As a result of the war and the severing of ties with Washington, the Arabs were drawn closer than ever to the Soviet Union, which responded with vigor. Even as the supporters of Israel gloated about the defeat of Soviet arms, Moscow quickly acted to rearm the Arabs. On June 21, Soviet President Nikolai V. Podgorny headed a diplomatic mission to Egypt, followed by stops in Syria and Iraq. In Cairo, he was warmly greeted by 200,000 cheering Egyptians. Preceding him by one day had been Marshal Matvei V. Zakharov, army chief of staff, accompanied by a staff of military experts.

Two days after Podgorny's arrival, the first Soviet planeload of weapons landed at Cairo West airport, signaling the start of a dramatic resupply effort. It was followed with increasing frequency by other planes. Within one week 130 aircraft were reported delivered, and after a fortnight two hundred Soviet cargo planes had landed, bring urgently needed defensive weapons like mortars, field guns and ammunition. Soon ships began arriving too with war matériel at the rate of two a week. The buildup lasted through the summer and winter, until by late 1968 all of Egypt's losses had been made up. Moscow was similarly generous with Syria and Iraq, quickly replacing their war losses with newer and better weapons.

Even more impressive than the Soviet arms supply operation was Moscow's willingness to increase its commitment to the Arab cause. The Kremlin acceded to a request by Nasser to supply the Egyptian Army with Russian military advisers and instructors down to the battalion level. Before, the Soviet presence had been relatively small, confined to weapons instructors and teachers in Egyptian military academies.

Within a short time, several thousand Soviet advisers arrived in Egypt. Under their guidance, Egypt's military forces were reformed, the officer corps significantly improved and the army greatly strengthened—exactly what Israel had tried to prevent by going to war. It was soon to be facing an Egypt stronger than ever.

The Soviet assistance did not come without a price tag. In return, the Soviets finally were granted preferential treatment at four Mediterranean harbors (Alexandria, Port Said, Mersa Matruh and Sollum), which they had long been seeking, as well as virtual control of seven air bases (Aswan, Beni Suef, Cairo West, El Mansura, Inchas, Jianaklis and Mersa Matruh). Now the Soviets too were stronger than ever in the region.

Repercussions of the war extended to Israel's relation with France, once its closest and most cherished foreign friend. It was France that had helped Israel with its nuclear program, starting as early as the late 1940s, and France which provided Israel the weapons it sought during most of the nineteen years of its existence. It was French planes that won the war for Israel (the promised U.S. Skyhawks had not yet arrived). Now this close relationship was about to be shattered and the embargo on arms shipments imposed at the start of the war continued indefinitely.

President Charles de Gaulle was angered that his advice to both sides not to fire the first shot had been ignored by Israel and he became the first leader to brand Israel the aggressor in public. In a statement on June 21, the aged French leader declared: "... France condemns the opening of hostilities by Israel. . . . France accepts as final none of the changes effected on the terrain through military action."

Those words brought enormous criticism on de Gaulle from France's largely pro-Israel population. The war had evoked an extraordinary outpouring of support for Israel from common Frenchmen and intellectuals, who demonstrated by the thousands for Israel. French newspapers reflected that support by broadly damning de Gaulle for his remarks. Typical was an editorial by the Socialist Party newspaper, *La Populaire,* which commented: "Except for some nuances, General de Gaulle thinks like Mr. Kosygin."

De Gaulle, no stranger to controversy, refused to relent. He pressed his message through his foreign minister, Maurice Couve de Murville. In an eloquent speech at the emergency meeting of the U.N. General Assembly, the French envoy declared that "the war has settled nothing and has made everything more difficult. . . . that war does not solve anything, that resorting to force is not a way to settle conflicts, is not only France's traditional position, but the basic principle of our organization's Charter."

He went on to list the many casualties of the war: "Three great powers have no more relations with one or other party—the Soviet Union with Israel, the United States of America and Great Britain with many Arab countries.... From the regional viewpoint ... all the elements of an indefinite struggle are now gathered.... Israel ... occupies territories belonging to the United Arab Republic, Jordan and Syria.... How can one expect, if it persists, that a similar state of affairs ... may prevail without bringing about incessant and dangerous incidents?"

Couve de Murville's words were prophetic.

The war was over but not the fighting. Only nine days after Couve de Murville spoke, on July 1, the first serious postwar scrimmage between Egyptian and Israeli troops broke out at the Suez Canal. Small groups of tanks and armored vehicles clashed on the northeast side of the canal around Port Fuad, the only position Egypt retained in the northern Sinai, and Qantara, thirty miles to the south, the major Israeli stronghold along the northern section of the canal.

As usual, each side blamed the other for the violation of the cease-fire arrangement. But the question of who fired first was less important than what the action portended. It was the beginning of a near daily series of increasingly violent incidents along the canal.

The clashes escalated from artillery exchanges the next day to more incidents until, on July 8, Israel launched an air attack across the canal. Israel announced the attack was aimed at Egyptian tanks and artillery; Egypt said six Israeli planes bombed Port Fuad and its sister city, Port Said, and killed one civilian and wounded seven. The next day an Israeli soldier was killed and two others wounded when their jeep ran over a mine south of Port Fuad. Day by day, the level of combat grew more vicious.

The fighting was escalating so swiftly that the Security Council convened on July 8 after the Israeli air attack in emergency session at the joint request of Egypt and Israel to try to halt the mounting combat. Two days later, the Council adopted by consensus a plan by U Thant to place thirty-two U.N. observers on both sides of the canal to prevent further violations. Egypt and Israel accepted, but only after both sides had hesitated and balked, particularly Nasser, who feared the creation of another permanent UNEF-like force on his territory.

Once again, an international corps of peace-keepers under the aegis of the United Nations traveled to the unsettled Middle East to try to bring tranquillity to the region.

Advance parties arrived on July 15, by which time the shooting had gotten so fierce that the observers on the Egyptian side were greeted by intense

Israeli artillery fire and on the eastern side by a low-level attack by Egyptian planes. The commander of the observers on the eastern side, Major A. Vitiello, a pilot himself, dryly reported to General Odd Bull that "this attack was very well carried out." But there were no U.N. casualties. Two days later, at 6 P.M. local time, four-man teams officially took up their observation duties on each side of the canal.

Their presence had an immediately calming influence and the canal zone fell silent—for the moment.

The fast action by the Security Council was in marked contrast to the inability of the members in the emergency session of the General Assembly to agree on the various Middle East proposals before them. The Assembly had now been in session since June 17, but still it had not managed to agree on a resolution. Although the vast majority of member states believed Israel should withdraw and all admitted that acquisition of territory was contrary to the U.N. Charter, they were prevented from agreeing by various other articles attached to each of the draft resolutions. The draft by the non-aligned nations of Asia and Africa, for instance, offered no clear prescription for the achievement of peace once withdrawal occurred. The Latin draft, on the other hand, made withdrawal conditional on a declaration of the end of the state of belligerency by the Arab nations.

When a vote was finally taken on July 4, both the Latin and nonaligned draft resolutions split the members and failed to get the necessary two-thirds vote. The nonaligned draft was supported by the Arabs, the Soviet Bloc and four European countries, France, Greece, Spain and Turkey, receiving fifty-three votes for and forty-six against, including the United States and Israel. The Latin draft was supported by most of the European nations, seventeen African nations and the United States; Israel abstained. But still it too managed to garner only a simple majority, fifty-seven to forty-three. In both votes, there were twenty abstentions.

Neither the American nor the Russian draft was brought to a vote since both were assumed to be incapable of winning the necessary support for passage.

The Assembly's inability to adopt a peace resolution infuriated the Arab world. Cairo Radio termed the U.S. position in the Assembly debates "final proof of American collusion with Israel," a view widely held throughout Moslem countries that American Independence Day.

Despite its failure to agree on a peace resolution, the Assembly did manage to pass two resolutions that same day. One was a humanitarian resolution similar to the one passed in the Security Council, and the other was on Jerusalem. It labeled Israel's claim to the city "invalid," and it called on the Jewish state to "rescind all measures already taken and to desist forthwith from taking any action which would alter the status of Jerusalem." The Jerusalem resolution passed with ninety-nine votes. There were no votes against, but twenty nations abstained, including the United States and Israel.

Still, those resolutions were no substitute for one that would outline peace measures. But the Assembly was mired. Only a forceful plea from Assembly President Abdur Rahman Pazhwak of Afghanistan saved the Assembly from disbanding in disgust at this point and throwing the problem back to the Security Council. Pazhwak pointedly noted to the members that "they have agreed that the time has come when peace in the Middle East must be made, finally and for all time." Second, he added, "There is virtual unanimity in upholding the principle that conquest of territory by war is inadmissible in our time and under our Charter." Finally, he said, "There was in addition a broad consensus that the political sovereignty and territorial integrity of states allow them a rightful freedom from threat of belligerency."

On the basis of Pazhwak's plea, the Assembly agreed to continue in session. But it was no use. Israel quickly rejected the resolution on Jerusalem, and when it was resubmitted on July 14 in response to Israel's rejection, it again carried ninety-nine to zero. This time there were eighteen abstentions, including again the United States.*

But the vote barely mattered. Israel again totally rejected the resolution. The emergency session of the Assembly dragged on unproductively until September 18, when it finally admitted its inability to find a formula for peace in the Middle East and returned the intractable problem to the Security Council.

The reality was that as long as Israel retained the support of the United States it could safely ignore Arab anger and the United Nations and go its own way. This it did throughout the summer. It tightened its grip on Jerusalem, tentatively and then more boldly set up settlements in the occupied territory in defiance of the Geneva Convention and world opinion, and encouraged Palestinians to flee across the Jordan River.

* Those abstaining on July 14: Australia, Barbados, Bolivia, Central African Republic, Colombia, Congo, Iceland, Jamaica, Kenya, Liberia, Madagascar, Malawi, Malta, Portugal, Rwanda, South Africa, United States, Uruguay. Absent were Botswana, Haiti, Malaysia, Maldive Islands. Israel did not participate.

The flow of refugees had dwindled immediately after the war and then resumed in force in mid-June when Israel set up its occupation machinery in the towns and villages of the West Bank. Throughout the rest of the month thousands of men, women and children crossed to the East Bank of the Jordan.

While the Israelis did not use force to make the Palestinians leave, they did encourage the exodus by their destruction of homes as in Qalqilya, tales of which quickly spread, and by providing buses and trucks in many villages to take Palestinians to the Jordan. Trucks with loudspeakers roamed through the West Bank announcing that transportation was available daily at the Damascus Gate of the Old City.

At the blasted Allenby Bridge, large groups of Palestinians crossed each day during the last half of June, the men lugging all the possessions they could carry, the women burdened by bulky sacks balanced on their heads. Children cried and Israeli soldiers cursed when the hordes of new refugees became confused and created blockages at the crude crossing. Occasionally the soldiers fired their weapons into the air to get the attention of the disoriented, disorganized refugees.

Once the homeless Palestinians crossed to the East Bank, they were on their own in the harsh desert. There was no shade, no water. Jordan had set up no administrative machinery to process them. The small country's resources had already been overwhelmed by its war losses.

Water, food, blankets and housing were the first needs of the refugees. Members of UNRWA, the United Nations Relief and Works Agency which had cared for the original refugees of 1948 for the past nineteen years, worked desperately to care for the new homeless. Tent cities were going up as fast as possible to provide at least basic shelter for the dispossessed.

One such tent city for seven thousand refugees was Wadi Daleil, thirty miles east of Amman in the open desert. *New York Times* correspondent Dana Adams Schmidt visited it on June 21 and reported: "Wadi Daleil is a hellish sort of place. . . . The wind sweeps up cones of yellow dust from the rock-hard clay desert. The whirling dust seems to consume the tents of refugees. However, some of the refugees have no tents. Some have improvised shelters with blankets draped over sticks. Others sit in tight family groups in circles with their backs to the world, headcloths tightly drawn, eyes shut, hands shielding faces from the sand. When the wind drops, the bare clay magnifies the heat of the summer sun. There is no shade. Water has to be brought in trucks. At night it is cold. . . . Except at the clinic, few latrines have been dug, and garbage accumulates among the tents, which are scattered apparently without plan across the desert. . . . Until everyone can be given a proper tent and cooking equipment, a truck moves through the camp once a day and soup is ladled to the refugees.

"Wherever the foreign visitors go a crowd gathers. 'What is your nationality?' they ask. To reply that one is an American is to invite violence."

The stories of the refugees all had a numbing sameness of despair and underlying hatred to them. Abdul Latif Husseini, a thirty-year-old bank clerk, was one of those who boarded a truck-and-bus convoy provided by Israel in Jerusalem on June 22 to take him on his journey into homelessness. Husseini was originally from Haifa but had fled to Jerusalem during the 1948 war. Now he was fleeing Jerusalem. He had been planning to get married at the end of the month and had already rented a house and spent $1,000 to furnish it, but then the war started. At its end, he discovered his bank was closed, his house damaged, and his furniture either damaged or stolen by looters. He was bitter.

"I can forget you slapping my face," he told *Washington Post* reporter Jesse W. Lewis, Jr., who made the convoy trip with him, "but I will pass this on to my children."

So too would many others pass on to their children their hatred of Israel and their bitterness at their fate. Fatah and the PLO and other resistance groups were suddenly getting a whole new group of highly motivated potential recruits for their cause.

Israel continued to refuse to allow those who changed their minds to return once they crossed the Jordan. Soldiers fired into the air and pointed machine guns at anyone who tried to cross back into the West Bank. After international protests, Israel announced that refugees would be allowed to return starting July 10. But when groups of Palestinians gathered at the bridges, they were turned back by Israeli soldiers saying they had no orders to allow them to enter the West Bank.

After an exchange of charges and countercharges between Israel and Jordan over who was responsible for preventing the refugees from returning to the West Bank, the two countries reached an agreement through the Red Cross on August 6 for seemingly unlimited return. An estimated 32,000 families representing 160,000 persons applied to return. But in the end Israel allowed only 14,056 Palestinians to move back to the West Bank.

It was not until the beginning of August that the minimal needs of all the new refugees on the East Bank were finally provided. By then, UNRWA estimated that 323,000 Palestinians had been turned into refugees by the war, 113,000 of them for the second time since 1948. The largest exodus was from the West to the East Bank, a total of 178,000 Palestinians, 93,000 of them former refugees. In Syria, 102,000 refugees had been created by the occupation of the Golan Heights, 17,000 of them second-timers, and another 38,000 in the Sinai, 3,000 of them repeat refugees.

By late summer, the region once again was stalemated. Israel's diplomatic position had solidified into four broad positions: 1) peace negotiations must be held directly between the Arab states and Israel, not through intermediaries; 2) no occupied land would be returned until secure boundaries could be negotiated; 3) settlement of the refugee problem had to be on the basis of peace and regional cooperation; and 4) the future of Jerusalem was nonnegotiable. These positions amounted to a prescription for no movement. Certainly no Arab nation would begin to talk on these terms, and no Arab leader, with pride already deeply wounded by the defeat on the battlefield, would consent to meet with Israel so soon after the war and thereby give the impression that he had been beaten into submission.

The Arabs made their continued opposition plain late in the summer. Between August 29 and September 1, thirteen Arab nations met in the Sudanese capital of Khartoum to formulate a joint policy toward Israel. They agreed to continue the political struggle against Israel, created a fund of $392 million to assist the damaged economies of Egypt and Jordan, and lifted the ineffective oil embargo that had been imposed by Algeria, Iraq and Kuwait on the second day of the war and later adopted by other Arab oil nations. They then enunciated three "no's":

"No peace with Israel, no negotiations with Israel, no recognition of Israel and maintenance of the rights of Palestinian people in their nation."

Both sides were now set in concrete.

The frustration of diplomatic stalemate soon vented itself in renewed fighting along the Suez Canal. The calm brought by the appearance of the U.N. observers along both sides of the canal lasted only until September 4 when the first serious cease-fire violation occurred since their arrival.

Observers at Port Tewfiq, opposite the port of Suez at the southern end of the canal and still in Egyptian hands, reported that two Israeli torpedo boats and a landing craft were warned by Egypt that they would be fired on if they continued northwest toward Port Tewfiq. The boats proceeded and shots were fired about a hundred meters in front of them, causing the boats finally to change course. Eight minutes later Israeli positions opened fire on both Port Tewfiq and Suez.

Soon the shelling spread north all along the 101-mile canal and involved mortar and tank fire. It continued for eight hours before General Bull could work out a cease-fire. One Israeli soldier was killed. Egypt reported Israeli shelling had destroyed Port Tewfiq and killed 44 and wounded 172 civilians.

"Every time something happens along the canal the Israelis take it out on our civilians," complained Suez Governor Hamed Mahmoud on September 8.

After this, firing in the canal area grew frequent. "The most trivial incident could lead to a violation of the cease-fire," General Bull wrote later. "The Egyptians would open fire on Israeli fighter aircraft, and though these usually kept to the East Bank, they were, even so, dangerously close to Egyptian positions, while the Israelis would fire on Egyptians trying to get their ships out of the canal."

By early autumn, it was becoming obvious to U.S. experts—if not the political leadership of the Administration—that Israel's actions were not contributing to peace. This was pointed out in a State Department cable drafted September 14 for transmission to the Tel Aviv Embassy, which noted "indications Israeli objectives may be shifting from original position seeking peace with no rpt no territorial gains toward one of territorial expansionism. Israel's refusal to authorize the return of all refugees desiring to resume residence on West Bank . . . and statements by senior Israeli officials quoted in American press give rise to impression that Israeli Government may be moving toward policy of seeking security simply by retaining occupied areas rather than by achieving peaceful settlement with Arabs."

The cable noted that Israel now seemed to be putting more emphasis on "form of settlement (direct negotiations and formal peace treaties) rather than substance. . . . There is concern . . . [this stance] could in fact become rationale for territorial acquisitions." It was important for Israel to demonstrate, the cable concluded, "that Israel sincerely wishes peaceful settlement above all."

As so often during this lamentable period, the Middle East experts in the State Department and White House were reading the situation clearly. But, presumably because of political considerations, the cable was never sent, once again depriving Israel of the advice and guidance of the United States.

Within two weeks of the aborted cable, Israel embarked on a cautious course of settlement in the occupied territories. Although Israeli leaders repeatedly vowed that they had no territorial ambitions, their actions indicated otherwise. Within four months of the war Jews began settling on occupied territory.

The first settlement on the West Bank was established at Kfar Etzion in a hilly area between Jerusalem and Hebron. Four Jewish settlements in the Etzion bloc had been overrun in 1948 and held thereafter by Jordan. Now on September 27, 1967, an advance group of twelve young men and three women, all born in the bloc and most of whom lost their fathers in the 1948 fighting, re-established Kfar Etzion as a *nahal*, a paramilitary agriculture post.

The government immediately denied that the *nahal* was to become a civilian settlement. It had been established, officials insisted, as a security garrison. However, at a ceremony inaugurating the *nahal*, parliament member Michael Hazani, according to a *New York Times* account of the event, "expressed the hope that the settlers would be the vanguard of thousands who would bring life to the surrounding barren hills." That was exactly what they were to become in the midst of Palestinian property.

The United States protested the move the same day, a State Department spokesman declaring that Israeli settlement in the West Bank was "inconsistent with the Israeli position, as we understand it, that they regard occupied territories and all other issues arising out of the fighting to be matters for negotiation." He added: "We have not been informed of any change in this policy."

Nor was Washington ever informed. Yet the creeping settlement of the occupied territories continued. By November there were fledgling settlements in the territories of Egypt, Jordan and Syria controlled by Israel. Though they numbered in total only five with several hundred people, they were the harbinger of a drive to settle all of the West Bank and the Golan Heights.*

Another settlement of a far more incendiary kind was also established in the Jewish Quarter of the Old City of Jerusalem. Jews had lived in the quarter before the 1948 war when they lost it to Jordan's Arab Legion and had to

---

* The settlements established in 1967: Yam and Sinai in the Sinai Peninsula; Meron Golan and Afik in Syria; and Kfar Etzion in Jordan. Despite official denials, there could be no doubt that the government was determined to establish settlements, as Dayan made clear in his memoirs nineteen years later. He wrote that as early as the fourth day of the war, June 8, 1967, "... I gave the policy directive ... to act in accordance with our intention to establish permanent Jewish settlements in the Mount Hebron and Jerusalem areas."

flee their homes. Now they began expelling the Arab residents of the quarter, who had since moved in. At first there were a few hundred expelled, but over the years as many as 6,500 Palestinians lost their homes. The first evictions started right after the war, on June 18, when families were accused of living in former synagogues or in security areas and were ordered to leave with little notice. By October, Israelis began moving into the quarter. Eventually they would control all of it, but for the moment they were content to absorb it house by house.

Skirmishing along the Suez Canal continued into the fall, increasingly taking a civilian toll in Egypt's canal cities. Partial evacuation of the towns had to be carried out to protect the civilians.

Then on October 21 occurred the most serious incident since the war. The Israeli destroyer *Elath,* sailing not far from where the *Liberty* had been attacked, was sunk by Egyptian missiles.

The 2,300-ton warship with a crew of 202, one of Israel's largest ships, was patrolling off Port Said at the edge of Egyptian territorial waters—Israel claimed it was thirteen and a half miles out at sea; Egypt said it was inside its twelve-mile limit—when crewmen saw a twenty-foot missile approaching. It was about six miles away and appeared to be headed off course from the ship. Suddenly its homing devices took over and aimed it straight at the vessel. Desperately the Israeli crew tried to shoot it down but failed. It hit amidships, its thousand-pound warhead exploding on impact.

A few minutes later a second missile slammed into the engine room. An hour and a half after that a third missile smashed into the sinking ship, sending it to the bottom. A fourth missile followed shortly, but the ship was already under the waves by then. Nonetheless it added to the destruction by exploding among the scores of survivors splashing in the sea.

Israel's losses were forty-seven dead and ninety-one wounded.

The sinking was the first by a missile in warfare. The CIA identified the missile as a Soviet-made SS-N-2 Styx surface-to-surface missile which flew at an altitude of three hundred to one thousand feet at near the speed of sound. The missiles had been fired from a distance of about thirteen miles from two Komar-class missile boats produced in the Soviet Union and given to Egypt in 1962 along with the missiles. In one quick incident, all the boastful postwar talk about the inadequacy of Soviet weaponry seemed somewhat exaggerated.

The CIA speculated that the Egyptians launched the attack—without Soviet advisers or instructors—because "the Egyptians have long been anxious to bolster the morale of their armed forces and probably hit the destroyer because they were confident the missiles could do the job. The destroyer presented what to them was an immediate provocation. . . . on July 14 the Egyptians served notice that all foreign vessels were to keep clear of Port Said by at least 50 miles."

Israel's response was violent.

Three days later, its guns zeroed in on Egypt's oil installations at the southern canal city of Suez and in a three-and-a-half-hour pounding involving artillery and planes knocked out 80 percent of Egypt's refinery capacity by destroying the El Nasser and the Suez refineries. Oil storage tanks were also hit and set ablaze.

Washington was worried about the massive retaliatory action, as it was about the destroyer sinking, and Walt Rostow urged the President to use the attack as a way to emphasize to Israel that it must try harder for peace. In a memorandum on the same day as the Israeli attack, October 24, Rostow wrote to Johnson: "This gives you a chance not only to lean on Eban on the necessity of their struggling for peace, but letting it be known quietly that . . . there is no future for Israel or the Middle East in this kind of mutual violation of the cease-fire."

Washington's concern grew more urgent three days later when seven Soviet ships boldly steamed into Egyptian waters. A destroyer, a communications ship and two supply vessels docked at Port Said and two submarines and a destroyer entered Alexandria harbor in a display of support for Egypt. The message to Israel was clear: lay off.

The message to the United States was equally clear, and worrisome. In a cable that same day to the embassy in Tel Aviv, Dean Rusk ordered the ambassador to meet with Eshkol. "You should underline the gravity of the situation which could emerge from further Israeli retaliatory actions against UAR or any other Arab state," he said.

Ambassador Barbour replied that he had received Foreign Ministry assurances that there would be no more retaliation, adding: "While there obviously still is considerable uncertainty here as to further Egyptian and, in fact, Soviet intentions, and Israeli public remains emotionally agitated to appreciable degree . . . indications seem to me to confirm GOI assurances that nothing further contemplated on their side. . . ."

Once again, the Soviet Union had flexed its muscle and once again Israel, with American prodding, had backed down. A superpower confrontation had again been averted. But the situation was volatile and dangerous. A diplomatic solution had to be found before the Middle East erupted again.

XXIV
THE TERRORISTS
RISE AGAIN

The urgent need to defuse the Middle East brought the Security Council back in session on October 24, within hours after Israel launched its heavy retaliatory attack against Egypt's oil facilities at Suez. The raid and other attacks on civilians had convinced Egypt to evacuate 300,000 persons from canal cities to prevent them from being held hostage by Israeli gunners. The evacuation represented another mass movement of population, more misery and hardship as a result of the Arab-Israeli conflict. Clearly something had to be done urgently to prevent further suffering.

After a day of discussions, the Council agreed on Resolution 240 on October 25 condemning violations of the cease-fire and demanding that the cease-fire be strictly observed. At the same time, U Thant reported that the number of observers at the canal would have to be increased from forty-three to ninety and their posts doubled to eighteen in order to observe the zone adequately.

These again were stop-gap measures meant to dampen passions. But in no way did they begin to meet the need to frame a resolution that would outline the basics of a settlement and also offer some practical method for achieving it. The fifteen members of the Council now devoted themselves to the herculean task the General Assembly had failed to accomplish.

Egyptian Foreign Minister Riad had flown to New York to attend the meeting, and the mood he found in the city did nothing to lift his spirits. "New York was seething with hatred for anything that was Arab," he wrote later. "Israel, the occupier, enjoyed support while the Arabs, the victims of

Israeli aggression, were regarded as the villains, deserving of punishment. I felt bitterness at the slanting of news; the main facts—who fired the first shot in the war, who was pursuing an expansionist policy, who was dealing savagely with the Palestinians living under the terror of military occupation— were ignored."

Arthur Goldberg did nothing to improve Riad's mood. Riad was distrustful of the U.S. envoy, and his suspicions were not allayed when one day he happened to be in the same hotel elevator with Goldberg and another man entered. Seeing Goldberg, the man raised his hat, introduced himself and said: "Like you, I am an American Jew living in New York. I have followed closely all your statements to the TV networks, and now I bow my head to you in thanks and gratitude. . . . We shall never forget the noble services you have extended to Israel."

Commented Riad later: "Goldberg smiled, though he was embarrassed at my witnessing this." The encounter seemed to symbolize for Riad the totally pro-Israel attitude of America.

Repeatedly the two men clashed during private talks aimed at finding a resolution with wording acceptable to both Israel and Egypt. One sore point for Riad was Goldberg's insistence on calling the war a "conflict." Riad insistently referred to it as "Israel's aggression." When Riad pointed out that it was Israel who had attacked, Goldberg replied: "Do not forget you were the ones to start the aggression against Israel. War, from our point of view, was declared the moment when you closed the Gulf of Aqaba, not with the Israeli military operations."

Riad responded heatedly by noting that the Gulf had been closed before 1956 and that when the Security Council had debated the issue in 1951 it did not consider the closure an aggressive act. Riad continued: "Furthermore, you speak as if it were an absolute defeat for us and we must submit to Israel's terms and conditions. We were defeated, but we did not yield, and we will never surrender. . . ."

After listening to Goldberg describe the problems of the Middle East, the Egyptian envoy commented: "There is no need for me to get to know Israel's position now, for the U.S. position conforms to that of Israel."

Although Riad's remark was made with emotion, it was largely true as it applied to public opinion. Americans were basically so supportive of Israel that the country was nearly automatically anti-Arab.

Abba Eban was in New York too for the Council session, and he was having a considerably more enjoyable time than Riad. Everywhere Israelis went they were hailed as heroes, wined and dined, interviewed and congratulated.

Eban had requested a private meeting with Johnson and the President granted it. He met with Eban and Eppy Evron in the White House for an hour on October 24. Johnson gave Eban a pro forma lecture about Israel's failure to consult with Washington before going to war and the dangers ahead. "Israelis should not forget what we have said about territorial integrity and boundaries," said Johnson. "We could not countenance aggression."

The rhetoric aside, Eban heard from the President what he really wanted to hear. "United States objectives and Israeli objectives are much the same in general," Johnson declared. Nothing could have been sweeter to Eban's ears. If the two countries were that close then Israel had retained the powerful friend it needed despite its flouting of the United Nations and the Geneva Convention.

The similarity of purpose, according to Eban, extended to an astonishing promise from the Administration that it would not back any Security Council resolution that Israel opposed.

"That meant we had a veto so far as the United States was concerned," Eban later noted. "[This] was a situation in which Israel's political weight was far greater than its parliamentary strength within the United Nations system." Indeed, with such unswerving support it meant that Israel could not lose in the coming Security Council actions.

Johnson's support did not come without a price, as a memorandum to the President from Jewish affairs adviser Harry McPherson had made clear. McPherson had informed Johnson the previous month that Eppy Evron was willing to perform a bit of personal campaigning for the President among Jewish groups around the country. "Eppy would like to know what he could say—with firmness—that would satisfy the people he talks to, and square with your needs," McPherson wrote. It was an offer similar to one made by an anonymous, but obviously powerful, Jewish supporter—perhaps Evron himself—more than a year earlier. "[Deleted] is ready to mount a systematic campaign to inform the Jewish community in America of what we have done for Israel," Walt Rostow wrote the President. "He has taken on his own a campaign within the Jewish community on Vietnam. The theme is as follows: The whole fate of Israel depends on the credibility of U.S. commitments. If the U.S. were to fail to meet its commitments in Vietnam, what good would its commitments be to Israel? I think this is a first-rate approach and I told him so."

Thus were such bargains struck, tacit, never directly connected, but a quid pro quo nevertheless: In return for Johnson's support for Israel, supporters of Israel would proselytize for Johnson's causes in the Jewish American community.

The shock, the humiliation, the numbness caused by their losses were slowly wearing off the Palestinians that fall to be replaced by one searing emotion: hatred.

Throughout the occupied territories and in the refugee camps the Palestinians in Fatah and other guerrilla organizations were beginning to stir. They represented a potentially formidable enemy. In addition to the refugees now in Jordan, Lebanon, Syria and Egypt, there were an estimated 800,000 Palestinians who had remained in what some Israelis were already calling Samaria and Judea, the ancient Hebrew names for the West Bank, and 450,000 in the crowded Gaza Strip. Fatah's organization and its imitators had been barely touched by the war and they now began their operations again. Through small actions at first, a hand grenade tossed here, a mine planted there, they began again fighting back.

It was the start of a campaign of terror the likes of which Israel had never encountered in its history.

Each month the incidents became more frequent and daring. By October they had already become numerous enough to be worrisome to Israeli authorities. On October 1 occurred the first raid from Jordan since the war when four Palestinian guerrillas crossed the Jordan River and penetrated three miles inside Israel in the Beth Shean Valley, shot to death a soldier and blew up a two-story building in the Israeli town of Hamadia. The next day an Israeli policeman was slightly wounded in Nablus when guerrillas fired on his jeep. On October 15, the guerrillas struck again across the Jordan River, blowing up a dining hall, generator and trailer truck in the kibbutz of Moaz Haim. This time they left behind leaflets signed by Fatah.

By November 7, there had been twenty-three incidents in the Beth Shean Valley alone. On that same day, seven Fatah infiltrators were killed and three others captured at the village of Sheukh near Hebron.

This rise of terrorism brought deep concern to Israeli authorities. They struck back with a harsh anti-guerrilla campaign that included imprisonment, internal exile, deportation, and the destruction of houses of terrorists or of those harboring them or of those simply suspected of being Fatah members. Several of these policies were in violation of the Geneva Convention, especially its article prohibiting collective punishment.*

* Article 33 states: "No protected person may be punished for an offense he or she has not personally committed. Collective penalties and likewise all measures of intimidation or of terrorism are prohibited. Reprisals against protected persons and their property are prohibited."

The reasons for these Draconian measures were explained by General Uzi Narkiss, the former head of the Central Command who was now the West Bank's military commander. "If you know the Arab mentality, you know this toughness is probably good," he told David Holden of the London *Sunday Times.* "I don't think they really understand any other language." Already there was a hint of superiority, a tinge of racism, evident in such remarks.

In practice, aspects of the policy were cruel to the innocent. Thus, in retaliation for the presence of the Fatah guerrillas at Sheukh, nine homes were blown up on November 8, forty damaged by the blasts and eight men were arrested. In Nablus, homes were razed and two hundred men were arrested after being identified by hooded informers as members of Fatah.

The entire village of Tiflig, near Nablus, was bulldozed into oblivion. Tiflig had been created by refugees of the 1948 war and had housed six thousand Palestinians, most of whom fled at the start of the latest war; it remained largely abandoned. Authorities justified Tiflig's destruction on the grounds that terrorists were using it as a staging area.

In Gaza, where the suppression was severest, 144 inhabited homes were razed in one night of destruction in a refugee camp. Twelve refugees were killed when Israeli soldiers fired into a mob trying to get at food stores at the United Nation's former UNEF site at Rafah near Gaza. A communal grave with twenty-three bodies was also discovered in the Gaza area, the circumstances of the mass deaths a mystery.

Thousands of young Gaza men were accused of sympathizing with the PLO and were given a harsh choice: prison or deportation. U.N. officials estimated between three to four thousand registered refugees were forced to leave the Gaza Strip because they were suspected of belonging to the Palestine Liberation Army. Any Gaza family choosing deportation was given a box lunch, a small bonus and free transportation to the banks of the Jordan. The occupation authorities in Gaza also carried out a reverse of Israel's publicized policy of allowing "family reunions," by which refugees separated from their families in the West Bank were supposed to be allowed to rejoin them. Refugees were told to submit for "census purposes" the names of those among them who had members earning income abroad. When names were supplied, Israel rounded up those on the lists and dumped them at the Jordan.

Deportation was soon to become a nearly routine practice throughout the occupied territories. The first of what were to become well over a thousand deportees in the next decade was the aged Sheikh Abdul Hamid Sayigh of Jerusalem, the head of the Supreme Moslem Council. His crime was that he had objected to Israeli interference in self-governing Moslem religious institutions. For that he was deported to Jordan on September 23.

Internal banishment also was employed against the Palestinians. Four Arab notables who challenged the legality of Israel's annexation of Jerusalem were exiled inside Israel. Even though their crime was largely the citing of the U.N. resolutions denouncing annexation and the U.N. Charter and international law, they were accused of "incitement to subversion" and were banished to Jewish villages in northern Israel. They included such well-known figures as Anwar Khatib, governor of Jordanian Jerusalem, and Abdel Mehsen Abdul Mehzar, a member of the Jordanian Jerusalem Municipal Council, which Israel had summarily disbanded on June 29.

The deportation and internal exile of such prominent individuals carried a potent message: Israel's rule was total; opposition to it would not be tolerated.

This was made clear by Israel's handling of less prominent Palestinians. Reports to the United Nations charged that common Palestinians were usually held in custody without being given a chance to petition a court, interrogated, routinely beaten and often tortured, and then dumped in the middle of one of the bridges across the Jordan. Israeli soldiers would not allow the deportees to return and the Jordanian authorities were left with no choice but to give refuge to yet more refugees.

Refugees trying to sneak back into the West Bank were dealt with harshly. Israeli soldiers, many of whom obviously did not agree with their government's policy, were used to keep returnees out. One disillusioned Israeli soldier wrote of his personal experiences as a guard along the Jordan: "Every night Arabs cross the Jordan from east to west. We blocked the passages . . . and were ordered to shoot to kill without warning. Indeed, we fired shots every night on men, women and children. . . . In the mornings we searched the area and, by explicit order from the officer on the spot, shot the living, including those who hid or were wounded. After killing them we covered them with earth or sometimes left them lying there until a bulldozer came to bury them."

By early winter, it was estimated by some observers that at least two hundred Palestinians had been killed trying to enter the West Bank without Israeli permission.

Moshe Dayan, like most officials in Israel and its many supporters abroad, defended the country's occupation policies as necessary for Israel's security and, in comparison with most occupations, benign. In fact, it became a cliché to describe Israel's occupation as the "most humane in history."

In his candid way, Dayan admitted in his memoirs, in a chapter titled

"Living Together," that "we had to take stern measures." The Army had to blow up houses, he wrote, to combat terrorism and "this caused a furor, particularly when the householder was well known. But it proved effective and deterred many." He also admitted the practice of deportation and justified it on the grounds that it too was "effective."

In his and most other accounts by Israelis and many Western news reports, the occupation often was depicted as a blessing for the Palestinians. Thus Dayan maintained ten years after the occupation began, and had already reaped endless violence and hatred, that occupation helped relations between Palestinians and Israelis. "On the whole, relations between the Arabs in the territories and the military administration were normal, as they were with the Jews of Israel," he claimed. "In the matters which affected their daily lives, the Arab community had no complaint. On the material side, their standard of living rose by leaps and bounds."

Dayan admitted that acts of terror infuriated the Israeli public but asserted that "they did not turn on the Arab workers and visitors in their midst. The differences of view did not develop into vendettas. The . . . freedom of movement . . . and the economic prosperity formed a sound basis on which the two nations could live together."

Rafik Halabi, an Israeli Arab, a Druse who retained his loyalty to Israel, remembered the public's attitude and actions differently. When patrons at a Jerusalem cinema discovered a Fatah bomb before it exploded October 8, an enraged mob of Israelis descended on the Arab section and "vented their wrath on Arab property and by beating anyone who crossed their path," Halabi later wrote.

A hint of racism also became an underlying feature of the occupation, as Halabi's experience illustrated on the day of the Jerusalem bomb scare. "Later that night," Halabi continued, "a Jewish policeman expressed the depths of his feeling by spewing out at me the epithet 'filthy Arab!' " It was an epithet Palestinians were to hear many times during the long years of occupation.

Nonetheless, Abba Eban too presented a rosy picture of the occupation in his memoirs, which were published in 1977. "The strange thing was the deference of the conquerors to the vanquished. A world hitherto closed in mystery was now open before us, and the old rhetoric about Arab-Israeli coexistence became more concrete. . . . For the Arab masses . . . the change had been too quick to be absorbed. Villages and small townships lived on in their typically self-contained structure, calmly, independent of central institutions. . . . They now knew that they were safe."

Actually, by that autumn of 1967 there probably was not a family in all of the West Bank and Gaza that felt safe. It is doubtful that there was a family in all of the occupied territories that had not personally experienced the loss of a member of the family as a refugee or seen or heard of a son dragged off to prison. Every Palestinian was painfully aware of the stories of confiscation and destruction of homes, of midnight arrests and beatings, of mysterious deaths, and of those searing, spiteful words: "filthy Arab."

Yet a picture had taken shape in the West of Israel the underdog, a triumphant nation more moral than others, holding itself to a higher standard, its occupation a model of civility. There was an almost childish innocence in this adoration bestowed on Israel, especially in the United States, by a Christian world thrilled by decisive action, suddenly shorn of its Holocaust guilt and happy to share in the joy of Jews everywhere. Even Israel's annexation of Jerusalem was being condoned that autumn in the United States. A Harris poll showed that 43 percent of the Americans approved of Israel's control of Jerusalem, compared to 33 percent against, and 42 percent favored more aid to Israel.

The Johnson Administration was determined to support Israel as far as it could, yet at the same time it recognized there was an urgent need to find a solution to the tensions that were already becoming acute in the Middle East. To that end, the United States and the nations of the world now again concentrated their efforts in the United Nations.

XXV
PASSAGE OF
U.N. RESOLUTION 242

The early part of November was consumed at the United Nations by a frantic round of Security Council meetings, statements and private consultations. Although under the U.N. Charter the Council could theoretically intervene militarily to halt aggression or recommend on its own the solution of a conflict, its actions could be no bolder than the degree of consensus of its members. With the two superpowers reflecting the positions of their clients in the Middle East, it was obvious that any agreement at all in the Council would be a considerable achievement.

On the positive side was the fact that the fifteen members of the Council seemed to be in general agreement that a resolution had to be passed calling for Israel's withdrawal and appointing a special U.N. negotiator to seek peace in the Middle East. The problem was the wording. Israel would not accept a resolution that demanded its withdrawal from "all the occupied territories," while the Arab nations maintained publicly that they would accept nothing less. All of the land under Israeli occupation had to be returned, the Arabs insisted, and until that condition was met they would not negotiate. The Israelis maintained that they were willing to give up most of the land but that they wanted prior political concessions for doing so.

Israel had taken the same stand in 1957, arguing that it should reap some political benefit from its conquests. But at the time President Dwight D. Eisenhower had refused on the grounds that such a barter violated the Charter of the United Nations and U.S. policy. He had rhetorically, but pointedly, asked during a nationally televised address: "Should a nation which attacks and occupies foreign territory in the face of United Nations disapproval be allowed to impose conditions on its own withdrawal? If we agreed that armed attack can properly achieve the purposes of the assailant, then I fear we will have turned back the clock of international order."

Eisenhower's position had not only been in the best idealistic tradition of the United States but also was the essence of high statesmanship. By his uncompromising stand, he stated for all the nations of the world to hear that America observed the principles of the U.N. Charter and was willing to support the weak against the strong.

The Johnson Administration, now facing an identical situation, displayed no such exalted ideals or level of statecraft. Instead, it embarked on a confused and at times an almost unbelievably naïve effort to find a solution. From the very beginning, it retreated from the principle upheld by Eisenhower and conceded that indeed Israel should be allowed to impose conditions on its withdrawal.

This was a fatal mistake. It plagued the Administration's actions throughout its handling of the crisis and it led directly to the Administration squandering nearly all of its energies on one narrow issue: crafting a withdrawal formula acceptable to Israel.

Implicitly, this meant that withdrawal would not be total, since at a minimum Israel demanded that changes be made in the 1949 armistice lines. It was not an unreasonable demand, since the Arab nations, too, agreed that some slight changes in the old armistice lines would be advantageous for both sides. After all, the lines had come into being willy-nilly, a reflection of the zones controlled by the contending armies when the fighting had finally stopped in 1949. In some cases villages were left cut in half, roads bisected and homes separated from their lands. A more rational and premeditated boundary would be advantageous for both sides.

But fundamental to this reasoning was the assumption that any changes made would be minor and that Israel would make reciprocal concessions for any small pieces of land it might gain in adjustments to the frontiers. It apparently never occurred to the American negotiators that if withdrawal was not required to be total, then Israel might later be able to argue—as it was to do—that its withdrawal did not have to be major.

The American position was not only naïve. It also reflected a fundamental inattention to the political realities in Israel. The Administration was ignoring the evidence that had accumulated over the months since the outbreak of war that there was by now broad sentiment in Israel to retain the captured territories. Further, the hardliners led by Menachem Begin were not talking about minor border adjustments. They wanted, as they had for decades, all of the West Bank, which they considered an integral part of *Eretz Yisrael.*

U.S. officials, lulled by the soothing assurances of Abba Eban, a man they trusted and who was patently ready to make concessions, failed to take into account how powerful Israel's nationalists had grown and how forcefully they would be helped if the United States did not insist on total withdrawal.

Instead, the Administration relied on Eban's repeated assurances that Israel sought no territory. Over the months, in doing so, it inadvertently helped undercut his and Eshkol's position in Israel in their struggle with the hardliners.

Yet on their face, Eban's assurances seemed dependable. After all, at the beginning of the war Eshkol had written Johnson that Israel had no "colonial" aspirations and was not seeking territorial aggrandizement. Throughout the summer Eban had repeated these soothing words. But as the months passed and it became clear that the United States would not demand total withdrawal, the Israeli position, under pressure from the nationalists, had subtly begun to harden.

This should have been obvious to the Administration on September 19. Eban on that day outlined for Goldberg current Israeli thinking on the borders. Israel, he said, would give all of the Sinai back to Egypt but keep the Gaza Strip. It would work out some territorial adjustments with Syria and in Jerusalem make some arrangement so that the Holy Moslem Quarter "would be put under Moslem control and sovereignty."

As for the West Bank, Eban explained that "it would be difficult for the citizens to understand the government simply turning the area back. Therefore, the Israeli government was thinking of two elements:

"(a) demilitarization of the West Bank with a U.N. inspection system and

"(b) some form of economic, customs or travel arrangements which would permit access to and larger cooperation with the area."

Even this relatively mild proposal was a departure from Israel's earlier positions, and caused Assistant Secretary of State Luke Battle to observe that it represented a hardening in Israel's position. A day after Eban's meeting with Goldberg, in a memorandum titled *Israel's Expanding War Aims*, Battle noted the new aims of the Israeli government to Rusk and observed that "they went beyond those supported by U.S. policy as enunciated in the principles of June 19 [in the speech given that day by President Johnson]."

Despite Battle's warning, the political leadership in Washington did not grasp the extent of change in Israel's position; it wasn't until Eban visited Washington in late October—more than a month later—that Rusk took the matter up with him. When the secretary of state reminded Eban of Israel's

June assurance that it had no territorial ambitions, the foreign minister bluntly replied: "That was before Syria and Jordan entered the war."

In a meeting the next day with Under Secretary Katzenbach and other U.S. officials, Eban was more conciliatory and reassured them that all Israel sought in terms of territory were "small security adjustments."

This assurance and subsequent conversations with Israeli officials "caused the United States to begin seeking a draft Security Council resolution which employed indefinite language on the withdrawal question," according to a secret State Department study concluded in the late 1970s.* It is apparent from the study that Eban and Rafael employed a series of threats, as well as assurances, to secure the Administration's agreement to use indefinite language. At one point, on October 26, Eban warned Goldberg, according to the secret study, that Israel's position on withdrawal was "simply and clearly that it would not withdraw from all territories that it had occupied." He added: "Pressure by the United Nations to get Israel back behind the June 5 lines . . . would strengthen the hands of those in the Israeli government who wanted to create a *fait accompli* by annexation." The study added: "Later that day, [Rafael said] that if the Security Council adopted a resolution unacceptable to Israel on the territorial-withdrawal issue, he was under instructions from the Cabinet to announce Israeli unwillingness to cooperate with a United Nations representative. The following day, Goldberg presented to Eban and Rafael a text incorporating less definite phraseology on the withdrawal question."

The decision by the United States to employ indefinite language on withdrawal was a tremendous victory for Israel's hardliners. Although U.S. officials and Eban apparently believed at the time that such a clause was useful simply as a bargaining tool to decide on minor border changes, in fact it gave Begin and others back in Israel the opportunity to argue not only about

* The study was commissioned at a time when the government of Menachem Begin was arguing that Israel had never agreed to withdraw from the West Bank. Seeking to reconstruct what actually had been agreed to in the turbulent aftermath of the 1967 war, which over the years had become the subject of hot dispute, the Carter Administration ordered a study based on U.S. documents. The documents, mainly classified State Department reports, involved memorandums of conversations made at the time, cables to and from Washington and various embassies, including a large number from the U.S. mission at the United Nations, and other reports on the progress and details of the talks that led to passage of Security Council Resolution 242. The study thus provides, for the first time, a documented history of what actually took place in the negotiations and the understandings of the parties as perceived by the State Department. Much of the following narrative is based on the study or supported by it.

the extent of withdrawal but even about the areas where withdrawal was called for. No one among the U.S. negotiators at the time apparently suspected that the use of indefinite language on withdrawal might eventually be employed to justify Israel's retention of all of the West Bank, the Golan Heights and Jerusalem.

In addition to giving in on the withdrawal issue, the United States accepted without hesitation the Israeli position that negotiations would precede withdrawal. This was made clear in a memorandum by Hal Saunders to Walt Rostow on October 31, in which he remarked that "we aren't about to press the Israelis to withdraw before they negotiate a settlement." This represented, although no doubt unwittingly, the final capitulation to Israel's position. There was almost no hope the Arabs would negotiate while their land was occupied—and no way Israelis, even the moderate ones, would abandon the West Bank without heavy U.S. pressure. Begin, Dayan and other hardliners, of course, were not prepared to give back the West Bank under any conditions, but now they had a perfect pretext to stall any withdrawal.

Once again U.S. officials underestimated the tactical advantage they had bestowed on Israel's hardliners. The assumption on the U.S. side was that negotiations would be technical and brief. This was the position officials sold to the Arabs. They completely failed to realize that the Israeli hardliners would use the negotiation issue as a gambit to forestall withdrawal on the West Bank by indulging in endless picayune arguments designed to prevent agreement.

Somehow the strength and determination of the Israeli hardliners continued to elude U.S. officials, in spite of the continually mounting evidence that Israel's position was not as conciliatory as Eban painted it or the Johnson Administration persisted in believing. A number of officials, particularly Hal Saunders, Luke Battle and the experts in the State Department's Near East division, were aware that as the weeks passed Israel's position was hardening. But the pro-Israel atmosphere of the time was so overwhelming that no one seemed capable of understanding the long-term import of that trend or of acting on it. Urgency and an unequivocal position on withdrawal were desperately needed to strike a deal while Israel was still flexible. But these were not forthcoming from the White House, and without them the chances for peace were inexorably seeping away.

One glaring clue ignored by the Administration that Israel's hardliners were getting the upper hand should have been detected in the attempt by Israel to work out a separate peace agreement with Egypt shortly after the war. Instead of seeking an overall settlement with all its Arab neighbors, the

Cabinet had decided secretly in August to try for a bilateral accord with Egypt. One effect of such a separate pact, of course, would be to neutralize Israel's most powerful enemy and thus relieve pressure on Israel for an agreement on the West Bank.

To Nasser, Israel promised to return all of the Sinai immediately if he signed a peace treaty between the two countries. But Nasser rebuffed the Israeli offer, realizing that a separate peace would leave Israel free to deal with the other Arab nations as it wished and that it would then be in such a commanding position that it would probably not give up the West Bank.

Nasser told King Hussein about the Israeli offer shortly before the king arrived in New York on November 2 to join in the Security Council negotiations. The two Arab leaders agreed that their primary effort must be directed at freeing the captive population of the West Bank.

"Nasser told me that the Sinai was not important compared to the Palestinians," Hussein related years later. "I should do anything I can to get back the West Bank, he said. He suspected Israel's motives and, I think, he felt personally responsible for what had happened to the people of the West Bank as a result of the war."*

Thus, with the Johnson Administration ignoring the accumulating evidence and still assuming that Israel planned near-total withdrawal, Hussein had arrived in New York with a plan agreed upon with Nasser. The king would be the spokesman for the Arabs, or at least Egypt and Jordan, and he would offer recognition of Israel in return for the captured territories, "total peace for total withdrawal," as he phrased it. Hussein hinted at his intentions on November 5 on CBS's *Face the Nation,* saying that the Arabs' offer "would mean that we recognize the right of all to live in peace and security" and that Nasser would grant Israeli shipping free passage in the Suez Canal and the Straits of Tiran. The next day he publicly assured reporters that Nasser shared his views. On November 8, the chief official spokesman for the Egyptian government, Mohammed H. Zayyat, confirmed publicly in Cairo that the Arabs recognized "the right of each party to security and freedom from fear of attack." Referring back to Egypt's signing of the 1949 Armistice Agreement with Israel, he added that "this document would guarantee the right of Israel to exist is self-evident. We do know Israel exists."

These public statements were less generous than they appeared. For while Hussein and Cairo were saying they recognized Israel's existence, they were

* The deal Nasser turned down is of course exactly what was accepted in 1979 by Nasser's successor, Anwar Sadat, when he signed the Camp David peace treaty with Israel, which gave Egypt no more than it could have gotten twelve years earlier. This does much to explain the disdain Hussein displayed toward Sadat and the treaty.

not going so far as to offer to recognize the Jewish state diplomatically. But that offer was being made secretly.

In a series of exhaustive secret meetings at the Waldorf-Astoria Towers in New York, where Eban, Hussein, Riad and Goldberg were all staying, the United States was laboriously working behind the scenes trying to forge an agreement that would be acceptable by both the Arabs and Israel.

The bargaining was intense and, as with almost everything else connected with the Middle East, complex and unorthodox. The Arabs did not trust Goldberg, or particularly like him either, because they felt he was abrasive, arrogant and condescending. So while he dealt personally with the Israeli delegation, another U.S. official carried on talks with the Arabs. Thus Goldberg would talk with the Israelis, then report what they had to say to the official and he in turn would go to Hussein's suite and relay the Israeli position. The process was then reversed. The official would tell Goldberg about Hussein's reactions and Goldberg would communicate them to the Israelis.

At the start of this awkward process, despite the coolness in their relations, Goldberg had personally met with Hussein the day after his arrival in New York to outline the U.S. position. According to the State Department study, "Goldberg told the King that the United States did not visualize a Jordan limited to the East Bank; that the United States was prepared to help obtain an appropriate Jordanian role in Jerusalem; and that the U.S. purpose was to create a context of peace in which Israeli withdrawal would take place and Jordanian territorial integrity and political independence would be protected."

Goldberg, according to the study, warned Hussein that the United States "could not guarantee that everything would be returned to Jordan; some territorial adjustments would be required. There must be a withdrawal to recognized and secure frontiers for all countries which were not the old armistice lines. Goldberg also noted that there must be a mutuality in adjustments."

By way of illustration—and indicative of how minor U.S. officials assumed the eventual changes would be—Goldberg said that if Jordan made an adjustment of the Latrun salient, that annoying bulge between Jerusalem and Tel Aviv, then "there ought to be some compensatory adjustment for it."

The next day, November 4, Goldberg managed to get an agreement from Israel on a withdrawal clause. Since it had already been agreed in the earlier text that the clause would contain indefinite language, two drafts were drawn up, both vaguely worded. One contained the phrase "withdrawal of all forces from territories occupied by them"; the language of the other included an even vaguer phrase calling for "withdrawal of armed forces from occupied territory." There was no mention of Israel or of "all the territories."

Goldberg showed Eban both versions. Eban predictably preferred the vaguer one and that was then adopted as the official U.S. wording. As the secret State Department study observed, "Having developed a phraseology on the withdrawal question acceptable to Israel, U.S. officials then sought to sell the phraseology to the front-line Arab states."

Significantly, the study added: "In so doing, U.S. officials emphasized that any territorial adjustments would be limited in nature and would not, of necessity, be detrimental to the Arab states."

Thus by the first week of November the U.S. position was established—and made clear to the Arab states. It would support adjustments to the armistice lines, but still it was assumed that they would entail only minor bits of land and that Israel's withdrawal would be nearly complete in return for peace.

As Hussein heard the assurances he became more optimistic. Such U.S. promises sounded not only good to him, but also believable. After all, the United States had once before forced Israel to return the fruits of its conquests. If America now promised that it would essentially do that again, then there could be little doubt that Washington had the power and the influence to do it. What Hussein failed to realize, however, was how strong Israel's influence in the United States had become since 1957.

So with the U.S. assurances still ringing in his ears, he traveled on November 6 to Washington, where, he had been promised, he would hear Secretary of State Rusk repeat them.

This indeed occurred. Rusk repeated that the U.S. would use its influence to get Israel out of most of the West Bank. In reporting on the meeting later to Johnson, Rusk explained "that the net effect of these assurances was that the United States was prepared to support the return of a substantial part of the West Bank to Jordan with boundary adjustments, and would use its influence to obtain compensation to Jordan for any territory it was required to give up." By way of example, Rusk told Johnson—as he and Goldberg had earlier told Hussein—that if Jordan gave up the Latrun salient "the United States would then use its diplomatic and political influence to obtain in compensation access for Jordan to a Mediterranean port in Israel."

In addition to all this, the secret study reports, "Rusk also repeated to the President the assurances given to Hussein concerning Jerusalem and concerning United States efforts to obtain for Jordan the best possible deal."

Hussein was euphoric, and he was about to become even more so. Two days later, on November 8, he met with Johnson in the White House and heard the President of the United States personally reaffirm the U.S. commitment. At one point Hussein asked Johnson how soon he could expect Israel to withdraw. "In six months," said Johnson, according to Hussein. Goldberg later gave the same timing for withdrawal, according to an aide of Hussein.

When Hussein returned to New York on November 10, he told Goldberg he was "extremely pleased" and "extremely satisfied" with his talks in Washington. According to the State Department study, "[Hussein] thought that his friends were ready to help with respect to Jordan, particularly to get the West Bank back, while recognizing that some adjustments might be required. . . . The nature of the U.S. meaning of withdrawal had been clarified to him."

The essence of the U.S. position, according to Hussein, was expressed by several officials in the phrase that withdrawal would mean only "minor reciprocal border rectifications." When Hussein asked Goldberg whether Israel agreed with the U.S. position, Goldberg assured him they did, according to the king.

The next day, November 11, Goldberg reported to Eban that Hussein had met with Arab delegations and said that he was "satisfied with the assurances given to him in Washington." The secret study added: "Evidently, Eban was aware of the assurances given to Hussein, as he did not question or comment upon Goldberg's statement."

In fact, according to King Hussein and a knowledgeable U. S. source who declines to be identified, there was no doubt that Eban had agreed to the U.S. assurances because they had been written down by the U.S. official who had been dealing with him in the secret meetings at the Waldorf and shown to him. When Hussein had personally asked Goldberg whether Israel accepted the terms, Goldberg's words, according to the king and the U.S. official, were: "Don't worry. They're on board."*

The United States did not make its assurances public, but they were conveyed privately to Great Britain and several Arab states. Goldberg person-

* The authors of the study, which was concluded in 1978, apparently were unaware of this written understanding, which in sum called for only minor and reciprocal border rectifications. It has disappeared from government files. But that it existed has been confirmed to me by both Hussein and the U.S. official who actually wrote it out on Waldorf stationery. He has declined to be identified. Questions to Goldberg, who has since denied that 242 called for only "minor" border changes, have gone unanswered.

ally met on November 15 with representatives from Iraq, Lebanon and Morocco and assured them, according to the study, "that the United States did not conceive of any substantial redrawing of the map. Goldberg emphasized the importance of this statement to the Arab diplomats and the fact that it had previously been made known to the parties."

While these negotiations went on secretly, public attention was focused on the maneuvering in the Security Council. On November 7, India, Mali and Nigeria had joined together to submit the first draft resolution on withdrawal. The draft was generally balanced and fair, but it contained two basic flaws in Israel's view.

The first objectionable phrase said "Israel should withdraw from all the territories occupied as a result of the recent conflict." The phrase "all the territories" was too strong for Israel and thus for the United States too. The other said that there should be a guarantee of navigation through international waterways, such as the Straits of Tiran, "in accordance with international law." This phrase meant that Egypt could press its contention that the straits were within its territorial waters and the whole matter would have to be adjudicated, thereby effectively keeping the waterway closed to Israel during the long period of litigation.

To overcome these objections, the United States submitted its own resolution the same day. Although Arthur Goldberg stoutly defended the draft as being fair to both sides, it was as objectionable to the Arabs as was the Afro-Asian draft to Israel. When Egypt's Riad read it, he complained that "this is nothing more than an Israeli draft under a U.S. name."

That was not quite the case, but it was true that the draft resolution had been designed to retain Israeli support. As a result, it contained the vague phrase already privately agreed upon with Israel: "withdrawal of armed force from occupied territory." There was no mention of Israel and no time frame attached to indicate *what* occupied territories. Since Israel contended that Jordan's claim to the West Bank and Egypt's to Gaza were both illegal and involved occupations, the parties could end up talking about Arab occupation rather than Israeli under the wording of the resolution. The Arabs also objected to the way the U.S. draft dealt with the waterway issue. It flatly declared there should be "freedom of navigation through international waterways in the area," completely ignoring Egypt's claims.

Informal soundings among the members showed that neither the U.S. nor the Afro-Asian draft could win the support of the necessary nine members for passage, much less the unanimity that was being sought. Without every member of the Council supporting a resolution, it was unlikely that either the Arabs or Israel would take it very seriously. Thus neither the Afro-Asian group nor the United States was anxious at this point to push for a speedy vote on its draft.

But movement was urgently needed. Tensions along the Suez Canal continued to build and the Council members were impatient and under public pressure to take some action. Clearly what was needed was a simple resolution that would reflect the private understanding the United States had given to Jordan and the Arabs and at the same time meet with Israel's approval.

The man who spearheaded the effort before the Security Council was Britain's highly popular representative, Lord Caradon, the former Hugh Mackintosh Foot, a gracious sixty-year-old product of England's old Colonial Office. Caradon had first served in the Middle East in 1929 and he brought a sensitivity and finely nurtured impartiality to the Council's deliberations. Caradon too now worked quietly behind the scenes to garner the support of the other permanent members of the Security Council and the ten nonpermanent ones.*

On November 16, Caradon introduced a British draft resolution that was so finely and precisely worded that it was a work of diplomatic art. It differed from the two earlier drafts, and a draft being worked up by the Latin countries, in calling for "withdrawal of Israeli armed forces from territories occupied in the recent conflict," artfully retaining the vague language Israel demanded by avoiding the use of *the* territories in the English text (though not in the texts of the U.N.'s four other official languages).†

Yet it added a phrase that clearly implied the missing *the:* "emphasizing the inadmissibility of the acquisition of territory by war."‡

* They were Argentina, Brazil, Bulgaria, Canada, Denmark, Ethiopia, India, Japan, Mali and Nigeria.

† Chinese, French, Spanish and Russian.

‡ Text of the resolution:

> *The Security Council,*
> *Expressing* its continuing concern with the grave situation in the Middle East,
> *Emphasizing* the inadmissibility of the acquisition of territory by war and the need to work for a just and lasting peace in which every State in the area can live in security,
> *Emphasizing further* that all Member States in their acceptance of the Charter of the United Nations have undertaken a commitment to act in accordance with Article 2 of the Charter,
> 1. *Affirms* that the fulfillment of Charter principles requires the establish-

The United States threw its full weight behind the British effort and, in the words of the secret State Department study, "used every effort to prevent the introduction of a Latin American draft, and resisted all attempts to introduce more specific language into the withdrawal clause in the British text. Moreover, the United States provided public assurances that it considered the U.K. draft to reflect fully the U.S. position on withdrawal, boundaries and peace."

However, the study added, "The United States did not during this period emphasize its position that it envisioned only limited boundary adjustments."

Despite that notable lapse, one about which the Arabs should have been suspicious, support for what was later titled Security Council Resolution 242 quickly grew. Jordan, armed with what it believed were ironclad assurances from the highest levels of the U.S. government, was willing to accept it and Egypt, although less trustful, agreed to acquiesce.

While the British draft was gaining support in the Security Council, it was beginning to dawn on some U.S. experts that the proposed resolution could open up some difficult problems. Hal Saunders expressed his worry more forcefully than ever before in a memorandum to Walt Rostow on November 20, citing "our serious concern that the *Israelis are hardening their position to the point where they will leave no room for the Arabs to negotiate.* While we have Eban's statements that negotiations are possible, we also have a for-

---

ment of a just and lasting peace in the Middle East which should include the application of both the following principles:

(i) Withdrawal of Israeli armed forces from territories occupied in the recent conflict;

(ii) Termination of all claims or states of belligerency and respect for and acknowledgment of the sovereignty, territorial integrity and political independence of every State in the area and their right to live in peace within secure and recognized boundaries free from threats or acts of force;

2. *Affirms further* the necessity

(a) For guaranteeing freedom of navigation through international waterways in the area;

(b) For achieving a just settlement of the refugee problem;

(c) For guaranteeing the territorial inviolability and political independence of every State in the area, through measures including the establishment of demilitarized zones;

3. *Requests* the Secretary-General to designate a Special Representative to proceed to the Middle East to establish and maintain contacts with the States concerned in order to promote agreement and assist efforts to achieve a peaceful and accepted settlement in accordance with the provisions and principles in this resolution;

4. *Requests* the Secretary-General to report to the Security Council on the progress of the efforts of the Special Representative as soon as possible.

mally communicated Israeli Cabinet decision, which shows no flexibility whatever even on the mechanics of negotiation." (Emphasis in original.)

The nature of the Israeli Cabinet decision remains secret, but it is obvious from Saunders' language that it was a distressing one. Nonetheless, the Johnson Administration maintained its course, supporting Resolution 242 and continuing to reassure the Arabs that all was well.

On the same day that Saunders wrote his memo an alarming development came from another quarter. On November 20, Soviet First Deputy Foreign Minister Vasily V. Kuznetsov, in New York for the Security Council meeting, introduced a rival Russian draft. Suddenly the hopes that agreement in the Council was near were dashed. All the minutely detailed negotiations of the secret hotel shuttle and the Council's considerations were in peril.

The Soviet draft returned to a clause specifically calling for Israel's withdrawal of all of its forces to the lines prior to June 5. Similarly, on the waterway issue, it called for passage "in accordance with international agreements," less restrictive than the Afro-Asian wording but leaving Egypt's claim open. Otherwise, it went beyond Caradon's draft by explicitly calling for Israel's recognition and an end to the arms race in the region, a clause also contained in the American draft.

Despite its positive aspects, the Soviet stance on withdrawal and the waterway doomed it in the eyes of Israel, the United States and several other members. Israel immediately rejected it outright, Eban declaring that it "does not meet the test of exact balance, acquiescence by the parties and workability." It appeared the Council was going to fail. Now apparently immovably deadlocked, the members decided to recess for two days to see if some compromise could be found.

Caradon had acceded to the recess because of another unexpected development. Soviet Ambassador Kuznetsov, a widely experienced and respected diplomat and an old friend of Caradon's, had asked to see the British diplomat alone that day before the meeting. When they were together, Kuznetsov said: "I want you to give me two days."

"I hesitated," recalled Caradon. "What would my government say? They might assume that the Russians wanted the time to gather more support for their ... resolution. But then Kuznetsov said something strange. He said: 'I am not sure that you fully understand what I am saying to you. I am personally asking you for two days.'"

Caradon said he realized that when Kuznetsov put his request on such a personal basis, "I knew that he would not work against me ... I knew I could trust him, as he trusted me."

Activity was feverish over the next two days. Informal polls of the delegations showed the British draft had the greatest support, but some delegations remained noncommittal and there was no clear indication how a vote on the various drafts would go.

The meeting reconvened at 4:00 P.M. on November 22, a half hour late. The United States, the Soviet Union and the Asian-African bloc all had agreed they would not press for a vote on their resolutions, so the deliberations of the Council were now focused solely on the British draft.

The time of voting "was a dramatic, unforgettable moment," Caradon recalled. As he watched delegates raising their hands in favor of the draft, he heard a loud cheer from the crowded gallery. "I turned to my right to see, much to my surprise and delight, Deputy Foreign Minister Kuznetsov of the Soviet Union with his finger raised voting for the British resolution and thus making it unanimous.

"Kuznetsov had made good use of the two days," Caradon observed. "He had come to the conclusion that a unanimous vote and full agreement were essential. He had gone back to his government and, I have no doubt, to Arab governments too, and he had persuaded them."

What had been thought impossible had been achieved. The Security Council with its representation of all the peoples of the world had unanimously agreed on a common approach to the Middle East as embodied in Resolution 242.

Far more significant was the unprecedented level of agreement between Israel and the Arabs reached in secret. If both sides stuck by their pledge to Goldberg, then there finally did seem a chance that some time in the future there might actually be hope that peace could be achieved in the Middle East.

Passage of Resolution 242 was a fitting conclusion to the six days in June that transformed the Middle East irreversibly. Like other efforts before and after, it gave the appearance of great accomplishment, but it had no substance without the cooperation of both sides directly involved in the Middle East. That was not forthcoming.

As the months passed and Israel dug in on the West Bank rather than withdraw, Jordan repeatedly reminded the United States of its secret agreement. But now Israel denied it had ever agreed to the terms of the understanding. And in a technical sense this was no doubt true. Certainly the Cabinet, with Begin and Dayan exerting powerful voices, could never have agreed to the return of the West Bank. Begin, in fact, would not even agree to Resolution 242.

347

Although Israel gave the impression publicly that it had accepted 242, and the news media reflected that impression, the fact was that as far as the Cabinet was concerned it had done no such thing. Nearly five months after its adoption by the Security Council, Hal Saunders reflected the confusion by remarking that "our feeling [is] that the Israelis have accepted [242] even though they won't say so specifically."

That was wishful thinking, an attitude that repeatedly misled U.S. administrations in their dealings with Israel. The reality was that nationalists like Begin had no intention at any time to return the West Bank. Others in the Cabinet like Eban and Eshkol were more flexible and more willing to seek an exchange of land for peace, but they were stymied by the intransigence of Begin's camp and the refusal of the Arab states to declare publicly and unequivocally that they were ready, unconditionally, to make peace.

The position of Eshkol and other moderates was also undermined by the unwillingness of the United States to exert its full influence and demand that Israel honor its commitments. Instead, Washington allowed the peace process to degenerate into a technical hassle over whether it called for immediate implementation, as the Arabs argued, or detailed negotiations, as Israel claimed. Soon Arabs and Israelis were accusing each other of a lack of good will and a refusal to act in good faith—charges that bore some truth on both sides.

Nonetheless, nothing could have played more into the hands of Israel's nationalists than this enervating, endless dispute, since it was obvious that the more time that passed the better became Israel's chances of retaining the territory. Further, Begin and others could properly argue that Washington's inaction indicated more loudly than its words that the United States was willing to acquiesce in the status quo. Why, if Israel could retain America's support and still keep the territory, should it gamble on returning land that could affect its security or territorial ambitions? Why should it be any more generous than its biggest protector demanded?

Thus Washington's refusal to take tough action helped the position of the nationalists. Eshkol, who had emerged from the war with his political support weakened because of his early hesitations, was in no position to wield strong leadership. His was a consensus government. As long as he was free from pressure by Washington there was no way he could force Begin and others to change their minds. Had Washington sternly demanded action, he might have had a chance. But without it, the peace initiative was doomed.

Over the years, as presidents came and went, the secret American understanding with Hussein was routinely reiterated to the king—though not publicly—by each new Administration, most recently by the Reagan Administration, as the United States' interpretation of 242.*

Despite such assurances, nothing happened. Israel, instead of showing signs of withdrawing, extended its occupation by building more and more Jewish settlements on land confiscated from Arab owners on the West Bank, on the Golan Heights and in East Jerusalem.

As the years went by, Hussein repeatedly threatened to make the secret agreement public, but on the advice of U.S. officials he remained quiet, if disillusioned. The officials believed that Hussein's release of the agreement would bring only embarrassment to Washington and anger from Israel—but no increased support for his position. By keeping the understanding secret, they calculated, Hussein would earn more good will in Washington than advantages he would achieve by going public.†

As the months passed, Israel continued to confuse security and biblical prophecy for peace. And the Johnson Administration, and others that followed, blindly continued to lend support, although unwittingly, to Israel's most extreme elements.

Such uncritical support obscured in the United States the ugly realities of the occupation and to some immeasurable extent encouraged the hardliners within Israel to turn their back on the nation's liberal and humane past. By

---

* An example of the latest of such assurances was given to Hussein by Secretary of State George Shultz in January 1983 after the king's meeting with President Reagan in late 1982. Shultz's letter stated that "the President believes, consistent with Resolution 242, that territory should not be acquired by war. He believes, as well, however, that Resolution 242 does permit changes in the boundaries which existed prior to June 1967 but only where such changes are agreed between the parties." On the status of Jerusalem, which all Israeli governments since 1967 have contended is Israeli territory and not negotiable, Shultz informed the king that "the United States considers East Jerusalem part of the occupied territories."

† Hussein revealed the arrangement in a speech before the World Affairs Council in Los Angeles on November 6, 1981. To anyone listening closely, it would have been obvious that he had a secret agreement when he said: "Since 1967, questions have been raised as to the true meaning of 242. . . . I asked for clarification of the withdrawal provision at the time and was told the United States was prepared to make a commitment that would be understood to require Israeli withdrawal from all the occupied territory of the West Bank, with 'minor reciprocal border rectifications' conditional on mutual agreement. . . . An essential part of the understanding as conveyed by the representatives of the United States was that Israel had acquiesced in the agreed interpretation of what Resolution 242 would require. The specific term used was that Israel was 'on board.' And furthermore, that six months would be the outside limit for its implementation."

This revelation received little public notice and the king was left with his irksome secret intact.

allowing Israel to retain its conquests, to annex Jerusalem, to settle the occupied territories, to inflict collective punishment on a defenseless people, the United States inadvertently gave succor to the most extreme political fringe in Israeli society, which in turn led within ten years to the election of the radical government of Menachem Begin.

Instead of living up to its own ideals and those of the United Nations Charter and leading Israel to do the same, the United States in effect promoted the illicit behavior of Israel. It was an Israel rendered so delirious by victory and release from anxiety that it had lost its moorings. In such an emotional atmosphere, it needed counseling and guidance from a strong friend.

This it did not get from Washington. Successive administrations were concerned with other, seemingly more pressing, problems and tantalized by the domestic political benefits of placating a powerful lobby. This lack of U.S. vision and Washington's indulgence in Israel's flouting of international standards were to prove a great tragedy for the Israeli people. For although the Arab nations had been defeated, they had not been conquered or destroyed. Their spirit, as that of the Palestinians, remained determined.

The world was to see the results of this tragic slide into passivity six years later, when the Arabs once again took to the battlefield to try to regain their land.

EPILOGUE

The 1967 war established beyond doubt a profoundly depressing trend in the Middle East. It demonstrated that each succeeding war is more brutal, bloodier and more destructive than the previous one. Thus casualties in 1956 amounted to 189 dead and 899 wounded for Israel and an estimated 1,000 killed and 4,000 wounded for Egypt in the Sinai fighting. Eleven years later, with newer weapons and better training, Israel lost 983 killed and 4,517 wounded in the three-front war. Combined Arab losses were about 4,296 killed and 6,121 wounded.

The 1973 war, the Middle East's first true modern war fought with massive armor, air and missile forces, was horrifying in its destructiveness. Estimated casualties were 2,838 Israelis killed, 8,528 wounded, and 508 taken prisoner or missing; the Arabs lost 8,528 killed and 19,549 wounded and had 8,551 taken prisoner or missing. Equipment losses were equally large: the sides together lost 495 aircraft, 61 helicopters, 1,250 armored personnel carriers and a staggering 3,394 battle tanks.

With the massive rearming of both sides with the latest and deadliest weapons available from the armories of the Soviet Union and the United States that has occurred at unprecedented levels since 1973, there can be no doubt that any future war would be far worse than ever.

Another depressing trend that the 1967 war confirmed was the proclivity of the superpowers to posture in militant confrontation against each other during fighting in the Middle East. In 1956, the Soviets rattled rockets against London, Paris and Tel Aviv and President Eisenhower was concerned enough to alert the Sixth Fleet to possible war. Confrontation became more direct and dangerous in 1967 when Kosygin flatly warned Johnson that Moscow was ready to use any means, including military, to stop the fighting. Johnson responded by aggressively moving the Sixth Fleet. The 1973 war ended with Washington and Moscow in even sharper confrontation. U.S. forces were put on a worldwide war alert before the crisis finally subsided.

With the increase in Soviet power, and especially the significant strengthening of its Mediterranean fleet, the next time may not end with such restraint.

From the distance of a decade and a half, it is safe, if not satisfying, to observe that the war of 1967 was the worst tragedy in the modern history of the Middle East. In the sixteen years since then, the region has been racked by more hatred, violence and bloodshed than at any time since the founding of the Jewish state. The mere listing of the major events makes a doleful litany: the war of attrition, Black September, the PLO terror campaign culminating in the Munich massacre, the traumatic 1973 war, the struggle for southern Lebanon that led to the near destruction of Beirut and, once again, the massacre and uprooting of thousands of Palestinian refugees leading to renewed hatred.

The single outstanding diplomatic achievement of the period, the 1979 Camp David peace treaty, in the final analysis seemed to be leading not to a lasting peace between Egypt and Israel but to a tenuous relationship of acrimony and increasing mutual suspicions. It certainly contributed to the assassination of President Anwar Sadat and there is every indication that more of the same, and perhaps worse, is in store. The Middle East, at the end of 1983, appears doomed to endure another long period of suffering, terrorism and probably, eventually, renewed warfare.

In 1967, Americans became so caught up in the reflected glory of Israel's triumph that they ignored or failed to realize how costly the war was to their own country. Yet the expense had been significant. Foremost, it worsened relations with the Soviet Union in the late 1960s. It undoubtedly gave added ammunition to Kremlin hardliners to increase further Russia's military might and its presence in the Middle East. Moscow has done both since then, and although the United States in the meantime has managed to woo away Egypt, there is every indication that Cairo soon will renew its ambassadorial-level relations with Moscow.

The war left America completely identified with Israel, and it relations with the Arab world became practically nonexistent. The result was that the Arabs believed they were left with no way to influence the festering conflict except by association with the Soviet Union and by war. When war finally came in 1973, Washington found itself without enough influence or credibility to prevent it. Nor could it head off the disastrous oil embargo that followed, which resulted in massive financial dislocations around the globe and one of the greatest transfers of wealth in history.

America's image, already tarnished by the unremitting conflict in Vietnam, widely perceived as a racial war, was further blemished in the eyes of the Third World by the 1967 war. Israel was generally regarded as an alien outpost of the West, a perception it did its utmost to reinforce, and its conquest of territory by force was abhorred and feared by weak nations, who worried that the same fate at the hands of powerful neighbors might befall them.

By steadfastly supporting Israel while it publicly and repeatedly defied the United Nations and its Charter, which Israel had sworn to uphold, the United States contributed to the weakening of the international body it had helped create.

Even graver, Washington's continuing support of Israel's occupation directly conflicted with three of the greatest ideals of the American republic: human rights, the inadmissibility of acquiring territory by force and the Wilsonian tenet that all people have the right of self-determination. All of these basic American ideals were flagrantly violated by Israel's occupation. Washington's acquiescence in this defiance over a period of so many years brought into question, in many parts of the world, the sincerity and reliability of the United States as a nation committed to its own widely proclaimed ideals.

Further, after the war the United States found itself Israel's only major friend. France finally severed its long-term weapons aid and as a consequence Washington became Israel's new arms supplier. The cost was considerable. Not only did the United States give to Israel its most advanced and sophisticated weapons, but by the 1980s it was directly paying for 37 percent of Israel's total defense budget. In fiscal 1983, U.S. military aid had climbed to $1.7 billion, nearly half of which ($750 million) was an outright grant and the rest a loan on extremely concessionary terms (a ten-year grace period followed by twenty years of repayment at low interest rates). This aid was in addition to economic support, which in 1983 amounted to $785 million, all of it in the form of a grant given directly to Israel without any controls.

Nor did the costs to America stop with direct aid to Israel. To assure Israel's peace treaty with Egypt, Washington in 1983 awarded Cairo $425 million in military and $750 million in economic aid, all of it outright gifts. Thus, the United States in 1983 had devoted 58 percent of all its Foreign Economic Support Funds to two countries, 30 percent to Israel and 28 percent to Egypt. (The rest, $1.125 billion, was divided up among thirty-one countries.)

Beyond aid, the United States also found itself by late 1983 with American troops stationed to the north and south of Israel and the Sixth Fleet to the west to help guarantee Israel's security. To the east was King Hussein's Jordan, which over the years the United States had supported in part because of its moderate attitude toward Israel. In the Sinai, Americans were serving with the Multinational Force and Observers organization that was established in 1982 when Israel finally returned the peninsula to Egypt. More than half of the force's two thousand troops and observers were Americans and the United States was picking up one third of the force's cost. In Lebanon, around 1,800 U.S. Marines were participating in a separate multinational force created as a result of Israel's invasion exactly fifteen years after the 1967 war. Off the coast was a large contingent of the Sixth Fleet, including three aircraft carrier task forces, plus the only U.S. battleship in commission, the *New Jersey*. Marine casualties were already well over two hundred and likely to go higher.

In addition to the financial costs to the United States, the 1967 war left the Suez Canal closed and major world trade routes in chaos. As in 1956, Egypt had scuttled ships to block the canal, and this time it would remain closed for years. In 1966, twenty-one thousand ships had transited the canal; now there would be none. The closure, according to a CIA report written on the second day of the war, would "temporarily disrupt world trade, necessitate expensive rerouting of commerce and compel adjustment in patterns of trade, particularly in crude petroleum. Western Europe, particularly Italy, will be the most seriously affected. A number of other countries will also be hurt. India and Pakistan, which receive large imports of grain from the United States through the Suez, will have to pay more to have grain shipped around Africa. . . . It will increase the landed cost of Iranian crude oil to Western Europe by some twenty percent, the average time required for . . . US grain deliveries to India from twenty-three days to twenty-nine days."

Although the United States had its own abundant petroleum supplies at the time, U.S. oil operations suffered. American oil companies were shut down briefly in Iraq, Libya and Saudi Arabia, and shipments to the United States and the United Kingdom were embargoed in those countries as well as Abu Dhabi, Algeria, Kuwait and Qatar. Algeria also took the opportunity to nationalize five U.S. oil firms. In addition, twenty-six thousand Americans had fled the Middle East; the 250 U.S. citizens in Jordan were finally flown out on June 11.

Then there was the tragedy of the *Liberty* with its heavy casualties. The survivors were all ordered not to speak with the press, and the incident was quietly brushed under the carpet. A naval board of inquiry accepted the Israeli version and duly pronounced the attack an accident. The crew was scattered to various commands and the *Liberty,* on which $20 million had been spent to convert it into a SIGINT ship and another $10 million on its electronics hardware, was decommissioned on June 28, 1968, and was sold for scrap for $101,666.66.*

The U.S. government asked Israel for only $7,644,146 to cover the loss of the *Liberty,* but for years Israel refused to pay and Washington did not press the matter. The reason for Washington's inactivity, Dean Rusk later observed tartly, was that "in light of our aid programs for Israel, we would, in effect, be paying ourselves." Israel finally agreed to partial payment thirteen years later at a time when its U.S. aid had soared to more than $2 billion annually, much of it in the form of outright grants. It agreed on December 18, 1980, to pay $6 million in three annual payments—if the United States agreed to drop interest payments on the original claim, which then totaled more than $10 million. President Jimmy Carter acquiesced and the matter was finally settled legally—but not emotionally. Members of the *Liberty* crew remained bitter toward their own government and toward Israel for the attack.

The government effort to downplay the incident followed the dead to their graves. The gravestone placed in Arlington National Cemetery, where six of the killed were interred, said merely: "Died in the Eastern Mediterranean." The inscription infuriated many of the survivors, who complained that it sounded as though the men had died in a Middle Eastern brothel rather than in combat. They eventually formed a survivors' association and through persistent pressure on the government had the inscription changed on October 6, 1982, to one reading: "Killed USS Liberty." It was not much of an improvement, but at least it was closer to the truth.

A similar concern to avoid reminders about the attack was displayed when Commander McGonagle was awarded the Medal of Honor, the nation's highest award. The written citation mentioned an attack by jets and torpedo boats, but did not identify their nationality. When the award was

---

* After litigation, the Israeli government paid $3,566,457 as compensation to the wounded on April 28, 1969. It voluntarily paid $3,323,500 to the families of the killed in June 1968.

presented on June 11, 1968, it was not by the President but by the secretary of the navy, and it was presented not in the White House but at the Navy Yard in Washington.

Despite all these efforts at removing the memory of the *Liberty,* many senior government officials were convinced, and remain so, that the attack, for whatever reasons, was deliberate. In a letter to survivor Jim Ennes, Dean Rusk wrote in 1981: "I still do not know at what level in the Israel government the attacks were launched, but I am convinced that it was not trigger-happy local commanders." His view was widely shared.

Thus, although the U.S.-Israel relationship remains strong, its costs to the United States were increasingly being questioned in 1983. A democratic, rational and enlightened Israel was worth the expense. An expansionist and ungrateful Israel working at odds against U.S. national interests might begin to be perceived as less worthwhile.

It is one of history's most sorrowful ironies that the Jews of Israel have created for the Palestinians their own diaspora and saga of suffering every bit as poignant as the Jews' own odyssey. In the process, the nature of Israel itself is changing, and may have already changed far more profoundly than is generally realized. Washington's acquiescence to Israel's hardliners directly contributed to the coming to power in 1977 of Menachem Begin. That watershed event signaled the triumph of harsh Old Testament mysticism over the liberal and rational Judaism that was practiced by many of Israel's early founders. Whether this triumph is only temporary, as many Israelis and their supporters hope, or whether it is permanent, as Begin and his fanatical supporters like Ariel Sharon and Moshe Arens believe, will largely determine the nature of the future Israel.

Begin's resignation on September 15, 1983, and his replacement by Foreign Minister Yitzhak Shamir as prime minister was not an encouraging development for Israeli liberals. Shamir was a sixty-seven-year-old carbon copy of Begin, a native of Poland (his original name was Yezernitzky) who emigrated to Palestine in 1935 and quickly became a member of the Irgun, the terrorist group Begin eventually headed. He soon joined an even more radical terrorist cell, Lehi, the Lohamei Herut Israel (the Fighters for the Freedom of Israel), better known as the Stern Gang, so named after its unbalanced leader, Abraham Stern.

The Stern Gang was responsible for numerous assassinations of British officials as well as the killing of Lord Moyne, the British resident minister in Cairo in 1944, and, it is widely suspected, the assassination of Count Bernadotte in Jerusalem in 1948. As one of the three leaders of the Stern Gang after Stern himself was killed by British police in 1942, Shamir planned and approved a number of assassinations, including Lord Moyne's—acts that Shamir years later still defended. "It was the only way we could operate because we were so small," he is quoted as saying in the late 1970s in Nicholas Bethell's book *The Palestine Triangle.* "So it was more efficient and more moral to go to selected targets. . . . We were aiming at a political goal. There are many examples of what we did to be found in the Bible—Gideon and Samson, for instance."

After Israel's establishment, Shamir joined the shadowy world of intelligence as a Mossad agent, operating mainly in Europe. He retired in 1965 and in 1973 was elected to the Knessset as a member of Begin's party. He rose quickly through the ranks and became speaker of the body when Begin came to power in 1977. While in that position Shamir opposed the Camp David peace accord with Egypt, in part because it pledged the two parties to U.N. Resolution 242, which Shamir never accepted. He became foreign minister in 1980, after Moshe Dayan's resignation, and in that post was criticized by the Israeli commission that studied the circumstances of the massacre of hundreds of Palestinians in the refugee camps of Sabra and Shatila in September 1982. The Kahan Commission found that Shamir had failed to act on warnings that the killings were taking place.

The changes in Israel can be seen in areas other than the character of its latest nationalist leaders like Begin and Shamir. In recent years more Israelis have left than immigrants arrived. According to a study by Israel's Ministry of Labor and Social Welfare, 510,528 Israelis emigrated and only 384,000 Jews immigrated in the period between 1969 and 1979. Many of the émigrés have moved to the United States, which now has an Israeli community equaling at least 10 percent of Israel's total Jewish population of 3.3 million.

These figures represent an enormous turnover of the Israeli population—a full 25 percent in ten years, according to the Labor Ministry study—and could be responsible for bringing about changes fundamental to the basic nature of Israel. No study apparently exists of the types of Israelis leaving and the new immigrants, but the impression of some observers is that the most moderate members of the society are the ones making up the majority of the new émigrés. In turn, the new immigrants appear to be largely extremists fired by Menachem Begin's brimstone vision. If so, the basic nature of Israel may already have dramatically altered to reflect more closely the views of Menachem Begin and Yitzhak Shamir. That is a dark vision whose fulfillment could have profoundly detrimental results for Israel.

In late 1983, the time of this writing, no one concerned about world peace can feel optimistic about the chances for finding a solution to the conflict in the Middle East. The Reagan peace plan appears a dead issue, spurned by Israel and the PLO and distrusted by the Arabs. The Soviet Union has introduced new and deadlier missiles, SAM-5s, along with thousands of Soviet advisers, in Syria, and Israeli officials are making threatening sounds toward Damascus. Lebanon, despite the withdrawal agreement with Israel, remains a quagmire, rent by communal violence, Arab-Israeli conflict and U.S.-U.S.S.R. competition.

Although Israel disavowed any territorial ambitions and promised an immediate withdrawal after dispersing the PLO, its actions have been different. It seems likely that Menachem Begin and Yitzhak Shamir will finally realize David Ben Gurion's and Moshe Dayan's old dream. The gist of that was recorded by former Prime Minister Moshe Sharett in his diary on May 16, 1955: "According to [Dayan], the only thing that's necessary for Israel to expand into part of Lebanon is to find an officer, even just a major. We could either win his heart or buy him with money, to make him agree to declare himself the savior of the Maronite population. Then the Israeli army will enter Lebanon, will occupy the necessary territory, and will create a Christian regime which will ally itself with Israel. The territory from the Litani River southward will be totally annexed to Israel and everything will be all right."

Shamir seems determined to absorb southern Lebanon either by outright occupation or, more likely, through the use of such surrogates as Saad Haddad, interestingly a Christian and a maverick major from the Lebanese Army. Only in one aspect was Sharett's diary entry essentially wrong. The Israelis are now dug in at the Awali River, which is north of the Litani.

It may already be too late to prevent the next war. Arab hatred by now has become so ingrained and Israeli intransigence so adamant that nothing short of a war may be capable of changing the attitude of either side. That does not, however, absolve the United States from doing its utmost to break the impasse, to live up to its words uttered in secrecy, as to King Hussein, and to try to prevent the explosion that is likely to come.

U.S. inaction in the past has already placed a great burden of guilt on it for Israel's increasingly bellicose behavior. Johnson, by his unrestrained support of Israel in the critical period immediately after the war, failed to give Israel the guidance it needed. His actions vitiated the authority of the moderates, reinforced the positions of the hardliners like Begin and encouraged their intransigent behavior. Nothing worse could have happened to Israel, for it turned Israelis from pioneers into occupiers, from a suffering people seeking peace into persecutors sowing hatred.

The Jewish American community must accept its share of responsibility in this tragic development. Like Lyndon Johnson, the community supported uncritically or passively acquiesced in whatever actions Israel took. Its silence denied tiny Israel the community's wisdom and, again, encouraged the reckless behavior of Israel's extremist elements.

Only when Washington and the Jewish American community realize that their responsibilities toward Israel extend beyond automatic support will there occur the chance of finally achieving Israel's security. Then a more moderate, more accommodating Israel may finally encourage moderates among the Arabs. Up to now, Israel's overwhelming strength and its unbending, aggressive policies have significantly contributed to the very militancy among the Arabs that Israel has repeatedly pointed to as the root cause of the Middle East conflict. But it has been Israeli militancy over the years—its refusal to deal with the refugee problem, its unprovoked launching of the 1956 war, its ruthless "retaliatory" raids, its arrogant flaunting of its superiority in the occupied territories—that has encouraged Arab extremists. Its unforgiving attitude and its unhesitant use of its mighty military forces to crush its enemies under whatever pretext has left the Arab world humiliated and frustrated, determined at whatever price to regain its pride.

It should be amply clear by now that Israel's security cannot be attained by further humiliating the Arabs. Eisenhower tried to tell Israel that more than a quarter of a century ago, and was roundly condemned for his wise counsel. His failure should not deter Israel's friends from trying again.

Of one thing there can be no question: It is only by living in friendship that Israel has a chance of living in peace. It cannot forever continue to blame the Arabs solely for the conflict. It takes two to fight, and both sides have been doing more than their share for thirty-five years. If they do not soon try to be friends, to be more openhearted and generous of spirit, more conscious and tolerant of the deep religious stirrings that motivate both peoples, no one can doubt that wars far more horrible than any witnessed in the Middle East await Arabs and Israelis alike.

Not only must Arabs and Israelis begin to reconsider their attitudes and actions toward each other, but Americans and Israelis should take a sober look at the increasingly complex relationship that has grown between them. It already has many unhealthy aspects, not the least of them being Israel's almost total dependence on the United States.

Despite such dependence, Israel under Menachem Begin seemed to delight in ignoring and at times defying U.S. interests and thereby making America an accessory, however unwilling, of such rash actions as the bombing of Iraq's nuclear facility and the inhumane siege and bombardment of Beirut with its thousands of innocent victims. No major power, certainly no democracy, should tolerate such defiance. Yet defiance may be an inevitable byproduct of the relationship itself. It is too early to assess Shamir's stewardship, but now at its beginning is a good time to re-examine the relationship.

Nearly two centuries ago, George Washington warned about the dangers of such a relationship in his memorable Farewell Address. It would be prudent and perhaps profitable for Americans and Israelis to reflect on his words today. They are uncannily prophetic in describing many aspects of the association that has emerged in recent years between the United States and Israel.

Washington said on September 17, 1796:

". . . a passionate attachment of one nation for another produces a variety of evils. Sympathy for the favorite nation, facilitating the illusion of an imaginary common interest, in cases where no real common interest exists, and infusing into one the enmities of the other, betrays the former into a participation in the quarrels and wars of the latter, without adequate inducements or justifications. It leads also to concessions to the favorite nation, of privileges denied to others, which is apt doubly to injure the nation making the concessions, by unnecessarily parting with what ought to have been retained, and by exciting jealousy, ill will, and a disposition to retaliate in the parties from whom equal privileges are withheld; and it gives to ambitious, corrupted or deluded citizens who devote themselves to the favorite nation, facility to betray or sacrifice the interests of their own country, without odium, sometimes even with popularity; gilding with the appearances of a virtuous sense of obligation, a commendable deference for public opinion, or a laudable zeal for public good, the base of foolish compliances of ambition, corruption, or infatuation.

"As avenues to foreign influence in innumerable ways, such attachments are particularly alarming to the truly enlightened and independent patriot. How many opportunities do they afford to tamper with domestic factions, to practise the arts of seduction, to mislead public opinion, to influence or awe the public councils!—Such an attachment of a small or weak, towards a great and powerful nation, dooms the former to be the satellite of the latter.

"Against the insidious wiles of foreign influence (I conjure you to believe me, fellow citizens), the jealousy of a free people ought to be *constantly* awake; since history and experience prove that foreign influence is one of the most baneful foes of republican government. . . ."

___CHRONOLOGY___

135 A.D.   The Jewish Diaspora begins.
After more than a millennium of living in Palestine, the end of the Jewish presence came when a general by the name of Bar Kochba rose up against Roman rule. He conquered Jerusalem and hoped to found another Israeli kingdom, but the Romans reacted mercilessly. The rebels were decimated and so many Israelis were carted off to the slave markets that one report said an Israeli slave could be bought for the price of a horse's ration. Emperor Hadrian moved to eradicate all aspects of Israeli national life. He renamed the Israeli province of Judea to Syria-Palestina and changed Jerusalem to Aelia Capitolina. He sternly decreed that henceforth Israelis could visit the sacred city only once a year to pray at the ruined Temple. Though small communities remained, the Israelis' days in Palestine were over, or so it seemed. They were now scattered around the world in the great Diaspora.

570   Mohammed born in Mecca.
Mohammed gave the world its third great monotheistic religion, borrowing heavily from both Judaism and Christianity, and claiming—as the Christians had to the Jews—that Islam was the enlightened successor of both of the older religions. His fiery teachings ignited a religious crusade that gave rise to one of the great civilizations. His converts poured out of the Arabian Peninsula and within a century conquered the Persian Empire, Egypt, most of northern Africa, half of Byzantine Asia, Spain and Palestine.

638   Jerusalem captured by the Arabs.
After a four-month siege, Jerusalem fell to the Arab army. It had become venerable to Islam after Mohammed had a vision that he was transported to the storied city by a winged horse which then used the old Jewish Temple Mount to take him to heaven and back. Moslems, "submitters to the will of God," proved to be more tolerant masters than Christians, who ruled Jerusalem under the Roman and later the Byzantium empires. The Moslems encouraged their captives to convert, which many of the Palestinians did, but when Jews and

others refused, they were allowed to live in Jerusalem and practice their religion openly in return for homage and tribute.

691   Moslems build shrine in Jerusalem.

Followers of Mohammed completed a shrine on the Temple Mount around the stone from which Mohammed began his heavenly trip, a sign of their reverence for Jerusalem and known as the fabulous Qubbet es Sakhra, better known in Christendom as the Dome of the Rock, which still graces the Temple Mount today. For most of the next twelve centuries Islam ruled Palestine and large sections of the Mediterranean and Eastern worlds with enlightenment, scientific achievement and tolerance. The ascendancy of Islam brought a golden age for Jews, particularly in Spain but also in Arab areas such as Egypt and Morocco between the tenth and thirteenth centuries. Restrictions imposed by Christians against the practice of their religion were repealed or ignored and Jews were allowed to enter fully in the life of most of the Islamic nations. In Spain, they enjoyed their greatest freedom and rose to positions of power and wealth as physicians, landowners, financiers and statesmen. During this tolerant age there was no major effort to re-establish a Jewish homeland in Palestine, though some few hearty Jewish pilgrims returned to the ancient hills of Judea and Samaria.

1099   Crusaders capture Jerusalem.

The explosive force of Islam shocked Christian Europe into a religious reawakening. Its answer to this alien threat was the First Crusade, whose members captured Jerusalem on July 15 and celebrated this memorable religious moment by slaying Moslem and Jew alike in a bloodbath that took at least seventy thousand lives.

1181   The beginning of modern anti-Semitism.

The revival of militant Christianity as signified by the Crusades began the modern period of anti-Semitism in Europe. The first Crusaders marched to the Holy Land over Jewish blood. In Speyer, Mainz, Trier, Cologne, Worms, Metz, Regensburg and Prague Diaspora Jews were slain indiscriminately in the name of Christ. Anti-Semitism raged through much of the Holy Roman Empire, and once again Jews moved eastward in Europe and southward to Arab lands to find tolerance in the Moslem empire.

1187   Arabs recapture Jerusalem.

The Ayyubid Sultan Saladin, a Kurd who proved to be one of Islam's most enlightened rulers, captured Jerusalem on October 2 with a minimum of bloodshed and a maximum of good will among the populace, including his Crusader victims. Crusaders reoccupied Jerusalem for fifteen years in the thirteenth century, finally losing it in October 1244, and then all of their presence in Palestine in 1291. From that time Jerusalem and Palestine remained in Moslem hands until the end of World War I.

1182   Jews expelled from France.

1215   Catholic Church decrees badges for Jews.

Official anti-Semitism was codified at the Fourth Lateran Council under the leadership of Pope Innocent III. The council decreed that Jews could not hold public office or employ Christian servants and that they must wear a distinctive garment or badge to distinguish them from non-Jews.

1290   Jews expelled from Britain.

1492   Jews expelled from Spain.

1493   Jews expelled from Sicily.

1495   Jews expelled from Lithuania.

1496   Jews expelled from Portugal.

1510   Jews expelled from Brandenburg.

1517   Palestine comes under control of Ottoman Turks.

The Moslem Turks opened Palestine to Jewish immigration, and over the sixteenth and seventeenth centuries several evangelical Jewish leaders led groups of Jews to settle in the Holy Land. By the early seventeenth century, there were reported to be twenty to thirty thousand Jews living in Safed, the largest Jewish community in Palestine.

1517   Martin Luther nails his theses to church door.

At noon on October 31, Luther affixed his theses, *Disputatio pro declaratione virtutis indulgentiarum,* on the main door of the Castle Church of Wittenberg, thus launching the great Reformation of the Catholic Church and the rise of Protestantism. The wave of religious toleration that slowly emerged from these events tended to mute anti-Semitism and make life for Jews in Europe somewhat more tolerable, although Luther himself in 1544 attacked Jews on charges of deicide.

1541   Jews expelled from Naples and Prague.

1648–49   Pogroms in the Ukraine takes the lives of thousands of Jews.

1775   Catholic Church issues *Edict Concerning the Jews.*

Under Pope Pius VI, the church called for restrictions on relations between Christians and Jews, and charges against Jews of deicide were alluded to in the edict.

1775 and 1789   The American and French revolutions.

The revolutions in the United States and France increased personal freedom and lessened religious bigotry throughout much of the Western world, and had the effect of making the lot of the Jews easier in the Christian countries. Jews were granted equal rights by the U.S. Declaration of Independence in 1776 and, briefly, by the Constituent Assembly of the French Revolution between 1790–91.

1796   Jews receive equal rights in Holland.

1798   Napoleon Bonaparte invades Egypt.

Napoleon's forces, seeking to oust Britain from its Asian empire, remained in the Middle East only three years before being defeated. But the young French general managed to penetrate across the Sinai wastes and kill and plunder as far north as Acre, where an Anglo-Turkish force finally stopped his advance in May 1799. A month before that, while in Palestine, Napoleon had attempted to secure the support of the area's few thousand Jews by telling the Chief Rabbi of Jerusalem on April 20: "Now is the moment, which may not return for thousands of years, to claim the restoration of civic rights among the population of the universe which has been shamefully withheld from you for thousands of years, your political existence as a natural right to worship Jehovah in accordance with your faith. . . ." His appeal was received warmly, but there were too few Jews to influence the battle. Palestine remained in the hands of the Turkish Ottoman Empire.

1830   Jews receive equal rights in France.

1849 Jews receive equal rights in Denmark.

1858 Jews receive equal rights in England.

1867 Jews receive equal rights in Austria-Hungary.

1870 Jews receive equal rights in Italy.

1871 Jews receive equal rights in Germany.

1874 Jews receive equal rights in Switzerland.

1876 Jews receive equal rights in Spain.

1878 Jews receive equal rights in Balkan States.

1881 Russian Jews begin moving to Palestine.
Under the official anti-Semitism and pogroms of tsarist Russia, Jews began fleeing Eastern Europe, some of them moving to Palestine. In two waves lasting up to 1891 an estimated twenty-five thousand—equal to the number of Jews then living in Palestine—arrived in Palestine, though few of them remained in the primitive country that was populated by a vast majority of Palestinians. The liberal secularism loosed by the revolutions in America and France started giving way in Europe to chauvinistic nationalism that in turn led to the open questioning of the loyalty of Jews to their adopted countries. Virulent anti-Semitism, symbolized by the 1894 Dreyfus affair in France, began again sweeping through Europe.

1882 Britain captures Egypt.
British concern for the security of its trade route to its rich colony of India led to the conquest of Egypt. The Suez Canal had been opened in 1869 and it represented the most direct route from Britain to its Asian empire. The British presence in Egypt eventually led to its expansion to other Middle Eastern regions.

1897 Zionist Organization founded.
The renewal of European anti-Semitism led to the establishment of the Zionist Organization, dedicated to the founding of a national homeland for Jews. Expression of the Jews' feelings was given the year before by Austrian journalist Theodor Herzl in his seminal book *The Jewish State*. He wrote: "In countries where we have lived for centuries we are still cried down as strangers." Jews, he added, needed a homeland "where we may at last have hooked noses, black and red beards, bow legs, without being despised for it . . . where the offensive cry 'Jew' may become an honorable appellation like German, Englishman, Frenchman. . . . We are a people—one people." Jews from fifteen countries, including a number from Europe, the United States and Palestine, gathered August 29 at the Stadt Casino in Basle, Switzerland, and established the Zionist Organization, whose aim, they declared, was "a Jewish homeland openly recognized, legally secured." Several areas for settlement of the homeland were considered, including Uganda. But when Palestine was finally chosen, a misleading motto spread: "A people without a land for a land without a people."

1914 World War I.
One of the results of the war that took an estimated eight million lives was the final dismemberment of the Turkish Ottoman Empire. At its peak in the sixteenth century the empire had extended east to Persia, including Palestine, north to the Ukraine, south along the Mediterranean coast to beyond Tunisia and west to the gates of Vienna. The empire had reached its height in 1529 when

Sultan Suleiman the Magnificent threatened Vienna and Central Europe. His failure started the long, slow disintegration that earned the empire the reputation of being the "sick man of Europe" and set generations of covetous European politicians plotting to hasten the death. But the empire proved resilient and at the time of World War I the Moslem Turks still retained Palestine and other territories. Suspecting British and French intentions to divide up what was left of the empire, Turkey joined with Germany and the Central Powers against the Allies—and lost the empire, including Palestine.

1916 Britain promises Arabs independence.

In an effort to gain Arab support in World War I, British High Commissioner to Egypt and the Sudan Sir Henry McMahon wrote a series of letters to Sharif Hussein ibn Ali of the Hejaz in Arabia (great-grandfather of the current king of Jordan, Hussein) pledging Arab independence. The four McMahon letters, written between August 30, 1915, and January 30, 1916, formed the legal basis for Arab expectations that the end of the war would bring them their own homeland, including Palestine, free of Ottoman rule.

1916 Britain and France divide up Middle East.

In a secret arrangement called the Sykes-Picot Agreement, London and Paris on October 23 agreed between themselves that after the war Britain would control the Baghdad part of the region, including Palestine, and France the Damascus part.

1917 Balfour promises Jews homeland in Palestine.

The British also sought to win the support of world Jewry in World War I by endorsing the idea of a national homeland for the Jews in Palestine. On November 2 British Foreign Secretary Arthur Balfour issued what has become known as the Balfour Declaration, proclaiming that "His Majesty's Government view with favor the establishment in Palestine of a national home for the Jewish people ... it being clearly understood that nothing shall be done which may prejudice the civil and religious rights of existing non-Jewish communities in Palestine ..." The declaration was denounced by Arabs and hailed by Jews. Thereafter it served as the Zionists' asserted basis for their aspirations to found in the ancient Holy Land a Jewish homeland, "openly recognized, legally secured." However, Britain maintained that it did not imply support for a Jewish state or Jewish control of all of Palestine.

1917 Jews receive equal rights in the Soviet Union.

1919 King-Crane Commission report on Palestine.

To ascertain local attitudes toward a Jewish national home in Palestine President Woodrow Wilson, who believed one of the goals of the war had been the principle of self-determination for all people, dispatched Henry C. King and Charles R. Crane on March 20 on a fact-finding mission to Palestine. On August 28 they issued their negative report. "The non-Jewish population of Palestine—nearly nine-tenths of the whole—are emphatically against the entire Zionist program," they reported. "There was no one thing upon which the population of Palestine was more agreed than upon this. To subject people so minded to unlimited Jewish immigration, and to steady financial and social pressure to surrender the land, would be a gross violation of the principle of self-determination just quoted, and of the people's rights, though it kept within the forms of law.... Yet the fact came out repeatedly in the commission's conference with Jewish representatives that the Zionists looked forward to practically complete dispossession of the present non-Jewish inhabitants of Palestine.... No British officer ... believed that the Zionist program could be carried out except by force of arms." The report was ignored and had no influence on American or British policy.

1920 First anti-Zionist riot by Palestinians.
The Zionist campaign to populate Palestine with Jews frightened and angered the native Palestinians. They feared that the Jews were intent on taking away their land and they expressed their suspicions by rioting. The first anti-Zionist riot occurred in April and resulted in the deaths of five Jews and the wounding of more than two hundred. Still the Zionist immigrants arrived.

1921 More Palestinian riots.
In May, Palestinians protesting continued Jewish immigration rioted in Jaffa and five rural settlements, killing 47 Jews and wounding 146. A British commission of inquiry under Sir Thomas Haycraft concluded: "The fundamental cause of the Jaffa riots ... was a feeling among the Arabs of discontent with, and hostility to the Jews, due to political and economic causes, and connected with Jewish immigration, and with their conception of Zionist policy as derived from Jewish exponents."

1922 Britain takes over Palestine and Jerusalem.
On July 24, under a League of Nations mandate, the still thriving British Empire took control of Palestine. It was a neglected and impoverished area, despite Zionist immigration, with fewer than a million inhabitants: 598,177 Moslems, 83,790 Jews, 71,464 Christians (many of them Palestinian Arabs) and 7,617 "others," in the words of the first official census. But as their spoils of war Britain and France enforced the secret Sykes-Picot Agreement they had concluded with each other early in the war. They divided the former territories of the Ottoman Empire between themselves, with France creating Lebanon out of Syria and being given the mandate over both of the countries. (Syria to this day has never officially recognized the existence of Lebanon and has no official diplomatic relations with it.) Britain created modern Iraq, Jordan and Palestine as separate administrative units for its mandate, which assured it in-depth protection of the Suez Canal. Britain had ruled Egypt since 1882, and with its new mandate nations it now had possession of an entire region from which any threat could possibly come to its vital waterway, which led to the "jewel of empire," Britain's fabulously profitable Indian colony. By controlling Iraq, along with its predominant position in the Persian Gulf, it also assured oil supplies for British industry and the Royal Navy, which had converted its ships from coal to oil in 1911. But Britain was caught in a dilemma. The McMahon letters and the Balfour Declaration had made contradictory promises to Arabs and Jews that London could not possibly honor.

1922 British White Paper on Palestine.
Stirred by Palestinian protests about British policy in Palestine, London issued a policy statement in June denying that the Balfour Declaration had supported the creation of a Jewish homeland in all of Palestine. "His Majesty's Government ... would draw attention to the fact that the terms of the Balfour Declaration do not contemplate that Palestine as a whole should be converted into a Jewish National Home, but that such a Home should be founded *in Palestine*.... The Secretary of State is of opinion that the declaration does not contain or imply anything which need cause either alarm to the Arab population or disappointment to the Jews."

1929   Jews chased from Hebron.
The ancient city of Hebron, fabled as the burial place of patriarchs Abraham, Isaac and Jacob, was venerated by Jew and Moslem alike. Riots touched off by suspicions of Jewish infringement on the Temple Mount in Jerusalem led to the murder of sixty Jews and the ouster of all other Jews in Hebron. Countrywide the casualty toll came to 133 Jews killed and 339 wounded during the disturbance between August 23 and August 29. Palestinians suffered 116 dead and 232 wounded.

1930   Shaw Commission report on Palestinian riots.
Britain appointed a commission under Sir Walter Shaw to investigate the causes of the 1929 riots. In March it reported, among other things: "The news that this expectation [of Jewish financial support for Zionist immigrants] had been realized would quickly spread and was, in our opinion, a cause of increased apprehension and alarm among all classes of Arabs." At the time there were in Palestine 771,174 Moslems, 164,796 Jews, 84,986 Christians and 9,628 others.

1933   Adolf Hitler becomes chancellor of Germany.
Hitler, born April 20, 1889, in Austria, son of a customs inspector, a high-school dropout, a World War I corporal, rejected by Vienna's Academy of Fine Arts and so poor he lived in the streets of Vienna as a bum, became chancellor of Germany on January 30. That night at a small private dinner in Berlin with his closest associates, he said: "Some foreign source today called me 'anti-Christ.' The only kind of anti I am is anti-Lenin." But he was anti many things, as many Jews already suspected. Jewish immigration into Palestine that year soared to 30,327. The year before it had been only 9,553. Immigration continued to climb sharply until it hit a prewar peak in 1935 of 61,854, causing continued distress and resentment among the Palestinians.

1937   Peel Commission report on Palestinian riots.
Riots and strikes by Palestinians throughout most of 1936 led to eighty Jews and an estimated thousand Palestinians being killed. London ordered another commission to investigate once again the causes of the violence. In June the commission headed by Lord Robert Peel reported that the underlying cause of the riots was the same as it had been since the 1920 riots: "The desire of the Arabs for national independence and their hatred and fear of the establishment of a Jewish National Homeland." Prophetically, the commission added: "It was believed by Palestinians that ... further growth of a Jewish homeland might mean the political as well as economic subjection of the Arabs to the Jews, so that, if ultimately the British Mandate should terminate and Palestine become independent, it would not be national independence in the Arab sense but self-government by a Jewish majority." By this time Jewish immigration had brought the number of Jews living in Palestine to 386,074 compared to 875,947 Moslems and 109,764 Christians.

1938   British study partition of Palestine.
A commission appointed to investigate ways to divide Palestine into Arab and Jewish nations, as recommended in the Peel Commission report, spent three months in Palestine studying the situation and then failed to agree on any practical plan. Another White Paper issued simultaneously with the commission's report gloomily concluded: "... the political, administrative and financial difficulties involved in the proposal to create independent Arab and Jewish States inside Palestine are so great that this solution of the problem is impracticable."

1939   London Conference on Palestine.

Unable to devise a workable plan of its own, the British government convened a meeting in London with Arab and Jewish representatives. The Arabs would not recognize the Jewish Agency of Palestine, which was the de facto government of the Jews in Palestine, so British officials had to meet separately with each side. In talks lasting from February 7 to March 15, Britain proposed that both sides start with the assumption that a Jewish nation could not occupy all of Palestine. The Arabs agreed but the Jews rejected the idea in principle and no agreement was reached.

1939   British White Paper on Palestine.

In an effort to clarify its mandate policy, which remained torn between Britain's conflicting promises to Jews and Palestinians alike, the British government in May issued a White Paper that spelled out its objectives and prepared the way for an end to the mandate. The British government had concluded, the paper said, "unequivocally that it is not part of their policy that Palestine should become a Jewish state." It added: "They . . . cannot agree that the McMahon correspondence forms a just basis for the claim that Palestine should be converted into an Arab state." Britain's objective henceforth would be "the establishment within ten years of an independent Palestine state . . . in which Arabs and Jews share in government in such a way as to ensure that the essential interests of each community are safeguarded." Because Jewish immigration was continuing as a result of Hitler's anti-Semitic policies in Germany and continued to be sharply protested by the Arabs, Jewish immigration for the coming five years, beginning in April 1939, would be limited to a total of 75,000 (Immigration the year before had equaled 12,868.) The paper added: "No further Jewish immigration will be permitted unless the Arabs of Palestine are prepared to acquiesce in it." Britain had also decided, said the paper, to prevent any futher Jewish purchase of land in Palestine. Jews at the time owned less than 6 percent of Palestine's 6,580,755 acres. The new policy was bitterly condemned at the Zionist Congress of 1939, which declared the Jewish people would not accept the status of a permanent minority in Palestine. The Arabs complained about the length of the transition period but they were generally well disposed to the British position.

1939   World War II.

The outbreak of war on September 1 turned the Palestine question into a sideshow, or so it seemed. By the time the war ended on May 8, 1945, in Europe and four months later in Asia on September 2, an estimated forty million persons had perished, including six million Jews. War's end brought the horrible revelations of Hitler's gas chambers and the currency of a despicable word: genocide. The incredible tales of the death camps—a mournful list that included such notorious names as Auschwitz, Belzec, Buchenwald, Lublin, Maidanek, Sobibor and Treblinka—sent a trauma of revulsion and disgust and shame throughout the West. It was a Christian nation, a nation that prided itself on its culture and Western civilization, that had committed one of the greatest atrocities in history against a lone and defenseless people. A tremendous swelling of sympathy engulfed the Western nations for the Jews and the Zionist aspiration to found a Jewish state. Such a state could give at long last succor and protection to the hundreds of thousands of homeless Jews in Europe's displaced persons' camps and a national home to all world Jewry. The Arabs, who had had no part in the atrocities, neither as oppressor nor victim, looked on with dismay as

370

sympathy for creation of a Jewish nation in Palestine spread throughout much of the Christian world.

1945 Roosevelt pledges support for Arabs.

President Franklin D. Roosevelt on February 14 met Saudi Arabian King Abdul Aziz ibn Saud aboard the U.S.S. *Quincy* in the Suez Canal and promised him that America would do nothing to harm the Arab cause in Palestine. He put his pledge in writing on April 5 in a letter to Saud: "Your Majesty will . . . doubtless recall that during our recent conversation I assured you that I would take no action . . . which might prove hostile to the Arab people. It gives me pleasure to renew to your Majesty the assurances which you have received regarding the attitude of my Government and my own, as Chief Executive, with regard to the question of Palestine and to inform you that the policy of this Government in this respect is unchanged." However, like so many politicians before and since, Roosevelt also had tried to pacify the Jews by supporting their cause, thus he fully backed the Palestine plank of the 1944 Democratic Convention which said: "We favor the opening of Palestine to unrestricted Jewish immigration and colonization, and such a policy is to result in the establishment there of a free and democratic Jewish commonwealth."

1946 Report of the Anglo-American Committee of Inquiry.

President Harry S Truman officially urged the British government in August 1945 to waive its five-year quota of 75,000 Jewish immigrants into Palestine and admit an extra 100,000 Jews from the displaced persons' camps in Europe. On April 20, the committee recommended that Truman's request be accepted but it added: "Jews shall not dominate Arab and Arab shall not dominate Jew in Palestine and Palestine shall be neither a Jewish state nor an Arab state." The British government feared the Arabs would react violently and declined to follow the commission's recommendation to increase immigration.

1946 Jewish terrorism spreads.

British limits on Jewish immigration to Palestine and also limits on the purchase of Arab land by Jews were bitterly resented in the Jewish community. Two underground terrorist groups, Lehi (Fighters for the Freedom of Israel), better known as the Stern Gang, and the Irgun Zvai Leumi (National Military Organization), resorted increasingly to violence against the British as the plight of European Jews became known. Many Jews now wanted to immigrate to Palestine but the British firmly enforced their quota on immigration, at times heartlessly turning back ships packed with desperate Jews seeking refuge in Palestine. The Jewish community in Palestine became enraged and its anger was taken out on the British by terrorists. They killed an average of two British policemen or troops a day in this period and attacked numerous British installations. The Stern Gang, whose leaders included Yitzhak Shamir, the foreign minister of Israel under the Begin government and in October 1983 Begin's successor, assassinated British Minister of State Lord Moyne in Cairo on November 6, 1944, and, it was widely suspected, United Nations representative Count Bernadotte of Sweden on September 17, 1948, in Jerusalem. On July 22, 1946, the Irgun terrorists, who were led by Menachem Begin, blew up a wing of the King David Hotel in Jerusalem, killing ninety-one Arabs, Britons and Jews. The two groups cooperated in the worst atrocity in Palestine in 1948 when on April 9 they attacked the small Arab village on Deir Yassin and killed 240 men, women and children, mutilating many of the bodies. Jewish terrorism became so vicious that in February 1947 all nonessential British civilians and military families were evacuated from Palestine. Though there were individual Arab terrorists, there was no organized terrorism during this period by the Arabs.

1946   Anglo-Arab London conference.

On September 9, representatives of the Arab states and British officials met to discuss the future of Palestine. Neither Jews nor Palestinians would at first attend the conference because they objected to Britain's plan to partition Palestine into Arab and Jewish nations. Though they later took part, both Jews and Palestinians rejected Britain's proposal that Jewish immigration be increased to ninety-six thousand per year, the Jews because they thought the figure too low and the Arabs because they thought it too high. London, debilitated by the war, drained by the cost of supporting 100,000 troops in Palestine, frustrated by the incessant attacks by Jewish terrorists, and restless to get out of the quagmire of Palestine, warned that "His Majesty's government are not prepared to continue indefinitely to govern Palestine themselves merely because Arabs and Jews cannot agree upon the means of sharing its government between them."

1947   Britain refers Palestine to the United Nations.

British Foreign Secretary Ernest Bevin informed the House of Commons on February 18 that Britain was unable to devise a workable solution acceptable to Arabs and Jews and therefore was referring the matter to the United Nations for resolution. "His Majesty's government have . . . been faced with an irreconcilable conflict of principles," Bevin said. "There are in Palestine about 1,200,000 Arabs and 600,000 Jews. For the Jews, the essential point of principle is the creation of a sovereign Jewish state. For the Arabs, the essential point of principle is to resist to the last the establishment of Jewish sovereignty in any part of Palestine. The discussions of the last month have quite clearly shown that there is no prospect of resolving this conflict by any settlement negotiated between the parties. We shall . . . ask the United Nations . . . to recommend settlement of the problem. We do not intend ourselves to recommend any particular solution."

1947   United Nations partitions Palestine.

On November 29, partition of Palestine into Arab and Jewish states was voted in the United Nations General Assembly by a thirty-three to thirteen majority. There were ten abstentions and one absent (Siam). The negative votes were cast by Afghanistan, Cuba, Egypt, Greece, India, Iran, Iraq, Lebanon, Pakistan, Saudi Arabia, Syria, Turkey and Yemen. The abstainers were Argentina, Chile, China, Colombia, El Salvador, Ethiopia, Honduras, Mexico, the United Kingdom and Yugoslavia. The Partition Plan awarded 56.47 percent of the land of Palestine to the proposed Jewish nation, though at the time there were 1,327,000 Palestinians and only 608,000 Jews in Palestine and Jews owned only 5.67 percent of the land. Nearly all of the rest was owned privately by Arabs or held as state domain for communal use by Palestinians. Jerusalem was declared a *corpus separatum* under international supervision and belonging to neither Arabs nor Jews. The Jewish Agency for Palestine immediately accepted the plan (although Begin and his Irgun denounced it); the Arabs rejected it. Despite widespread opposition within the State Department and at the Pentagon, President Truman ordered the government to actively support partition. He ignored a prescient memorandum sent him on September 22 by Loy W. Henderson, chief of the State Department's Office of Near Eastern and African Affairs. Henderson cautioned that partition was "not only unworkable; if adopted, it would guarantee that the Palestine problem would be permanent and still more complicated in the future." Then he commented on an issue that was causing concern among Jews and non-Jews alike. "The stress on whether persons are Jews or non-Jews is certain to strengthen feelings among both Jews and Gentiles in the United States and elsewhere that Jewish citizens are not the same as other citizens." He said his views were shared by "nearly every member of the Foreign Service or of the Department who has worked to any appreciable extent on Near Eastern problems." Yet political pressure to support partition was enormous. Under Secretary of State Robert A. Lovett said afterward that he had "never in his life been subject to as much pressure." Truman recalled: "I do not think I ever had as much pressure and propaganda aimed at the White House as I did in this instance."

1948   State of Israel proclaimed.

The British ended their mandate at midnight, May 14. But by 8 A.M. the Union Jack was hauled down from its last perch in Jerusalem and British troops began withdrawing early. Exactly eight hours later, at 4 P.M., David Ben Gurion, already acting as prime minister, stood in a Tel Aviv museum before two hundred select guests and declared that Israel now existed as an independent Jewish state. "Exiled from the land of Israel, the Jewish people remained faithful to it in all the countries of their dispersion, never ceasing to pray and hope for their return and the restoration of their national freedom," he said. The official declaration added: "We extend our hand in peace and neighborliness to all the neighboring states and their peoples, and invite them to cooperate with the independent Jewish nation for the common good of all. The State of Israel is prepared to make its contribution to the progress of the Middle East as a whole." No mention was made of the new nation's borders. When the matter had come up at a meeting with Jewish leaders before statehood, Ben Gurion dismissed the idea of mentioning borders by saying: "Why should we bind ourselves?" On orders from President Truman, the United States recognized Israel ten minutes after its creation, becoming the first nation to do so. Fighting between Jews and Palestinians had been going on intermittently since announcement of the Partition Plan the previous year and now full-scale war broke out. Armies of Egypt, Transjordan, Iraq, Lebanon and Syria invaded. When the fighting ended in 1949 the frontiers of Israel were enlarged from 5,893 square miles envisioned in the Partition Plan to 7,993 square miles, equal to 77.4 percent of Palestine. Approximately 725,000 Palestinians—nearly 60 percent of the Arab population—had been uprooted from their homes, in some cases driven out of them by Jewish terrorists, and turned into refugees. There was no truth to claims at the time that Arab leaders had appealed to the Palestinians in radio broadcasts to leave Palestine. There were now 1,013,000 Jews in the territory controlled by Israel and only 160,000 Palestinians. Jews occupied more than four hundred formerly Arab villages and towns, took over the empty Palestinian homes and shops, and settled in as the new owners. The Palestinians crowded into crude refugee camps in the surrounding Arab countries.

1956   Israel, Britain and France attack Egypt.

On October 29, Israel attacked Egypt in collusion with Britain and France in an effort to topple Gamal Abdel Nasser, the greatest Arab leader of his time. With British and French aerial and naval protection, the Israelis quickly conquered the Gaza Strip and the whole of the Sinai Peninsula. But President Dwight D. Eisenhower, invoking the U.N. Charter against the conquest of land by force, was appalled by the shoddy exercise and demanded that Israel return the captured territory to Egypt. Despite months of resistance by Israel and enormous pressure by the Israeli lobby in the United States, Eisenhower stuck by his position. His threat to impose sanctions against Israel and rescind the tax-free status of large contributions to it by private Americans finally forced Israel to surrender its war gains on March 16, 1957.

NOTES

PROLOGUE

Page
17 They began arriving: Sachar, H. M., *A History of Israel.*
17 The first rough: Elon, *The Israelis.*
17 Jerusalem itself was: *Ibid.*
17 Their total number: *Ibid.* Also see Sachar, H. M., *op. cit.*
17 Turkish authorities, fearful: Ben-Sasson, H. H. (ed.). *A History of the Jewish People.* Cambridge: Harvard University Press, 1976.
17 The concern of: *Ibid.*
17 Many of the: Sachar, H. M., *op. cit.*
18 Before the founding: Sachar, Abram Leon. *A History of the Jews.* New York: Alfred A. Knopf, 1974.
18 That began to: *Ibid.*
18 German Jews began: *Ibid.*
18 By the time: *Ibid.*
18 By World War I: *Ibid.*
18 National policy remained: Morison, Samuel Eliot. *The Oxford History of the American People.* New York: Oxford University Press, 1965.
19 In 1921, Congress: *Ibid.*
20 The pogrom of: Sachar, H. M., *op. cit.*
21 The movement was: *Ibid.* Also see Epp, *Whose Land Is Palestine?*
21 A powerful Zionist: Elon, *op. cit.*
21 When it officially: Epp, *op. cit.*
21 The first of: *Ibid.* Also see Sachar, H. M., *op. cit.*
22 Though East Europeans: Sachar, H. M., *op. cit.*
22 Yet the surge: Epp, *op. cit.*
22 In a far-ranging: Britannic Majesty's Government. *The Political History of Palestine Under British Administration.*
23 On November 29: Sachar, H. M., *op. cit.*
23 They bitterly noted: Epp, *op. cit.*
23 As a result: *Ibid.* Also see Cattan, *Palestine, the Arabs and Israel.*

CHAPTER 1

Page
31 Shortly after 7 A.M.: Dupuy, *Elusive Victory.*
32 For the past: *Ibid.*
32 The 725,000 Palestinians: UN A/6797*, *Report of the Special Representative's Mission to the Occupied Territories,* 15 Sept. 1967. Also see O'Ballance, *Arab Guerilla Power: 1967–1972.*
32 The groundwork for: Hirst, *The Gun and the Olive Branch.* Also see, Nyrop, *Jordan,* and Stephens, *Nasser.*
33 His caution was: Interview with King Hussein, Amman, Jordan, Aug. 3, 1983.
33 The battle "must": Hirst, *op. cit.*
33 The name of: Schleifer, *The Fall of Jerusalem.* Also see O'Ballance, *op. cit.*
33 He was actually: Cooley, *Green March, Black September.*
33 By 1964, despairing: Hirst, *op. cit.*
34 The first public: *Ibid.*
34 But then on: *Ibid.*
34 Other attacks soon: U.N. S/7277, letter from the representative of Israel to the president of the Security Council, 2 May 1966.
34 A U.N. observer: *Ibid.*
34 "Although boastful and": *Ibid.*
35 Although Fatah was: Hirst, *op. cit.*
36 As Israeli Ambassador: U.N. S/PV.1323, 18 Nov. 1966.
36 That point was: U.N. S/7277, *op. cit.*
36 On the night: U.N. S/7275, letter from the representative of Israel to the president of the Security Council, 2 May 1966.
36 The Mixed Armistice: U.N. S/7325, Annex, 16 May 1966.
37 But on February 23: Petran, *Syria.*
37 The spy, Eliahu: Aldouby, Zwy, and Jerrold Ballinger. *The Shattered Silence.* New York: Lancer Books, 1971.
37 He had provided: *Ibid.*
37 On April 18: Khouri, *The Arab-Israeli Dilemma.*
38 Israel retaliated on: *Ibid.*
38 On August 15: *Ibid.*
38 No longer, announced: *Ibid.*
38 Prime Minister Levi: *Ibid.*
38 Major General Yitzhak: *Ibid.*
38 On October 7: *Ibid.*
39 "We are not": Draper, *Israel and World Politics.*
39 Tensions between Israel: Laqueur, *The Road to War.*
39 The next day: *Ibid.*
39 Privately, the Soviets: Interview with James Critchfield, former CIA Mideast expert, June 1, 1983, McLean, Va.
39 On November 4: Brecher, *Decisions in Crisis.*
39 The U.N. Security: Khouri, *op. cit.*
40 Public anger had: U.N. S/PV.7587, 18 Nov. 1966.
40 On November 12: *Ibid.*
40 At dawn on: All details of the raid are based on U.N. S/7593, 18 Nov. 1966; and *Time,* Nov. 25, 1966.
41 "When a sovereign": Weizman, *On Eagles' Wings.*

CHAPTER II

Page
42 Correspondent Joe Alex Morris: Washington *Post,* Nov. 15, 1966.
43 Over the years: Newhouse, John. *The New Yorker,* Sept. 19, 1983.
44 Still, Hussein's rule: Snow, *Hussein.*
44 One of the worst: Washington *Post,* Nov. 25, 1966.
44 Jerusalem had been: *Time,* Dec. 2, 1966; *New York Times,* Nov. 27, 1966.
44 On the same: U.N. S/PV.1328, 25 Nov. 1966.
45 Ambassador Michael Comay: *Ibid.*
45 Jordan's Ambassador Mohammad: *Ibid.*
46 Footnote: U.N. S/PV.1324, 21 Nov. 1966.
46 Prime Minister Levi: *New York Times,* Nov. 27, 1966.
46 Born in 1924: General Odd Bull to the author, letter,1/5/83, called Weizman "the greatest Israeli general." There can be no doubt that it was Weizman's patient and loving development and training of the Air Force which made it the lethal force that, in effect, won the 1967 war in the first day.
47 As he later: Weizman, *On Eagles' Wings.*
47 Like Begin's mentor: Ofira Seliktar, "Israel: The New Zionism," *Foreign Policy,* Summer, 1983. Also see Brenner, Lenni. *Zionism in the Age of the Dictators.* Westport, CT: Lawrence Hill, 1983.
48 He spoke six: CIA biography, Biographic Registry, 31 Aug. 1967; declassified 7/20/81.
49 Their efforts were: W. W. Rostow to the President, confidential memorandum, May 31, 1966, 2:00 P.M.; declassified 1/16/79.
49 King Hussein immediately: President Johnson to Embassy Amman, State Department cable 90603, immediate secret, Nov. 23, 1966; declassified 9/10/83.
50 Over the years: Laqueur, *The Road to War.*
51 Shukairy was publicly: *Time,* July 8, 1966.
51 "In this country": *Ibid.*
51 The attacks piqued: Draper, *Israel and World Politics.* Also interview with King Hussein, Aug. 3, 1983, Amman, Jordan.
52 On March 6: Ro'i, Yaacov. *From Encroachment to Involvement.* New York: John Wiley & Sons, 1974.
52 By April 18: *Ibid.*
52 Without apparently realizing: Interview with James Critchfield, June 1, 1983, McLean, Va.
52 It had, the: *Ibid.*
52 The Middle East was: Petran, *op. cit.*
53 From this time on: Critchfield, *op. cit.*
53 The fears of: *Ibid.*
53 "The Israelis were": Interview with Richard Helms, June 16, 1983, Washington, D.C.
54 "We believe that": *Ibid.*
54 Two months later: *Ibid.*
54 Suddenly, in March: Bull, *War and Peace in the Middle East.* In a letter to the author, 1/25/83, Bull stated: "The days before the General Armistice Agreement was signed (20 June 1949) identical cables were sent from the Israeli Minister of Foreign Affairs to Israeli diplomatic representatives abroad stating, i.e., 'The demilitarized areas will remain free of armed forces but normal civilian life will be resumed under our full sovereignty.' This was not made known for either the UN representative or the Syrian members during

Page

the negotiations which led to the agreement. In 1951 during an ordinary meeting of the Mixed Armistice Commission, an Israeli member claimed full responsibility in the D-Zone. Neither the UN nor the Syrian Government agreed. Here I believe the UN made a great mistake—in my opinion this Israeli claim was a violation of the armistice agreement and should have been brought up to the Security Council. In those days, Security Council rulings were accepted. Arab farmers were thrown out followed by illegal Israeli cultivation—the result: many violations of the armistice agreements followed by shootings."

55 A fire fight: Draper, *op. cit.*

55 Then on January: *Ibid.*

55 Walworth Barbour, the: Tel Aviv Embassy to secstate, secret cable 2390 signed by Barbour, 10:41 A.M., 17 Jan. 1967; declassified 4/16/81.

55 Israel launched a: Khouri, *The Arab-Israeli Dilemma.*

56 Israel's sense of: *Facts on File Yearbook 1967.* Also see Hirst, *The Gun and the Olive Branch.*

56 Syria's President Attassi: Draper, *op. cit.*

56 Hussein's prime minister: *Facts on File Yearbook 1967.*

56 The repeated airing: Draper, *Present History.*

57 "Israel can be": Draper, *Israel and World Politics.*

57 Nasser's position became: Khouri, *op. cit.*

57 *Al Quds,* a: Draper, *Israel and World Politics.*

57 Nasser took to: Laqueur, *op. cit.*

57 From Syria's perspective: Draper, *Israel and World Politics.*

58 Egypt's prime minister: *Ibid.*

58 Observers in the: Richard Helms interview, 6/16/83, Washington, D.C.; Bull to the author, letter, 4/27/82.

58 "I don't think": Bull, *ibid.*

58 "Are you people": Weizman, *On Eagles' Wings.*

58 On May 11: Draper, *Israel and World Politics.*

58 On May 12: The story was based on a background briefing by Gen. Yariv. For details see Cooley, *Green March, Black September.* Also see top secret/nodis State Department Administrative History, written 1968, *United States Policy and Diplomacy in the Middle East Crisis, May 15–June 10, 1967.* The study covers 155 pages and was declassified and sanitized 9/16/83.

59 That same day: Charles W. Yost, "How It Began," *Foreign Affairs,* Winter 1968.

59 Syria was concerned: U.N. S/7885, letter from the representative of Syria to the president of the Security Council, 15 May, 1967.

59 Nasser tended to: Heikal, *The Sphinx and the Commissar.*

59 Israel denied the: Brecher, *Decisions in Israel's Foreign Policy.*

59 As the National: Saunders, *Terrorist Organizations of the Present Crisis,* undated. A handwritten note says it was written "for McGeorge Bundy sometime prior to June 19th, 1967."

60 The fall of: Glassman, Jon D. *Arms for the Arabs: The Soviet Union and War in the Middle East.* Baltimore: The Johns Hopkins University Press, 1975.

60 Unity was one: James Critchfield interview, 6/1/83, McLean, Va.

60 In fact, the: Critchfield, *op. cit.*

CHAPTER III

Page

61 Prime Minister Levi: Amos Elon, "Letter from the Sinai Front," *Commentary,* August 1967.

62 On January 23: Brecher, *Decisions in Israel's Foreign Policy.*

63 At that moment: Rabin, *The Rabin Memoirs.*

64 "Israel wants to": Brecher, *op. cit.*

64 At his Gaza: Rikhye, *The Sinai Blunder.*

65 In the heavy: *Ibid.*

67 "We are witnessing": *Facts on File Yearbook 1967.*

67 In the same: *Ibid.*

68 By that afternoon: Brecher, *op. cit.*

68 Israeli apprehensions increased: Rabin, *op. cit.*

68 Even before U Thant: Rikhye, *op. cit.*

68 Rikhye notified U Thant: *Ibid.*

69 Of the seven: *Ibid.*

69 By the next: Charles W. Yost, "How It Began," *Foreign Affairs,* Winter 1968.

69 That morning Rikhye: Rikhye, *op. cit.*

70 Rafael replied that: U.N. A/6730/Add.3, 26 June 1967.

70 Repeated requests over: Brecher, *Decisions in Crisis.*

70 Foreign Minister Riad: U.N. A/6730/Add.3, 26 June 1967.

71 Kony took the: *Ibid.*

71 He pointed out: *Ibid.*

71 At 7 P.M. that: *Ibid.*

71 That same day: Laqueur, *The Road to War.*

71 Despite such provocations: Tel Aviv Embassy to secstate, secret cable, 3640, 10:52 A.M., May 18, 1967; declassified 12/6/79.

72 The next day: U.N. S/7906, 26 May 1967.

72 Shortly before dusk: Rikhye, *op. cit.*

73 That same May: Brecher, *Decisions in Israel's Foreign Policy.*

CHAPTER IV

Page

74 Secret messages were: Johnson to Eshkol, secret cable, May 17, 1967; declassified 2/12/81, but, interestingly, the complete text was printed as early as 1970 in Bar-Zohar's book, *Embassies in Crisis.*

74 Neither Johnson nor: W. W. Rostow to the President, secret memorandum, Urgent Message to Eshkol, May 17, 1967, declassified 9/20/83.

75 The Soviet Union: *Facts on File Yearbook 1967.*

76 In one brief: Maclear, Michael. *The Ten Thousand Day War.* New York: St. Martin's Press, 1981.

76 At least 100,000: *Facts on File Yearbook 1967.*

76 Expressing both his: *Ibid.*

77 In it, Eshkol: Bar-Zohar, *op. cit.*

77 "Our main formal": W. W. Rostow to the President, secret memorandum, May 19, 1967; declassified 5/1/78.

78 "The President may": Saunders to W. W. Rostow, NSC memorandum, May 19, 1967.

79 By 1967, when: Urofsky, *We Are One!*

79 Only 187 emigrated: *Ibid.*

79 With their prosperity: Isaacs, *Jews and American Politics.*

Page
79 Thus concentrations of: Washington *Post,* June 7, 1967.
80 When Kennedy informally: Urofsky, *op. cit.*
80 After Kennedy's assassination: Miller, *Lyndon.*
80 Commented Jewish lobbyist: *Ibid.*
80 The ways in: W. W. Rostow to the President, secret memorandum, May 21, 1966, 4:05 P.M.; declassified 3/13/79.
81 Another study, written: Unsigned memorandum to the President, preliminary draft, undated but internal evidence indicates it was composed in the winter of 1966–67.
83 "This is the": Saunders to W. W. Rostow, NSC memorandum, undated.
83 The loan was: W. W. Rostow to the President, confidential memorandum, July 29, 1966; declassified 3/13/79.
83 The President authorized: LBJ/JJ/mf, memorandum, Oct. 8, 1966, 11 A.M.
83 He funded the: Washington *Post,* Jan. 13, 1976.
83 When his bank: *New York Times,* Sept. 16, 1976.
83 The list reported: Unsigned memorandum, *US HELP FOR ISRAEL 1964–1966,* Nov. 2, 1966.
84 Far more significant: Unsigned secret memorandum, *HOW WE HAVE HELPED ISRAEL,* May 19, 1966; declassified 3/13/79. Also, unsigned classified memorandum, *What We Have Done for Israel,* NEA/IAI:2/8/67; declassified and sanitized 4/16/81.
84 Instead of sending: mf, unaddressed memorandum, Nov. 10, 1966.
85 To this end: Vice President to secretary of state, letter, Mar. 15, 1966, #6711.
85 Rusk tried to: Rusk to Vice President, secret letter, Mar. 31, 1966; declassified 5/16/77.
85 On May 1 he: Vice President to W. W. Rostow, memorandum, May 1, 1966.
85 The White House: D. W. Ropa to Bromley Smith, confidential memorandum, *Israeli-Vietnamese Relations,* May 2, 1966; declassified 3/12/79.
86 That same day: Saunders to WWR, secret memorandum, May 2, 1966; declassified 3/12/79.
86 The secret aid: State Department Administrative History, *United States Policy and Diplomacy in the Middle East Crisis, May 15–June 10, 1967,* top secret/nodis, 1968; declassified 9/16/83. This document says the request included at least two elements, an appeal for 200,000 gas masks and a recommendation that a U.S. destroyer visit Elath.
86 A note six: WWR to the President, untitled memorandum, May 24, 1967, 11:55 A.M.
86 He sent a: Quandt, *Decade of Decisions.*
87 Partly in return: Cable from Ambassador Battle, *Extent of U.S. assurances to Israel in 1957 with reference to the withdrawal of Israeli forces from Sinai,* May 25, 1967; see attached; *Aide-Mémoire Handed to Israel's Ambassador Abba Eban by Secretary of State John Foster Dulles, 11 Feburary 1957.*
87 No Israeli flagship: Rikhye, *The Sinai Blunder.*
87 On the other: Laqueur, *The Road to War.*
87 Foreign Minister Abba: Eban, *An Autobiography.*
87 As part of: Brecher, *Decisions in Israel's Foreign policy.*
88 The Saudis announced: Brecher, *Decisions in Crisis.*
88 On May 20, the: Damascus Domestic Service in Arabic, Foreign Broadcast Information Service, 20 May 1967, 0415 GMT.
88 On May 21, Egypt: *Facts on File Yearbook 1967.*
88 Illusions were so: *Time,* June 9, 1967.

NOTES

Page

88 Nasser, by now: Sadat, Anwar. *In Search of Identity.* New York: Harper & Row, 1978.

88 "Now with our": *Ibid.*

89 "Under no circumstances": Cairo Domestic Service in Arabic, Foreign Broadcast Information Service, 23 May 1967, 0400 GMT.

CHAPTER V

Page

90 Chief of Staff: Rabin, *The Rabin Memoirs.*

90 Next to get: Eban, *An Autobiography.*

90 "We are now": Cairo Domestic Service in Arabic, Foreign Broadcast Information Service, 23 May 1967, 0400 GMT.

91 Even the moderate: Eban, *op. cit.*

91 But first he: Rabin, *op. cit.*

91 The civilian-fighter: Elon, *The Israelis.*

92 Eshkol informed Rabin's: Rabin, *op. cit.* Text of the letter is in state priority cable 198955, secret, 5/21/67; declassified 10/14/83.

92 Indeed, the other: *Ibid.*

92 And Aharon Yariv: Rabin, *op. cit.*

92 Eshkol demurred: *Ibid.*

92 "If we ignored": *Ibid.*

92 Eban, like others: Eban, *op. cit.*

93 Despite their deepened: *Ibid.*

93 According to Eban's: *Ibid.*

93 In summing up: Rabin, *op. cit.*

93 In the past: Brecher, *Decisions in Israel's Foreign Policy.*

94 From his Tel: Eugene V. Rostow, University of Texas Oral History Project, interview, Dec. 2, 1968.

94 Rostow managed to: *Ibid.*

94 "We should be": Bar-Zohar, *Embassies in Crisis.*

94 He added that: Eban, *op. cit.*

94 Moshe Dayan, the: Bar-Zohar, *op. cit.*

94 But the committee: Eban, *op. cit.*

94 When they learned: Bar-Zohar, *op. cit.*

95 That May 23: *Ibid.*

95 As Israeli historian: *Ibid.*

95 Reflecting the urgency: Eban, *op. cit.*

CHAPTER VI

Page

96 U Thant found: Rikhye, *The Sinai Blunder.*

96 "Various of our": EYES ONLY draft of letter to President Johnson with handwritten revisions, apparently by LBJ, 5/22/67; declassified 5/8/81.

97 Johnson had gone: Heikal, *Nasser: The Cairo Documents.* Also see memorandum from office of the Chief of Protocol, the State Department, to James Jones, the White House, Sept. 12, 1966.

98 Beyond that, Nasser: Heikal, *op. cit.*

98 Nasser's image was: *Ibid.* Also, Lucius D. Battle, Oral History, Lyndon Baines Johnson Library, Nov. 14, 1968.

Page
99 Through the public: Lucius D. Battle interview, Jan. 21, 1983, Washington, D.C.
99 He forcefully let: *Ibid.*
99 Battle's plain words: *Ibid.* Also see Battle to Secretary of State, Cairo secret cable 2251, Dec. 30, 1964, 2 P.M., declassified 10/7/76, which mentions Sabry's role.
99 "The American ambassador": Heikal, *op. cit.* Compare with the Foreign Broadcast Information Service text, 23 Dec. 1964, 1710 GMT, Cairo Domestic Service in Arabic, which has a less inflammatory interpretation. Nonetheless, the CIA's later analysis would seem to support Heikal's version.
100 A Central Intelligence: Intelligence memorandum, CIA, Office of Central Intelligence, 24 Dec. 1964; declassified 11/1/76.
100 Another reason for: Battle interview, *op. cit.*
100 Indeed, one of: Heikal, *The Sphinx and the Commissar.*
101 At least as: Peres, Shimon. *David's Sling.* London: Weidenfeld and Nicolson, 1970.
101 By 1960 Nasser: Nutting, *Nasser.*
101 About one hundred: Steven, *The Spymasters of Israel.*
101 Nasser recklessly boasted: *Ibid.*
101 The Israeli secret: *Ibid.*
101 Starting September 11: *Ibid.*
102 The CIA had: Peres, *op. cit.*
102 By the time: Rusk to the President, secret memorandum, Jan. 22, 1965; declassified 10/6/76.
102 The month before: Unsigned to Bundy, secret memorandum, Apr. 6, 1965; declassified 6/3/77.
103 Typical was a: Benjamin H. Read to Bromley Smith, Department of State memorandum on "Congressmen and Senators, with quotes, who have made statements over the past year on PL-480 to the UAR," Nov. 11, 1965.
103 The next day: *Ibid.*
103 "CIA piece is": Battle to secstate, secret cable 1758, Nov. 19, 1964, 8:42 A.M.; declassified 3/29/77.
103 "Dean Rusk again": Komer to the President, confidential memorandum, Jan. 21, 1966, 12:15 P.M.; declassified 1/16/79.
104 In a memorandum: Komer to the President, secret memorandum, Feb. 23, 1966, 10:30 A.M.; declassified 1/16/79.
104 In fact, as: *New York Times,* Mar. 16, 1976.
104 As was his: Heikal, *Nasser: The Cairo Documents.*
104 He received his: *Ibid.*
105 When the Egyptian: *Ibid.*
105 Though Nasser despised: Nutting, *op. cit.*
106 An invitation to: Heikal, *Nasser: The Cairo Documents.*
106 Nasser believed the: Nutting, *op. cit.*
107 Yemen charged the: *Facts on File Yearbook 1967.*
107 The truth was: Interview with Richard Nolte, 1/11/83, Washington, D.C.
107 In their long: Battle interview, *op. cit.*
108 The next day: *Ibid.*
108 The man selected: Baltimore *Sun,* Feb. 2, 1968.
108 Rusk, consumed like: Nolte inteview, *op. cit.*
108 As Nes later: Baltimore *Sun, op. cit.*
108 Indeed, when Nasser: Riad, *The Struggle for Peace in the Middle East.*

CHAPTER VII

Page
109   One of the: Brecher, *Decisions in Crisis.*
109   Roche labored on: Roche to the President, secret memorandum, dated May 22, 1967, but probably written May 23; declassified 1/5/82.
110   "Jewish pressure groups": Miller, *Lyndon.* Despite Roche's assertion that Johnson had a number of telephone conversations with Jewish groups that day, the President's Daily Diary shows that LBJ had twenty-six calls up to the time of his speech, none of them with any major Jewish leader. However, according to Michael Brecher's *Decisions in Crisis,* it was Roche himself who read Eppy Evron the original State Department draft. Whoever it was who was toying with the Jewish community, Johnson or Roche himself, I have used Roche's account since it vividly reflects the basic reality of the anxiety experienced in the Jewish community.
111   They had begun: President's Daily Diary, May 23, 1967.
111   Rusk that May: Johnson, *The Vantage Point.*
112   Evron cabled Jerusalem: Brecher, *Decisions in Israel's Foreign Policy.*
112   "The United States": White House press release, *Remarks of the President on the Near East Situation,* May 23, 1967.
112   But at the: *New York Times,* April 26, 1968, stories on Goldberg's resignation which rehash his U.N. career.
112   "I must frankly": Washington *Post,* May 4, 1965.
113   Only that day: President's Daily Diary, May 23, 1967.
113   Eppy Evron the: W. W. Rostow memorandum to the President, May 24, 1967, 11:55 A.M.
113   Moscow's reaction to: Brecher, *Decisions in Crisis.*
113   The day before: Johnson, *op. cit.*
114   The closure of: Lall, *The UN and the Middle East Crisis, 1967.*
114   The reaction in: State Department Administrative History, *United States Policy in the Middle East Crisis, May 15–June 10, 1967,* top secret/nodis, 1968; declassified and sanitized 9/16/83.
115   Rabin increased his: Rabin, *The Rabin Memoirs.* Also see Dayan, *Story of My Life.*
115   On the evening: Rabin, *op. cit.*
116   Rabin called on: *Ibid.* Also see Dayan, *op. cit.*
116   The next day: Rabin, *op. cit.*
117   What happened next: Weizman, *On Eagles' Wings.*

CHAPTER VIII

Page
120   With these disturbing: Eban, *An Autobiography.*
120   Seven years before: de Gaulle, Charles. (Terence Kilmartin, trans.) *Memoirs of Hope: Renewal and Endeavor.* New York: Simon and Schuster, 1971.
120   "But she is not": Compare with Michael Bar-Zohar in *Embassies in Crisis,* wherein he asserts that Ben Gurion made no such remark. Bar-Zohar, who wrote a highly informative biography of Ben Gurion, says that "General de Gaulle's version of his conversation with Ben Gurion is inaccurate to say the least." Whether it is accurate or not, de Gaulle was not known as a prevaricator and he obviously believed Ben Gurion sought enlarged frontiers.

Page

The point is important since it obviously influenced de Gaulle's attitude and actions toward Israel.

120   Before Eban could: Eban, *op. cit.*
120   De Gaulle was sitting: *Ibid.*
121   His next stop: *Ibid.*
122   "When Dayan is": Prittie, *Eshkol.*
123   Dayan finally recognized: Dayan, *Story of My Life.*
123   The campaign became: Prittie, *op. cit.*
123   "I knew in": Dayan, *op. cit.*
123   Dayan itched to: *Ibid.*
124   "When we knew": Rikhye, *The Sinai Blunder.*
125   "They say that": *Ibid.*
125   "I told them": *Ibid.*
126   Dean Rusk briefed: Memorandum for the Record, Record of National Security Council Meeting . . . Discussion of Middle East Crisis, May 24, 1967; declassified and sanitized 5/8/81.
128   Around August 15: Steven, *The Spymasters of Israel.*
129   Later that day: Secstate to Amman Embassy, confidential flash cable 1524, May 24, 5:22 P.M.; declassified 11/13/81.
129   The answer came: Embassy Amman to secstate, confidential flash cable 2192, May 24, 1967, 6:05 P.M.; declassified 11/13/81.
129   One of the: National Security Agency/National Security Service, top secret study titled *Attack on a [deleted] the U.S.S. Liberty (S-[deleted],* 1981; declassified and (heavily) sanitized, undated.

CHAPTER IX

Page

131   Johnson had been: Johnson, *Vantage Point.*
131   He said nothing: Rafael, *Destination Peace.*
131   Israel faces a: Rabin, *The Rabin Memoirs.*
132   Whatever the cause: Eban, *An Autobiography.*
133   Democratic Senator Paul: *Ibid.*
133   Rusk gasped.: Rafael, *op. cit.*
134   "I do not": *Ibid.*
134   President Johnson arrived: President's Daily Diary, May 25, 1967.
134   At the end: W. W. Rostow to the President, memorandum, May 25, 1967, 6 P.M.
135   By 7 P.M. Johnson: President's Daily Diary, *op. cit.*
135   Vice President Humphrey: *Ibid.*
135   A character trait: Cohen, Warren I. *Dean Rusk.* Totowa, N.J.: Cooper Square Publishers, 1980.
136   Eban had known: Eban, *op. cit.*
136   At their dinner: Brecher, *Decisions in Israel's Foreign Policy.*
136   Rusk in the: President's Daily Diary, *op. cit.*
136   In reporting his: Breacher, *op. cit.*
137   "President Johnson has": Bar-Zohar, *Embassies in Crisis.*

CHAPTER X

Page

138 The harshly militant: Cairo Voice of the Arabs in Arabic, speech by President Gamal Abdel Nasser, 1935 GMT, 26 May 1967.

139 The article was: Laqueur's *The Road to War* carries the complete text as Appendix Five.

139 To calm the: Draper, *Present History.*

139 It was about: Eban, *An Autobiography.*

140 President Johnson had: Interview, Richard Helms, May 11, 1983, Washington, D.C.

140 But when Eban: Eban, *op. cit.*

141 Said General Wheeler: Bar-Zohar, *Embassies in Crisis.*

141 Rusk that day: Rusk to the President, secret memorandum, *Your Conversation with the Israeli Foreign Minister,* May 26, 1967; declassified and sanitized 6/11/82.

142 Under a heading: W. W. Rostow to the President, secret memorandum on *Meeting in the Middle East,* May 26, 1967, 1:30 P.M.; declassified 12/13/82.

143 All of Johnson's: President's Daily Diary, May 26, 1967.

143 Wheeler reviewed the: Quandt, *Decade of Decisions.*

144 Evron went to: Brecher, *Decisions in Israel's Foreign Policy.*

144 While Evron was: *Ibid.*

144 In his detailed: *Ibid.*

144 To avoid publicity: *Ibid.*

145 Eban had first: Eban, *op. cit.*

145 "What a President": *Ibid.*

145 "I know that": *Ibid.*

146 Johnson declared: Johnson, *The Vantage Point.* Also see secret/nodis memorandum of conversation, nine pages heavily sanitized, Lois Nivins to Kay Herbert, 5/30/67, for the official U.S. record of these talks; declassified 9/21/83.

146 Johnson and his: President's Daily Diary, May 26, 1967.

146 ". . . regarding the straits": Unsigned secret draft to the President, 5/26/67; declassified 9/21/83 (although Eban had printed part of the text in his 1977 memoirs).

146 "What do you": Eban, *op. cit.*

146 As Eban departed: Eugene V. Rostow, University of Texas Oral History Project, interview, Dec. 2, 1968.

146 Johnson's mood apparently: President's Daily Diary, May 26, 1967.

146 Secretary McNamara said: In a letter to the author, 4/12/83, Christian explained Johnson's apparent change in mood: "Johnson was much more pessimistic after the meeting and it is correct that his first reaction was that he had not headed off war. . . . It is probable that subsequent conversations gave the President more encouragement and that late that evening he was making more positive statements. This might have been a case of 'whistling past the graveyard' on his part."

147 Eban went straight: Eban, *op. cit.* Also see Rafael, *Destination Peace.*

147 The general had: Rabin, *The Rabin Memoirs.*

147 Impatient and unsatisfied: *Ibid.*

CHAPTER XI

Page
150 Moscow's actions had: James Critchfield interview, June 1, 1983, McLean, Va.
150 At 3 A.M. that day: Heikal, *Nasser: The Cairo Documents.*
150 At about the: Bar-Zohar, *Embassies in Crisis.* Also see Brecher, *Decisions in Israel's Foreign Policy.*
151 The prime minister: Brecher, *Ibid.*
151 At that time: *Ibid.*
152 As head of: Bell, J. Bowyer. *Terror Out of Zion.* New York: St. Martin's Press, 1977. Also see Bethell, Nicholas. *The Palestine Triangle.* New York: G. P. Putnam's Sons, 1979, and Brenner, Lenni. *Zionism in the Age of the Dictators.* Westport, CT: Lawrence Hill, 1983.
152 So intent on: Tillman, *The United States in the Middle East.*
152 When the plan: *Ibid.*
152 Begin's militant and: *Ibid.*
152 Begin's proposition to: Brecher, *op. cit.*
153 In frustration, Eshkol: *Ibid.*
153 As for working: *Ibid.*
153 Allon retained close: *Ibid.*
154 As spokesman for: *Ibid.*
154 He went to: *Ibid.*
155 He strongly urged: *Ibid.*
155 Eshkol refused. But: Brecher, *Decisions in Crisis.*
155 Israelis were showing: Bar-Zohar, *op. cit.*
155 Though Eshkol had: Brecher, *Decisions in Israel's Foreign Policy.*
156 Lyndon Johnson began: President's Daily Diary, May 27, 1967.
156 Only the day: Washington *Post,* May 26, 1967. Goldberg letter to author, 1/17/83.
156 An hour later: President's Daily Diary, *op. cit.*
156 The previous day: Ginsburg to W. W. Rostow, letter, May 26, 1967. Name File: David Ginsburg, LBJ Library. Johnson wrote Ginsburg a letter, apparently in response to another letter from him, in the midst of the war on June 9, 1967. "Dear David: I am deeply grateful for your warm and wise note of encouragement. . . . As ever, it is a comfort and inspiration to have you as a companion on another hard but hopeful journey."
156 Johnson decided after: President's Daily Diary, *op. cit.*
156 Accompanying the President: *Ibid.*
157 Krim's wife, an: *American Men and Women of Science,* Vol. 3, *The Physical and Biological Sciences.* New York: R. R. Bowker Co., 1972. Also interview with Mathilde Krim, 7/28/83, New York City. Biographical details come from the interview.
158 U Thant had used: Text sent to the President by W. W. Rostow and received at the ranch at 3:03 P.M., 27 May 1967, followed by *Summary and Evaluation,* untimed and unsigned.
158 More important, an: W. W. Rostow to the President, top-secret memorandum, received at the ranch 5:19 P.M., 27 May 1967; declassified and sanitized 5/8/81. Part of the text excised as late as 1981 had actually been printed in Bar-Zohar's 1970 book, *Embassies in Crisis,* page 130, reading: "If Israel begins hostilities, the Soviet Union will come to the aid of the attacked countries." A variation of it appears in Brecher's 1974 book, *Decisions in Israel's Foreign Policy,* page 398. It reads: "The Soviets state that if Israel starts military action, the Soviet Union will extend help to the attacked States."

CHAPTER XII

Page
160 Abba Eban arrived: Eban, *An Autobiography.*
160 Even Levi Eshkol: Brecher, *Decisions in Israel's Foreign Policy.* Also see Prittie, *Eshkol.*
161 As Eban observed: Eban, *op. cit.*
161 Although Eban had: *Ibid.*
161 Rabin, sitting in: Rabin, *The Rabin Memoirs.*
162 Dressed in a: Washington *Post,* May 19, 1967.
163 "We used to": Text of Nasser's remarks received at the ranch at 6:25 P.M., 28 May 1967.
164 That night he: President's Daily Diary, May 28, 1967. Also see Shogan, Robert. *A Question of Judgment.* New York: Bobbs-Merrill Co., 1972.
165 The message from: Brecher, *op. cit.*
165 In addition to: Eban, *op. cit.*
165 Rusk had appended: Brecher, *op. cit.*
165 It was that: *Ibid..* Also see Eban, *op. cit.*
165 Only Transportation Minister: Brecher, *op. cit.*
166 Israelis on that: Eban, *op. cit.*
166 He was nearly: Prittie, *op. cit.*
166 Eshkol had never: Brecher, *op. cit.*
167 Snapped one disgusted: Amos Elon, "Letter from the Sinai Front," *Commentary,* August 1967.
167 Chief of Staff: Rabin, *op. cit.*
167 "You can and": Bar-Zohar, *Embassies in Crisis.*
168 Also, as each: Crosbie, Sylvia Kowitt. *A Tacit Alliance.* Princeton, N.J.: Princeton University Press, 1974.
168 At the end: Eban, *op. cit.*
168 He left the: Bar-Zohar, *op. cit.*
168 Although he was: President's Daily Diary, May 29, 1967.
169 Eight church leaders: *New York Times,* May 28, 1967.
169 The Zionist Organization: *Facts on File Yearbook 1967.*
169 The latest casualty: *Ibid.*
169 And only that: *Ibid.*
169 One of Johnson's: Wattenberg to the President, memorandum, May 31, 1967, received 11 A.M.
169 Senator Jacob Javits: W. W. Rostow to the President, confidential memorandum CAP67459, received 5:47 P.M., 27 May 1967; declassified 2/1/82. Also, W. W. Rostow to the President, confidential memorandum CAP67473, received 9:33 P.M., 28 May 1967; declassified 2/1/82.
170 "We'll set a": LBJ/JJ/mf, 5/27/67, 9:30 P.M., with note: "JJ relayed to Walt Rostow."

CHAPTER XIII

Page
171 Hussein's decision had: Vance, Vick, and Pierre Lauer. *Hussein of Jordan.* London: Peter Owen, 1968.
171 "Now, eleven years": Complete text in *New York Times,* May 31, 1967.
171 As Abba Eban: Eban, *An Autobiography.*
171 After listening to: Vance and Lauer, *op. cit.*
172 Its Article 1: Complete text in *New York Times,* May 31, 1967.

Page

172 At a stroke: Dupuy, *Elusive Victory.*

172 Hussein later explained: Vance and Lauer, *op. cit.*

172 Although Hussein's concern: Addressed to "Lois," White House memorandum, 9/14/66.

172 Two days later: W. W. Rostow to Henry Wilson, memorandum, Sept. 19, 1966.

173 In an internal: *Ibid.*

173 All through the: *Time,* Jan. 13, 1967.

173 The pact, and: Snow, *Hussein.*

173 The Cairo ceremony: *New York Times,* May 31, 1967.

174 "The Soviet Union": *Washington Post,* May 30, 1967.

174 The misunderstanding had: Heikal, *The Sphinx and the Commissar.*

175 Casualties in Israel: Bar-Zohar, *Embassies in Crisis.*

175 As soon as Levi: Eban, *op. cit.*

175 Walt Rostow only: Brecher, *Decisions in Israel's Foreign Policy.*

175 And on the: Eban, *op. cit.*

176 In the event: Unaddressed and signed "Jim," memorandum, 5/30/67, 7:35 P.M. The complete text: "Rostow says both he and Rusk have talked to John W. Finney who wrote the piece and Tom Wicker about the injustice and inaccuracy of the story today. Walt does not know what the NY Times will do about it however. George Christian talked to Max Frankel who agreed that the story should not have been printed."

176 The next day: Dick Moose to W. W. Rostow, memorandum, May 31, 1967.

176 Eshkol and Eban: Eban, *op. cit.* Also see Brecher, *op. cit.*

176 Amit, a sabra: Brecher, *Decisions in Crisis.*

176 He was also: Interview with James Critchfield, 6/1/83, McLean, Va.

176 Amit later explained: Brecher, *Decisions in Crisis.*

176 Eshkol and Eban also: *Ibid.*

177 President Johnson and: Johnson, *The Vantage Point.*

177 This suspicion was: Brecher, *Decisions in Israel's Foreign Policy.*

177 His weakness was: Johnson, *op. cit.*

177 With Ambassador-designate: Battle interview, Jan. 21, 1983, Washington, D.C.

177 In addition to: *Ibid.*

178 In a long: Lisbon Embassy to secstate and White House, EYES ONLY cable 1517 from Robert Anderson, June 2, 3:25 P.M.; declassified and sanitized, 12/9/82.

179 Notification of Mohieddin's: Battle interview, *op. cit.*

180 On his side: Heikal, *Nasser: The Cairo Documents.*

180 The *Intrepid*'s passage: Washington *Post,* June 2, 1967.

180 In fact, both: W. W. Rostow to the President, secret memorandum, received 11:04 A.M., 29 May 1967; declassified 4/5/82. Handwritten on the memorandum is: "If everybody agreeable—go on with it. Pres. told Walt."

180 Despite his suspicions: Cairo Embassy to secstate, secret cable 8397, received 6:20 P.M., June 2, 1967; declassified 8/27/82.

180 On June 1: Eban, *op. cit.*

181 Typical of their: Baghdad Domestic Service in Arabic, Foreign Broadcast Information Service, 1100 GMT, 1 June 1967.

181 "Those who survive": Draper, *Israel and World Politics.*

181 His first report: Brecher, *Decisions in Israel's Foreign Policy.*

181 In Israel it: Interview with Helms, 8/2/82, Washington, D.C.; letter from

Page

    McNamara, 2/1/83. McNamara wrote: "I was absolutely opposed to an Israeli attack and made my position very clear."

182   Amit's report was: Eban, *op. cit.*

182   In one meeting: Bar-Zohar, *op. cit.*

182   At another time: Weizman, *On Eagles' Wings.*

183   One day Weizman: *Ibid.*

183   British journalist and: Kimche, Jon. *There Could Have Been Peace.* New York: The Dial Press, 1973.

183   A White House: In a memorandum from Saunders to Rostow, Sept. 28, 1967, he was identified as "Peter Rosenblatt who has recently visited Israel. You will recall that he works for Bill Leonhart and has numerous Israeli connections."

183   Weizman later touched: Weizman, *op. cit.*

184   Dayan promptly accepted: Curtis G. Pepper, "Hawk of Israel," *New York Times Magazine,* July 9, 1967.

184   At the same: Brecher, *Decisions in Israel's Foreign Policy.*

184   The spy ship: Ennes, *Assault on the* Liberty. In a letter to the author, 4/11/83, Ennes wrote: "The crew was 286 men before Rota, but 292 after we picked up three Marines and three NSA civilians. Most of the crew were regular 'general' service Navy types, and the 'spooks' or CTs (then officially known as Communication Technicians) were assigned to the Naval Security Group."

CHAPTER XIV

Page

186   At about 11 A.M.: Quandt, *Decade of Decisions.*

187   In addition to: *Ibid.*

187   This view was: Wheeler to the Secretary of Defense, secret memorandum JCSM-310-67, 2 June 67; declassified 2/2/82.

187   Rusk had received: Cairo Embassy to secstate, secret cable 8362 by Yost, 1:01 P.M., 2 June 1967; declassified 8/10/81.

188   And, if the network: Nearly every official I interviewed who was serving at this time believed that Israel had access to America's highest secrets relating to the Middle East.

188   "While I realize": Yost cable, *op. cit.*

188   As Ambassador Harman: Quandt, *op. cit.*

188   Nothing had been: Eban, *An Autobiography.*

189   Eshkol, Allon, Dayan: Rabin, *The Rabin Memoirs.*

190   With Amit's departure: Helms interview, 8/2/82, Washington, D.C.

190   On June 3: State Department Administrative History, *United States Policy and Diplomacy in the Middle East Crisis, May 15–June 10, 1967,* secret/nodis, 1968; declassified and sanitized 9/16/83.

190   "As now written": Saunders to W. W. Rostow, memorandum titled *The President's Saturday Speech.* June 1, 1967.

190   But Johnson could: Office of the White House Press Secretary, *Remarks of the President at the New York State Democratic Dinner,* June 3, 1967, 7:10 P.M.

191   His remarks were: *New York Times,* June 4, 1967.

191   Johnson went from: *Ibid.*

191   While at the table: Miller, *Lyndon.*

191   Footnote: *Ibid.*

191   The President, his: President's Daily Diary, June 3, 1967.

191   Amit and Harman: Brecher, *Decisions in Crisis.*

Page
192 A letter from: Johnson to Eshkol, secret letter, June 3, 1967; declassified 4/5/82. That the Administration was suspicious of an imminent Israeli attack and feeling a sense of urgency is indicated by a memorandum sent by Saunders to Johnson attached to the letter. In it, Saunders cautioned the President: "It may be urgent that we put this letter on record soon." Secret memorandum, 2:50 P.M., June 3, 1967; declassified 4/5/82.
192 Nor did a warning: Bar-Zohar, *Embassies in Crisis.*
192 Eban dismissed de Gaulle's: Eban, *op. cit.*
192 A Soviet warning: Dagan, Avigdor. *Moscow and Jerusalem.* New York: Abelard-Schuman, 1970.
193 That Saturday Dayan: Brecher, *op. cit.*
193 To further create: Bar-Zohar, *op. cit.*
193 One who remained: *Ibid.*
193 Indeed, Arab forces: Dupuy, *Elusive Victory.*
194 Little appreciated, however: *Ibid.*
194 The official decision: Eban, *op. cit.*
194 In order to mask: *Ibid.*
194 The communiqué achieved: *Ibid.*
194 They would have: Brecher, *op. cit.*
195 Eshkol that Sunday: Moskin, *Among Lions.*
195 In Egypt that: Charles W. Yost, "How It Began," *Foreign Affairs,* Winter 1968.
195 Columnist James Reston: *New York Times,* June 4, 1967, Reston column.
196 In a story: *New York Times,* June 5, 1967. Reston's front-page story is next to the headline:

ISRAELI-EGYPTIAN BATTLE ERUPTS;
PLANES AND TANKS ARE IN ACTION;
CAIRO REPORTS ATTACKS FROM AIR.

196 Anthony Nutting, the: Nutting, *Nasser.*
196 Imprudently, Nasser expressed: Cairo Domestic Service in Arabic, Foreign Broadcast Information Service, 1730 GMT, 4 June 1967.
196 Correspondent Flora Lewis: *Washington Post,* June 5, 1967.
197 Aboard the *Liberty:* Ennes, *Assault on the* Liberty.
197 Walt Rostow that: Bar-Zohar, *op. cit.*
197 Lyndon Johnson that: President's Daily Diary, June 4, 1967.

CHAPTER XV

Page
201 Israeli reconnaissance had: Churchill, Randolph S., and Winston S. *The Six Day War.* Boston: Houghton Mifflin Company, 1967.
201 In the underground: Weizman, *On Eagles' Wings.*
202 Hod had told: Schiff, Zeev. *A History of the Israeli Army (1807-1974).* San Francisco: Straight Arrow Books, 1974.
202 They had planned: Dupuy, *Elusive Victory.*
202 Unknown to the: Riad, *The Struggle for Peace in the Middle East.*
202 Tension was palpable: Weizman, *op. cit.*
203 One hundred eighty-three: Dupuy, *op. cit.*
203 Before 11 A.M.: Herzog, *The Arab-Israeli Wars.*
203 Israel's loss was: Dupuy, *op. cit.*
203 Before noon, Jordanian: *Ibid.*

Page
204 As a General: Eban, *An Autobiography*. He identifies the officer as Brigadier
    General Zeevi.
204 Even before the: Weizman, *op. cit.*
204 "He had no": Moskin, *Among Lions.*
204 Stoically, Hussein said: Interview with King Hussein, 8/7/83, Amman, Jor-
    dan.
204 At 8:30 A.M. that: Bull, *War and Peace in the Middle East.*
205 Hussein was not: Snow, *Hussein.*
205 In addition, Moshe: Dayan, *Story of My Life.*
205 "They started the": Moskin, *op. cit.*
205 As he later admitted: Sachar, H. M., *A History of Israel.*
205 Jordanian guns opened: *Ibid.*
205 And, in a brutal: Interview with King Hussein, 8/7/83, Amman, Jordan.
206 At 1:30 P.M.: Bull, *op. cit.*
206 At 3:52 P.M.: *Ibid.*
206 Women and children: Howard to author, letter, 2/5/83. Howard writes that he
    was at Government House receiving his introductory briefing when "the brief-
    ing officer suggested we 'take a break' for a while as the sound of distant
    shooting could be heard. In the ten years of my service which followed, I never
    did receive the end of that briefing! Making my way with others to the roof of
    Government House, I was greeted by Colonel Mick Johnson, the Deputy
    Chief of Staff UNTSO, who pointed across the valley towards the Old City of
    Jerusalem. 'It's the anachronism of the age,' he exclaimed, as we saw Israeli
    soldiers dismounting from their 20th Century tanks and clambering on scaling
    ladders over the 16th Century wall of Sultan Suleiman the Magnificent."
    Howard's mention of Israelis attacking the Old City this early seems prema-
    ture since officially the assault did not start until the next day, although of
    course there may have been earlier raids.
207 Unknown to Howard: Bull, *op. cit.*
207 Footnote: *Ibid.*
207 While Bull was: Eban, *op. cit.*
207 Interior Minister Shapira: Moskin, *op. cit.*
208 "We are going": Eban, *op. cit.*
208 Most of Jordan's: Dupuy, *op. cit.* Dupuy says (p. 291) the Old City was held by
    only one battalion of Jordanian reservists whose heaviest weapons were two
    120mm mortars. Also see Schleifer, *The Fall of Jerusalem,* who also puts the
    number of Jordanian troops inside the city at battalion strength. There were,
    he says, 480 men, all reservists, inside the walls.
208 As Justice Minister: Moskin, *op. cit.*
208 "There was no": *Ibid.*
208 No minutes were: *Ibid.*
208 Abba Eban realized: Eban, *op. cit.*
208 *New York Times:* Eric Pace, "Cairo Diary," *New York Times Sunday Maga-
    zine,* July 2, 1967.
209 Foreign Minister Mahmoud: Riad, *op. cit.*
209 Israel's forces were: Dupuy, *op. cit.*
209 The crew of: Ennes, *Assault on the* Liberty. Also, Ennes to author, letter,
    4/11/83, in which he explains: "Dave Lewis, who headed the SIGINT effort,
    had authority to release messages without showing them to the Captain. The
    message was prepared by Dave and may not have been seen by McGonagle.

Page

In any case . . . the request was official, and it was scornfully declined by Admiral Martin."

210 Washington's first official: Quandt, *Decade of Decisions.* Also, for exact time, Bar-Zohar, *Embassies in Crisis.*

210 Less than two: Tel Aviv Embassy to secstate, limited official use flash cable 3924, 4:05 A.M., 5 June 1967.

210 Within minutes of: Tel Aviv Embassy to secstate, secret flash cable 3928, 5:27 A.M., 5 June 1967; declassified 8/27/82.

211 Lyndon Johnson was: President's Daily Diary, June 5, 1967.

211 "War has broken": Bar-Zohar, *op. cit.*

211 Saunders worked on: Interview with Saunders, 5/16/83. Along with Lucius Battle, Richard Helms and most other officials interviewed, Saunders said he assumed the Israelis had attacked first.

211 Other calls to: President's Daily Diary, June 5, 1967.

211 Rusk had wanted: Johnson, *The Vantage Point.*

211 When Sergeant Paul: President's Daily Diary, *op. cit.*

211 Before he could: *Ibid.*

211 He also took: Interview with Mathilde Krim, 7/28/83, New York City. Though Mrs. Krim said she was quite certain the President knew by this time who had fired the first shot, as she said she was, she declined to go into details.

212 Communist Premier Aleksei: White House list of all hot-line calls, *WASHINGTON–MOSCOW 'HOT LINE' EXCHANGE,* undated. It shows twenty exchanges between June 5 and June 10.

212 Footnote: Johnson, *op. cit.*

212 Rusk's message was: White House list of hot-line exchanges, *op. cit.* Although Quandt says in *Decade of Decisions* that Rusk's cable was sent the routine way, the list notes say Kosygin's message was communicated and then "relay of Rusk to Gromyko message on hostilities." It is possible of course that Rusk's message was sent routinely earlier and then repeated on the hot line.

212 After carefully studying: White House list of hot-line exchanges, *op. cit.*

212 Press secretary Christian: A memorandum for the record dictated by Harold Saunders on Dec. 13, 1968 (some of the records of this period were written many months later because officials had been too busy to write them at the time), gives the circumstances of how the release was written.

212 He added that: White House press secretary release, *Statement by Press Secretary George Christian,* June 5, 1967.

213 It occurred during: Department of State, *Transcript of press and radio news briefing,* Monday, June 5, 1967, 12:48 P.M.

213 McCloskey had remembered: McCloskey interviews, 11/12/82 and 4/15/83, Washington, D.C.

214 Several minutes later: AP Bulletin #94, 1:28 P.M., June 5, 1967.

214 The reaction was: *New York Times* and *Washington Post,* June 6, 1967.

214 Earlier in the day: President's Daily Diary, June 5, 1967.

215 Less than an hour: Department of State release, *Transcript of background press briefing,* 5:03 P.M., June 5, 1967.

215 The commotion grew: White House release, *Statement of Hon. Dean Rusk,* June 5, 1967.

216 He also received: Marvin to the President, memorandum, 6:55 P.M., June 5, 1967.

216 Before the day: Joe Califano to the President, memorandum, 9:55 P.M., June 5, 1967.

Page
216 The President also: Roche to the President, personal memorandum, 11:05 A.M., June 5, 1967.
216 As a breather: President's Daily Diary, June 5, 1967.
216 At one point: *Ibid.*
216 He had lunch: *Ibid.*
216 Johnson worked into: W. W. Rostow to the President, secret memorandum, 9:40 P.M., June 5, 1967; declassified 3/3/83.
217 At about the: W. W. Rostow to the President, secret memorandum, June 5, 1967; declassified 10/18/82.
217 It was 9:53 P.M.: President's Daily Diary, June 5, 1967.
217 Johnson finally went: *Ibid.*

CHAPTER XVI

Page
218 "Will His Majesty": Snow, *Hussein.*
219 Chief of Staff: Rabin, *The Rabin Memoirs.*
219 The possibility that: *CIA intelligence information, cable #8444g, subject: 2) Soviet claims of sighting of United States aircraft over Ismailia,* 7 June 1967; declassified and sanitized 11/7/80.
220 To the ship's: Ennes, *Assault on the* Liberty.
220 Nasser made another: Riad, *The Struggle for Peace in the Middle East.*
220 The secretary of state: White House release, *Statement of Hon. Dean Rusk,* June 5, 1967.
220 In fact, there: Based on interviews with numerous officials, including Battle, Critchfield, Helms, McCloskey, Nolte and Saunders.
220 Riad immediately went: Riad, *op. cit.*
220 *He had been: Nolte interview, 1/11/83, Washington, D.C.*
221 *The crux of: Riad, op. cit.*
221 Secretary of State: White House release, *Statement of Secretary Dean Rusk outside West Lobby,* 9:05 A.M., June 6, 1967.
221 On instructions from: Cairo Embassy to secstate, secret flash cable 8567, 12:35 P.M., 6 June 1967; declassified 8/10/81.
221 In a message: Roche to the President: EYES ONLY memorandum, June 6, 1967. Roche starts his message: "Text: Isaiah 26, 10: 'If favor is shown to the wicked, he does not learn righteousness; in the land of uprightness he deals perversely.' "
222 Telegrams protesting McCloskey's: Silberman to Harry C. McPherson, Jr., telegram WA1948 PD, 8:39 P.M., June 6, 1967.
222 Democratic and Republican: *Facts on File Yearbook 1967.*
222 Senator Charles H.: *Ibid.*
222 Senator Wayne Morse: *Ibid.*
222 David S. Broder: *Washington Post,* June 7, 1967.
223 In a memorandum: Katzenbach to the President, memorandum, June 6, 1967.
223 Lyndon Johnson had: President's Daily Diary, June 6, 1967.
223 At 5:34 o'clock: White House list of *WASHINGTON-MOSCOW 'HOT LINE' EXCHANGE,* undated. Also see Johnson, *The Vantage Point.*
224 Although the fighting: Dupuy, *Elusive Victory.* Also see Herzog, *The Arab-Israeli Wars.*
224 On the day: Rafael, *Destination Peace.*
224 In addition, Rafael: Moskin, *Among Lions.*

Page
224 He had sympathetic: *Ibid.*
224 As it turned out: Lall, *The UN and the Middle East Crisis, 1967.*
225 Although the Council: *Ibid.*
226 Despite this delay: Eban, *An Autobiography.*
226 Goldberg and Fedorenko: Rafael, *op. cit.*
226 Walt Rostow that: W. W. Rostow to the President, memorandum, 11 A.M., June 6, 1967. Attachment says Rostow also sent the memorandum EYES ONLY to Rusk and McNamara, "State-1223, DOD-1225, 6 June."
227 A few hours: W. W. Rostow to the President, confidential memorandum, 4 P.M., June 6, 1967; declassified 9/16/80.
227 Less than an: White House hot-line list, *op. cit.*
227 Eban's first act: Rafael, *op. cit.*
227 The Council finally: Lall, *op. cit.*
227 Israel had won: Eban, *op. cit.*
228 With the world: *Ibid.*
228 The speech was: *Ibid.*
228 But the diplomatic: Lall, *op. cit.*
228 Jordan immediately accepted: Rusk to Amman Embassy, secret flash cable 4112, 11:30 P.M., 6 June 1967; declassified 7/8/81.
228 It had been: Unnamed to Tel Aviv Embassy, flash cable 4095, 8:30 A.M., 6 June 1967; no classification indicated.
228 Despite King Hussein's: Dupuy, *op. cit.*
228 The Israeli Air: *Ibid.* Also see Schleifer, *The Fall of Jerusalem,* and Forrest, *The Unholy Land.*
228 A cable from: Amman Embassy to secstate, secret flash cable 4098A, 2:33 P.M., 6 June 1967; declassified and sanitized 4/5/81.
229 Egypt found the: Cairo Embassy to secstate, confidential flash cable 8618, 5:16 P.M., 6 June 1967; declassified 8/10/81.
229 Footnote: Nolte interview, *op. cit.*
229 Egypt's charges of: *Facts on File Yearbook 1967.*
229 Perhaps more than: Dupuy, *op. cit.*
230 A CIA appraisal: Helms to Walt Rostow, secret study, *ISRAELI OBJECTIVES IN THE CURRENT CRISIS—SOVIET POLICY AND MISCALCULATION,* 6 June 1967; declassified 1/23/81.
230 In Washington, the: President's Daily Diary, June 6, 1967.
230 At that time: National Security Agency/Central Security Service, *Attack on a [deleted] the U.S.S. Liberty (S-[deleted],* 1981; no declassification date.

CHAPTER XVII

Page
231 It was 4 A.M.: Gur, Lieutenant General Mordechai. *The Battle for Jerusalem.* New York: Popular Library, 1978.
231 Only a few: Dupuy, *Elusive Victory.*
231 Shortly before 10 A.M.: Moskin, *Among Lions.*
232 Now the blue: *Ibid.*
232 At 10 A.M., Motta: *Ibid.*
232 "I, General Shlomo": *Ibid.*
232 A short while: Gur, *op. cit.*
233 "I felt this": Moskin, *op. cit.*
233 At a press: *Ibid.*

Page
233 Eshkol arrived at: *Ibid.*
233 We have come: Sachar, H. M., *A History of Israel.* Sachar calls the song "Jerusalem the Golden," but among Americans in Israel it was called "Jerusalem of Gold."
233 The prime minister: Moskin, *op. cit.*
234 Later that day: *Ibid.*
234 Apparently the fall: President's Daily Diary, June 7, 1967.
234 Two of his: *Ibid.*
234 "Once there is": Joe Califano to the President, memorandum, 10:15 A.M., 7 June 1967. Name File: Abe Fortas, LBJ Library.
235 Mathilde Krim also: Marvin to the President, memorandum, 1:25 P.M., 7 June 1967. Name File: Mathilde Krim, LBJ Library.
235 "The United States": *Ibid.*
235 The President was: President's Daily Diary, June 7, 1967.
235 Abe Feinberg also: Rostow to the President, handwritten note, 6/7/67.
236 Later in the day: Unsigned and unaddressed memorandum starting: "Mrs. Arthur Krim thinks Mr. Rostow should know ..." 6/7/67. Name File: Mathilde Krim, LBJ Library. A covering sheet from W. W. Rostow addressed the memorandum to the President at 3:55 P.M., June 7, 1967.
236 That concern seemed: Joe Califano to the President, 6:05 P.M., 7 June 1967. Name File: David Ginsburg, LBJ Library.
236 Even two junior: Larry Levinson and Ben Wattenberg to the President, confidential memorandum, 7:45 P.M., 7 June 1967. Name File: Ben Wattenberg, LBJ Library; no declassification date.
237 Premier Kosygin that: Unsigned text of Johnson's message, 11 A.M., 7 June 1967; declassified 3/25/80.
237 Kosygin obviously thought: Tel Aviv Embassy to secstate, secret cable 4237, 10:14 P.M., 7 June 1967; declassified 7/8/81.
237 Ambassador Barbour cabled: *Ibid.*
237 The Soviets also: Lall, *The UN and the Middle East Crisis, 1967.*
238 Abba Eban repeated: *Ibid.*
238 But the deception: Amman Embassy to secstate, secret flash cable 4125, 3:11 P.M., 7 June 1967; declassified 7/8/81.
238 Indeed, Hussein's losses: Dupuy, *op. cit.*
239 Ambassador Burns in: Amman Embassy, cable 4125, *op. cit.*
239 Inexplicably, Washington failed: Secstate to Tel Aviv Embassy, secret flash cable 208985, 10:40 P.M., 7 June 1967; declassified 7/8/81.
240 Five minutes after: White House Situation Room to the President, memorandum, 10:45 P.M., 7 June 1967.
240 "... many Egyptian wounded": Elon, "Letter from the Sinai Front," *Commentary,* August 1967.
240 In Cairo, Nolte: Cairo Embassy to secstate, secret cable 8670, 6:56 P.M., 7 June 1967; declassified 8/10/81.
241 While Nolte worried: Pace, "Cairo Diary," *New York Times Sunday Magazine,* July 2, 1967.
241 *Times* reporter Eric: *Ibid.*
242 That night the: Ennes, *Assault on the* Liberty.
242 But there was: National Security Agency/Central Security Service study, *Attack on a [deleted] the U.S.S. Liberty (S-[deleted],* 1981; no declassification date.
242 A Joint Chiefs: *Ibid.*

Page
242 By bureaucratic blunder: *Ibid.*
243 But when he: Ennes, *op. cit.*
243 McGonagle thought for: *Ibid.*
243 That night he: *Ibid.*
243 In Washington, Wednesday: President's Daily Diary, June 7, 1967.
243 The purpose of: Harold H. Saunders, secret memorandum for the record, *National Security Council Meeting, Wednesday, June 7, 1967,* Jan. 7, 1969; declassified 8/9/82.
243 Actually, there was: This comes from several of E. Rostow's co-workers who prefer to remain anonymous but whose integrity I trust.
243 In a memorandum: George Christian to the President, memorandum, June 7, 1967. Name File: Eugene Rostow, LBJ Library.
243 Wally Barbour, the: Tel Aviv Embassy to secstate, secret cable 3988, 8:30 A.M., 7 June 1967; declassified 7/8/81.
244 In one of: Saunders, *National Security Council Meeting, Wednesday, June 7, 1967, op. cit.*
244 The President did: President's Daily Diary, June 7, 1967.
244 But the outside: *Ibid.*
245 At the moment: Ennes, *op. cit.*

CHAPTER XVIII

Page
246 "Our losses were": *New York Times,* June 9, 1967.
246 But he was: *Ibid.*
247 Estimated Jordanian losses: Dupuy, *Elusive Victory.*
247 An estimated twenty: Amman Embassy to secstate, confidential cable 4141, 7:28 P.M., 8 June 1967; declassified 7/8/81.
247 Economically, Hussein's losses: Nyrop, *Jordan.*
248 With the atmosphere: *New York Times,* June 9, 1967.
248 There were other: Ennes, *Assault on the* Liberty.
248 The sea was: In a letter to the author, 3/15/83, Ennes wrote: "I know the official reports say visibility ten miles, but visibility was *unlimited* in all directions. We could see mountains 50 or more miles away, could see clearly the buildings and the minaret at El Arish 12 and 13 miles away, could still clearly see the smoke coming from El Arish 12 and 13 miles away, could still clearly see the smoke coming from El Arish when it was 25 miles away shortly before the attack. The only factor limiting our vision was the curvature of the earth."
249 As one of: National Security Agency/Central Security Service study, *Attack on a [deleted] the U.S.S. Liberty (S-[deleted],* 1981; declassification undated.
249 Obviously the gunners: Ennes, *op. cit.*
250 On its wings: Ennes, *Assault on the* Liberty.
250 In Cairo that: Pace, "Cairo Diary," *New York Times Sunday Magazine,* July 2, 1967.
250 "I guess this": Nolte interview, 1/11/83, Washington, D.C.
250 "Almost total defeat": Cairo Embassy to secstate, secret flash cable 8687, 8:01 A.M., 8 June 1967; declassified 8/10/81.
251 There were by: Pace, *op. cit.*
251 The State Department: Secstate to Cairo Embassy, secret flash cable 209179, 10:10 A.M., 8 June 1967; declassified 8/10/81.

Page
251 Israeli reporter Amos: Elon, "Letter from the Sinai Front," *Commentary,* August 1967.
251 To an urgent: Riad, *The Struggle for Peace in the Middle East.*
251 An official of: Cairo Embassy to secstate, secret flash cable 8697, 1:19 P.M., 8 June 1967; declassified 8/10/81.
251 Throughout that Thursday: Pace, *op. cit.*
252 Though the bodies: *Washington Post,* June 10, 1967.
252 Ambassador Wally Barbour: Tel Aviv Embassy to secstate, confidential cable 4013, 9:42 P.M., 8 June 1967; declassified 7/8/81.
252 The Hebrew press: *New York Times,* June 10, 1967.
252 The U.S. Consulate in: Jerusalem Consulate to secstate, confidential flash cable 1053, received 9:46 A.M., 8 June 1967; declassified 7/8/81.
252 Secretary of State: Secstate to Tel Aviv Embassy, secret flash cable 209182, 10:56 A.M., 8 June 1967; declassified 7/8/81.
253 A delegation of: Rabin, *The Rabin Memoirs.*
253 Ambassador Barbour, closely: Tel Aviv Embassy to secstate, secret flash cable 4007, 12:37 P.M., 8 June 1967; declassified 7/8/81.
254 The Syrians had: Dayan, *Story of My Life.*
254 At 1:10 P.M. (7:10 A.M.): Unless otherwise noted, all details of the attack based on Ennes, *op. cit.,* and National Security Agency/Central Security Service Study, *op. cit.*
255 Crouching on the: Ennes letter to the author, 1/6/81. Ennes wrote that the fire was caused by "napalm which burned furiously on the outside bulkhead of the radio shack."
255 The message was: In a letter to the author, 3/15/83, Ennes wrote that the *Saratoga*'s skipper, Captain Joseph Tully, immediately ordered planes into the air. When the carrier *America* failed to follow suit, "Tully flashed, 'WTH' (what the hell?) . . . but got no reply and moments later got an order from the flagship (Admiral Martin) to recall his airplanes."
256 It was not: COMSIXTHFLT TO RUFPBK/UNSINCEUR, secret flash cable, June 8, 1967; declassified 3/28/78.
257 At about the: USDAO to Rudlkd/Cincusnayeur, secret cable, 6/16/67; declassified 8/13/82.
257 An effort to: State Department Administrative History, *United States Policy and Diplomacy in the Middle East Crisis, May 15–June 10, 1967,* top secret/nodis, 1968; declassified and sanitized 9/16/83.
258 In Washington, President: President's Daily Diary, June 8, 1967.
258 Johnson replied that: Unaddressed and unsigned text, 11:35 A.M., 8 June 1967; declassified 3/25/80.
258 A minute after: President's Daily Diary, June 8, 1967. Also see Ennes, *op. cit.*
258 "We have a flash": W. W. Rostow to the President, memorandum, 9:50 A.M., 8 June 1967.
258 "We have just": National Security Agency/Central Security Service Study, *op. cit.*
259 At his regular: White House press office transcript, *News Conference #866-A,* 11:18 A.M., 8 June 1967.
259 In fact, while: President's Daily Diary, June 8, 1967. On Clifford's role in the U.S. recognition of Israel, see Wilson, Evan M. *Decision on Palestine.* Stanford, Cal.: Hoover Institution Press, 1979.
259 Although there was: Ennes, *op. cit.*

Page
260 In the end, Clark: *Ibid.*
260 Footnote: *Ibid.*
260 Thus that afternoon: National Security Agency/Central Security Service Study, *op. cit.*
260 If Johnson or: *Washington Post,* June 9, 1967.
261 Afterward, Medhi was: *Ibid.*
261 Despite the crises: President's Daily Diary, June 8, 1967.
261 Hurriedly, Johnson took: *Ibid.*
261 Now, as the: Heikal, *Nasser: The Cairo Documents.*
262 Egypt officially reported: Dupuy, *op. cit.*
262 Israeli losses were: *Ibid.*
262 At 5 P.M. Washington: Riad, *op. cit.*
262 Eight hours later: Lall, *The UN and the Middle East Crisis, 1967.*
262 The survivors aboard: National Security Agency/Central Security Service Study, *op. cit.*
262 Two thirds of its: Ennes, *op. cit.*
263 Commander McGonagle, enraged: In a letter to the author, 3/15/83, Ennes wrote: "McGonagle told the QM, 'Tell him I said to go fuck himself.' The signalman asked, 'Really?' McGonagle said, 'No, just tell him "No, thank you." ' But someone nevertheless sent the 'Go fuck yourself' message."
263 Frustrated, someone in: Ennes letter to the author, 6/6/82.

CHAPTER XIX

Page
264 Yitzhak Rabin was: Rabin, *The Rabin Memoirs.*
264 Yet Rabin years: *Ibid.*
264 Weizman expressed equal: Weizman, *On Eagles' Wings.*
265 Footnote: Bamford, James. *The Puzzle Palace.* Boston: Houghton Mifflin Company, 1982.
266 Israel claimed in: Lall, *The UN and the Middle East Crisis, 1967.*
266 The U.S. proposal: *Ibid.*
266 Early Friday afternoon: *Ibid.*
267 There then began: *Ibid.*
267 Their successes were: Dupuy, *Elusive Victory.*
267 By afternoon, Cairo: Pace, "Cairo Diary," *New York Times Sunday Magazine,* July 2, 1967.
267 When Nasser finally: *Ibid.*
268 The country briefly: *Ibid.*
268 The news of: *Facts on File Yearbook 1967.* Also see *New York Times,* June 10, 1967.
268 In Washington, Dean: Department of State release, *TRANSCRIPT OF BACKGROUND PRESS BRIEFING, FRIDAY, JUNE 9, 1967, 5:05 P.M.*
270 A headline in: Ghareeb, Edmund, *Split Vision.*
270 Columnist Mary McGrory: *Ibid.*
270 *Time* magazine printed: *Time,* July 14, 1967.
271 On the same day: *New York Times,* June 10, 1967.
271 He also agreed: *Ibid.*
271 That brought to: *Ibid.*
271 Outright contributions were: *New York Times,* June 9, 1967.
271 By the time: Urofsky, *We Are One!*

NOTES

Page
271 Many also volunteered: *Ibid.*
272 By coincidence, this: *Ibid.*. Also see *Washington Post,* May 30, 1967. Urofsky misspells Beys Afroyim's name "Efroyim." Justice Black wrote the majority opinion, arguing that the government did not have the right to "rob" Afroyim of his citizenship. He was joined by Justices Black, Brennan, Douglas, Fortas and Warren; against were Clark, Harlan, Stewart and White. The ruling made it legal for all Americans theoretically to vote in foreign elections. But in reality this affected mainly though not exclusively Jewish Americans residing in Israel since they did not have to take a loyalty oath (and thereby renounce their American citizenship) to gain Israeli citizenship. As Jews, they automatically were granted Israeli citizenship.
272 Corporations contributed to: Urofsky, *op. cit.*
272 There was a: *New York Times,* June 10, 1967.
272 The *Intermountain Jewish:* Urofsky, *op. cit.*
272 Arthur Waskow, an: *Ibid.*
273 Lyndon Johnson that: President's Daily Diary, June 9, 1967.
273 He took time: *Ibid.*
273 An aide noted: *Ibid.*
273 Bundy too, though: McG. Bundy to the President, memorandum, *The 6:30 Meeting,* 6:15 P.M., 9 June 1967.
273 Later in the: President's Daily Diary, June 9, 1967.
274 He also took: White House release, *NEWS CONFERENCE #868-A,* 11:25 A.M., 9 June 1967.
274 However, Ensign Malcomb: Ennes, *Assault on the* Liberty.
274 The first ship: *Ibid.*

CHAPTER XX

Page
276 Syrian fears were: Lall, *The UN and the Middle East Crisis, 1967.*
278 The Chinese Communist: *Facts on File Yearbook 1967.*
278 At 7:30 A.M.: *Ibid.*
278 Other East Bloc: *Ibid.*
278 After an initial: Brecher, *Decisions in Israel's Foreign Policy.*
278 Chairman Mao Tse-tung: Cooley, *Green March, Black September.*
278 Almost simultaneously with: Bull, *War and Peace in the Middle East.* In a letter to the author, 3/15/83, Bull says that the scheduled 2 P.M. meeting actually took place only at 2:30 P.M. local time "as Dayan had been delayed on an inspection of the Golan front." Bull estimated he received Dayan's initial call "not later than 7 A.M. EDT [1 P.M. local time]."
278 The earlier false: Petran, *Syria.*
279 Kosygin reinforced the: White House hot-line exchange list, undated.
279 He requested that: Johnson, *The Vantage Point.*
279 Johnson was still: President's Daily Diary, June 10, 1967.
279 Johnson got to: *Ibid.*
279 He flatly informed: Johnson, *op. cit.*
279 The strong message: *Ibid.*
279 "The atmosphere was": Helms, memorandum for the record, *Hot Line Meeting June 10, 1967,* Oct. 28, 1968; declassified and sanitized 2/26/82. Also see Helms's Oral History for the LBJ Library, 4/4/69.
279 Johnson, his appetite: President's Daily Diary, June 10, 1967.

Page
279 "Don't you think": Helms's Oral History, *op. cit.*
280 McNamara picked up: Johnson, *op. cit.*
280 No one said: *Ibid.*
280 Meantime, Johnson also: *Ibid.*
281 He immediately asked: Rafael, *Destination Peace.*
282 Bull set the: Lall, *op. cit.*
282 Sixteen hours after: Pace, "Cairo Diary," *New York Times Sunday Magazine,* July 2, 1967.
283 Nasser was never: Sadat, Anwar. *In Search of Identity.* New York: Harper & Row, Publishers, 1978.
283 During the early: Pace, *op. cit.*
284 Yisrael Galili, the: *Washington Post,* June 11, 1967.
284 In Washington, the: White House list of hot-line exchanges, undated.
284 Johnson had remained: President's Daily Diary, June 10, 1967.
285 A memorandum to: Bromley Smith to the President, confidential memorandum, 5:30 P.M., 11 June 1967; declassified 2/13/82.
285 He referred to: Lall, *op. cit.*
285 Finally, as he: *Ibid.*

CHAPTER XXI

Page
289 Floodlights were set: Halabi, *The West Bank Story.* Also see Hirst, *The Gun and the Olive Branch* and Benvenisti, Meron, *Jerusalem: The Torn City.* Jerusalem: Isratypeset, 1976.
289 Footnote: Report of the National Lawyers Guild, 1977 Middle East Delegation, *Treatment of Palestinians in Israeli-Occupied West Bank and Gaza.* New York: National Lawyers Guild, 1978.
290 One reason publicly: Kollek, Teddy, and Amos Kollek. *For Jerusalem.* Jerusalem: Steimatzky's Agency Ltd., 1978.
290 Other *faits accomplis:* UN A/6797*, report of the special representative on his mission to the occupied territories, 15 Sept. 67. Also see Mayhew and Adams, *Publish It Not . . .*
290 Some of the: Davis and Mezvinsky: *Documents from Israel 1967–1973.*
292 Sister Marie-Thérèse: Hirst, *op. cit.*
292 Similar scenes occurred: Davis and Mezvinsky, *op. cit.*
292 One of the other: UN A/6797*, *op. cit.* Also see Schleifer, *The Fall of Jerusalem.*
292 In fact, Moshe: Dayan, *Story of My Life.*
292 Similar reprisals occurred: UN A/6797*, *op. cit.*
293 In the streets: Hirst, *op. cit.*
293 The scene at: *Ibid.*
293 Raymonda Tawil, a Palestinian: Tawil, *My Home, My Prison.*
293 Footnote: Dayan, *op. cit.*
294 There was nothing: *Time,* June 23, 1967.
294 Widespread looting was: UN A/6797*, *op. cit.* Also see Benvenisti, *op. cit.*
294 Abdullah Schleifer, a Jew: Schleifer, *op. cit.*
294 Looting in some: UN A/6797*, *op. cit.*
295 The provincial capital: *Ibid.*
295 Sister Marie-Thérèse: Hirst, *op. cit.*

Page

295   There were reports: UN A/6672, 12 July 1967, report of the Secretary-General on the withdrawal of UNEF.

295   Nor were the: *Ibid.*

296   Moshe Dayan later: Dayan, *op. cit.*

296   A British free-lance: Mayhew and Adams, *op. cit.*

297   With only a few: For instance, a headline in *The New York Times* on June 23, 1967, read: "Israeli Occupation of Jordan Area Is Termed Gentle."

297   The French daily: Hirst, *op. cit.*

297   Praise came from: *Facts on File Yearbook 1967.*

298   In a Gallup: *Washington Post,* June 12, 1967.

298   A count of letters: Benjamin H. Read to W. W. Rostow, memorandum, *Public mail on the Arab-Israeli crisis addressed to Secretary of State,* June 8, 1967.

298   In a report: McPherson to the President, letter, 9:10 A.M., 11 June 1967.

298   Israeli's supporters were: *Facts on File Yearbook 1967.*

299   In Israel, Moshe: *Ibid.*

299   Levi Eshkol reiterated: *Ibid.*

299   The President was: *Washington Post,* June 19, 1967.

299   Democratic leaders attending: *Facts on File Yearbook 1967.*

300   Johnson luxuriated that: President's Daily Diary, June 11, 1967.

CHAPTER XXII

Page

301   On Tuesday, June: W. W. Rostow to the President, memorandum, 11:55 A.M., 13 June 1967.

301   The 1,358th session: Lall, *The UN and the Middle East Crisis, 1967.*

302   Only several hours: White House release, *PRESS CONFERENCE NO. 102,* 12:10 P.M., 13 June 1967.

302   No formal decision: Telephone interview with Harold Saunders, May 10, 1983, Washington, D.C.; also see Saunders' thoughtful reflections in a post-mortem of the crisis written in late 1968, titled *The Middle East Crisis, Preface, Introduction,* Dec. 20, 1968, top secret; declassified 10/14/83. Saunders writes that the United States made two major decisions in May and June: "First, we 'decided' at the outset of the crisis to try to restrain Israel from trying to settle its own problems militarily. . . . As far as I can tell, our decision, if discussed at all, was taken more by instinct than by decision. It is understandable that many big 'decisions' are made this way because they involve fundamental philosophies—for example, war can never lead to anything good—that are not easily put aside and are often not even questioned. . . . To me [this decision] was the most fascinating part of the first half of this dramatic period, and yet I never heard it discussed. . . . Second, we 'decided' after war broke out to go for a full Arab-Israeli settlement and not just for another truce. Again, the men around the President just started talking this way—apparently at first with little discussion of what was possible. Events played their role, especially when the Soviet Ambassador at the UN—whether by error or by design—finally agreed to a simple cease-fire which left conquering Israeli forces in control of highly advantageous military and negotiating positions. Israel's position may have been the governing one in our 'decision.' . . . Israeli officials in Washington—especially the Israeli Minister, Ephraim Evron—were closer to high American officials than were Arab representatives. But much more important, we were convinced that we just could not move Israel against its will."

Page
302 At the United: Lall, *op. cit.*
303 The Council concluded: *Ibid.*
303 Footnote: *Ibid.*
303 Top delegations from: *Facts on File Yearbook 1967.*
304 At the first: *New York Times,* June 18, 1967.
304 The government leaked: *Ibid.*
304 The next day: *New York Times,* June 19, 1967.
304 As *The New: New York Times,* June 19, 1967.
304 Israel's public restraint: Bromley Smith to the President, confidential memo-
        randum, June 11, 1967; sanitized and declassified 12/13/82.
305 The popularity of: Isaac, *Israel Divided.* Also see Sachar, H. M., *A History of Israel.*
305 One of the: Isaac, *op. cit.*
305 In a 1938: *Ibid.*
305 Moshe Moskowitz, a: *Ibid.*
306 Explained Zvi Shiloah: *Ibid.*
306 Nor, most importantly: *Facts on File Yearbook 1967.*
306 Lyndon Johnson spent: President's Daily Diary, June 17 and 18, 1967.
307 Shortly before dinner: *Ibid.*
307 The President read: *Ibid.*
307 Johnson enunciated: *New York Times,* June 20, 1967.
307 Abe Feinberg telephoned: Marvin to the President, 6:30 P.M., 19 June 1967.
308 Saying he planned: President's Daily Diary, June 19, 1967.
308 Kosygin's speech was: *New York Times,* June 20, 1967.
308 Arthur Goldberg answered: *Ibid.*
308 During the course: *Ibid.*
309 While the 122: *New York Times,* June 24, 1967.
309 There was a sobering: President's Daily Diary, June 23, 1967.
309 Johnson immediately flew: *Ibid.*
309 At 12:41 P.M. Sunday: President's Daily Diary, June 25, 1967.
309 The two sides: *Ibid.*
310 Johnson made his: *Ibid.*
310 Kosygin did not: *New York Times,* June 26, 1967.

CHAPTER XXIII

Page
311 On June 27: *Washington Post,* June 28, 1967.
311 The next day: *Washington Post,* June 29, 1967.
312 They more than: *National Geographic,* April 1983.
312 Inside the new: UN A/6717, mission of the personal representative to Jerusa-
        lem, 12 Sept. 1967.
312 That same night: Kollek, Teddy, and Amos Kollek. *For Jerusalem.* Jerusalem:
        Steimatzky's Agency Ltd., 1978.
312 Footnote: Mattar, Ibrahim. *Journal of Palestine Studies,* Vol. XII, No. 4, Sum-
        mer 1983.
312 Benvenisti, Meron. *Jerusalem: The Torn City.* Jerusalem: Isratypeset, 1976.
313 At dawn on: *New York Times,* June 30, 1967.
313 In all, fifty-five: Benvenisti, *op. cit.*
313 "Many Jews were": Kollek, *op. cit.*

Page
313 Abba Eban declared: UN A/6753*, Report of the Secretary-General, 10 July 1967.
313 Indeed, that was: UN A/6717, *op. cit.* Also see Schleifer, *The Fall of Jerusalem,* and *Washington Post,* June 23, 1967.
313 The United States: *New York Times,* June 23, 1967.
314 Despite this straightforward: Lall, *The UN and the Middle East Crisis, 1967.*
314 On June 21: Glassman, Jon D. *Arms for the Arabs.* Baltimore: The Johns Hopkins University Press, 1975.
314 Within one week: *Ibid.*
314 The buildup: Pollock, David. *The Politics of Pressure.* Westport, Conn.: Greenwood Press, 1982.
314 Even more impressive: Heikal, *The Sphinx and the Commissar.*
315 The Soviet assistance: Kaplan, Stephen S. *Diplomacy of Power.* Washington, D.C.: The Brookings Institution, 1981. Kaplan notes that Albania had terminated Soviet use of the naval base at Vlonë in 1961, and since then the Russians had been seeking naval facilities and air bases in the eastern Mediterranean.
315 In a statement: *New York Times,* June 22, 1967.
315 He pressed his: Lall, *op. cit.*
316 Only nine days: *Facts on File Yearbook 1967.*
316 The clashes escalated: *Ibid.*
316 The fighting was: Lall, *op. cit.*
316 Advance parties arrived: Bull, *War and Peace in the Middle East.*
317 When a vote: Lall, *op. cit.*
317 The Assembly's inability: *New York Times,* July 5, 1967.
317 Despite its failure: Lall, *op. cit.*
318 Footnote: *Ibid.*
319 The flow of refugees: *New York Times,* June 21, 1967.
319 At the blasted: *New York Times,* June 11, 1967. Also see Hirst, *The Gun and the Olive Branch,* and Forrest, *The Unholy Land.*
319 Once the homeless: *New York Times,* June 22, 1967.
319 One such tent: *Ibid.*
320 The stories of: *Washington Post,* June 22, 1967.
320 Israel continued to: *New York Times,* July 11, 1967. Also see Hirst, *op. cit.*
320 After international protests: Hirst, *Ibid.* Also see Joe Alex Morris, Jr.'s story in the *Washington Post,* July 11, 1967.
320 After an exchange: *New York Times,* Aug. 7, 1967.
320 An estimated 32,000: UN A/6797*, report on the mission of the special representative to the occupied territories, 15 Sept. 1967.
320 By then, UNWRA: *Ibid.*
321 The Arabs made: *Facts on File Yearbook 1967.*
321 The frustration of: Bull, *op. cit.*
322 "Every time something": *New York Times,* Sept. 9, 1967.
322 After this, firing: Bull, *op. cit.*
322 This was pointed: State to Amembassy Tel Aviv, secret cable 2942, 9/14/67; declassified 3/5/79. Written by hand on the top is the notation: "Not sent." In an interview with Harold Saunders on Aug. 30, 1983, Washington, D.C., he said he had no memory of the cable but he suggested there may have been reasons for not sending it other than political. He speculated the contents may have been communicated orally or included in other cables.

Page
323 Although Israeli leaders: *Facts on File Yearbook 1967.* Also see *New York Times,* Sept. 28 and 29, 1967, and *Washington Post,* Nov. 16, 1967.
323 The first settlement: *New York Times,* Sept. 28, 1967.
323 However, at a ceremony: *Ibid.*
323 The United States: *Washington Post,* Sept. 19, 1967.
323 Footnote: Ann Lesch, "Israeli Settlements in the Occupied Territories," *Journal of Palestine Studies,* Autumn 1978.
323 Another settlement of: *Ibid.* Also see *New York Times,* June 19, 1967.
324 Now they began: Lesch, *op. cit.*
324 Then on October 21: *New York Times,* Oct. 23, 1967.
324 The sinking was: CIA Directorate of Intelligence, secret Special Report, *The Threat of the Guided Missile Patrol Boat,* 17 Nov. 1967; declassified 6/4/79.
324 The CIA speculated: Arthur McCafferty to W. W. Rostow, memorandum, Oct. 23, 1967.
325 Three days later: *Washington Post,* Oct. 25, 1967.
325 "This gives you": W. W. Rostow to the President, memorandum, 5 P.M., 24 Oct. 1967.
325 Washington's concern grew: *Washington Post,* Oct. 28, 1967.
325 In a cable: Secstate to Tel Aviv Embassy, secret cable 60511, 27 Oct. 1967; declassified 3/5/79.
325 Ambassador Barbour replied: Tel Aviv Embassy to the President, secret cable 1328, 27 Oct. 1967; declassified 3/5/79.

CHAPTER XXIV

Page
326 The urgent need: Lall, *The UN and the Middle East Crisis, 1967.*
326 Egyptian Foreign Minister: Riad, *The Struggle for Peace in the Middle East.*
327 Arthur Goldberg did: *Ibid.*
327 Eban had requested: Unsigned memorandum of conversation, Oct. 24, 1967; declassified 2/16/82.
328 "That meant we": Eban, *An Autobiography.*
328 Johnson's support did: McPherson to the President, memorandum, 5:10 P.M., Sept. 20, 1967.
328 It was an offer: W. W. Rostow to the President, confidential memorandum, 9:15 A.M., June 10, 1966; declassified and sanitized, 3/13/79.
329 By October they: *Facts on File Yearbook 1967.*
329 On October 15: *Ibid.*
329 By November 7: *Ibid.*
330 The reasons for: *Washington Post,* Nov. 17, 1967.
330 In practice, aspects: *Ibid.*
330 The entire village: *New York Times,* Nov. 30, 1967.
330 In Gaza, where: *Washington Post,* Nov. 27, 1967.
330 U.N. officials estimated: United Nations *Annual Report of the Secretary-General on the Work of the Organization, 16 June 1966–19 June 1967.*
330 Any Gaza family: Schleifer, *The Fall of Jerusalem.*
330 The occupation authorities: *Ibid.*
330 The first of: Ann Lesch, "Israeli Deportation of Palestinians from the West Bank and the Gaza Strip, 1967–1978," *Journal of Palestine Studies,* Winter 1979.

Page
331 Four Arab notables: *Washington Post,* Aug. 1, 1967. Also see Halabi, *The West Bank Story.*

331 Reports to the: UN A/6797*, report on the mission of the special representative to the occupied territories, 15 Sept. 1967.

331 Refugees trying to: *Washington Post,* Nov. 27, 1967.

331 One disillusioned Israeli: Schleifer, *op. cit.* Schleifer explains the origin of this personal tale: "That fall [1967] an obscure, hopelessly isolated but brave group of Israeli New Left students and writers published in their 'underground' Hebrew newspaper *Nimas* (Fed Up) an anonymous account of guard duty along the Jordan by a troubled reservist. According to the editor, his story has been corroborated by other soldiers whose names they could not reveal."

331 Moshe Dayan, like: Dayan, *Story of My Life.*

332 Rafik Halabi, an Israeli: Halabi, *op. cit.*

332 A hint of: *Ibid.*

333 A Harris poll: *Washington Post,* Oct. 9, 1967.

CHAPTER XXV

Page
334 On the positive: Lall, *The UN and the Middle East Crisis,* 1967.

334 "Should a nation": *New York Times,* Feb. 21, 1957.

335 From the beginning: Noring, Nina J., and Walter B. Smith II. *The Withdrawal Clause in UN Security Council Resolution 242 of 1967.* Washington, D.C.: Department of State, February 1978, classified secret/nodis.

335 But fundamental to: Dean Rusk, Eugene Rostow, Walt Rostow, Richard Helms, Lucius Battle, Harold Saunders, Ambassador to Jordan at the time Findley Burns and others have all said to the author that they expected an early and substantial withdrawal by Israel. Rusk wrote in a letter to the author, Aug. 23, 1983, "It was clear to me at the time that Resolution 242 was somewhat flexible with regard to territories. . . . The purpose of this flexibility was to permit minor adjustments in the western frontier of the West Bank, for demilitarization measures in the Sinai and the Golan Heights and for a fresh look at the future of the city of Jerusalem. Resolution 242 never contemplated the movement of any significant territories to Israel." Eugene Rostow, in a letter to the author, Sept. 22, 1983, wrote: "I shared the general view that the modification of the armistice lines . . . would not involve major territorial changes if the Arabs moved quickly."

336 This should have: Noring and Smith, *op. cit.*

336 A day after: *Ibid.*

336 Despite Battle's warning: *Ibid.*

337 In a meeting: *Ibid.*

337 This assurance and: *Ibid.*

338 This was made: Saunders to W. W. Rostow, secret memorandum, *Eshkol's Knesset Speech Yesterday,* Oct. 31, 1967; declassified 9/15/81. Also, in a letter to the author, 10/7/83, Dean Rusk wrote: "It was not the understanding that Resolution 242 required Israeli withdrawal prior to the settlement of the other issues encompassed by that resolution. In one sense, Resolution 242 was an agenda for negotiation. Our thought at the time was that these several points would be negotiated in one general package and that bits and pieces of it would not be broken off for separate treatment."

405

Page

This position of course lent itself to a basic and insurmountable disagreement between the Arabs and the Israelis. Israel argued later that negotiations must be wide-ranging and, in the opinion of the Arabs, so inclusive that they would have amounted to a renegotiation of the principles already embodied in 242. They believed, as Hussein and others have related to me, that the principles were already set down in 242 and that negotiations should be strictly limited to the implementation of those principles, in other words, withdrawal by Israel to lines established in limited negotiations.

338   One glaring clue: Aronson, Shlomo. *Conflict and Bargaining in the Middle East.* Baltimore: The Johns Hopkins University Press, 1978. Also Isaac, *Israel Divided.*

339   But Nasser rebuffed: Interview with King Hussein, Aug. 7, 1983, Amman, Jordan.

339   Nasser told King: *Ibid.*

339   "Nasser told me": *Ibid.*

339   Hussein hinted at: *Facts on File Yearbook 1967.*

339   On November 8: *Ibid.*

340   Thus Goldberg would: U.S. Intelligence source who declined to be identified.

340   Since it had: Noring and Smith, *op. cit.*

341   Goldberg showed Eban: *Ibid.*

341   As Hussein heard: Hussein interview, *op. cit.* Also interview with Zaid Rifai, who at the time was the king's private secretary and sat in on most of the meetings with U.S. officials, Sept. 16, 1983, Washington, D.C.

341   This indeed occurred: *Ibid.* Also Hussein interview, *op. cit.*

341   In reporting on: Noring and Smith, *op. cit.*

342   At one point: Hussein interview, *op. cit.*

342   Goldberg later gave: Rifai interview, *op. cit.*

342   When Hussein asked: *Ibid.* Also Hussein interview, *op. cit.*

342   In fact, according: Hussein interview, *op. cit.*

342   The United States: Noring and Smith, *op. cit.*

342   Goldberg personally met: *Ibid.*

343   On November 7: Lall, *op. cit.*

343   To overcome these: *Ibid.*

343   When Egypt's Riad: Riad, *op. cit.*

343   Informal soundings among: Noring and Smith, *op. cit.*

344   On November 16: Lall, *op. cit.*

345   The United States: Noring and Smith, *op. cit.*

345   Hal Saunders expressed: Saunders to W. W. Rostow, secret memorandum, *Your Talk with Herzog,* 11/20/67; declassified 9/14/83.

346   On November 20: Lall, *op. cit.*

346   Suddenly the hopes: Caradon, Lord, et al. *UN Security Council Resolution 242: A Case Study in Diplomatic Ambiguity.* Given the secret understandings, the celebrated ambiguity seems misplaced in the title of a study of this supposed seriousness.

346   Israel immediately rejected: Lall, *op. cit.*

346   Caradon had acceded: Caradon, *op. cit.*

347   The time of: *Ibid.*

347   As the months: Hussein interview, *op. cit.*

347   But now Israel: *Ibid.* Also see Noring and Smith, *op. cit.*

347   Begin, in fact: Brecher, *Decisions in Israel's Foreign Policy.*

Page
348 Although Israel gave: Aronson, *op. cit.* Also see Brecher, *Decisions in Israel's Foreign Policy* on the peculiar history of Israel's handling of the 242 issue.
348 Nearly five months: Memorandum of conversation between Rowland Evans, Harold H. Saunders and John W. Foster, April 15, 1968. Unclassified.
348 Eshkol, who had: Polloch, David. *The Politics of Pressure.* Westport, Conn.: Greenwood Press, 1982.
348 Over the years: Hussein interview, *op. cit.* Also U.S. intelligence sources who decline to be identified.
349 Footnote: The text was supplied by a U.S. source who declined to be identified, but who retains close ties in Jordan and the U.S. government.
349 As the years: Hussein interview, *op. cit.* Also Rifai interview, *op. cit.*
349 The officials believed: Interview with Harold Saunders, Aug. 28, 1983, Washington, D.C.
349 Footnote: Official text of Hussein's speech released by the Kingdom of Jordan, 11/6/81.

EPILOGUE

Page
351 Thus casualties in: Dupuy, *Elusive Victory.*
351 Eleven years later: *Ibid.*
351 The 1973 war: *Ibid.*
353 Not only did: Report by Controller General of the United States, *U.S. Assistance to the State of Israel,* June 24, 1983.
353 In fiscal 1983: *Ibid.*
353 To assure Israel's: *Ibid.*
354 Beyond aid, the: *Ibid.*
354 The closure, according: CIA Directorate of Intelligence, confidential study, *Impact of the Closure of the Suez Canal on World Trade,* June 1967; declassified 11/7/80.
354 Although the United: *Facts on File Yearbook 1967.*
355 The survivors were: Ennes, *Assault on the* Liberty.
355 The crew was: Bamford, James. *The Puzzle Palace.* Boston: Houghton Mifflin Company, 1982.
355 The reason for: Rusk to Ennes, letter, Sept. 10, 1981.
355 They eventually formed: *The USS Liberty Newsletter,* December 1982.
355 A similar concern: Ennes, *op. cit.*
356 In a letter: Rusk to Ennes, letter, *op. cit.*
356 Shamir was a: *Time,* Sept. 12, 1983. Also see for some of his early exploits: Frank, Gerald. *The Deed.* New York: Simon and Schuster, 1963.
356 The Stern Gang: Frank, *Ibid.* Also see Bethell, Nicholas. *The Palestine Triangle: The Struggle for the Holy Land 1935-48.* New York: G. P. Putnam's Sons, 1979. Bethell's book contains some interesting interviews with Shamir on his views of assassination.
357 After Israel's establishment: *New York Times,* Sept. 2, 1983.
357 In recent years: *New York Times,* Aug. 19, 1981.
357 If so, the: For an interesting discussion of the changes in Israel during the time of Begin's premiership, see *A Compassionate Peace: A Future for the Middle East,* a report prepared for the American Friends Service Committee, New York: Hill and Wang, 1983.
358 The gist of: Rokach, *Israel's Sacred Terrorism.*

SELECTED
BIBLIOGRAPHY

Antonius, George. *The Arab Awakening.* New York: Paragon Books, 1979.

Bar-Zohar, Michael. *Embassies in Crisis.* Englewood Cliffs, N.J.: Prentice-Hall, Inc., 1970.

Brecher, Michael. *Decisions in Crisis.* Berkeley: University of California Press, 1980.

———. *Decisions in Israel's Foreign Policy.* London: Oxford University Press, 1974.

Britannic Majesty's Government. *The Political History of Palestine Under British Administration.* New York: British Information Services, 1947.

Bull, General Odd. *War and Peace in the Middle East: The experiences and views of a U.N. observer.* London: Leo Cooper, 1973.

Caradon, Lord, et al. *UN Security Council Resolution 242: A Case Study in Diplomatic Ambiguity.* Washington, D.C.: Institute for the Study of Diplomacy, Georgetown University, 1981.

Cattan, Henry. *Palestine, the Arabs and Israel: The Search for Justice.* London: Longman, 1969.

Cooley, John. *Green March, Black September: The Story of the Palestinian Arabs.* London: Frank Cass, 1973.

Davis, Uri, and Norton Mezvinsky (eds.). *Documents from Israel 1967–1973: Readings for a Critique of Zionism.* London: Ithaca Press, 1975.

Dayan, Moshe. *Moshe Dayan: Story of My Life.* New York: William Morrow and Company, Inc., 1976.

Draper, Theodore. *Israel and World Politics: Roots of the Third Arab-Israeli War.* New York: The Viking Press, 1968.

———. *Present History.* New York: Random House, 1983.

Dupuy, Trevor N. *Elusive Victory: The Arab-Israeli Wars, 1947–1974.* New York: Harper & Row, Publishers, 1978.

Eban, Abba. *An Autobiography.* Jerusalem: Steimatzky's Agency Ltd., 1977.

Elon, Amos. *The Israelis: Founders and Sons.* New York: Holt, Rinehart and Winston, 1971.

Ennes, James M., Jr. *Assault on the Liberty: The True Story of the Israeli Attack on an American Intelligence Ship.* New York: Random House, 1979.

Epp, Frank H. *Whose Land Is Palestine?* Grand Rapids, Mich.: William B. Eerdmans Publishing Company, 1974.

Forrest, A. C. *The Unholy Land.* Old Greenwich, Conn.: The Devin-Adair Company, 1972.

Ghareeb, Edmund (ed.). *Split Vision: The Portrayal of Arabs in the American Media.* Washington, D.C.: American-Arab Affairs Council, 1983.

Halabi, Rafik. *The West Bank Story.* New York: A Helen and Kurt Wolfe Book, Harcourt Brace Jovanovich, Publishers, 1981.

Heikal, Mohamed. *Nasser: The Cairo Documents.* London: New English Library, Mentor Edition, 1973.

————. *The Road to Ramadan: The inside story of how the Arabs prepared for and almost won the October war of 1973.* London: Collins, 1975.

————. *The Sphinx and the Commissar: The rise and fall of Soviet influence in the Middle East.* New York: Harper & Row, Publishers, 1978.

Herzog, Chaim. *The Arab-Israeli Wars: War and Peace in the Middle East from the War of Independence Through Lebanon.* New York: Random House, 1982.

Hirst, David. *The Gun and the Olive Branch: The roots of violence in the Middle East.* New York: Harcourt Brace Jovanovich, 1977.

Hurewitz, J. C. (ed.). *Soviet-American Rivalry in the Middle East.* New York: Praeger Publishers, 1971.

Isaac, Rael Jean. *Israel Divided: Ideological Politics in the Jewish State.* Baltimore: The Johns Hopkins University Press, 1976.

Isaacs, Stephen D. *Jews and American Politics.* Garden City, N.Y.: Doubleday & Company, 1974.

Johnson, Lyndon Baines. *The Vantage Point: Perspectives of the Presidency 1963-1969.* New York: Holt, Rinehart and Winston, 1971.

Kerr, Malcolm H. *The Arab Cold War: Gamal 'Abd Al-Nasir and his Rivals. 1958-1970.* 3rd ed. New York: Oxford University Press, 1971.

Khouri, Fred J. *The Arab-Israeli Dilemma.* Syracuse, N.Y.: Syracuse University Press, 1968.

Lall, Arthur. *The UN and the Middle East Crisis, 1967* (revised edition). New York: Columbia University Press, 1970.

Laqueur, Walter. *The Road to War.* Middlesex, England: Pelican Books, 1970.

————. *The Struggle for the Middle East: The Soviet Union and the Middle East 1958-68.* Baltimore, Md.: Penguin Books, 1972.

Lesch, Ann Mosely. *Israel's Occupation of the West Bank: The first two years.* Santa Monica, Cal.: The Rand Corp., ARPA Order No. 189-1, undated.

Mayhew, Christopher, and Michael Adams. *Publish It Not . . . The Middle East Cover-up.* London: Longman, 1975.

Medzini, Meron (ed.). *Israel's Foreign Relations: Selected Documents, 1947-74.* Jerusalem: Ministry of Foreign Affairs, 1976.

Meyer, Lawrence. *Israel Now: Portrait of a Troubled Land.* New York: Delacorte Press, 1982.

Miller, Merle. *Lyndon: An Oral Biography.* New York: G. P. Putnam's Sons, 1980.

Moskin, J. Robert. *Among Lions: The definitive account of the 1967 battle for Jerusalem.* New York: Arbor House, 1982.

National Laywers Guild. *Treatment of Palestinians in Israeli-Occupied West Bank and Gaza: National Lawyers Guild Report of the 1977 Middle East Delegation.* New York: National Lawyers Guild, 1978.

Nutting, Anthony. *Nasser.* London: Constable, 1972.

Nyrop, Richard F. (ed.). *Jordan: A country study.* Washington, D.C.: The American University, 1980.

O'Ballance, Edgar. *Arab Guerilla Power: 1967–1972.* London: Faber and Faber, 1973.

Petran, Tabitha. *Syria.* New York: Praeger Publishers, 1972.

Prittie, Terence. *Eshkol: The man and the nation.* New York: Pitman Publishing Corporation, 1969.

Quandt, William B. *Decade of Decisions: American Policy Toward the Arab-Israeli Conflict.* Berkeley, Cal.: University of California Press, 1977.

Rabin, Yitzhak. *The Rabin Memoirs.* Boston: Little, Brown and Company, 1979.

Rafael, Gideon. *Destination Peace: Three Decades of Israeli Foreign Policy, a Personal Memoir.* London: Weidenfeld and Nicolson, 1981.

Riad, Mahmoud. *The Struggle for Peace in the Middle East.* London: Quartet Books, 1981.

Rikhye, Indar Jit. *The Sinai Blunder.* London: Frank Cass, 1980.

Roberts, Samuel J. *Survival or Hegemony? The Foundations of Israeli Foreign Policy.* Baltimore, Md.: The Johns Hopkins University Press, 1973.

Rodinson, Maxime. *Israel and the Arabs.* New York: Pantheon Books, 1968.

Rokach, Livia. *Israel's Sacred Terrorism: A Study Based on Moshe Sharett's Personal Diary and Other Documents.* Belmont, Mass.: Association of Arab-American University Graduates, 1980.

Sachar, Howard M. *A History of Israel from the Rise of Zionism to Our Time.* Jerusalem: Steimatzky's Agency Ltd., 1976.

Schleifer, Abdullah. *The Fall of Jerusalem.* New York: Monthly Review Press, 1972.

Snow, Peter. *Hussein: A biography.* London: Barrie & Jenkins, 1972.

Stephens, Robert. *Nasser: A political biography.* London: Allen Lane, Penguin Press, 1971.

Steven, Stewart. *The Spymasters of Israel.* New York: Macmillan Publishing Co., 1980.

Stone, I. F. *Underground to Palestine and Reflections Thirty Years Later.* New York: Pantheon Books, 1978.

Tawil, Raymonda Hawa. *My Home, My Prison.* New York: Holt, Rinehart and Winston, 1979.

Tillman, Seth P. *The United States in the Middle East: Interests and Obstacles.* Bloomington, Ind.: Indiana University Press, 1982.

Turki, Fawaz. *The Disinherited: Journal of a Palestinian Exile.* New York: Monthly Review Press, 1972.

Urofsky, Melvin I. *We Are One! American Jewry and Israel.* Garden City, N.Y.: Anchor Press/Doubleday, 1978.

Weizman, Ezer. *The Battle for Peace.* New York: Bantam Books, 1981.

————. *On Eagles' Wings: The personal story of the Israeli Air Force.* Jerusalem: Steimatzky's Agency Ltd., 1976.

Acknowledgments

Research outside the Johnson Library was greatly facilitated by Andrew Mayer, an indefatigable ferret of obscure and out-of-date material and a conscientious reader of the manuscript.

There are others to thank. Members of The Library, who shared their company and wit: first reader Hanja Cherniak, regular readers Cheryl Bennett, Robert T. Fleetwood, Jr., James Killpatrick and Donald H. Lund (president), and associates Tom Berret, Frank Burns, Don Carlson, Tom Chakeres, Punch Coomaraswamy, Jackie Grimes, Ben Gurtizen, James McIlhenny, Richard Powell, Marvin Stone and Mo Sussman. Then there are James Ennes, Janine Hamann-Orci, Cornish Hitchcock, Jan Schumacher, Steven E. Smith, Francis Vautier and, especially, Michael McDonald, all of whom were more generous in their help than could be reasonably expected. Belinda Salzberg was particularly helpful in many ways, from reading certain sections of the manuscript to aiding in research.

There are two others without whose support this book literally would not exist, certainly not at this time: Robbin Reynolds, who has been a supporter and a source of encouragement for years, and another old friend, Dennis Mullin, whose knowledge of the aromas and byways of the Middle East is nonpareil.

Finally, there are those who read the manuscript in detail and offered numerous and helpful suggestions and criticisms. William Brubeck and Murray J. Gart, both shrewd and knowing observers of the Middle East, were unselfish in their time and counsel, and they contributed many insights into the complex subject. And last, Joni Evans, who for the second time has gone through the long and occasionally difficult process of editing one of my manuscripts. She brings one of publishing's most discerning and astute editor's pencils to the task. On this book, she was aided by Marjorie Williams, who contributed her own considerable editing talents.

And last, for his nobility, Rajah.

INDEX

About the Author

Donald Neff is the author of *Warriors at Suez: Eisenhower Takes America into the Middle East.* He has reported for the York *Dispatch,* United Press International, the Los Angeles *Times* and *Time* magazine, where he also served as a correspondent, writer and senior editor for sixteen years. His assignments have included tours in Japan, Vietnam and Israel as well as Texas, California and New York. Among his journalism awards, the most recent is the Overseas Press Club's citation for the best magazine article in 1979 for *Time*'s cover story "The Colombia Connection."

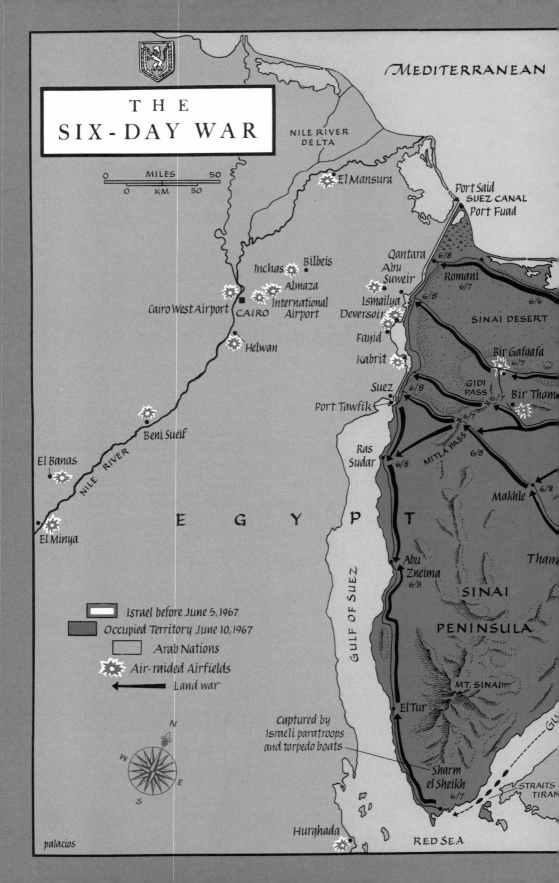

THE SIX-DAY WAR

MEDITERRANEAN

NILE RIVER DELTA

MILES 0 — 50

KM 0 — 50

El Mansura

Port Said
SUEZ CANAL
Port Fuad

Qantara
Abu Suweir
6/8
Romani
6/7
6/6
Inchas Bilbeis
Almaza
Cairo West Airport
International
Airport
CAIRO
Ismailya
6/8
Deversoir
SINAI DESERT
Bir Gafgafa
6/7
Fayid
Helwan
Kabrit
GIDI
PASS
Bir Tham
6/7
Suez
6/8
Port Tawfik
6/7
Beni Sueif
Ras
Sudar
6/8
MITLA PASS
6/8
El Banas
NILE RIVER
E G Y P T
Makhle
6/8
El Minya

GULF OF SUEZ
Abu
Zneima
6/8
Tham
SINAI
PENINSULA

Israel before June 5, 1967
Occupied Territory June 10, 1967
Arab Nations
Air-raided Airfields
Land war

MT. SINAI

El Tur

N
W   E
S

Captured by
Israeli paratroops
and torpedo boats

Sharm
el Sheikh
6/7

STRAITS
TIRAN

GU

Hurghada

RED SEA

palacios